Landscape Architecture

Landscape

John Ormsbee Simonds

Architecture

A Manual of Site Planning and Design

A completely revised edition of
Landscape Architecture:
The Shaping of Man's Natural Environment

Written as a companion piece to
Earthscape:
A Manual of Environmental Planning

McGraw-Hill Book Company

New York   St. Louis   San Francisco   Auckland   Bogotá   Hamburg   London   Madrid
Mexico   Montreal   New Delhi   Panama   Paris   São Paulo   Singapore   Sydney   Tokyo   Toronto

101112131415 HALHAL 9987654321

ISBN 0-07-057448-0

The editors for this book were Joan Zseleczky and Beatrice E. Eckes, the designer was Jan V. White, and the production supervisor was Teresa F. Leaden. It was set in Trump by York Graphic Services, Inc.

Printed and bound by Halliday Lithograph.

Library of Congress Cataloging in Publication Data

Simonds, John Ormsbee.
  Landscape architecture.

  "A Completely revised edition of Landscape architecture; the shaping of man's natural environment; written as a companion piece to Earthscape, a manual of environmental planning."
  Bibliography: p.
  Includes index.
  1. Landscape architecture. 2. Building sites—Planning. I. Title.
SB472.S58 1983   712   82-12721
  ISBN 0-07-057448-0

This text is gratefully dedicated

To my teachers, whose gifts to all who would accept them were the open mind, the awakened curiosity, the discerning eye, and the compelling vision of that which is higher, wider, deeper, and greater—and worth the striving for . . .

To my students, who in thoughtful agreement or in lively dissent have proved a reverberating sounding board and provided a stimulating climate for discussion and research . . .

To my partners and colleagues in practice, for whom the planning of a better environment for living is a strong and vital compulsion . . .

And to my lovely wife, Marjorie, and now grown-up children, who have encouraged the rewriting of this book.

Contents

Foreword ix

The Hunter and the Philosopher 1

1. Fundamentals 3

The Human Animal 3
Nature 9
The Ecological Basis 11
Landscape Character 13
Natural Forces, Forms, and
Features 22
The Built Environment 29

2. Land 33

As Heritage 33
As Resource 35
Land Grants 37
Land Rights 38
Land Surveying 38
Land Use 39

3. Water 47

Planning Approach 48
Water as a Resource 49
Water as Landscape Feature 51
Water-Related Site Design 54

4. Plants 63

Plants in Nature 64
Introduced Plantations 65
Plant Identification 66
Gardening 67
The Planned and Planted
Landscape 68

5. Climate 77

The Planetary Framework 77
Climate and Response 78
The Cold Region 80
The Cool-Temperate Region 80
The Warm-Humid Region 82
The Hot-Dry (Desertlike) Region 82
Microclimatology 84

6. Site   **91**

Site Selection   *91*
Site Analysis   *94*
Environmental Impact Assessment   *96*
The Conceptual Plan   *105*
Site-Structure Expression   *111*
Site-Structure Plan Development   *120*
Site-Structure Unity   *122*
Site Systems   *126*
Site Development Guidelines   *130*

7. Spaces   **135**

Site Volumes   *135*
The Base Plane   *152*
The Overhead Plane   *156*
The Verticals   *158*

8. Visible Landscape   **173**

The View   *173*
The Vista   *177*
The Axis   *180*
The Symmetrical Plan   *186*
The Asymmetrical Plan   *190*
Visual Resource Management   *195*

9. Circulation   **197**

Motion   *197*
Pedestrian Traffic   *208*
Automobile Traffic   *213*
Rail, Water, and Air   *228*
People Movers   *233*
Integrated Systems   *235*

10. Structures   **237**

Composition   *237*
Structures in the Landscape   *247*
The Defined Open Space   *250*

11. Habitations   **255**

Dwelling-Nature Relationships   *255*
Human Needs and Habitat   *258*
Variations on a Theme   *261*

12. Community   **265**

The Group Imperative   *265*
Form Order   *267*
New Directions   *267*

13. The City   **277**

Cityscape   *277*
Problems   *281*
Possibilities   *284*
The New Urbanity   *285*

14. Region   **289**

The Family   *290*
The Cluster   *291*
The Neighborhood   *292*
The Community   *293*
The City   *295*
The Region   *296*

15. Environment   **301**

Philosophic Orientation   *301*
A New Planning Order   *303*
A Need for the Visionary   *305*
Lifting Our Sights   *307*

Epilogue   **309**

Bibliography   **317**

Quotation Sources   **319**

Illustration Credits   **321**

Index   **323**

Foreword

Landscape Architecture has been written in response to the need for a book outlining the site-planning process in clear, simple, and practical terms.

It introduces us to an understanding of *nature* as the background and base for all human activities;

Describes the planning constraints imposed by the *forms, forces, and features of the natural and the built landscape*;

Instills a feeling for *climate* and its design implications;

Discusses *site selection and analysis*;

Instructs in the planning of workable and well-related *use areas*;

Considers the volumetric shaping of exterior *spaces*;

Explores the possibilities of *site-structure organization*;

Searches out the lessons of history and contemporary thought in the planning of expressive *human habitations* and *communities*; and

Provides guidance in the creation of more efficient and pleasant *living environments* within the context of the city and the region.

It is not proposed that the reader will become, per se, an expert land planner. As with training in other fields, proficiency comes with long years of study, travel, observation, and professional experience. The reader should, however, gain through this book a more keen and telling awareness of our physical surroundings. One should also gain much useful knowledge to be applied in the design of homes, schools, recreation areas, shopping malls, trafficways . . . or any other project to be fitted into, and planned in harmony with, the all-embracing landscape. This, at least, has been the express intent.

Landscape Architecture

The hunter and the philosopher

Once there was a hunter who spent his days tracking the wide prairies of North Dakota with his gun and dog and sometimes with a small boy who would beg to trot along. On this particular morning hunter and boy, far out on the prairie, sat watching intently a rise of ground ahead of them. It was pocked with gopher holes. From time to time a small striped gopher would nervously whisk from the mouth of his den to the cover of matted prairie grass, soon to reappear with cheek food pouches bulging.

"Smart little outfits, the gophers," the hunter observed. "I mean the way they have things figured out. Whenever you come upon a gopher village, you can be sure it will be near a patch of grain where they can get their food and close by a creek or slough for water. They'll not build their towns near willow clumps, for there's where the owls or hawks will be roosting. And you'll not be finding them near stony ledges or a pile of rocks where their enemies the snakes will be hiding ready to snatch them. When these wise little critters build their towns, they search out the southeast slope of a knoll that will catch the full sweep of the sun each day to keep their dens warm and cozy. The winter blizzards that pound out of the north and west to leave the windward slopes of the rises frozen solid will only drift loose powder snow on top of their homes.

"When they dig their dens," continued the hunter, "do you know what they do? They slant the runway steeply down for 2 or 3 feet and then double back up near the surface again where they level off a nice dry shelf. That's where they lie—close under the sod roots, out of the wind, warmed by the sun, near to their food and water, as far as they can get from their enemies, and surrounded by all their gopher friends. Yes, sir, they sure have it all planned out!"

"Is our town built on a southeast slope?" the small boy asked thoughtfully.

"No," said the hunter, "our town slopes down to the north, in the teeth of the bitter winter winds and cold as a frosty gun barrel." He frowned. "Even in summer the breezes work against us. When we built the new flax mill, the only mill for 40 miles, where do you think we put it? We built it right smack on the only spot where every breeze in the summertime can catch the smoke from its stack and pour it across our houses and into our open windows!"

"At least our town is near the river and water," said the boy defensively.

"Yes," replied the hunter. "But where near the river did we build our homes? On the low, flat land inside the river bend, that's where. And each spring when the snows melt on the prairie and the river swells, it floods out every cellar in our town."

"Gophers would plan things better than that," the small boy decided.

"Yes," said the hunter, "a gopher would be smarter."

"When gophers plan their homes and towns," the boy philosophized, "they seem to do it better than people do."

"Yes," mused the hunter, "and so do most of the animals I know. Sometimes I wonder why."

1

Fundamentals

Intelligence, by one definition, must be "the ability to respond adaptively to the environment"—i.e. "the ability to plan a course of action based upon information gained through the senses."

John Todd Simonds

One characteristic of animal behavior is that it is dominated by the physical presence of what the animal wants or fears. . . . Man has freed himself from this dominance in two steps. First, he can remember what is out of sight. The apparatus of speech allows him to recall what is absent, and to put it beside what is present; his field of action is larger because his mind holds more choices side by side. And second, the practice of speech allows man to become familiar with the absent situation, to handle and to explore it, and so at last to become agile in it and control it.

Jacob Bronowski

Animals . . . live in the extensional world—they have no symbolic world to speak of. There would seem to be no more "order" in an animal's existence than the order of physical events as they impinge on its life.

S. I. Hayakawa

People are animals, too. We still retain, and are largely motivated by, our natural animal instincts. If we are to plan[1] intelligently, we must acknowledge and accommodate these instincts; the shortcomings of many a project can be traced to the failure of the planner to recognize this simple fact.

The human animal

Homo sapiens (the wise one) is an animal (a superior type, we commonly assume, although neither history nor close observation altogether supports this assumption).

A human standing in the forest, with bare skin, weak teeth, thin arms, and knobby knees, would not look very impressive among the other creatures. As an *animal*, the bear with powerful jaws and raking claws would clearly seem superior. Even the turtle seems more cunningly contrived for both protection and attack, as do the dog, the skunk, and the lowly porcupine. All creatures of nature, upon reflection, seem superbly equipped for living their lives in their natural habitat and for meeting normal situations. All except the humans.

Lacking speed, strength, and other apparent natural attributes, we humans have long since learned that we can best attack a situation with our minds. Truth to tell, we have little other choice.

We alone of all the animals have the ability to weigh the factors of a problem and reason out a response. We are able to learn not only from our own experiences but also from the disasters, the triumphs, and the lesser experiences of untold thousands of our fel-

---

[1]The terms *plan, planning,* and *planner,* as used in this text, refer to the planning of our physical environment by architect, landscape architect, engineer, and urban or regional planner, working separately or, ideally, in close collaboration.

lows. We can borrow from, and apply to the solution of any problem, the accumulated wisdom of our species.

Our essential strength—the very reason for our survival and the key to all future achievement—is our unique power of perception and deduction. *Perception* (making oneself aware of all conditions and applicable factors) and *deduction* (deriving, through reason, an appropriate means of procedure) are the very essence of planning.

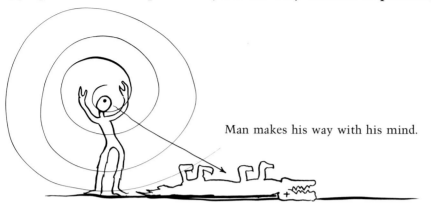

Man makes his way with his mind.

Down through the dim chaotic ages, the force of the human mind has met and mastered situation after situation and has raised us (through this planning process) to a position of supremacy over all the other creatures of the earth.

We have in fact inherited the earth. This vast globe on which we dwell is ours, ours to develop further, as an agreeable living environment. Surely, we with our twinkling minds should by now have created for ourselves a paradise upon this earth.

Have we? What have we done with our superlative natural heritage?

We have plundered our forests.

A consequence of the violation of nature.

We have ripped at our hills and laid them open to erosion and ever-deepening gullies.

We have befouled our rivers until even the fish and other wildlife have often been killed or driven off by the stench and fumes.

Our trafficways are lined with brash commercial hodgepodge and crisscrossed with senseless friction points.

We have built our homes tight row on row, with little thought for refreshing foliage, clean air, or sunlight.

Looking about us with a clear and critical eye, we find much to disturb and shock us. Our cluttered highways, sprawling suburbs,

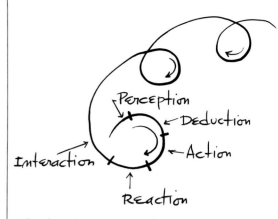

The thought processes of *perception-deduction* are in turn implemented by the physical processes of *action, reaction,* and *interaction.* These five dynamic drives form ever-repeating cycles and spin the intricate webbing of all human life.

And what is man? Amongst other things he is an organism endowed with a multiple organ, the brain, supported by the senses and the glands, in which the formative property of organic processes is applied to the memory records of experience. The brain orders its own records, and all mental processes express this basic activity. Art and science, philosophy and religion, engineering and medicine, indeed all cultural activities are based on the ordering of experience and the exploitation of the resulting design.

Lancelot Law Whyte

Ecology is the science of life or living matter in all its forms and phenomena interacting with the physical environment.

Everything we have to do to live, nature makes us do with lust and pleasure.

Seneca

White-tailed deer.

To the Etruscan all was alive; the whole universe lived; and the business of man was himself to live amid it all. He had to draw life into himself, out of the wandering huge vitalities of the world. The old idea of the vitality of the universe was evolved long before history begins, and elaborated into a vast religion before we get a glimpse of it. When history does begin, in China or India, Egypt, Babylonia, even in the Pacific and in aboriginal America, we see evidence of one underlying religious idea: The conception of the vitality of the cosmos, the myriad vitalities in wild confusion, which still is held in some sort of array: and man, amid all the glowing welter, adventuring, struggling, striving for one thing, life, vitality, more vitality; to get into himself more and more of the gleaming vitality of the cosmos. That is the treasure.

D. H. Lawrence

To be wholly alive a man must know storms, he must feel the ocean as his home or the air as his habitation. He must smell the things of earth, hear the sounds of living things and taste the rich abundance of the soil and sea.

James Michener

and straining cities offend more often than they please.

We are the victims of our own building. We are trapped, body and soul, in the mechanistic surroundings we have constructed about ourselves. Somewhere in the complex process of evolving our living spaces, cities, and roadways, we have become so absorbed in the power of machines, so absorbed in the pursuit of new techniques of building, so absorbed with new materials that we have neglected our human needs. Our own deepest instincts are violated. Our basic human desires remain unsatisfied. Divorced from our natural habitat, we have almost forgotten the glow and exuberance of being healthy animals and feeling fully alive.

Many contemporary ailments—our hypertensions and neuroses—are clearly no more than the physical evidence of rebellion against our physical surroundings and frustration at the widening

We are trapped in the fuming workings of our own machinery.

gap between the environment we yearn for and the stifling, artificial one we planners have so far contrived.

Life itself is dictated by our moment-by-moment adjustment to our environment. Just as the bacterial culture in the petri dish must have its scientifically compounded medium for optimum development and the potted geranium cutting its proper and controlled conditions of growth to produce a thriving plant, so we—as complicated, hypersensitive human organisms—must have for our optimum development a highly specialized milieu. It is baffling that the nature of this ecological framework has been so little explored. Volumes have been written on the conditions under which rare types of orchids may best be grown; numerous manuals can be found on the proper raising and care of guinea pigs, white rats, goldfish, and parakeets; but little has been written about the nature of the physical environment best suited to human culture. Here is a challenging field of research.

The naturalist tells us that if a fox or a rabbit is snared in a field and then kept in a cage, the animal's clear eyes will soon become dull, its coat will lose its luster, and its spirit will flag. So it is with humans too long or too far removed from nature. For we are first of all animals. We are creatures of the meadow, the forest, the sea, and the plain. We are born with the love of fresh air in our lungs, dry paths under our feet, and the penetrating heat of the sun on our skin. We are born with a love for the feel and smell of rich, warm earth, the taste and sparkle of clear water, the refreshing coolness of foliage overhead, and the spacious blue dome of the sky. Deep down inside we have for these things a longing, a desire sometimes compelling, sometimes quiescent—but always it is there.

It has been proposed by many sages that, other things being equal, the happiest person is one who lives in closest, fullest harmony with nature. It might then be reasoned: Why not restore humans to the woods? Let them have their water and earth and sky, and plenty of it. But is the primeval forest—preserved, untouched, or simulated—our ideal environment? Hardly. For the story of the human race is the story of an unending struggle to ameliorate the forces of nature. Gradually, laboriously, we have improved our shelters, secured a more sustained and varied supply of food, and extended control over the elements to improve our way of living.

What alternatives, then, are left? Is it possible that we can devise a wholly artificial environment in which to better fulfill our potential and more happily work out our destiny? This prospect seems extremely doubtful. A perceptive analysis of our most successful ventures in planning would reveal that we have effected the greatest improvements not by striving to subjugate nature wholly, not by ignoring the natural condition or by the thoughtless replacement of the natural features, contours, and covers with our constructions, but rather by consciously seeking a harmonious *integration.* This can be achieved by modulating ground and structural forms with those of nature, by bringing hills, ravines, sunlight, water, plants, and air into our areas of planning concentration, and by thoughtfully and sympathetically spacing our structures among the hills, along the rivers and valleys, and out into the landscape.

We are perhaps unique among the animals in our yearning for order and beauty. It is doubtful whether any other animal enjoys a "view," contemplates the magnificence of a venerable oak, or delights in tracing the undulations of a shoreline. We instinctively

The visual clutter of strip roadside development.

seek harmony; we are repelled by disorder, friction, ugliness, and the illogical. Can we be content while our towns and cities are still oriented to crowded streets rather than to open parks? While highways slice through our communities? While freight trucks rumble past our churches and our homes? Can we be satisfied while our children on their way to school must cross and recross murderous trafficways? While traffic itself must jam in and out of the city, morning and evening, through clogged and noisy valley floors, although these valley routes should, by all rights, be green, free-flow-

. . . and when he looked
At sky or sea, it was with
 the testing eyes
Of the man who knows the
 weather under his skin,
The man who smells the weather
 in the changed breeze
And has tried himself against it
 and lived by it.
It is a taut look but there is
 a freedom in it.
Stephen Vincent Benét

These are the Four that are
never content, that have never
been filled since the Dews
began . . .
Jacola's* mouth, and the
glut of the Kite, and the
hands of the Ape, and the Eyes
of Man.
Rudyard Kipling
*Jacola is the hyena.

There is that stupendous whole of a constructed environment, which, like fate, envelops civilized life. It must not be allowed to conflict seriously with . . . natural laws. . . .
We are convinced that patient research, starting from the elementary and progressing to the complex, can indeed gradually remodel the constructed world about us, to reach new levels of organic wholesomeness. . . .
The ancient idea of a world wisely ordered to function affords an emotional gratification that has shown eminent and long-tested survival value. It is the inspiration for all planning and designing.
Richard J. Neutra

In all, let Nature never be forgot.
....
Consult the Genius of the Place in all.

Alexander Pope

Genius of place symbolizes the living ecological relationship between a particular
location and the persons who have derived from it and added to it the various
aspects of their humanness. No landscape, however grandiose or fertile, can
express its full potential richness until it
has been given its myth by the love,
works, and arts of human beings.

René Dubos

There is a creature native to Kenya
called the flattid bug, and I was introduced to it in Nairobi, some years ago,
by the great Dr. L. S. B. Leakey. What
Dr. Leakey introduced me to was a
coral-coloured flower of a raceme sort,
made up of many small blossoms like
the aloe or hyacinth. Each blossom was
of oblong shape, perhaps a centimetre
long, which on close inspection turned
out to be the wing of an insect. The colony clinging to a dead twig comprised
the whole of a flower so real in its seeming that one could only expect from it
the scent of spring. . . .

The coral flower that the flattid bug imi-
tates does not exist in nature. The flattid
bug has created the form . . . from each
batch of eggs that the female lays there
will always be at least one producing a
creature with green wings, not coral, and
several with wings of in-between shades.

I looked closely. At the tip of the insect
flower was a single green bud. Behind it
were a half dozen partially matured blossoms showing only strains of coral. Behind these on the twig crouched the full
strength of flattid bug society, all with
wings of purest coral to complete the colony's creation and deceive the eyes of
the hungriest of birds.

Leakey shook the stick. The startled
colony rose from its twig and filled the
air with fluttering flattid bugs. They
seemed no different in flight than any
other swarm of moths that one encoun-
ters in the African bush. Then they returned to their twig. They alighted in
no particular order and for an instant the
twig was alive with the little creatures
climbing over each other's shoulders in
what seemed to be random movement.
But the movement was not random.
Shortly the twig was still and one beheld
again the flower. The green leader had
resumed his bud-like position with his
vari-coloured companions just behind.
The full-blown rank-and-file had resumed its accustomed places. A lovely
coral flower that does not exist in nature
had been created before my eyes.

Robert Ardrey

ing parkways leading into spacious suburbs and the open countryside beyond?

Planners, we must face this disturbing fact: our urban, suburban, and rural diagrams are for the most part ill-conceived. Our
community and highway patterns bear little logical relationship to
one another and to our topographical, climatological, physiological,
and ecological base. We have grown, and often continue to grow,
piecemeal, haphazardly, without reason. We are dissatisfied and
puzzled. We are frustrated. Somewhere in the planning process we
have failed.

Sound planning, we can learn from observation, is not achieved
problem by problem or site by site. Masterful planning examines
each project in the light of an inspired and inspiring vision, solves
each problem as a part of a total and compelling concept which
upon consideration should be self-evident. Stated simply, a central
objective of all physical planning is to create a more salubrious living environment—a more secure, effective, pleasant, and rewarding
way of life. Clearly, if we are the products of environment as well
as of heredity, the nature of this environment must be a vital concern. Ideally it will be one of order and of beauty, where tensions
and frictions have been in the main eliminated, where we can
achieve our full potential, and where, as the planners of old Peking
envisioned, man can live and grow and develop "in harmony with
nature, God and with his fellow man."[2]

Such an environment can never be created whole; once created,
it could never be maintained in static form. By its very definition it
must be dynamic and expanding, changing as our requirements
change. It will never, in all probability, be achieved. But striving
toward the creation of this ideal environment must be, in all landscape design, at once the major problem, the science, and the goal.

All planning must, by reason, meet the measure of our physical
dimensions. It must also meet the test of our senses: sight, taste,
hearing, scent, and touch. It must also consider our habits, responses, and impulses. Yet it is not enough to satisfy the instincts
of the physical animal alone. One must satisfy also the broader
requirements of the complete being.

As planners, we deal not only with areas, spaces, and materials,
not only with instincts and feelings, but also with ideas, the stuff of
the mind. Our designs must appeal to the intellect. They must
fulfill hopes and yearnings. By empathetic planning, one may be
brought to one's knees in an attitude of prayer, or urged to march, or
even elevated to a high plane of idealism. It is not enough to accommodate. Good design must delight and inspire.

Aristotle in teaching the art and science of persuasion, held that
to appeal to any person an orator must first understand and *know*
that person. He described in detail the characteristics of men and
women of various ages, stations, and circumstances and proposed
that not only each person but also the characteristics of each person
be considered and addressed. A planner must also know and understand. Planning in all ages has been an attempt to improve the
human condition. It has not only mirrored but actively shaped our
thinking and civilization.

With our prodigious store of knowledge we have it within our
power to create on this earth a veritable garden paradise. But we are
failing. And we *will* fail as long as our plans are conceived in
heavy-handed violation of nature and nature's principles. The
most significant feature of our current society is not the scale of our
developments but rather our utter disdain of nature and our seeming contempt for topography, topsoil, air currents, watersheds, and

[2]Translation from a manuscript in the possession of H. H. Li, descendant of architects to the imperial family.

Rape by the carryall.

our forests and vegetal mantle. We think with our bulldozers, plan with our 30-yard carryalls. Thousands upon thousands of acres of well-watered, wooded, rolling ground are being blithely plowed under and leveled for roads, homesites, shopping centers, and factories. Small wonder that so many of our cities are (climatologically speaking) barren deserts of asphalt, masonry, glass, and steel.

For the moment, it seems, we have lost touch. Perhaps, before we can progress, we must look back. We must regain the old instincts, relearn the old truths. We must return to the fundamental wisdom of the gopher building a home and village and the beaver engineering a dam. We must apply the planning approach of the farmer working from day to day in the fields, fully aware of nature's

Roots.

forces, forms, and features, respecting and responding to them, adapting them to a purpose. We must develop a deeper understanding of our physical and spiritual ties to the earth. We must rediscover nature.

Nature

Nature reveals itself to each of us according to our interests. To the naturalist, nature unfolds a breathtaking wonderland of spiderweb, egg mass, and fern frond. To the miner, nature is the tenacious yet prodigious source of minerals—coal, copper, tungsten, lead, silver. To the hydroelectric engineer, nature is an abundant reservoir of power. To the structural engineer, nature in every guise is an elo-

A plant.   Weeds in snow.

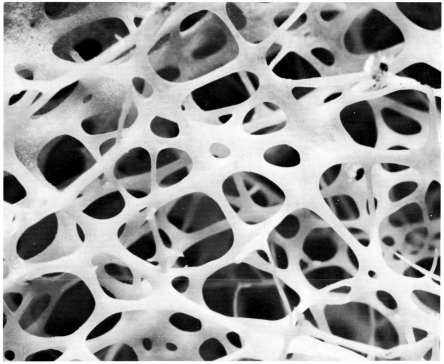

Bone cell structure.

Civilizations have risen and fallen without apparently perceiving the full import of their relations with the earth.

Lewis Mumford

From the dawn of China's primitive folk religion, the relationship between man and nature has been conceived as a deep, reciprocal involvement in which each can affect the other. As the forces of nature can bring prosperity or disaster to man, so can man disrupt the delicate balance of nature by his misdeeds, for Heaven, Earth and man constitute a single, indivisible unity, which is governed by cosmic law (tao). . . .

No boundaries may be drawn between the supernatural world, the domain of nature, and that of man. Hence, if this sensitive organism is to function easily, man must do his part; when he conforms to natural law, society enjoys peace and tranquility; when he transgresses it, both Heaven and nature are disturbed, the intricate machinery of the cosmos breaks down, and calamities ensue.

The World's Great Religions

Improbable as it may sound, it is a fact that the contemporary architect or engineer faces few problems in structural design which nature has not already met and solved. By our own standards, her designs are structurally more efficient and esthetically more satisfactory than ours.

We should—to paraphrase that forthright pre-Civil War critic, Horatio Greenough—learn from nature like men and not copy her like apes. But the truth of the matter is that we have only recently perfected the means whereby her structures can really be understood.

Fred M. Severud

For centuries European art has turned its back on the fundamental conception of nature in art, and Western man has imagined himself and nature as being in antithesis. In reality, his much-vaunted individuality is an illusion, and the truth which the Orient now reveals to him is that his identity is not separate from nature and his fellow-beings, but is at one with her and them.

Christopher Tunnard

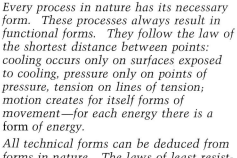

Crystals.   Marine plant forms.

Every process in nature has its necessary form. These processes always result in functional forms. They follow the law of the shortest distance between points: cooling occurs only on surfaces exposed to cooling, pressure only on points of pressure, tension on lines of tension; motion creates for itself forms of movement—for each energy there is a form of energy.

All technical forms can be deduced from forms in nature. The laws of least resistance and of economy of effort make it inevitable that similar activities shall always lead to similar forms. So man can master the powers of nature in another and quite different way from what he has done hitherto.

If he but applied all the principles that the organism has adopted in its striving toward useful ends, he will find there enough employment for all his capital, strength and talent for centuries to come. Every bush, every tree can instruct him, advise him, and show him inventions, apparatuses, technical appliances without number.

Raoul France

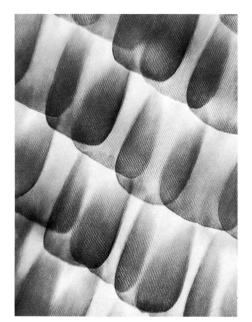

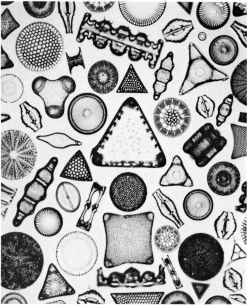

Wing scales of a butterfly.   Diatoms.

Nature's ingenious process of pollination. As the honeybee lands and presses into the blossom after nectar, it triggers the flower stamen, forcing it down in an arc to make contact with and deposit pollen on the bee's body. Bee, flower, mechanism—what have we humans made to compare?

Interaction between man and environment in the West is abstract, an I–It relationship; in the East it is concrete, immediate, and based on an I–Thou relationship. Western man fights nature; Eastern man adapts himself to Nature and nature to himself. These are broad generalizations and, like all generalizations, should be taken with a grain of salt. But I believe that they may help to explain some of the essential differences out of which the different attitudes of East and West to life and environment develop and which are each in its own right destined to play its part in the transformation of the present and the future.

E. A. Gutkind

In Spengler's most moving passage, where he identifies the "landscape" as the base of the "culture," he says that . . . man . . . is so held to it by myriad fibres, that without it life, soul, and thought are inconceivable.

Stanley White

Kyoto, as an illustrious example of oriental land planning, was laid out in accordance with the precepts of geomancy. These deal with the location and design of land use patterns and structural forms in response to, and in harmony with, the paths of energy flow through the earth and the atmosphere.

To the western mind this practice may seem dubious. In the more mature cultures its efficacy is unquestioned. Unfortunately its principles have been veiled in religious mysticism and never clearly defined in technological terms.

Let it be said only that historically architects, planners, and engineers have expressed in their constructions an intuitive feeling for those geologic conditions and natural forces which have shaped and continue to govern the physical landscape and which have a powerful influence on all elements introduced. Such pervasive conditions include surface and subsurface rock formations, strata, cleavages, fissures, drainageways, aquifers, mineral seams, and deposits and lines and upwellings of electrical energy flow. They include also the air currents, tides, variations in temperature, solar radiation, and the earth's magnetic field.

The contemporary planner can only bring to bear a diversified training in such related fields as geology, chemistry, physics, astronomy, and hydrology and hope in time to develop a fuller understanding of cause, effect, and relationships.

Kyoto,
Mountain green,
And water clean.

Sanyō Rai

The biosphere of the planet Earth is divided into several major habitats: the aquatic, the terrestrial, the subterranean, and the aerial.

quent demonstration of the universal principles of form creation to be understood and applied.

To the physical planner, nature reveals itself as the eternal, living, formidable, yet beneficent setting for every project and plan. It is essential to the success of our efforts that we come to know and understand nature, just as a hunter is at home with nature—drinks of the springs, uses the cover, hunts into the prevailing winds, knows when the game will be feeding on the beechnuts and acorns of the ridges and when on the berries in the hollows, and senses the coming of a storm and instinctively seeks out shelter, and just as a sailor is at home on the sea—reads the shoal, senses the sandbar, interprets the sky, and observes the changing conformation of the ocean bottom. Just so must planners be conversant with all facets of nature, until for any major tract of land, local building site, or landscape area we can instinctively recognize the natural characteristics, limitations, and fullest possibilities. Only by being thus aware can we develop a system of harmonious relationships.

History shows us inspiring examples of humanized landscapes planned in harmony with nature. One such example was the breathtakingly beautiful preindustrial city of Kyoto as it existed at the turn of the century.[3] Until only recently it could be said: "Set amidst a national forest of pine and maple trees, Kyoto overlooks a broad river valley in which clear mountain water slides and splashes between great mossy boulders. Here in ordered arrangement are terraced the stone, timber, and paper buildings of the city, each structure planned to the total site and fitted with great artistry to the ground on which it stands. In this remarkable landscape each owner considers his land a trust. Each tree, rock, and spring is considered a special blessing from his gods, to be preserved and developed, to the best of his ability, for the benefit of city, neighbors, and friends. Here, as one overlooks the wooded city or moves through its pleasant streets, one realizes the fullest meaning of the phrase 'the stewardship of land.' Kyoto is a city of great harmonies, great order, and great beauty, because from broadest concept to smallest detail *it was planned that way.*"[4]

The ecological basis

From the time of earth's beginnings there has evolved an interacting, counterbalancing framework for all life. This life matrix, or *biosphere,* born of earth, air, fire, and water, comprises the whole of our living environment.

It is as vast as the space between the basalt floor of the deepest ocean bed and the highest rarefied reaches of the outer ionosphere.

It is as awesome as the towering thunderheads, the roaring hurricane, and the crashing surf.

It is as tough as the granite hulk of a mountain.

It is "as fragile as frost at dawn."[5]

The biosphere, so fearfully and wonderfully contrived, is home to countless plant and animal communities that range in type and size from the invisible virus cluster to the roaming elephant herd or the pod of sounding whales. The biosphere is home as well to all members of the human race. As yet we have no other.

We are just beginning to learn the extent to which all organisms

[3]With the rapid industrialization of Japan many philosophic tenets developed over 3000 years of unbroken cultural evolution, which had guided all lives, thought, and land planning, have been tragically abrogated. Even Kyoto, the nation's cultural capital, while still one of the loveliest cities of the world, has felt the disruptive impacts.

[4]First edition (1961) of *Landscape Architecture*, p. 14.

[5]Ernest Braun and David E. Cavagnaro, *Living Water.*

are interrelated and interdependent and the sometimes critical effects of almost imperceptible changes in the temperature, chemistry, moisture content, soil structure, air movements, and water currents on our habitat. The slightest change in the delicate web of life may have repercussions throughout the whole of a natural system such as that of a marsh, pond, watershed, or receiving ocean basin.

While soil and adequate water supply are essential to all living matter, their life-giving, life-sustaining energy is ultimately derived from the sun. This is received and transmitted through many life-supporting processes, such as evapotranspiration, osmosis, capillary action, fermentation, and oxidation. But it can be said that the underlying basis of all higher forms of life is the process of *photosynthesis*, which takes place in the chlorophyll cells of waterborne phytoplankton and land-based plants. Here, carbon dioxide is consumed in the presence of air, sunlight, and water, producing carbohydrates and free oxygen. These two component products are essential to life.

As living, breathing human beings, inextricably related to all other organisms and creatures, we are utterly dependent upon the life-giving productivity of the remaining un-built-upon landscape areas of the earth. Should their life-support functions be diminished or disrupted to the point that they fail, we would then cease to exist. Only very recently, in the face of burgeoning population growth, rising indices of pollution, and the rapid depletion of our land and water reserves, has such a catastrophe seemed a remote possibility. Today, however, those scientists best able to assess trends and conditions have this very much on their minds.

What does all this mean to the planner, the designer of communities, the highway engineer, or the builder of home and garden? Simply that the integrity of the natural or cultivated landscape and the quality of the water within it and the air above it are to be in all ways protected. Land areas can no longer be treated as little more than pictorial stage sets of forest, billowing grass, limpid water, or lavender hills in profile amid which constructions can be blithely aligned or indiscriminately plunked. It is no longer acceptable that any land area be considered an isolated private domain, to be shaped at will to the heart's desire or carved up unfeelingly into cold geometric patterns. No smallest parcel can any longer be considered apart from all other contiguous land and water areas or those of the extensional environment. For it is now well recognized that each draws upon the other and in turn affects them. Ecologically, all land and water areas are interconnected and interrelated.

It is fundamental to intelligent land and resource planning that the natural systems which protect our health and well-being be understood and sustained.

That those most sensitive and productive, together with nature's superlatives, may be *preserved* in their natural condition;

That protective support areas be *conserved* and devoted to limited and compatible uses;

That the less critical areas selected for *development* be so planned as to do no significant harm to their environs;

And that all land use plans be so conceived as to bring people into the best possible relationships with each other and with the living landscape.

Natural systems supply, transport, treat, and store water; modify the climate; oxygenate and purify the air; produce food; treat or assimilate waste; build land; maintain beaches; and provide protection from hurricanes . . .

If essential components are destroyed, or if the system as a whole is overstressed, the process will break down and the system will fail.

Albert R. Veri et al.

Life-support systems are those functions of nature which must be maintained in order to support human (and other) life. The primary functions include the production of carbohydrates through the process of photosynthesis and the provision of available water through the workings of the hydrologic cycle.

The hydrologic cycle is the continuous process in which water moves by evaporation and transpiration to the atmosphere, falls to the land as precipitation, and flows toward the receiving water bodies, principally the oceans.

The basic premise of science is that the physical world is governed by certain predictable rules.

Landscape character

Looking down at the surface of our globe or moving in any direction across it, we find areas where there is an apparent harmony or unity among all the natural elements—ground forms, rock formations, vegetation, and even animal life. We may say of these areas that they possess a naturally produced *landscape character*. The more complete and obvious this unity, the stronger the landscape character.

Let us imagine that we have been dropped into the uplands of Utah's great spruce forest. All about us rise wild and rugged slopes of rock bristling with tall evergreen spires that tower against the sky. The deep, shadowy ravines are choked with great boulders and fallen trees. Melting snow drips or trickles from the crevices or gurgles underneath the tangled forest duff. White water rushes and foams from high ledge to chasm, cascading toward the stillness of a mountain lake that lies below, deep blue at its center, shading to pale green along its gravelly edges. Here all is in harmony, all is complete. Even the brown bear lumbering close to shore is clearly native to this place. The leaping trout, the wading tern, the caw-caw of the flapping crow are part of this scene, part of its *landscape character.*

The blazing Arizona desert, the fetid, dripping Georgia swamp, the bleak and desolate arctic tundra, the flat sedge island waterland off Barnegat Bay, each has its own distinctive landscape character, and each evokes in the observer a strong and distinctive emotional response. No matter what the natural landscape character of an area and no matter what the mood it produces in us—exhilaration, sadness, eeriness, or awe—we experience a very real pleasure in sensing the unity and harmony of the total scene. The more nearly complete this "oneness" and "wholeness," the greater the pleasure of the observer. The degree of evident harmony or unity of the various elements of a landscape area is a measure not only of the pleasure induced in us but also of the quality we call *beauty*. For beauty by definition is "the evident harmonious relationship of all sensed components."

Shoals off Mozambique, from 20,000 feet.

Pond lilies.

Natural landscape beauty is of many varying qualities, which include:

The picturesque	The bizarre	The delicate	The stark	The majestic
The ethereal	The idyllic	The graceful	The serene	The bold

Natural landscape character, too, is of many categories, including:

Mountain	Lake	Canyon	Pond	Dune
Sea	Forest	Desert	Prairie	Stream
River	Plain	Swamp	Hill	Valley

Each of these and other types may be further subdivided. A *forest* landscape character, for instance, might be one of the following subtypes:

Oak	White pine	Timberline	New Jersey river
Beech	Red pine	Valley	New Jersey coastal
Cedar	Yellow pine	Swamp	New Jersey plain
Maple	Loblolly pine	Jungle	Rocky Mountain
Hemlock	Piñon pine	Tropic	Adirondack
Mangrove	Pitch pine	Arctic	Alpine
Cypress	Himalayan pine	Alaskan	Redwood
Fir	Scotch pine	Burmese	Mixed hardwood
Cottonwood	Austrian pine	Bornean	
Teak	Norway pine	Lebanese	

An area of land that has common distinguishing visual characteristics of landform, rock formations, water forms, and vegetative patterns is termed a *landscape type*.

When the major type is broad or diversified, there may be defined within it *landscape subtypes* of significant differentiation.

Dunes, New Mexico.

Cactus forest.

Monterey coast.

Wyoming waterfall.
Florida gulf coast.

Each of the myriad examples that come to mind is itself a distinctive landscape type. For each type, the more closely an area or any object within it approaches the ideal (or has the most of those qualities that we associate with perfection in a given type), the more intense is our pleasure.

The absence of beauty we call *ugliness*. Ugliness results from a sensed lack of unity among the components or the presence of one or more incongruous elements. Since that which is beautiful tends to please and that which is ugly tends to disturb, it follows that a visual harmony of all parts of a landscape is desirable.

With only the visual aspects of site character in mind, it would seem that in developing a natural area we should do all that we can to preserve and intensify its inherent landscape quality. We should therefore eliminate objects that are out of keeping, and we may even introduce objects to increase or accentuate this native character.

Elimination of incongruous elements In all planning, as in life, the elimination of an incongruous element usually effects an improvement.

Let us suppose, for example, that we have wandered into a giant sequoia forest and stand in silent awe of the tremendous upward thrust of the redwood boles and their imposing timeless grandeur. And then suppose that on the forest floor we should happen to notice a neatly cultivated bed of pink petunias. The same petunias in a suburban garden bed might make quite a pleasant splash. But to find them here in the redwood forest would first surprise and then annoy us. They would annoy us because our experience would tell us that in this natural redwood grove petunias are out of place. They would set up unpleasant visual and mental tensions, and should we come often enough to this place, it is possible, even probable, that we would ultimately root them out with the toe of our boot. We would be eliminating an element that was in conflict with the natural landscape character.

An incident from the author's own experience further illustrates this point. As a small boy he spent summers in a camp on Lake George in the backwoods of Michigan. At the lower end of this lake he found a spot that he came to consider his private bullfrog pond. It was a clearing in the cattails, jammed with mossy logs and stumps and closed almost tight with the pads of water lilies. When he waded quietly through the cattails, he would spy huge green-black bullfrogs floating among the pads or squatting dreamily on the logs. These he hunted for their saddles, which were most welcome at the family table. Every day he visited his pond, lying hour after hour on a log, motionless, with a whittled birch rod poised ready for a frog to surface. It was an idyllic world of cedar smell, sunlight, patrolling dragonflies, lapping water, and contentment.

One morning he found that a battered yellow oil drum had been washed into his frog pond by a storm. He pushed it outside the cattails. Next morning it was back. Again he pushed it from the pond, farther this time but not far enough. Finding it once again floating jauntily among the lily pads, he shoved it out and went for a

The elimination of an incongruous element will usually effect an improvement.

Landscapes for living

Exemplary outdoor places and space

rowboat. With the anchor rope he towed the drum to the deepest part of the lake, bashed a jagged hole in its top with an ax head, and scuttled it. As he watched it slowly founder, he wondered why he had felt such anger at an old, rusty metal barrel. Years later, when the author recollected the pond in terms of its landscape character, he realized at last why the drum had to go. It was a disturbing, inharmonius element in the minilandscape, and it had to be removed.[6]

Introduction of accentuating elements   If it is true that the elimination of certain elements from an area can improve its landscape quality, it follows that other elements might be *introduced* with the same result. To accentuate the landscape quality of a site within or abutting a cactus desert, for instance, we might remove an old tire that had been tossed there and replace it with a clump of fine native cactus plants gathered from the surrounding sandy draws. Or we might plant a single picturesque Joshua tree that would reflect and articulate the area's mood or landscape expression.

To sum up, then, the landscape character of any area may be developed or intensified by eliminating any negative elements and by accentuating its positive qualities.

To improve a landscape or land area intelligently we must not only recognize its essential natural character but also possess knowledge that will enable us to achieve the optimum development of that character.

During the Ming dynasty in China this art was so highly refined that within a single garden of a few acres one might experience lofty mountain scenery, a misty lakeshore, a bamboo grove at the edge of a quiet pond, a pine-sheltered forest overlook, and a cascading waterfall. And, through the skill of the designer, the transition areas between viewing points were so masterfully contrived as to be fully as pleasant and dramatic as the major views themselves.

Use as a landscape factor   Up to this point we have considered the natural landscape as something to be observed, as in some of our larger parks, for example, or along scenic parkways, or at the better resort hotels. In such cases a person becomes a microvisitor, permitted only to enter an area inconspicuously, observe respectfully, and leave unobtrusively. But there are relatively few areas that can be reserved in their pristine state or developed solely for the display of their natural beauty.

We generally consider land in terms of use. At this point one is quite likely to ask: "What's all this talk about beauty and landscape character? What I want to know is, how can this property be *used?*"

But the hard, cold fact of the matter is that the most important factor in considering the use of land is a thorough understanding of its landscape character in the broadest sense. For the planner must

Big South Fork National River and Recreation Area, Tennessee and Kentucky.

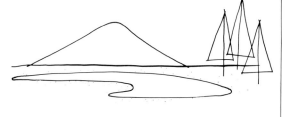

In the natural landscape a human being is an intruder.

---

[6]Yes, it *has* also occurred to the author in retrospect that there are better places in which to dispose of oil drums than the bottom of a lake.

These Japanese homes of hewn timber seem completely in character with the ancient grove that is their site.

first comprehend the physical nature of the site and its extensional environment before it is possible to:

1. Recognize those uses for which the site is suited and which will utilize its full potential.

2. Introduce into the area only those uses which are appropriate.

3. Apply and develop such uses in studied relationship to the landscape features.

4. Ensure that these applied uses are integrated to produce a modified landscape that is functionally efficient and visually attractive.

5. Determine whether or not a project is *unsuited* and would be incongruous not only on the immediate site but in the surrounding environs as well and thus appear to be misplaced, unfit, and (by definition) ugly. Such an improper use would be disturbing not only aesthetically but practically, for an unsuitable use forced upon a parcel of land generates frictions that may not only destroy the most desirable qualities of the landscape area but preclude proper function as well.

Since we are repelled by disorder, the discordant, and that which is ugly, since we are instinctively drawn to that which is harmonious and well formed, and since most artifacts and developments are designed to please, it follows that resultant beauty is a highly desirable attribute.

It works well; there is an efficient arrangement of all the parts. *It looks good;* it is beautiful; *I like it.*

Anything planned in the landscape affects the landscape. Each new plan application sets up a series or reactions and counterreactions not only about the immediate site but upon its extensional environment as well. This environment may extend a great distance in any direction and include many square miles.

In considering the development of any area of the earth's surface we must realize that this surface is a continuous plane. A project applied to this plane affects not only the specific site but all flow past it. Each addition or change, however minute, imposes upon the land certain new physical properties and visual qualities. It can thus be seen that the planner is engaged in a continuing process of landscape modification.

Landscape organization   The untouched landscape is in repose, a repose of equilibrium. It has its own cohesive, harmonious order in which all forms are an expression of geologic structure, climate, growth, and other natural forces. In the primeval forest or upon the open plain, the human is an intruder. If one penetrates the wilderness by trail or road, one may either roll with the topography and develop expressive harmonies or buck the terrain and generate destructive frictions. As human activity in an area increases, the landscape becomes more and more organized; agreeably if the orga-

State University of New York at Buffalo.

Esthetic impacts influence us at all moments. Consciously, or in most cases subconsciously, they provoke friendly or hostile reactions. . . . Their impacts on . . . decisions reach even into the most practical problems, into the shaping of things of daily use—cars, bridges—and above all, of our human environment.

Siegfried Giedion

Is it not yet conceivable that a well-designed and well-placed building, a bridge or road, can be an addition rather than a menace to the countryside?

Christopher Tunnard

nization is one of fitting relationships, disagreeably if the relationships are chaotic or illogical. The development of any area may entail a concentration of its natural landscape character, an integration of nature and construction, or the creation of a wholly built complex of spaces and forms. In any case, the commendable plans are those that effect a resolution of all elements and forces and create a newly unified landscape of dynamic équilibrium.

The planned landscape   We are all familiar with humanized landscape areas in which everything seems to be working well together. We recall pleasant stretches of New England farmland, western ranch territory, or Virginia plantation country. In or near such areas, we experience a sense of well-being and pleasure. We say that a certain town or region is quaint, delightful, or picturesque. What we probably mean is that we subconsciously sense certain qualities of compatibility that appeal to us. These we like. Other places of disorder, confusion, pollution, "bad taste," or "poor planning," are "ugly" and bother us. If we were traveling, these would be bypassed. We would prefer not to live in or near them.

The negative qualities of such places are those we would attempt to eliminate in any replanning process; the positive qualities are those we would strive to retain and accentuate. It would seem to follow as a guiding principle that *to preserve or create a pleasing site character all the various elements or parts must be brought into harmony.*

We make much of this word *harmony*. Do we mean to imply that everything should blend with or get lost in the landscape as through protective coloration or camouflage? No, but rather that the planner, in addressing a land-water holding, from small plot to vast acreage, will so integrate the structural and topographical forms as to produce the best possible fit. If the completed project seems to blend with the landscape, it is the happy result of an inspired design rather than the mistaken aim of an uninspired designer.

Contrast   It is known that the form, color, or texture of a handsome object can be emphasized through contrast. This principle applies as well to planning in the landscape and is exemplified by the bridges of the brilliant Swiss engineer Robert Maillart. All who have seen them marvel at the lightness and grace of the white reinforced-concrete arches that span the wild mountain gorges in Switzerland and Bavaria. Surely the lines and materials of these structures are foreign to the natural character of the craggy mountain background. Are they *right* for such a location? Or would the bridges have been more suitable if constructed of native timbers and stone?

In our national parks bridges have usually been built of indigenous materials. Although some may quarrel with this policy, it has produced many bridges of high design quality and spared the park-using public from more of the typical fluted and fruited cast-metal or balustraded cast-stone monstrosities that clutter up so many of our American river crossings.

Village of Cedarwood, Boca West, Florida.

To me the quest of harmony seems the noblest of human passions. Boundless as is the goal, for it is vast enough to embrace everything, it yet remains a very definite one.
Le Corbusier

The Salginatobel Bridge, Switzerland, leaps the wild chasm as lightly and surely as a native stag.

In his bridge design, however, Maillart has simply and forthrightly imposed a necessary function—a highway crossing—on the natural landscape. He has expressed with logical materials and refreshing clarity the force diagram of his structures. Moreover, by sharply contrasting his elegantly dynamic bridges and the rugged mountain forest, he has dramatized the highest qualities of each. The gorges seem more wild, the bridges more precise, more eloquent.

As another application of the principle of contrast, we may recall in color theory that to produce an area of greenest green a fleck of scarlet may be brought into juxtaposition. To make a spot of scarlet glow with fire, an artist brings it into contrast with the greenest possible background.

It follows that before introducing contrasting elements into a landscape it would be well to understand the nature of the features to be accentuated. The contrasting elements will then be contrived to strengthen and enrich the visual impact of these natural features. Conversely, to emphasize certain qualities of the structure or component introduced, one will search the landscape and bring into contrasting relationship those features that will effect the desired contrast.

A further principle in the use of contrast, as illustrated by the work of Maillart, is that of two contrasting elements one must dominate. One is the feature; the other, the supporting and contributing backdrop. Otherwise, with two contrasting elements of equal power, visual tensions are generated that weaken or destroy, rather than heighten, the pleasurable impact of the viewing experience.

We have said that to create a pleasing character for an area all components must work together in harmony. We find striking examples that seem to violate this precept: Maillart's bridges, for instance, and Frank Lloyd Wright's Falling Water at Bear Run. At first appraisal these structures would seem to be completely alien to their surroundings. Yet with study one senses in each a quality of fitness—of spirit, purpose, material, and form.

The precision and whiteness of the concrete forms contrast boldly with the natural forms, colors, and textures of the site. Yet the structure seems at home here. Why? Perhaps because the massive cantilevered decks recall the massive cantilevered ledge rock. Perhaps because the masonry walls that spring from the rock are the same rock tooled to a higher degree of refinement. Perhaps because the dynamic spirit of the building is in keeping with the spirit of the wild and rugged woodland. And perhaps because each contrasting element was consciously planned to evoke, through its precise kind and degree of contrast, the highest qualities of the natural landscape.

Cone nebula, 2000 light-years away.

Natural forces, forms, and features

We have come to learn through the centuries that the spinning orb on which we live is a minor planet suspended in limitless space—an infinitesimal speck of matter in the universal scheme of things. Yet it is our world—vast, imponderable, and wonderful to us, a world of marvelous order and boundless energy. It is illumined and warmed in rhythmic cycles by the heat of our sun, bathed in a swirling atmosphere of air and moisture. Its white-hot core is a seething mass of molten rock; its thin, cool crust, pocked and creased with hollows and ridged with hills, mountain ranges, and towering peaks. The greater part of its area is immersed in saltwater seas, which ebb and flow with heaving tides and are swept to their depths by immense and intricate patterns of current.

The earthscape From the ice-sheathed poles to the blazing equator, the earthscape varies endlessly. Wandering over it for something close to a million years, the human earth dwellers have learned first to survive and later to thrive through a process of adaptation. This process, if wisely continued, should gain for us an ever-improving way of life. The study of the human-nature relationship is as old as humans themselves. In long-range perspective it is probably still a very young science, but, everything considered, it is the most basic science of all.

In our lifetime, we have for the first time scaled earth's highest peak, plumbed its deepest ocean trench, and penetrated outer space. We are tempted to believe that we have conquered nature.

We have learned to unleash the awesome power contained within the atom. Now we must learn the means by which to control it.

There are those who hold that in the era ahead we will finally subject nature to our control. Let us not delude ourselves. Nature is not soon to be conquered by puny man.

Conquer nature! How can we conquer nature? We are—blood, bone, fiber, and soul—a very part of nature. We are spawned of nature, rooted in nature, nourished by nature. Our every heartbeat, every neural impulse, and every thought wave, our every act and effort are governed by nature's all-pervading law. Conquer nature! We are but fleeting traces of life in nature's eternal process of evolving life and growth. Conquer nature! It is far better that we turn again to nature's way to search out and develop an order consonant with the universal systems, that our living may tap the vital nature forces, that our cultural development may have orientation, that our form building, form organizing, and form ordering may have meaning, that we may know again the rich, pulsing harmonies of life at one with nature.

The history of our progress on this earth is the history of an increasing understanding of nature's vitalities and powers. The wisdom of the wisest among us is no more than a comprehension of the simplest natural principles. The knowledge of our most perceptive scientists is gained through a faint insight into the wonder of natural phenomena. Our labored development is the development of those sciences that reveal to us a way of life more closely *attuned to nature's immutable way.*

Those of the forests, jungles, and sea are keenly sensitive to their natural surroundings and instinctively shape their living patterns to comply with nature's rhythms and cycles. They have

learned that to do otherwise is to court inevitable disaster.

Years ago the urge to wander to strange new lands led the author to live for some months in lonely, exotic British North Borneo (Sabah). There he came to be profoundly impressed by the tremendous joy of the people in simply being alive—exultantly healthy and happy sons and daughters of nature. On the islands all live not only close to nature but *by* nature. Their whole life is guided day by day and hour by hour by the sun, the storms, the surf, the stars, the tides, the seasons. A full moon and an ebbing tide give promise of successful milkfish spearing on the shoal. The wheeling and screeching of the birds give warning of an approaching storm. In the quiet freshness of early morning a hunter may draw his little daughter to his side and, crouching, point a long brown finger to the peak of Mount Kinabalu looming high above the palm fringe. "Tiba, little Tiba," he may caution. "Look now at the clouds on the mountaintop. Soon it will be blowing and raining there, and the streams will be rushing full. So stay away from the banks today and play at home with your mama."

On the islands, clearly, the closer one's life is adapted to nature, the happier one's life will be. But not only on the islands. This observation is fully as true of our life on our farms and in our suburbs and cities. Sometimes we tend to forget this salient fact as we go about our living and planning for living. And often this forgetting is the root of much distress.

The city of Toronto, for example, is surging northward into an area many miles from its harbor on Lake Ontario. Aside from the convenience of the lakeshore, the summer temperature there is often 20° cooler and the winter temperature 30° warmer than in the districts of new building concentration.

A popular ski resort in Pennsylvania was laid out with the major runs facing south and southwest, directly exposed to the melting winter sun. On the same property, undeveloped northerly slopes have excellent snow on 2 days for every day on which the planned slopes are usable.

In many cities along the Ohio, Missouri, and Mississippi rivers from 10 to 25 percent of the developed land area is inundated at least once every 35 years.

A perceptive architect has noted that not 1 percent of all the buildings in his contemporary city give evidence of having been planned with any regard for prevailing winds, solar radiation, or natural thermodynamics. The meanest thatched hut in Borneo is planned in well-considered relation to all three. It is a jolting experience to reflect on the natural-landscape potential of the site on which our city is built and to realize the pathetic results of our city-building efforts.

If our planning is basically a studied attempt to improve our living environment, it would seem only logical to proceed in full awareness of the sweep of the sun, the air currents, the peaks and hollows of the earth, rock and soil strata, vegetation, lakes and streams, watersheds, and natural drainageways. If we disregard them, we will engender countless unnecessary frictions and costs and preclude those experiences of fitness and compatibility that can bring so much pleasure and satisfaction to our lives.

Major landscape elements   There are dominant natural landscape forms, features, and forces that we can alter little, if at all. We must accept them and adapt ourselves and our planning to them. These unchangeable elements include such topographical forms as mountain ranges, river valleys, and coastal plains; such features as precip-

Tao, the Way—the basic Chinese belief in an order and harmony in nature. This grand concept originated in remote times, from observation of the heavens and of nature—the rising and setting of the sun, moon, and stars, the cycle of day and night, and the rotation of the seasons—suggesting the existence of laws of nature, a sort of divine legislation that regulated the pattern in the heavens and on earth. It is worth noting that the original purpose of ritual was to order the life of the community in harmony with the forces of nature (tao), on which subsistence and well-being depended.
Mai-mai Sze

Gravity is one of man's greatest enemies. It has shaped man himself, conditioned his body as well as his thoughts, and put its unmistakable stamp upon his cities. Thus in the narrow winding valleys of the world, life is a continual battle with gravity. One must live on the valley's bottom, or "fight the slope" until his dying days.
Grady Clay

The first chart of the Gulf Stream was prepared about 1769 under the direction of Benjamin Franklin while he was deputy postmaster general of the colonies. The board of customs in Boston had complained that the mail packets coming from England took two weeks longer to make the westward crossing than did the Rhode Island merchant ships. Franklin, perplexed, took the problem to a Nantucket sea captain, Timothy Folger, who told him this might very well be true because the Rhode Island captains were well acquainted with the Gulf Stream and avoided it on the westward crossing, whereas the English captains were not. Folger and other Nantucket whalers were personally familiar with the stream because, he explained, "In our pursuit of whales, which keep to the sides of it but are not met within it, we run along the side and frequently cross it to change our side, and in crossing it have sometimes met and spoke with those packets who were in the middle of it and stemming it. We have informed them that they were stemming a current that was against them to the value of three miles an hour and advised them to cross it, but they were too wise to be counselled by simple American fishermen."
Rachel Carson

The Great Wall of China, raised in the third century B.C. against the invasion of the Tatars, extended for 1400 miles along the northern border. This fortress-wall, built through supreme effort, was a deliberate attempt to extend and reinforce the protective conformation of the mountain ridges.

itation, frost, fog, the water table, and seasonal temperatures; and such forces as winds, tides, sea and air currents, the process of growth, solar radiation, and gravity.

These we analyze to the extent necessary to make an accurate assessment of their influence and effects. Then, if wise, we will shape our plans in full awareness of, and response to, the constraints and possibilities. Such considerations are fundamental to the plac-

A harbor, a town, and every structure within it fitted to the topography.

ing of cities, the zoning of a community, the projected alignment of highways, the siting of industries, or the orientation and layout of a single home or garden.

The majority of the notable planning projects of any age demonstrate with clarity the adaptation of a structure or activity area to the landscape in such a way that the best qualities of each were made to complement the other. In such works not only the constructed elements but the natural elements as well appear to have been designed by the planner, as in one sense they were, for all were considered together as integral parts of the total conceptual plan.

Minor landscape elements   There are also landscape elements of lesser consequence, such as hills, groves, and streams, that we as planners *can* modify. In their planned development there are four general courses of action. Let us illustrate these varying approaches with the hill as an example:

Preservation of the natural form.   The landscape character of a hill may be such that its optimum yield or use is realized if it is carefully preserved from change. In its undisturbed state it might better produce its crop of timber, maple sap, nuts, or fruit. Throughout the United States we find huge tracts of land that have been set aside in their natural state as game preserves, parks, forests, or regional open space. Many a village or town in Japan is nestled among hills or islands that have for centuries been left undisturbed by decree, in the best interest of the community.

Destruction of the natural form.   A hill or knoll may be eliminated by grading, it may be split with a deep highway cut, it may be inundated by an impoundment, or it may be buried in construction. If any such treatment is proposed, its original landscape character need not be a consideration except as it poses a physical problem.

Alteration of the natural form.   The native aspect of a hill may be altered or changed completely by modifying its shape through grading, construction, or other types of development. Such changes may be detrimental and result in a denuded, eroded, or hacked-up mound, or they may effect an improvement, as in the terraced hills of Bali, with their contoured rice paddies, quiet pools, clear trickling water, and abundant crops.

Accentuation of the natural form.   The essential landscape character of a hill may be intensified. Its apparent height and ruggedness may be increased to such a degree, for instance, that a small knoll may be made to appear mountainous.

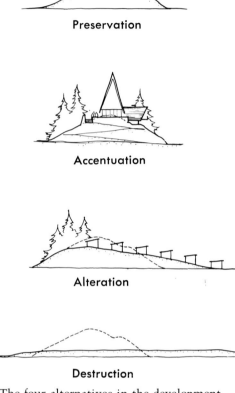

Preservation

Accentuation

Alteration

Destruction

The four alternatives in the development of a hill.

The Alhambra Palace of Granada, Spain, with the snow-covered Sierra Nevada in the distance. This assemblage of fortresslike structures fitted to the crest of the natural rock escarpment borrows both position and power from the native site.

Let us assume for example that we are the owners of a resort hotel in New Hampshire to which summer guests come each season for fresh air, rest, and quiet. We have noticed that many of the guests, when they tire of the rocking chairs set on the wide front porch, walk the easy path to the top of a nearby rise from which they can view the countryside. It occurs to us that "the hill" has become an important part of the resort life, and we decide during the off-season to "improve" this feature by giving it more interest and affording more of a climb to its top.

First, by transplanting a patch of hemlocks, we block off the easy path that led toward the hill and break a new path to a spring that bubbles from the rocks at its base. From this spring a view is opened up across the steepest face of the hill to a weathered old pine, which hides the hilltop beyond. A rough trail leads up through a pile of lichen-splotched rocks to a fallen tree trunk, on which the hiker can sit and rest. Already the hemlocks and spring and rocks have given a new perspective to the hill. Next the path winds easily *down* through a native birch clump to the far side of the hill, to a place where the only way ahead leads steeply up the roughest, wildest part of the hillside. Up, down, and around the trail leads, from ferny ledge to fallen tree, to view, and finally to a point where it breaks out on top. There we place a rough stone slab for a seat, in the shelter of a windblown juniper.

Next summer when our guests leave the porch and set out to "walk" to the hilltop, they find themselves hiking and climbing over a beautiful natural terrain they have never seen before. Through tangled wild-grape cover, around narrow granite outcrops, pulling themselves from rock to rock, they carefully pick their way until they finally reach the summit. They have made it! Nothing, they may think as they rest enjoying the view, is more exhilarating than mountain climbing. While 800 feet away and 200 feet below them, the oldsters sit rocking on the veranda, looking placidly out

The Red Rocks Amphitheater, Denver, Colorado. This magnificent outdoor space has been conceived in studied harmony with the existing terrain.

(left) Mont Saint-Michel, France, surrounded by its rushing tides and reached only by causeway—a sensitive and powerful adaptation of structure to natural forces and forms.

(right) The precise lines of this residence and the rough character of the rocky slope are both enhanced by their well-planned juxtaposition.

at "the hill." For our purpose we have eliminated the negative aspects of our hill and accentuated its positive qualities.

Any area of the natural landscape—mountain slope, island, hillside, or bay—can be developed in this manner.

Early in his career the author was engaged by the Michigan State Department of Parks in the planning of several campgrounds. His first assignment was to develop a site in northernmost Michigan as a state park for tourists, who would come to experience the joys of "wilderness living." Upon arrival at the park site, he found a large white "Public Park" sign at the entrance of a farm road that led in through a flat field of wild carrots to a trailer parking lot beside a muddy pond—not much of a wilderness campsite.

The planner's first step was to spend several weeks exploring the tract to become acquainted with all its natural features, good and bad. His aim was to utilize these features to the utmost. He proposed, in short, to intensify the native landscape quality of the site.

As a first step in the improvement program, the entrance road was moved from the open field to the thickest stand of balsam. Here a rough trail was carved through the rock and snaked up a ridge between the tree trunks, so that a camper's car or trailer could just squeeze through. The caretaker's sagging clapboard cottage with its red-and-white-painted window boxes was demolished and replaced with a rough-sawn slab cabin near the base of a towering pine. This change was made because the camper's first impression of the campsite would be of this venerable tree and the cabin in its shadow, and first impressions are usually the most lasting.

The site's main attraction, a spring-fed pond, was drained, scooped out, and developed as a natural swimming pool with a clean sand and gravel bottom. Above it, a large area of water was impounded to form a settling basin, and here the marsh birds, muskrats, and other wildlife could be seen from a timber bridge that was arched across the dam. At the lower end of the swimming pool a second bridge was built across the waterfall and spillway, where large speckled trout rolled and swam in the sparkling water of the pool below.

Trails were slashed through the densest cover and between the most jagged ledges. Every point of interest was strung on the new trail system like an offset bead.

In one of the more remote areas, a colony of beavers inhabited a stream, where they had built a dam. Much thought was given to

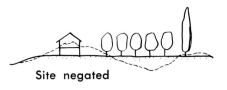

The natural site profile

Site negated

Site dramatized

The essence of land planning for any project:

1. Seek the most suitable site.
2. Let the site suggest plan forms.
3. Extract the full site potential.

The Rinshun Pavilion. In the Japanese tradition structures and site are wholly complementary.

the best way of displaying these shy creatures, a prize in any park. It was decided that to view them the hikers must find their way along an unmarked game trail as it threaded tenuously through a deep cedar swamp until, from the sloping trunk of a great fallen tree that overhung the dam, the hikers could look down to "discover" the beaver workings below them.

In the development of any land or water area, the landscape designer will focus on the essential effect to be conveyed (one inherent in the site). By emphasis, by articulation, and by the creation of progressive sequences of revealment, the observer will be led to discover the positive features of the locale and thus exact its full pleasurable impact.

The built environment

We have considered natural landscape elements and their importance in the planning process. Constructed forms, features, and lines of force are major planning factors too.

As we look at any road map, we find it crisscrossed with lines of various kinds and colors that we recognize as highways, minor roads, streets, railroads, ferryboat routes, and even subways. These lines seem innocuous enough on paper. But those of us who have zoomed along with the streaming traffic of a turnpike, or stood by the tracks as the *Limited* roared by, or tried to maneuver a catboat through the churning wake of a ferry will agree that the map lines tracing their path indicate powerful lines of force. Such lines are essential to the movement of people and goods, but unfortunately they may also be lethal. Every few minutes someone in the United

States is killed by an automobile, and the incidence of serious injury is much higher. It must occur to us, if we ponder these facts, that we planners have as yet failed to treat transportation routes with the proper respect, or else we have not yet learned to design them with foresight and imagination.

There are countless other features of the built environment that, if perhaps less dominant, still have great effect on our planning. To understand their importance we might list a few that deserve investigation in project siting. For openers the list will include:

> Peripheral streets
> Walkway access
> Adjacent structures and uses
> Structures to be demolished
> Unstable fill to be removed
> Subsurface construction
> Energy sources and supply
> Utility leads and capacities
> Applicable zoning
> Building code and regulations
> Easements
> Deed restrictions

This sampling may in itself seem formidable, but it does not include such additional considerations as neighborhood character, general site aspects, mineral rights, amenities, public services, and so forth. Any one of these features might well spell the failure or success of an enterprise. The list will differ considerably of course with projects of such varying types as a residence, school, shopping mall, or marina.

A prescribed planning procedure   If our plans are to respond to a wide variety of contrived and natural givens, how do we proceed? It is proposed that, starting down the list, each item in turn will be studied as to where the problems and possibilities lie. We will then maximize all possible benefits and reduce or eliminate, insofar as feasible, any negative aspects. An ingenious solution has often converted a liability into an asset.

Villa Gamberaia   To the east of Florence has been reconstructed the war-ravaged country villa Gamberaia, built in 1610 by Gamberelli for the duke of Zenobi Lapi and once considered one of the most beautiful villas in Italy. Yet when it was planned, there were those who said that the site was in all ways impossible and that the villa should never be built. In many ways these critics were right, for most of the landscape factors seemed detrimental. The property was unusually small. It was split by a busy trade road with its attending confusion and dust. The property to the north of the road was steep and rocky. The buildable area had only a passable view to the south, and the major view, to Florence and the cathedral, lay to the west—into the hot, cruel, slanting rays of the evening sun.

But for reasons that would seem all too familiar to the planner of today, the duke was determined to build there. It can be surmised that he forcefully declared:

He already owned the property.

It had long belonged to his family and had sentimental value.

There were few better sites available, and they were frightfully expensive.

On the other hand, if he didn't use this property, who knows when he could sell it.

Besides, he wanted his villa right here.

Time was of the essence. He must waste no more time in hunting for a better site. He must get this program rolling.

He had engaged a good architect to build it here, and if this architect couldn't do it, the duke would find another who could.

One can imagine Gamberelli roaming the site, noting each facet of the landscape, carefully observing each tree, each rocky outcrop, each varying sector of the view. At last he felt confident that the unfortunate features of the site could be minimized by imaginative handling and the commendable features highlighted to create a delightful villa. After all, the passing road did provide good access to Florence; there was a view of the city; the land did slope generally to the south for warmth in the early spring and late fall. The northern cliff, although craggy, was covered with gnarled and picturesque trees. Best of all, a mountain stream could be tapped to provide a flow of that most essential element, clear, cool water. Gamberelli set to work.

To connect the divided property and to provide a point of high interest at the road, he constructed across it a great walled ramp supported by a wide, deep arch through which the traffic could pass. In the shaded court thus formed by the walls and steep road shoulders he set the entrance gate that would lead to the house and gardens. The residence he fitted to the solid rocky contours of the slope, raising it above the entrance gate for privacy and a command of the best exposures.

Southward from the structure he leveled a garden panel, which terminated at a wall of clipped trees. This effectively screened all but a selected arc of the southerly view, brought into sharp focus and modulated into a rich montage by dark-green arches of architecturally treated foliage.

To the east and parallel with this panel, Gamberelli developed a long axis through the tangled trees and across the road by a ramp to sculpture and a quiet pool set amid tall cypress trees at the extreme limit of the duke's land. This long axial vista not only completed the unification of the split property but gave a pleasant impression of great distance and expansive freedom within the limited property confines. Moreover, the cypress and narrow vista accentuated, by telling contrast, not only the wild but also the precipitous natural character of the site.

While the western view was unpleasant in the late afternoon, Gamberelli must have reasoned, it was most pleasant for the rest of the day. This view was screened from the other garden areas, but from the west terrace it was displayed in full sweep. In the evening, after the sun had dropped behind the horizon, the western sky, ablaze with high color or muted in pastel twilight, served as a backdrop to Florence and its bridges, domes, and spires. Then, from the terraced gardens of Gamberaia, with their splashing fountains and scent of boxwood and lemon trees, the view was of such haunting beauty that the memory of those who saw it could never let it fade.

The changing landscape The most constant quality of the landscape is the quality of change. We are forever tugging and hauling at the land, sometimes senselessly, destroying the positive values, and sometimes intelligently, developing a union of function and site with such sensitivity as to effect an improvement, as at Villa Gamberaia. Whenever constructions are imposed on a site, its character is thereby modified.

Landscape evolution is a continuing process. At its best it is an ongoing exercise by which compatible uses are brought into harmonious interaction with our natural and built environs.

The ultimate principle of landscape architecture is merely the application and adjustment of one system to another, where contrasting subjects are brought into harmonious relationship resulting in a superior unity called "order."
Stanley White

2

Land

How often in their ceaseless wanderings over the face of the earth must men have paused as they topped the ridge or gained the pass to study the lay of the land?

Each topographic form had its message. Mountains were forbidding; craggy ravines were perilous; broad valleys, beckoning. Prairies, plains, and savannas stretched to the far horizons to be laboriously crossed on foot, on horseback, by travois, or by lumbering wagon trains.

Wherever their urgings or headings led them, our forebears avoided the unfavorable situation and sought those conditions within the landscape best suited to their needs. Sometimes these were as immediate as water, food, or forage; sometimes, as permanent as fortification or homestead. With the same atavistic instinct each of us by habit still constantly surveys the landscape about us to avoid areas of hazard or discomfort, to trace the most favorable path, and to attain the most suitable situation. This feel for the land is inborn; it is in our bones and blood.

As heritage

For many thousands of years our predecessors have gathered the bounty of the grasslands, waterways, and forests without causing significant damage. As they fished, set their snares, or hunted game, they left the land and waters as they found them. Their canoes glided silently through the unspoiled wilderness, their horses were tethered, and their herds grazed without lasting disruption of the natural cover. Their early encampments left no lasting scars and were soon overgrown. Even the first settlements and clearings fitted to the slopes and water edges were of little ecologic consequence.

As populations increased, however, the effects of people's workings have become more and more evident. Blazed trails have become roadways. Scattered farms have been consolidated to push back the marsh and woodland, sometimes to extinction. The early villages on the banks of a stream have swallowed the stream and usurped the banks of the nearby river. Village and town limits have been extended relentlessly outward to be interconnected with additional roads and with railways and often canals. Within a few bustling centuries our native American landscape has been transformed into an expanse of farmsteads, subdivisions, burgeoning cities, sprawling industrial complexes, and far-flung transportation systems. Often the only vestiges of wilderness left are those isolated fringes too difficult of access, too deep in the ooze, too dry, or too close to the rock for economic development.

Where the uses of land have been well suited to the sites, the resulting farms, roadways, and communities may be in all ways agreeable. We have flown over such settlements that seem nestled into the countryside. We have traveled inviting roads that weave pleasantly through the landscape, introducing us to woodland, meadow, streams, well-ordered fields, orchards, and abundant valleys. We have delighted in towns that seem to have blossomed spontaneously upon the crown of a hill or in cities terraced gracefully down to the river edge or harbor.

Well-suited developments intelligently planned can produce an integration of designed forms and modified landscape superior to the original. The best of the indigenous features can be preserved and incorporated. Or they may be conserved for limited uses and to maintain the native setting. The natural attractions may thus be enjoyed and appreciated daily to enrich the living experience. Such installations convey a sense of stability and fitness. They "sing" in the landscape, and they sing in harmony.

Where, however, the uses imposed are unsuited, where they are awkward in plan or clumsy in execution, the result is distressing to both the eye and the intellect. Moreover, the disruptive consequences may be costly, even catastrophic. For the immutable

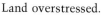

Land overstressed.

forces of nature have a way of rejecting those built intrusions which violate the land.

If humankind is to thrive—yea, even *survive*—it is incumbent upon us to study and apply those principles by which we can bring our species and nature into symbiotic balance. The problems of encroaching civilization, the imperiled land, and the increasing need for its stewardship have together become our heritage.

As resource

Land and the waters that lap its edges, flow across its surface, seep into its upper soil strata, and move within its deep aquifers are our ultimate resources. Mismanaged, they may be lost to us forever, and our national wealth and well-being proportionately diminished.

Before dividing our remaining land reserves into fragmented ownership parcels, it would be good to look at them in their wholeness to see what functions they now perform as farmland, forest, and open space. New patterns for their preservation, conservation, or necessary development can then take form. It is a matter of priorities, of seeing that each broad area of land is devoted to its most reasonable uses and that all land areas together are formed into logical systems. Only within such an overall context can each integral parcel be planned as a related and contributing part.

Soil bank Perhaps the most crucial function of our un-built-upon land areas is that of topsoil reservoir. This vital substance is the basis of all agricultural productivity. It occurs, where it still exists, as a thin mantle of weathered rock intermixed with organic matter in depths ranging from a few inches to a few feet. This rich skim overlaying the subsoils and naked rock may be thousands of years in the making. Once lost, it is gone forever. We in the United States have dissipated in the span of five centuries well over one-third of our vital topsoil endowment. It has been scooped, hauled, or washed and blown away to the rivers and thence transported to the sea. This is a loss no nation can afford. The disastrous consequences of misuse and waste of topsoil are to be observed in most of the arid regions of the world.

Topsoil washed from the uplands to become the silt of the rivers.

Every day some 12 square miles of American farmland is usurped by development.

Each state, county, or municipality has as one of its chief responsibilities a plan for the conservation and best use of the lands within its jurisdiction.

Landowners have the responsibility so to use their property as to protect its natural values and cause no harm to neighbors.

Almost imperceptibly the relationship of society to the land has changed, to a point at which the public good now largely transcends the rights of the individual.

The topsoil mantle is teeming with life. Scoop up a handful almost anywhere, and you are holding a cosmos of microscopic organisms and cells of regeneration.

Food　All forms of life derive from the land and its cover of soil. There, in the chlorophyll of rooted plants, carbon dioxide and moisture are transformed by the energy of the sun into the basic sugars and starches of our food chain. This is a miracle of chemistry occurring only when the conditions are right. The resulting types of vegetation and animal life vary endlessly from patch to patch and from region to region. It is only recently that we have come to understand how closely all are interrelated.

When any area of land is disturbed, the delicate balances are shifted and the repercussions of change may be felt many miles away. This is not to imply that all natural or cultivated food-yielding land should be left unmodified. Often, with husbandry, its nutrient yield may be increased, and for many types of terrain there may be more important uses. It is rather proposed that in land planning and utilization the most productive areas are to be defined and protected. This is fully as true in the layout of a residential property as in the comprehensive planning of a state.

Habitat　The land is our terrestrial home not only for the human species but for all living organisms, which together comprise the biomass of the planet Earth.

Ecology has taught us that all organisms and creatures are interacting and interdependent; that all are contributors and have their necessary functions in the biologic scheme of things; that the mountains, forests, marshes, and rivers together form a *community*

Egret in natural habitat. Those who fail to understand the oneness of the natural systems are in many ways impoverished.

without definable limits; and that the integrity of the component natural systems must somehow be preserved.

While each living plant or animal can be seen to lay claim to its necessary living space, such patterns of use have been fluid, transient, and intermittent, changing as environmental conditions change. In the past, such "territories" have formed spontaneously across the land and water surface of our planet, leaving the Good Earth time to heal between uses in preparation for new and often higher forms of life.

It is only within very recent times that members of the human race have seen fit to claim sole rights in land. This newly acquired compulsion to *own* land and take a permanent *fix* has become epidemic. Today, whole regions of the earthscape have been marked

All of North America was occupied, after a fashion, by Indians, whose home it was and who obtained their living from the land.

The Indian concept of land ownership was completely different from that of the whites. The Indian regarded land as something to be used and enjoyed, even to be defended against trespassers, but not to be owned exclusively by one person, nor ever to be bought and sold in the commercial sense.

When the white man sought to buy land from Indians, the latter might agree and accept a purchase price or gift, yet not understand what the white man meant. It was not simply that white men drove sharp bargains or that Indians reneged on bargains accepted, though there was some of each; more importantly, there was never a genuine meeting of minds. . . .

Marion Clawson

off by boundary posts and line fences, only to be further divided and subdivided, again and yet again.

Most such property ownership demarcations have been made on a wholly haphazard, geometric basis, without regard for topographic conformation.

Reason would tell us that if land *must* be parceled and subdivided (our entire culture seems now to be operating on this premise), new lines of ownership should be brought into consonance with the boundaries of functioning land and water systems. It would seem obvious that neither property lines nor development patterns should transect or disrupt the crest of a ridge, the continuity of a flowing stream, or the organic unity of a tidal estuary.

Not only should our remaining undisturbed land be so apportioned as to express and accommodate the natural form order, but the presently fragmented landholdings must in many cases be reassembled and more logically defined. Over the ensuing years, through the emerging techniques of land use planning, zoning, redevelopment, reclamation, and resource management, the mutilated landscape may be restored to fairer form and to a healthful wholeness. This is not implausible. Nature is slow but inexorable in its progressions, leveling constructions that are artificial, erasing lines that are arbitrary. Nature is patient and has immense powers of recuperation and regeneration. Once we gain fuller understanding of its processes and laws and recommit our society to a supportive nature-human relationship, we can literally recreate the landscape as a more bountiful earthly habitat.

Land grants

In the United States rights in land have flowed to individuals, corporations, and agencies mainly from government—from colonial powers in earlier times and later by acts of Congress.

Through the century following the Louisiana Purchase in 1803, the United States disposed of almost 1 billion acres of land held in the public domain. At first, the more important dispositions were those made to the states in support of public schools and the land-grant colleges. Then followed allotments for wagon roads, canals, and the building of railroads. In the last-named case the entrepreneurs were usually given alternate sections within a broad swath contiguous to the railroad right-of-way. The price of the remaining sections was then doubled to provide the government as much revenue as it otherwise would have received and to reflect the fact that the presence of transportation increased the raw-land values. The Homestead Act of 1862 extended rights in land to settlers, who by 5 years of homesteading and the making of certain improvements could obtain a clear title at the going rate of $1.25 per acre. Military bounties, Indian rights, and grants to encourage such activities as timber culture, mining, irrigation, and reclamation were to swell the dispositions to date to almost half of the total land area of fifty states, which is in the aggregate about 2.3 billion acres.

In Alaska today, the land-grant saga continues. From the time of the Alaska Purchase in 1867 until the Alaska Statehood Act of 1958 the federal government owned almost the whole of the territory, which is approximately one-fifth as large as all the contiguous states put together. In the act Congress promised to transfer to the state of Alaska ownership in 103 million acres of the 375 million total. Another 40 million acres (plus a $1 billion bonus) have since been awarded in settlement to Eskimos, Indians, and Aleuts who successfully pressed their claim of prior occupancy. Yet other vast tracts of Alaskan wilderness are being considered as new national parks and national monuments.

It can be seen that from our country's beginnings to the present time the dynamics of land transfer, ownership, and use have had profound political, social, and economic implications. The story of land exploration, land hunger, land transactions, regulation, and use (and too often *abuse*) is the story of America. Land is our ultimate resource. We must plan for its conservaton, regulation, and development on a more scientific basis. We must learn to use it more wisely.

Land rights

Once in private ownership, land can be readily used or sold as a valued commodity. A factor of use or sale is of course the ability to define and prove rights of ownership by clear title to the property. Such proof presupposes a survey and the establishment on the ground of stakes, monuments, or other markings by which the property boundaries can be identified. Further, there must be a means by which a lot or parcel may be so described as to differentiate it from and relate it to all other landholdings. Finally, there is need for a systematic and orderly means of recording land descriptions and titles.

In the United States, by comparison, we are fortunate in our system. In many Latin American countries, for instance, few of these conditions pertain. There, accurate surveys seldom exist; rights in land are often clouded and in dispute, and the systematic recording of titles is not yet a fact of life. Much land has been preempted by squatters, now backed by traditional sentiment in favor of the pioneer and against those who own or believe they own superseding rights to the land. Such vague and chaotic conditions of property ownership lead to a lack of commitment, investment, and improvement by those not certain of established rights and give force to a growing movement toward massive land reform.

Land surveying

The original land survey has left an indelible mark upon those parts of the United States to which it was applied. There was much to commend the system. As Marion Clawson has noted, we are a rectilinear country, divided into squares and oblongs like a haphaz-

Land definition by transit and rod.

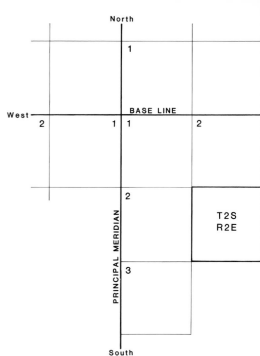

Within each region of the U.S. an east-west <u>base line</u> and north-south <u>principal meridian</u> have been established, and to these all subsequent land subdivision and title descriptions are related. <u>Townships</u> are numbered north and south of the base line, and <u>ranges</u> east and west of the principal meridian.

The principal units of land within counties are <u>townships</u>, six miles on a side, comprised of 36 <u>sections</u>, each approximately 1 mile square.

6	5	4	3	2	1
7	8	9	10	11	12
18	17	16	15	14	13
19	20	21	22	23	24
30	29	28	27	26	25
31	32	33	34	35	36

TOWNSHIP 2 SOUTH
RANGE 2 EAST

<u>Sections</u> are further subdivided as shown. Lots or parcels are described by bearings and distances or "metes and bounds" from stated reference points within a given area of the survey grid.

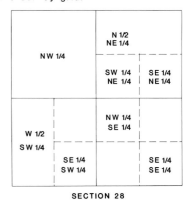

SECTION 28
(640 acres)

Diagrammatic system of land surveying

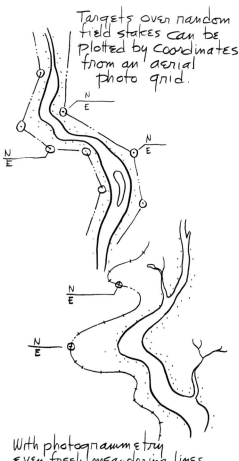

Targets over random field stakes can be plotted by coordinates from an aerial photo grid.

With photogrammetry even freely meandering lines can be plotted for property description and recording – with a trace of the line and coordinates on an aerial map for the record.

Only when all or part of the boundary line needs be staked or monumented is a field crew needed.

Meandering property lines are easily established.

An analogy: that in its land and resource planning each state be considered as a developing farmstead. An astute farmer would study the lay of the land until he came to understand it—its nature, constraints, and possibilities. He would then so lay out (and continually adjust) the working components—living quarters, barn, pens, fields, orchard, and lines of connection—as to bring them into best relationship to each other and to the land-water holding. He would plan the whole and each new element in such a way as to conserve and take full advantage of the land's best features: the ground forms, the woodlot, the spring, the drainageways, the soil, and the natural covers.

Not only is such a farm (state) more productive,

Not only is it more efficient,

Not only is it more agreeable as a place to live and work,

It is also the best possible investment for the farmer, his wife, and their heirs.

ard checkerboard, with the lines running directly north-south and east-west.

Roads typically follow the surveyed section lines even though this means going up and down hills instead of around them. Farmers tend to lay out their fields parallel to the boundaries of their land even though this may mean cultivating up and down the slope rather than along the contours. Much erosion has been caused or accelerated in this way. Some land experts, observing these types of bad land use, have been highly critical of the rectilinear land survey, and argue for modification.

Perhaps the time has now come. The crude surveying instruments and the need for range lines cleared through forest and swamps made the mechanical grid quite reasonable in its time. But now with the advent of photogrammetry, laser sighting, computer techniques, and electronic traverse computation it is time for a whole fresh look at the process of land description and measurement. A gradual land *resurvey* to follow and respond to natural topographical conformation is clearly in order. Governmental regulation could now require that future land surveys and dispositions be based, as appropriate, on more logical parcel boundaries to meet sound land use criteria.

Land use

We Americans, with a seemingly inexhaustible land reserve, have been extremely wasteful. We have claimed, cleared, and too often exploited, then moved on, to do it all over again. It is only now, with open land at a premium, that we have begun to understand the need for husbandry.

There are many examples of land well used—among them New England villages fitted to the topography, the Amish farmsteads of Pennsylvania, Maryland tobacco fields, Florida citrus groves, Wis-

Cherry orchards in Michigan: preservation, conservation, and sound development.

consin dairy farms, wheat and corn fields of the prairies, ranch lands of the plains, and bean fields, vineyards, and orchards along the west coast—and across the breadth of the land well-tended homesites and gardens.

In the good examples we may perceive these simple precepts of sound land management:

Learn to read the landscape,
to comprehend the grandeur of its geologic framework,

to understand the vital workings and interdependence of the land and water systems,

to discern in each form and feature the unique expression of nature's creative process.

Let the land's nature determine its use.

And so address each measure of the landscape as to reveal, through our planning, use, and treatment, its highest qualities.

Land use implications   When land passes from one ownership to another, certain legal rights are transferred with the property. Unless otherwise so specified in the deed or governing regulations, these include the right to use, cultivate, mine, perform earthwork, remove the soil or vegetation from the land, or build upon it.

Running with the land are also certain responsibilities, many firmly established by our land law tradition. It is unlawful, for instance, to cause damage by directing an increased flow of storm water runoff onto a neighbor's property. It is not lawful to alter grades significantly along a property line, or to create off-site earth slippage, erosion, or siltation, or to generate undue air, water, noise, or visual pollution. Other more recent restrictions dealing with such matters as wetland protection, beach access, erosion control, and unregulated grading are still to be fully tested in the courts.

Since most sites were acquired in the first place because they were attractive or had other positive qualities, it might well be proposed as a general rule that *the less modification, the better.* A fundamental principle of landscape design is to "plan *to* the site," letting the natural contours, conditions, and covers dictate the building and landscape forms.

Where for one reason or another it may be desirable to alter the grades, as to provide required use areas or to dispose of excavated foundation materials, the topsoil on disturbed areas should first be stripped and stockpiled. The revised contours will then be reshaped to accommodate the proposed uses, to express the meld of natural and constructed elements, and to enhance the building-site composition.

The *carrying capacity* of a land-water area is the population or level of activity that can be sustained for a given length of time without depletion of the resources or breakdown of the biological (natural) systems.

Adapt to the landforms:

To diminish landscape disruption

To reduce the costs of earthwork

To prevent the wasting of topsoil

To preclude the need for erosion control and replanting

To make use of existing drainageways

To blend into the natural scene

By means of site reconnaissance and soil surveys the most productive land can be designated for lawns, gardens, or crop production or be preserved in its natural state. Areas of thin soil, poor or excessive drainage, or underlying rock are prime candidates for projected development.

Homes, roadways, and cities belong on areas of low productivity.

The natural ground forms are best accepted as givens. They are the resolution of myriad forces at work over a long span of time. To adapt to them is to harmonize with the forces and conditions by which they have evolved.

We abuse land because we regard it as a commodity belonging to us. When we see land as a community to which we belong, we may begin to use it with love and respect. . . .

That land is a community is the basic concept of ecology, but that land is to be loved and respected is an extension of ethics.

Aldo Leopold

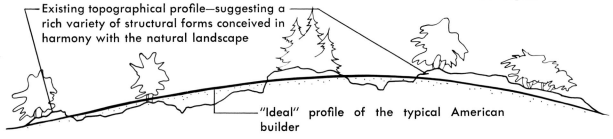

— Existing topographical profile—suggesting a rich variety of structural forms conceived in harmony with the natural landscape

"Ideal" profile of the typical American builder

The code of the American subdivider and homebuilder (as it would seem to the casual observer)

Axiom 1. Clear the land. Axiom 2. Strip the topsoil (or bury it and haul in new if this saves one operation). Axiom 3. Provide a "workable" land profil. (that is, as flat as possible). Axiom 4. Conduct all water to storm sewers (or else to the edge of the lot). Axiom 5. Build a good wide road—inexpensive but wide. Axiom 6. Set the house well back for a big front yard. Axiom 7. Keep the fronts even (this looks neat). Axiom 8. Hold to a minimum sideyard. Axiom 9. Throw on some lawn seed.

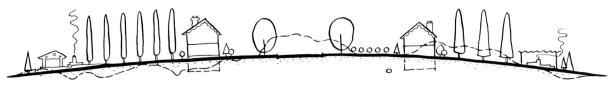

The American suburbanite dream (as seemingly interpreted by the suburban builder and by our present building restrictions)

A revised topography by courtesy of the bulldozer and carryall. The boulders are buried, the natural cover stripped, the brook "contained" in storm sewer or culvert. The topsoil is redistributed as a 4-inch skin over sand, clay, or rock. There sprouts a new artificial fauna of exotic nursery stock.

This is our constructed paradise.

A better way is building *with* nature and in compression, which provides the human scale and charm we find so appealing in the older cultures, in which economy of materials and space dictated a close relationship of structure and landscape form.

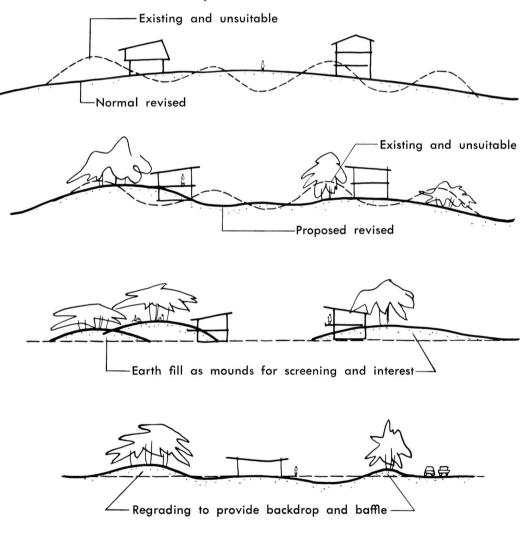

Existing and unsuitable

Normal revised

Existing and unsuitable

Proposed revised

Earth fill as mounds for screening and interest

Regrading to provide backdrop and baffle

If we must use our earthmovers to create a new landscape (and sometimes we must), let us use them to create a landscape of topographical interest and pleasant and useful forms.

EARTH FORMS

Protected,
Uncertain bearing,
Rich, deep soil,
Moist to wet,
Often flood-prone.

Prevailing Wind

Thin soil,
Rocky base,
Exposure to sun,
breeze, and
storms.

Earth forms are eloquent statements
of the constraints and possibilities

New land shapes may create
a sculptural quality often lacking
in the existing topography.

The significant rise or depression
is a limit of visual space.

Cut and fill
in balance

Cut slopes - blended out -
add interest to a roadway

or home site.

Engineered

Naturalized

Embankment

Landscape Curve

Shaped Slope

Gully   Swales

Ditch

Mound   Knoll

Blending or simulation of
natural ground forms

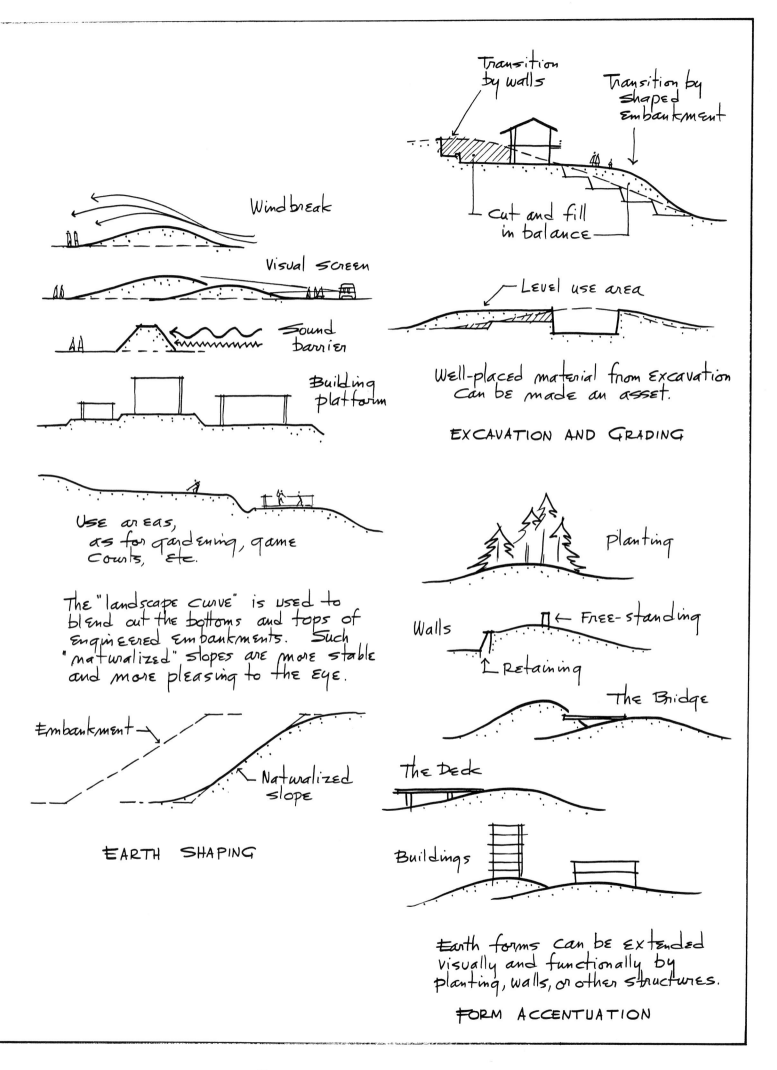

Windbreak

Visual Screen

Sound Barrier

Building platform

Use areas, as for gardening, game courts, etc.

The "landscape curve" is used to blend out the bottoms and tops of engineered embankments. Such "naturalized" slopes are more stable and more pleasing to the eye.

Embankment →

Naturalized slope

EARTH SHAPING

Transition by walls

Transition by shaped embankment

cut and fill in balance

Level use area

Well-placed material from excavation can be made an asset.

EXCAVATION AND GRADING

Planting

Walls — Free-standing

Retaining

The Bridge

The Deck

Buildings

Earth forms can be extended visually and functionally by planting, walls, or other structures.

FORM ACCENTUATION

SLOPE RETENTION

The range of slope stabilization methods includes:

Knitting the soil surface by seeding or the application of a mulch such as wood chips or shredded bark. The prior cross-raking of the slope face is recommended procedure.

Mulch

Selected trees, shrubs, and vines (indigenous preferred)

Planting

Plant roots and detritus knit and hold the surface soil layers.

Dumped or placed fragments of broken stone

Rubble

Stone-filled baskets of wire mesh or wicker

Gabions

Treated bags filled with dry sand-cement mortar

Mortar bags

Facing of dry or grouted units of stone or cast concrete

Rip-rap

A laid-up "crib" of interlocking wood, metal, or concrete members filled with rock ballast

Cribbing

Interlocking sections of steel or pre-cast concrete

Piling

Cut or un-cut stone laid up with open joints

Dry-stone wall

Cast wall may be left rough — with form board or exposed aggregate texture.

Porous backfill

Reinforced-concrete retaining wall

Masonry, cut stone, or brick, with mortar

Porous backfill

Below frost

Perf. drain

Footing

Poured concrete with stone or ceramic facing

Interception gutter on back slope to swale

Porous fill

Below frost

Perforated drain

Footing

SLOPE STABILIZATION

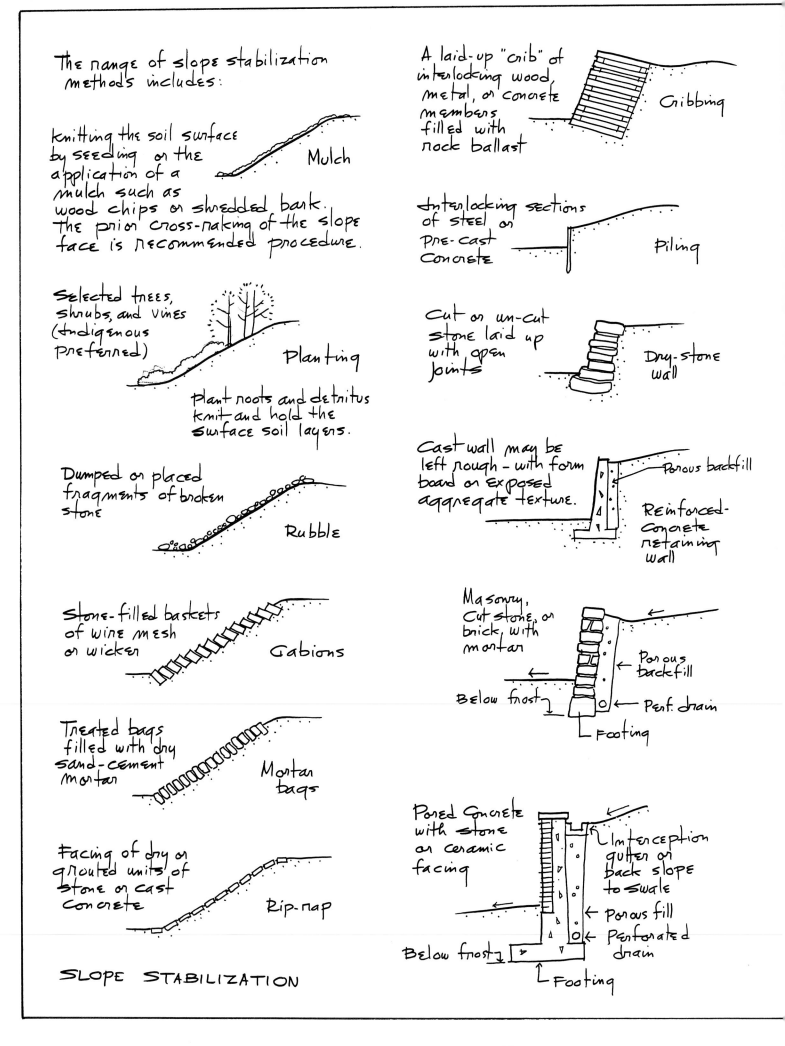

Precipitation

Surface run-off

Loading

Fill

Slump Position

Subsurface Water

Plane of Slippage

Note: The interception of surface storm water flow from above — by gutter or diversion swale — is a prerequisite to all effective slope treatment. The accommodation of subsurface flows to and around — or through — the retention materials or structures is also essential to preclude the damming of water.

With the introduction of water fill material becomes plastic and tends to slump with a rotary motion.

SLOPE DYNAMICS

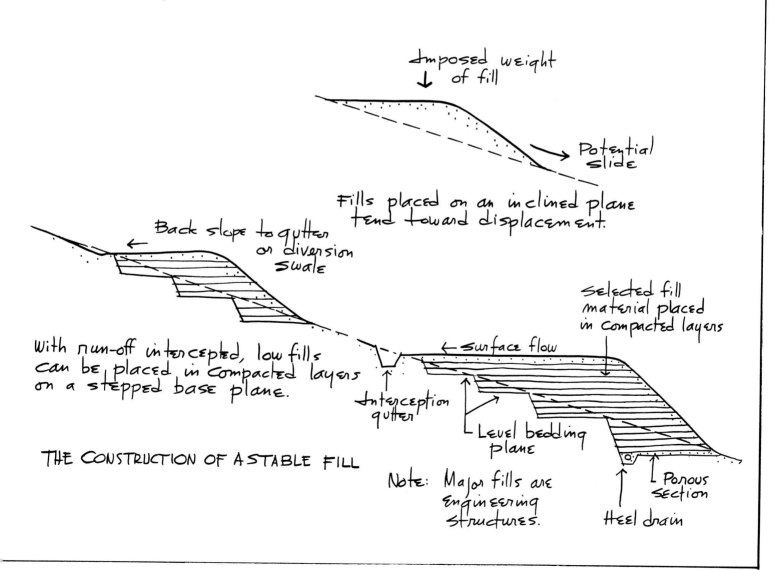

Imposed weight of fill

Potential Slide

Fills placed on an inclined plane tend toward displacement.

Back slope to gutter or diversion swale

Selected fill material placed in compacted layers

With run-off intercepted, low fills can be placed in compacted layers on a stepped base plane.

Surface flow

Interception gutter

Level bedding plane

THE CONSTRUCTION OF A STABLE FILL

Note: Major fills are Engineering structures.

Heel drain

Porous Section

Water

3

Free water is the shining splendor of the natural landscape. From the bubbling spring and upland pool to the splashing stream, rushing rapids, waterfall, freshwater lake, and brackish estuary and finally to the saltwater sea, water has held for all creatures an irresistible appeal. To some degree we humans still seem to share with our earliest predecessors the urgent and instinctive sense that drew them to the water's edge.

Perhaps at first they were drawn only for drink, to lave hot and dust-streaked bodies, or to gather the bounty of mollusk and fish. Later, water for the cooking pots would be dipped and carried in gourds, skins, hollow sections of bamboo, and jars of shaped fire-baked clay. Perhaps our affinity for water has increased with the discovery of its value in gardens and irrigation and with the knowledge that only with moisture present can plants flourish and animals thrive. It may be because in the deep, moist soils of the bottomlands the grasses are richer, the foliage more lush, and the berries larger and sweeter. Here too the refreshing breeze seems more cool and even the song of the birds more melodious.

In the past, fresh water in all its forms has been used, and too often misused or wasted, as if these were God-given privileges. Except in irrigated lands, where water rights and supply are jealously guarded, there has been little concern for what is happening upstream or downstream unless the flow should be cut off or increased to the point of flooding.

Water *flows*, inevitably, from source to receiving ocean basin. This continuity of rivulets, streams, and rivers can be readily observed. Not so obvious are the sequential and interacting relationships of the ponds, lakes, and wetlands. These too are links in the chain of flow. They are affected not only by the things that happen at their sides but by all that transpires within the upper watersheds or the subsurface aquifers that feed and help sustain them. These same subsurface water-bearing, water-transporting, water-yielding strata provide, also, the groundwater essential to farmland, meadow, and forest and to maintaining the level of the well fields from which our water supplies are drawn.

Water and water areas well used can benefit all who live within their sphere of influence. If, however, they are unwisely used, contaminated, or wasted, dependent life is thereby threatened, sometimes with minor loss or inconvenience, sometimes with major disaster, as by devastating drought or overwhelming flood.

It is only recently that entire river basins have come to be studied as unified and interrelated systems. Such a rational approach increases rather than limits the possibilities of fuller use and enjoyment and sets a workable framework within which all subareas may then be better planned.

Planning approach

Any consideration of the flow of surface or subsurface water leads one to the obvious conclusion that only comprehensive planning and resource management make any sense at all. A parcel-by-parcel approach to the use of river-basin lands can only fracture the contiguous water-related matrix and disrupt the natural systems.

Problems The problems to be precluded are those of rapid runoff, erosion, siltation, flooding, drought, and contamination. Simply stated, *any use that causes one or more of these abuses to any significant degree is improper and can no longer be condoned.* It can

If there is magic on the planet, it is contained in water . . . its substance reaches everywhere; it touches the past and prepares the future; it moves under the poles and wanders thinly in the heights or air. It can assume forms of exquisite perfection in a snowflake, or strip the living to a single shining bone cast up by the sea.

Loren Eiseley

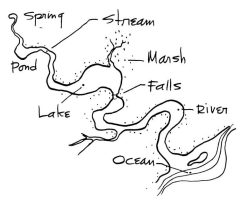

From upland spring to ocean outfall the river basin, river, and all its tributaries are part of a unified system.

Corruption.

There is magic in moving water

Fountains in the landscape

be left to biologists and legal experts to define a *significant* impact. But it can no longer be left to individuals or groups to determine whether or not their activities may cause harm to their neighbors, no matter if the "neighbors" live next door or at the river mouth 1000 miles downstream.

What happens in the wheat fields of North Dakota can have a telling effect on the workings of the lower Missouri and Mississippi rivers. What happens or doesn't happen on the forest slopes of the upper James may decimate the wildfowl yield of the distant salt marsh or contaminate the oyster beds of Chesapeake Bay. In Florida a cloud of spawning shrimp may die where the Apalachicola River debouches because of an oil spill on a tributary two states away.

Possibilities   If there may be *problems,* there are *possibilities* also. These include the *preservation* of those areas of wilderness or wild river yet unspoiled. They include the *conservation* and compatible uses of those river-related areas which are rich in soils, cover, or scenic quality and which in their natural or existing state are important contributors to our ecological well-being. The possibilities include the restoration of depleted farmlands and delapidated urban wastelands to productive use by regrading, soil stabilization, and replanting of eroded slopes and slashings. Well-planned agricultural districts, recreation lands, towns, and cities could then be clustered within a green-blue surrounding of field, forest, and clean water, linked with parklike transportation ways. Far more than many may realize we are already well on our way to such a concept, and ethic, of land and water management.

Proficient land and site planning at any scale will help solve the water-related *problems* and ensure that the *possibilities* are fully realized. The level of performance should be continually improved in the light of increasing public support and advancing technology. It is quite possible that within the span of our lifetimes wide reaches of our land and waterways may be restored to the fairer form that our naturalist friends Thoreau, Muir, and Aldo Leopold once found so wholesome and exhilarating.

Water as a resource

In planning the use of land areas in relation to waterways and water bodies a reasonable goal would be to take full advantage of the benefits of proximity. These benefits would seem to fall within the following categories.

Water supply, irrigation, and drainage   When these are important considerations, the area of more intensive use will be located near the sources. Those site functions requiring the most moisture in the soil or air will be given location priority. The efficiency of pumping and gravity flow will have much to do with plan layouts.

Irrigated fields will be established below points of inlet where possible and be so arranged that lines or planes of flow will slope

gently across the contours to achieve maximum percolation and continuity.

Drainage will be maintained whenever possible along existing lines of flow, with the natural vegetation left undisturbed. It would be hard to devise a more efficient and economical system of storm drainage than that which nature provides. Runoff from fertilized fields or turf will be directed to on-site detention swales or ponds so that the water may be filtered and purified before reentering the source or percolating into the soil to recharge the water table.

Water use in processing   When drawn from surface streams or water bodies for use in cooling, washing, or other processes, water of equal quantity and quality is to be returned to the source. Makeup water may be supplied from wells or public water supply systems.

Transportation   When waterways, lakes, or abutting ocean are to be used for the transport of people or goods, the docking installations and vessels are to be so designed and operated that the functional and visual quality of the waters is at all times assured.

Microclimate moderation   The extremes of temperature are tempered by the presence of moisture and by the resulting vegetation. This advantage may be augmented by the favorable placement of plan areas and structures in relation to open water, irrigated surfaces, or water-cooled breeze.

Habitat   Lakeshores, stream edges, and wetlands together form a natural food source and habitat for birds and animals. When flora and fauna are to be protected, the indigenous vegetation is to be allowed to remain standing whenever feasible to the natural edge of growth, and continuous swaths of cover are to be left intact to permit wildlife to move from place to place unmolested. The denser growth is usually concentrated along the water edge and converging swales.

Recreational use   Our streams and water bodies have long provided our most popular types of outdoor recreation such as boating, fishing, and swimming. Along their banks and shores is found the accretion of cottages, mobile home parks, and campsites that attest to our love of water. It is proposed that in long-range planning, with few exceptions, all water areas and edges should be acquired and made part of the public domain. Sheathed in green and incorporated within the regional open-space network, such landscape features would provide a recreational environment second to none.

Scenic values   For most people the glimmer of sunlight on open water is sure to elicit an exclamation of discovery and delight. The feelings may be expressed as a shout of triumph or as a silent upsurge of the spirits. But the sight and *sounds* of water evoke a sense of pleasure. It would seem that we are so acutely attuned to the language of water—the trickle and gurgle of ice melt, the splash of

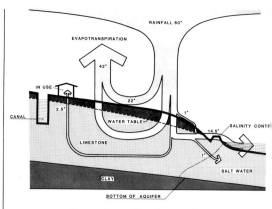

Coastal aquifer dynamics

It can be seen from this diagram, which shows present conditions pertaining along much of the southeastern coast, that only a small fraction of the annual rainfall is actually consumed. Here as elsewhere, by the scientific reduction of evapotranspiration and surface runoff, the available supply of potable water can be significantly increased.

The qualities of water are infinite in their variety.

In depth water may range from deep to no more than a film of surface moisture.

In motion, from rush to gush, plummet, spurt, spout, spill, spray, or seep.

In sound, from tumultuous roar to murmur.

Each attribute suggests a particular use and application in landscape design.

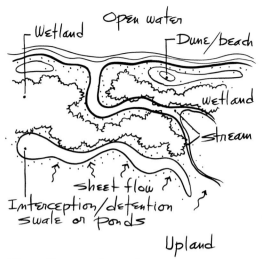

The rudiments of sound water management

- Confine development to the uplands.

- Protect the wetlands, streams, and water bodies by leaving adequate fringes of vegetation.

- Preserve and utilize the natural drainageways.

- Minimize excavation and grading.

- Preclude soil erosion by providing sheet flow and well-knit ground covers.

- Detain heavy surface runoff in swales or ponds to provide regulated flows, filtering, and groundwater recharge.

- Return to the earth or its receptor water of quality and quantity equal to that withdrawn.

the stream, the lapping of water on lakeshore, the surf crash, even the cry of shorebirds—that we can almost see with our ears.

A glimpse, a view, an unfolding panorama of the aquatic landscape is a scenic superlative.

Streams and water bodies are the punctuation marks in the reading of the landscape. They translate for us the landforms and the story of their geologic formation. They introduce and develop the regional theme. They set the mood; they articulate; they intensify. They give the essential meaning. What is a prairie without its sloughs? A meadow without its meandering brook? A mountainside without its cascade? A valley without its river?

Site amenity   Fortunate is the landowner whose property includes or borders upon an attractive stretch of water or affords even a distant view. In landscape and architectural planning a chief endeavor will be the devising of relationships that exact the full visual and use possibilities.

Water as landscape feature

Most attributes of nature—the hills, the trees, the starlit sky—are usually taken for granted, but the value of free water is not. Where it exists, as in the form of pond, stream, lake, or ocean, the adjacent landholdings are eagerly sought. They are prized as sites for parks and parkways, for homes, institutions, resort hotels, and other commercial ventures. It could almost be stated as a law of land economics that "the closer a site to open water, the higher its value as real estate."

Manage   In considering the site development of any landscape area, a first concern is the protection of the surface and subsurface waters both as to quality and as to quantity. *Quality* is maintained by precluding contamination in any form, as by the flow or seepage of pollutants, by groundwater runoff charged with chemicals or nutrients, by siltation, or by the introduction of solid wastes. The assurance of acceptable water *quantity* is a matter of irrigation or of detaining surface runoff in swales or ponds to prevent the flooding of streams or water bodies, to sustain the level of the underlying water table, and to replenish the deep-flowing aquifers.

Utilize   Since propinquity to water is so highly desirable, since there is only so much water area and frontage to go round, and since the protection of our water and edges has become so critical in our environmental planning, it would seem reasonable that all water-oriented land areas should be planned in such a way as to reap the maximum benefits of the water feature while protecting its integrity. This goal often resolves itself into the simple device of expanding the actual and visual limits of water-related land to the reasonable maximum. This is not as difficult as it might seem.

In practice, the rim of frontage is extended landward from the water edge in such a manner as to define an ample protective

sheath. This variform vegetated band, at best following the lines of drainage flow and responding to the subtle persuasions of the topography, will provide frontage for compatible development and serve as access to the water. The possible variations are limitless, but the principle remains always the same.

Each variable diagram must stand the test of these three underlying conditions:

1. All related uses are to be compatible with the water resource and landscape.

2. The intensity of the introduced uses must not exceed the carrying capacity or biologic tolerance of the land and water areas.

3. The continuity of the natural and built systems is to be assured.

If these three principles are adhered to, it can be seen that all land-water areas, from homesite to region, can be planned and developed in such a way that both scenic quality and ecologic functions can be maintained.

Open water is fast disappearing from the American scene. Expanding agricultural lands continue to follow the drainage ditches and tile fields across prairie wetlands and everglades. The urgent compulsion to dredge and fill, while slowed by recent conservation legislation, continues to "reclaim" the marsh, the cedar bog, and the mangrove strands. Rivers, lakes, and oceanfront are being hidden from public view behind a rising wall of apartments and office towers.

Is it not too late?
It is not too late!

Protect Where water features exist, protect them. Work to preserve not only the open water but the supporting watershed covers, the natural holding ponds, the swampland, the floodplain, the feeding streams and the vegetation on their banks, the coastal wetlands, the landward dunes, and the outward reefs or sandbars.

In the planning of every water-related project site there is an opportunity to demonstrate sound management principles. Each well-designed example not only serves the interest of the client but also stands as a lesson to others.

Rediscover Many water features of great potential landscape value have been bypassed in the process of building construction. At the time it was perhaps too expensive to drain or fill them or to establish stable foundations in the sand or muck at their sides. They remain "out back" or "yonder," often in their natural state, waiting to be reclaimed by the community as parkland or open space. Preserved or modified, they may be rediscovered and featured in new public or private landscape development.

Restore Again, a spring, a pond, or a section of stream may have

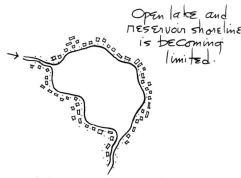

Avoid the water-edge ring of roads and buildings that seal off water bodies and limit their use.

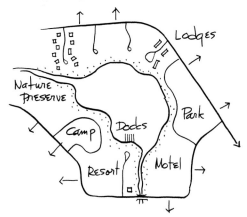

By expanding the traffic-free lake environs to include park, wildlife preserve, and public areas as well as private cottages and resorts, the use and enjoyment of the lake (and surrounding real estate values) are enhanced.

Present liability; potential community asset.

been enclosed in a culvert and buried in fill. Or it may have been used as a dumping ground and covered with brush and trash. Sometimes, to add to the disgrace, such water features have been shamefully polluted with oils and chemicals and are coated with scum. In most urban and suburban precincts and often in the open countryside, there are to be found such unrecognized landscape treasures waiting to be reclaimed.

San Antonio River. This once trash-littered stream has been converted to a delightful urban blueway.

In the shaping of water bodies it is desirable that the outline be curvilinear, rather than angular, to reflect the undulating nature of water.

Often to provide more efficient use of the bordering land the pond or lake is first excavated along straight lines, which are then softened by curvature and by rounding the intersections.

Since in most methods of excavation, as by dragline or pans, straight, deep cuts are more economical, the central body of a lake is often a rectangle or a polyhedron in shape, with a widened perimeter shelf sloped to the deeper excavation pit and trimmed to more natural form.

From no point along the shore should the expanse of the water surface be seen in its entirety. If possible, the shoreline should be made to dip out of sight at several points to add interest and to set free the observer's imagination. By this design device not only is the water body made more appealing but its apparent size is increased.

Preplan Sometimes in the necessary process of mining or in the excavation of open extraction pits, there exists the need to create new water areas. From the air in some regions these can be seen to dot the landscape, usually in the form of dull rectilinear dragline creations. Each may now be recognized as a lost opportunity. With advanced planning and sometimes little additional cost, these pits and the bordering property area could have been shaped into new and attractive waterscapes, with free-form lakes, grassy slopes,

Homes grouped around a preplanned excavation site: Miami Lakes, Florida.

and tree-covered mounds. This reasonable preplanning approach, as a condition of obtaining excavation permits and combined with soil conservation and afforestation, provides the opportunity to preclude new scars on the countryside and, instead, to create new landscapes from the old. With enterprise, many existing extraction pits could be acquired, reshaped, and transformed into highly attractive and valuable property.

Water-related site design

In the development of land-water holdings special care is required in the delineation of use areas, in the location of paths of vehicular and pedestrian movement, and in site and building design.

Natural streams and water bodies   Where these exist, they represent the resolution of many dynamic forces at work—precipitation, surface runoff, sedimentation, clarification, currents, wave action, and so forth. It can be seen that to alter a natural stream, pond, or lake will set in motion a whole chain of actions and interactions that must then be restored to equilibrium. It is soon learned, therefore, that a first consideration in the site planning of water-related areas is to leave the natural conditions undisturbed and build up to and around them.

In their existing state the banks of streams and rivers are lined by a fringe of grasses, shrubs, and trees that stabilize soils and check the sheet inflow of surface storm-water drainage. The bank faces are held in place by stones, logs, roots, and trailing plants that resist currents and erosion.

Lakeshores and beaches, armored with wave-resistant rock or protected by their sloped edges of sand or gravel, are ideally shaped to withstand the force and wash of wind-driven waves. Even the quiet pond or lagoon is edged with reeds, sedges, or lily pads which serve the same purpose.

Where a water feature such as a spring, pond, tidal marsh, or lake occurs in nature, it is usually a distillate of the surrounding landscape and a rich contributor to its ecologic workings and the scene. Such superlatives are to be in all ways protected. This is not to preclude their use and enjoyment, for the purpose of sensitive planning is to ensure protection while facilitating the highest and best use.

Impoundments   At a miniscale a trickling rivulet can be impeded by a few well-placed stones to increase its size and depth. By the construction of a proper dam larger and deeper pools can be created for fishing, swimming, or boating or as landscape features.

At a greater scale huge reservoirs or lakes may be impounded for water storage, flood control, or the provision of hydroelectric energy. Provided the drawdowns are not too severe or frequent, such large impoundments offer the opportunity for many forms of water-related recreation and often become the focal attraction for extensive regional development. To assure their maximum contribution and benefits all major reservoirs and the contiguous lands around them should be preplanned before construction permits are issued, with dedication provided for necessary rights-of-way and for appropriate public and private uses.

From the smallest dam to the largest, the location must be well selected to assure its stability, for a failure and surging washout can bring serious problems downstream. Water levels are to be studied in relation to topographical forms so that the edges of the pond or lake may create a pleasing shape well suited to adjacent paths of

Often, and particularly in large parks and nature preserves, the migratory aspect of beaches and shores is acknowledged, and they are allowed full freedom to assume and constantly adjust their natural conformation. This eminently sound approach deserves far wider application.

Beaches are built and rebuilt by the forces of ocean currents, storms, and tides. They are essentially temporary, since the forces that built them can also alter them beyond recognition—sometimes during a single great storm. Even the most costly stabilization projects have proven ineffective against . . . beach evolution.

Albert R. Veri et al.

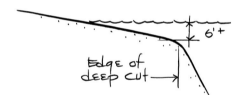

For safety a beach should slope to a depth exceeding a swimmer's height (6 feet plus) before reaching a deep-cut line.

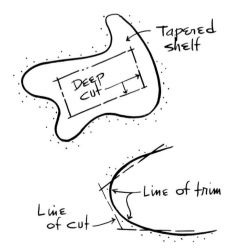

Rectilinear excavation pits can be reshaped by supplementary grading to create free-form lakes.

The Springs, Longwood, Florida. Here upwellings of crystal-clear water have been featured as the crown jewels of a planned community.

movement, use areas, and structures.

Where the feeding streams are silt-laden or subject to periodic flooding, upstream settling basins with weirs and a gated bypass channel will be required.

Paths, bridges, and decks   People are attracted to water. It is a natural tendency to wish to walk or ride along the edge of a stream or lake, to rest beside it enjoying the sights and sounds, or, in the case of streams, to cross to the other side.

These desires are to be accommodated in site planning. Routes of movement will be aligned to provide a variety of views and will in effect combine to afford a visual exploration of lake or waterway. It is fitting that water-edge paths or drives be undulating in their horizontal and vertical curvature and constructed of materials that blend into the natural scene. At points where water-oriented uses are intensified or where the meeting of land and water is to be given more architectural treatment, the shapes and materials of the pathways and use areas will become more structural too.

Overlooks may be as unprepossessing as a bench in the widened bend of a path. Or they may be decked, terraced, or walled, to bring the user into the most favorable relationship to the water for the purpose intended, be it viewing, relaxing, fishing, diving, or entering a boat.

Bridges too are designed with regard for much more than function. At their best they provide an exhilarating experience of crossing. Seen from many directions and angles, they are to be given sculptural form. Every bridge is to be designed with utmost simplicity as a clear expression of its materials, structure, and use. Each will derive its character from the locality and the nature of the site.

Water edges   The meeting of land and water presents a line of special planning significance.

It has been noted that where the uses are mild and where the banks or shores are attractive, they are best left essentially undisturbed. As water-related uses are intensified and the need for space increased, the degree of edge treatment is correspondingly increased

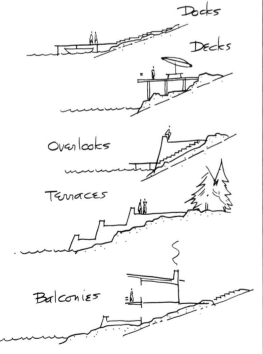

Utilize the slope of the banks.

until in some instances it may become entirely architectural.

In water-edge detailing these are some of the fundamentals to be kept in mind:

Minimize disruption.   Where the banks or shores are stable, the less treatment the better.

Maintain smooth flows.   Avoid the use of elements that obstruct currents or block wave action.

Slope and armor the banks, if necessary, to absorb energy where flows are swift or wave impact strong.

Attain access to water of desired depth by the use of docks, piers, or floats with self-adjusting ramps.

Avoid the indiscriminate use of jetties and groins or the diverting of strong currents.   The effects are often unpredictable.

Design to the worst conditions.   Consider recorded water levels and the height of wind-driven surf.

Preclude flooding.   Hold the floor level of habitable structures above the 100-year-flood stage.

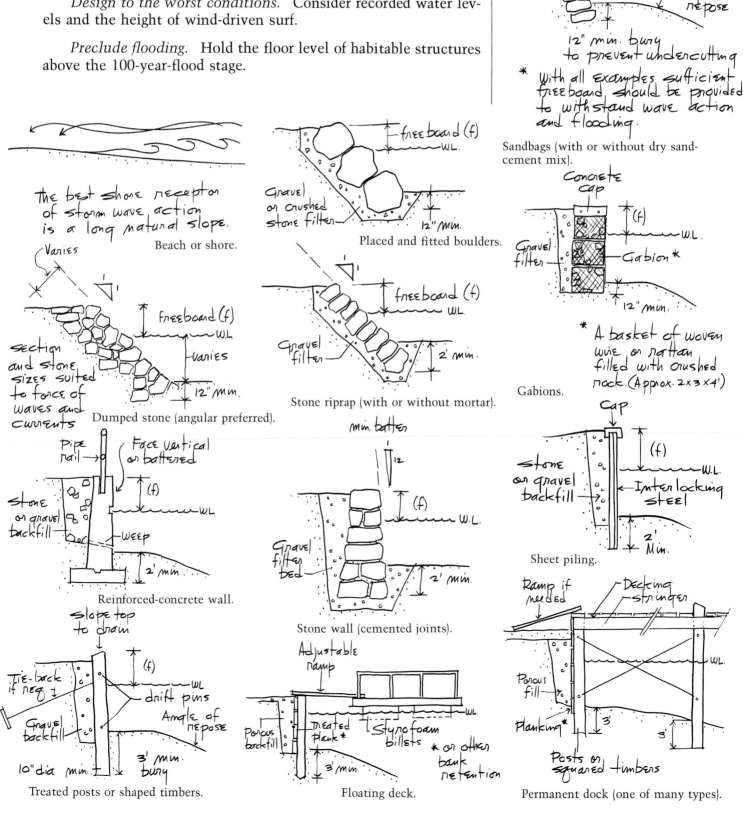

Where the natural shore or stream bank is stable, it is usually best left undisturbed.

Natural bank.

* With all examples sufficient freeboard should be provided to withstand wave action and flooding.

Sandbags (with or without dry sand-cement mix).

Gabions.

* A basket of woven wire or rattan filled with crushed rock. (Approx. 2 × 3 × 4')

The best shore receptor of storm wave action is a long natural slope.

Beach or shore.

Placed and fitted boulders.

Dumped stone (angular preferred).

section and stone sizes suited to force of waves and currents

Stone riprap (with or without mortar).

Sheet piling.

Reinforced-concrete wall.

Stone wall (cemented joints).

Treated posts or shaped timbers.

Floating deck.

Permanent dock (one of many types).

Promote safety by the use of handrails, nonslip pavement, buoys, markers, and lights.

Use weather- and water-resistant materials, fastenings, and equipment. Corrosion and deterioration are constant problems along the waterfront.

Prevent the direct flow of polluted surface runoff into receiving waters. Such runoff should be intercepted and treated, or filtered by the use of detention swales.

Pools, fountains, and cascades   It is hard to imagine any planned landscape area—patio, garden, or public square—that would not benefit by the introduction of water in natural or architectural form. Its sound, motion, and cooling effects give it universal appeal.

Water has become symbolic. It connotes and promotes refreshment and stimulates verdant growth. Its presence converts desert into oasis.

Where water is abundant and its use is to be featured, as in urban courts, malls, or plazas, its treatment is often carried to an exhilarating scale and high degree of refinement. Many a city is

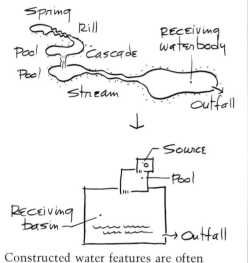

Constructed water features are often abstracted from nature.

Cascades, Commercial Place, Norfolk, Virginia.

The water in many city reservoirs is hidden from public view. In its storage and processing it could be used to refresh and beautify urban surroundings.

remembered for the delight of its exuberant fountains and rushing cascades.

In even the smallest garden, water also has its essential place. Wherever plants are used, for example, irrigation is needed and is to be considered in the design. A trickling spout or well-placed spray can moisten and cool a patch of gravel mulch, a bed of ivy, or a square of sunlit paving. The simplest container of water placed out for the birds adds interest and refreshment, as does a quiet pool, a dripping ledge, or a splashing fountain. Such water features, easy to devise and construct, can yield long hours of watching and listening pleasure.

STREAMS AND RIVERS

Where a water feature – such as a spring, pond, stream, river, lake, or tidal marsh – exists in nature, it is usually a distillate of the surrounding landscape and a rich contributor. Such superlatives are to be in all ways protected. This is not to preclude their use and enjoyment, for the purpose of sensitive planning is to ensure and facilitate both.

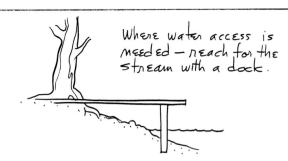

Where water access is needed – reach for the stream with a dock.

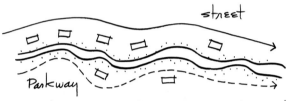

<u>A stream is a natural drainageway.</u>

Avoid cutting or blocking the flow with grading or construction.

<u>Streams and rivers are subject to high-velocity flow.</u>

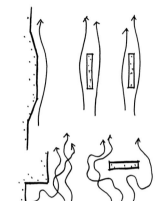

Piers, abutments, or other structures introduced into the channel should be of slip-stream design

Rather than produce turbulence.

street

Parkway

<u>A stream is a lineal plan element.</u>

Align paths of movement, and structures, in harmony with the line of flow.

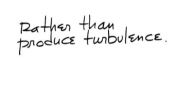

⌐ Flood level

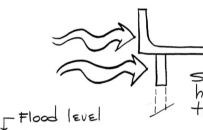

Swift flood waters have enormous thrust.

<u>Floods are an ever-present threat on most waterways.</u>

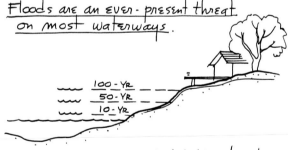

100-YR
50-YR
10-YR

Build habitable structures only above the 100-year flood stage.

⌐ Flood level

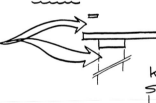

Keep low bridge spans thin in section to avert displacement.

RESPONSIVE DESIGN

Channel

Cutting force

<u>Streams and rivers are dynamic.</u> Their currents and water-borne sediments are powerful cutters and eroders.

Leave the banks undisturbed. With their natural conformation and matting of interlaced roots they are well suited to resist undercutting and cave-in.

<u>Stream crossings are costly and disruptive.</u>

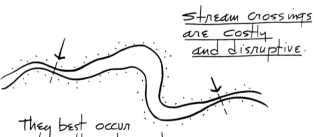

They best occur where the channel is narrow and the banks are high and stable. In shallow, gravelly areas a ford may be all required.

Utilize the fall of the stream to create occasional pools, rapids, and waterfalls.

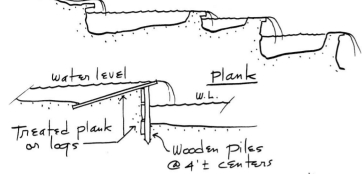

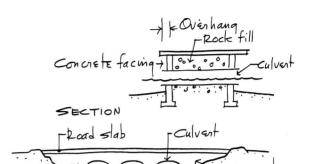

Plank

water level

W.L.

Treated plank or logs

Wooden piles @ 4'± centers

Earth

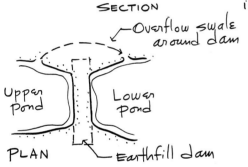

Level of water and by-pass inlet

Clay fill placed in compacted layers

W.L.

Sheet piling core is desirable.

SECTION

Overflow swale around dam

Upper Pond

Lower Pond

PLAN

Earthfill dam

Concrete

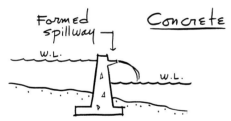

Formed spillway

W.L.

W.L.

Note: The failure of even a low dam can have disastrous downstream effects. Expert advice is recommended.

POND-IN-STREAM CONSTRUCTION

In the development of water-related areas care is required in the designation of use areas, the location of interconnecting paths of vehicular and pedestrian movement, and in the site and building design.

Path or roadway

Compacted-earth Culvert. Concrete or Corrugated metal. Opening cut to shape of fill.

W.L.

SECTION

Earth Fill With Culvent

Overhang

Rock fill

Concrete facing

Culvert

SECTION

Road slab

Culvert

W.L.

Concrete

ELEVATION

Formed Concrete with Rock Fill

STREAM CROSSING WITH CULVERTS

The conversion of a drainage ditch into an attractive waterway

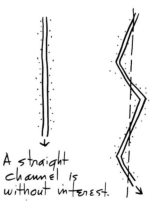

A straight channel is without interest. To improve:

First, divert the alignment.

Then, widen the bends. Place the excavated material inside the bends and shape into elongated mounds to give apparent reason for the stream deflection.

Using native materials, plant the rises with taller trees, leaving the outside of the curves in low ground covers.

NEW STREAM CONSTRUCTION

POOLS, FOUNTAINS, CASCADES

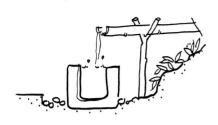

A water feature may be as simple as a trickle from a spring-fed tube into a brimming basin

A quiet reflecting basin of any size or shape can be constructed of such varied materials as metal, concrete, brick, granite sets, or redwood. Potted plants may be grouped around. Evaporated water is easily replenished with hose or watering can.

Or a tumultuous rush of cascading water in an urban plaza.

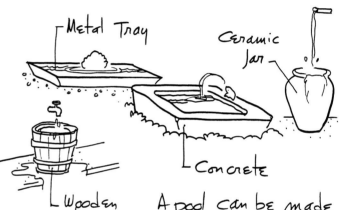

Metal Tray

Ceramic Jar

Concrete

Wooden Tub

Most garden areas would be improved by the introduction of water in some form, such as . . .

A pool can be made of many types of containers. The water source may be the garden hose, a faucet, a spout, a dripping slab of ledgestone.

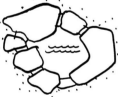

A few rough stones and simple basin . . .

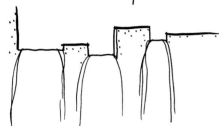

A formed pool and jet . . .

Seat pool
(Patio or Courtyard)

On an overflowing jar set in a bed of gravel.

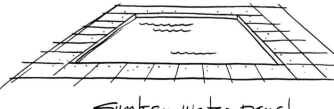

Sunken water panel

POOLS

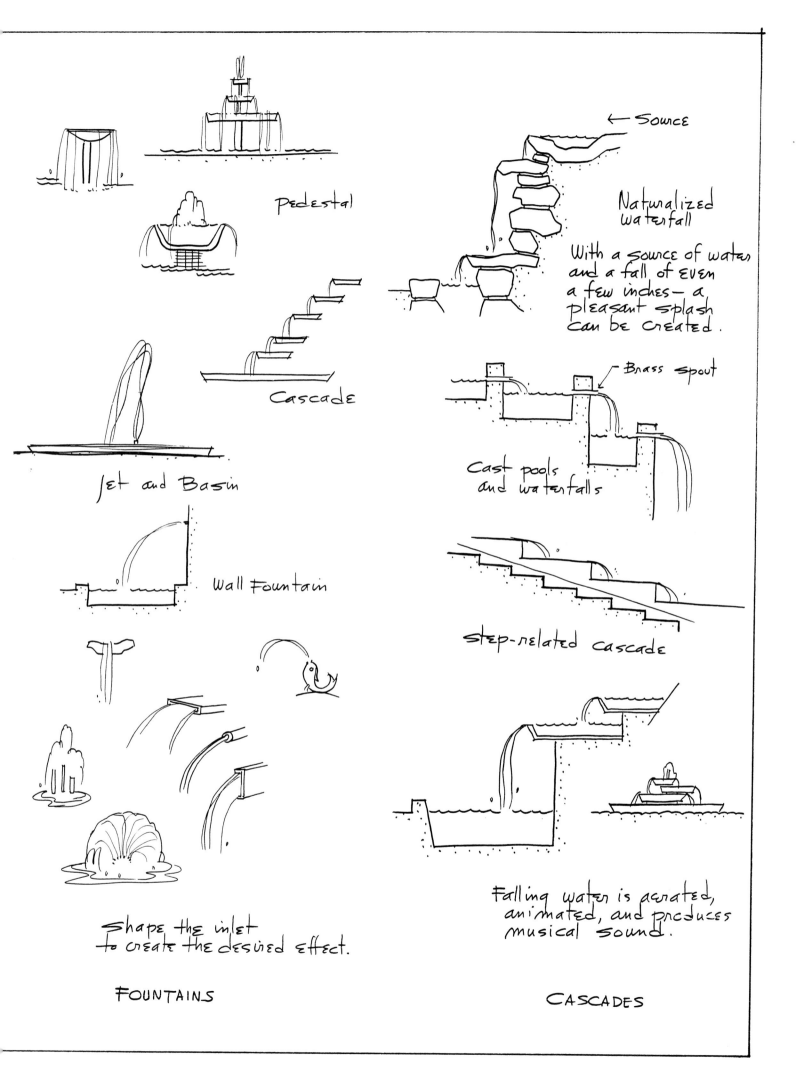

Pedestal

Cascade

Jet and Basin

Wall Fountain

Shape the inlet
to create the desired effect.

FOUNTAINS

← Source

Naturalized
waterfall

With a source of water
and a fall of even
a few inches— a
pleasant splash
can be created.

Brass spout

Cast pools
and waterfalls

step-related cascade

Falling water is aerated,
animated, and produces
musical sound.

CASCADES

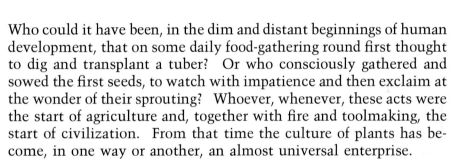

4

Plants

Who could it have been, in the dim and distant beginnings of human development, that on some daily food-gathering round first thought to dig and transplant a tuber? Or who consciously gathered and sowed the first seeds, to watch with impatience and then exclaim at the wonder of their sprouting? Whoever, whenever, these acts were the start of agriculture and, together with fire and toolmaking, the start of civilization. From that time the culture of plants has become, in one way or another, an almost universal enterprise.

Botany, as a field of scientific inquiry, has grown from the early classification of plants and their systematic study. Linnaeus, sensing a need to better understand the relationships, established the botanical orders and introduced the concept of standardized nomenclature. With over 250,000 plant species known to exist, it is doubtful that more than a few thousand yet remain unclassified. The rambling sorties of the first botanists have given way to well-organized expeditions. In more recent times plant explorers such as E. H. Wilson and David Fairchild have ranged the world, from the jungles of Africa to the Mongolian deserts and the peaks of the lofty Himalaya, in search of specimens for herbaria and botanic garden collections and for introduction to our gardens and farms.

Early attempts at selective plant breeding and cross-pollination have led to more sophisticated techniques of hybridization. The pioneering feats of the plant breeder Luther Burbank excited enthusiastic interest and produced a tantalizing array of new and superior roses, potatoes, oranges, plums, and other improved plant varieties. Today, plant crossing, plant selection, and seed radiation are creating a veritable cornucopia of hardier, more disease-resistant grains, more luscious fruits, more nutritious vegetables, and more attractive ornamental plants.

The science of horticulture holds great promise. Yet, in our exuberant pursuit of new and improved plant varieties we tend to ignore the vast and marvelous store of indigenous plants that surround us. They have evolved over countless centuries in nature's selective scheme of things. Each is a miracle of evolutionary adaptation and survival—the resultant of all natural forces. Each, where and as it stands, represents the highest form of plant life that the given situation can produce and for the time being sustain. We are only beginning to understand the essential functions of plants in our biosphere or the full extent of their contributions to the environment in which we work and live.

Plants in nature

The vegetal growth that covers most of our globe occurs in myriad forms that range from the towering redwoods of the Pacific coast forest to the microscopic plankton of our streams, freshwater bodies, and teeming saltwater seas. This wonder world of vegetation provides the habitat and basic food supply of all living creatures.

Food chain   In the green chlorophyll cells of plants, and only there, the energy of the sun is transformed into the simple starches at the base of the biologic food chain. In this process of photosynthesis plants draw moisture from the air and soil and in the presence of sunlight convert carbon dioxide into free oxygen and carbohydrates. It is in this vital miracle of chemistry that both the oxygen we breathe and the simple starches upon which all life depends are produced and replenished.

Some are consumed directly by humans as in vegetables and fruits. Most reach our tables, however, through a complex spiral that begins with the lower forms of grazing organisms of land and sea and moves through a succession of increasingly larger and more complex herbivores and carnivores. Finally the essential carbohydrates become our fare as fish, game, or butchered livestock. It can be seen that as plant life is diminished, life in all its varieties is thereby diminished too.

Transpiration   It is not only the free oxygen produced by plants that refreshes the air. Water drawn by the plants from the soil and the water table is given off by foliage as vapor through *evapotranspiration*. This cooling and moisturizing function contributes to the growing conditions for other plants and to creature comfort as well. Where it is lacking, arid desert conditions exist.

Climate control   Plants ameliorate the climate in other ways also. They serve as buffers against a storm. Their foliage and mat of fallen leaves protect the soil against drying winds and sun. Even in wintertime their branches, twigs, and stems form a mesh to retain and transmit solar heat and help protect soils from freezing temperatures.

Water retention   Plants retain the moisture that falls as precipitation—as droplets of dew or rain on their leaves, in the crevices of their bark, in the fountain of woody yet aqueous cells that comprise their internal structure, and in the fibrous mat of detritus and roots that cover and penetrate the earth. Water retained is water allowed to cleanse the air or to seep into the topsoil and subsurface aquifers. Runoff unchecked is erosion in the making, with siltation as a result.

Soil building   In the cycle of living and dying, plants return to the earth their decaying fibers and cells to provide humus and deepen the film of topsoil. This slowly accreting and vital substance, if protected from erosion, increases available nutrients and moisture and the earth's fecundity.

Detritus   The fallen leaves, fruits, stems, and rotting wood that are not retained by the soil as humus are washed away in the stream and river systems to enrich the broth of the tidal estuaries. This organic material in turn becomes food for new aquatic plants and for oysters and spawning shell and fin fish.

Productivity   Long before our progenitors gathered their first handfuls of berries or dragged in the first game to their campfires, the forests, prairies, and waters had provided provender for a vast and voracious domain of insects, fish, reptiles, soaring birds, and roving animals. Today, natural conditions would be much the same as they were a million years ago were it not for the ascendancy of humankind. Human hands first learned to strip and store nature's bounty, then to harvest the grass, grain, and timber, and finally to push back and destroy the natural covers to make room for garden patches, fields, and settlements. Too often we humans have gained our abundance at the expense of the earth's other inhabitants. The destruction of vegetative cover and wildlife has now reached devastating proportions. It is only within very recent times that we have paused to consider the consequences. More recently yet have we begun to understand the direct and fragile relationships that exist between the whole biologic realm of animals and plants.

Introduced plantations

The propagation and cultivation of plants for food and fiber is a logical extension of the nomadic way of life. Nature's yield of forage, cereals, vegetables, nuts, and fruits was often sporadic and scattered. The farm field, orchard, and vineyard have increased the bounty manyfold, while barns, silos, storage cellars, and bins have sustained the supply.

Where the smaller farms of the cabin builder, rail splitter, and horse-drawn plow were adjusted to the topography, the streams, wetlands, and forest were usually preserved. It is mainly in nineteenth- and twentieth-century America, with our mechanized equipment and our pioneering "Clear the land! Drain the marsh!" complex that we have wrought so much damage to the natural landscape order and ecological matrix. It need not be so. In many of our rural areas today, as in Germany, England, and Scandinavia, we

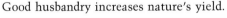

Good husbandry increases nature's yield.

find instructive examples of agriculture, settlements, and nature in symbiotic balance. In such cases the supply of food and cover is often *increased,* to the benefit of all.

Reforestation   Within the past century concern for the vanishing wilderness has been cause for the setting aside of millions of acres of state and national forest, wildlife refuge, parkland, and conservation lands. In addition, vast areas of cutover forest have been reestablished, and new plantations of trees (afforestation) have been installed on depleted or eroded lands as watershed protection, wildlife management preserves, and shelterbelt windscreens and for timber and other crop production. These commendable programs have received and deserve wide public support and are to be expanded.

The built landscape   As centers of trade were established to serve the farmlands, as ports and harbors expanded, as first meandering rural roads, then sweeping highways and transcontinental railways traced their paths across America and cities formed at their crossings, the landscape of nature gave way. It was a rapid and disheartening retreat.

It is disturbing to look about us at most of our developments—at the extent of the destruction of vegetation and the earth conformation, the degradation of lakes and waterways, the pollution of air and countryside. It is saddening to envision the landscape that once existed and to realize the superbly agreeable communities that, with intelligent planning, might otherwise have been.

A new American landscape is taking form. There are encouraging signs. We find in our rural, suburban, and urban areas many examples of land well used and natural features preserved. Many farmsteads, homes, and communities have been planned in sympathetic response to their topographical settings, and extensive areas of open space have been acquired to conserve scenic mountain slopes, riverbanks, and shores. Unfortunately, however, the good examples are far outnumbered by the bad.

It is not a lost cause—far from it. We have learned that the wanton destruction of our earthscape can be precluded, that defilement and pollution can be stopped, that eroded land can be restored, that towns and cities can in time be rebuilt, and that the natural vegetation can be reestablished. Moreover, we are learning much about our ecology, we are developing a whole new science of resource management, and we are constantly increasing our knowledge of community and landscape planning. Within the next few decades it will be well within our capacity to preserve or restore our major natural systems and reshape our constructed environment more responsibly. In this endeavor the preservation and creative use of plants will play an essential role.

Plant identification

A Sunday afternoon visit to the botanical garden is usually sufficient to awaken an interest in plants. As a start in attaining a broader knowledge it is well to learn to identify those plants within view of your residence windows—by their form, bark, twigging, buds, foliage, flower, and fruit. The range can then be extended to yard and to neighborhood. Beyond the town or city limits, in the field or woodland, lies a wealth of plants to be recognized and admired in all seasons of the year. Finally, for many enthusiasts the quest will eventually lead out along the streams and rivers and into the wilderness. There, in undisturbed nature, is to be found the

Rooftop gardens such as these may be the forerunners of terraced garden cities.

66

realm of plants as they were created. For those who understand what they see, it is a profoundly moving experience.

For the initiate the simplest plant guide will suffice as a start on the trail of exploration, but think twice before scanning the pages: they may lead you a very long way.

Gardening

When the settlers beached their rough landing boats on our eastern shores, they brought with them the carefully tended seeds,roots, and cuttings of our first gardens. Our gardens now stretch from sea to sea. For most Americans the love of plants and gardening seems to be inherent.

Those of us whose work it is to help plan our living environment can learn from this. It is our hope that this feeling for plants and their care may extend to the care of *all* vegetation and the waters and soil which support it; that the best of our wilderness and wild rivers may yet be preserved; that our vulnerable watersheds may be reforested and protected; that essential marshes may be restored and reflooded; that our remaining dunes may be replanted to bearberry and juniper, to fox grape and pine, or reseeded to their cover of sea oats; that our clustered communities can be planned within and around an all-embracing open-space framework of farmland and forest; and that our homes and schools may be planned as gardens and our cities as garden parks.

Plants in landscape design.

The planned and planted landscape

Many involved in land planning think of plants as no more than horticultural adjuncts to be arranged around construction projects which are otherwise complete. Nothing could be further from the truth. Vegetation and existing ground cover are in fact one of the primary considerations in the selection and planning of most properties. To a large extent they establish the site character. They hold the soils, modify the climate, provide windbreak and screen, and often define the conformation of use areas.

Plants in the landscape are either those existing in their natural habitat or those which have been introduced. Since established plants by the very fact of their existence have proved themselves to be suited to the site, it would seem logical to preserve them, at least until the need for their removal has been thoughtfully determined. Persons who have had occasion to replace vegetation, often carelessly destroyed, know the problems and costs involved.

When, however, new plantings are prescribed, they are to be given careful consideration, for a single inappropriate plant can alter or destroy the visual quality of a landscape or disrupt its ecological balance. Conversely, well-conceived plantings can do much to transform an otherwise dull and barren site into a more useful, comfortable, and pleasant place to be.

Each and every plant installed should serve a predetermined purpose. It is to be selected as the best of the available alternatives to suit the specific growing conditions and the precise design requirements, for planting design of excellence is a blending of science and art.

In preparing the planting layout for garden, campus, industrial park, or new community the approach is much the same. The aim is to enhance in all ways possible the routes of movement and the usable areas of the site. The following time-tested principles are offered as a guide:

Preserve the existing vegetation. Streets, buildings, and areas of use are to be fitted amid the natural growth insofar as practicable. The landscape continuity and scenic quality will thus be assured; the cost of site installation and maintenance will be reduced; and the structures, paved surfaces, and lawns will be richer by contrast.

Slope and watershed protection.

Windscreen.

Overhead space definition and canopy.

Enframement.

Backdrop.

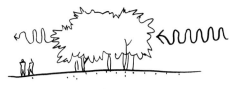

Noise abatement.

Shade.

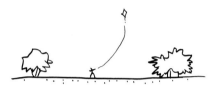

Ground space definition.

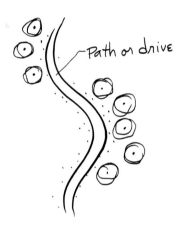

Path or drive

Plan reinforcement.

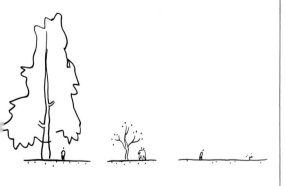

Scale induction.

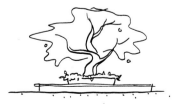

Ornamentation.

Select each plant to serve its intended function. Experienced designers first prepare a rough conceptual planting diagram to aid in making detailed plant selections. The diagram is usually in the form of an overlay to the site construction drawings. On it are sketched out area by area the outlines, arrows, and notes to describe what the planting is to achieve, as for example:

Light shade here.

Screen unsightly billboard.

Cast tree silhouette on wall.

Reinforce curve of approach drive.

Use ground cover and spring bulbs.

Plant specimen magnolia against evergreens.

Enframe valley view.

Shield terrace from glare of athletic field lights.

Provide enclosure and windscreen for game court.

The more complete the conceptual diagram and notes, the easier the plant selection, and the better the final results.

Trees are the basics. If tree selection and placement are sound, the site framework is well established. Often little additional planting will be needed.

Group trees to simulate natural stands. As a rule, regular spacing or geometric patterns are to be avoided. Trees in rows or grids are best reserved for limited urban situations where a civic or monumental character is desired.

Use canopy trees to unify the site. They are the most visible. They provide the dominant neighborhood character and identity. They provide sun filter and shade and soften architectural lines. They provide the spatial roof or ceiling.

Install intermediate trees for understory screening, windbreak, and visual interest. They are the enframers, particularly suited to the subdivision of a larger site into smaller use areas and spaces. As a category they include many of the better accent plants and ornamentals and may be used as individual specimens.

Utilize shrubs for supplementary low-level baffles and screens. They serve as well to provide enclosure, to reinforce pathway alignments and nodes, to accentuate points and features of plan importance, and to furnish floral and foliage display. They can also be used (sparingly) for hedges.

Treat vines as nets and draperies. Various types can be planted to stabilize slopes and dunes, to cool exposed walls, or to provide a cascade of foliage and blossoms over walls and fences.

Install ground covers on the base plane to retain soils and soil moisture, define paths and use areas, and provide turf where required. They are the carpets of the ground plane.

In all extensive tree plantings select a theme tree, from three to five supporting secondary trees, and a limited palette of supplementary species for special conditions and effects. This procedure helps to assure a planting of simplicity and strength.

Choose as the dominant theme tree a type that is indigenous, moderately fast-growing, and able to thrive with little care. These are planted in groups, swaths, and groves to provide the "grand arboreal framework" and overall site organization.

EXAMPLE BY REGION

	Northern Michigan	West Coast Bay Area	Central Arizona	Southwest Florida
	Resort	University	Urban Park	Community
Theme Tree	White Pine	Cal. Live Oak Eucalyptus	Washingtonia Palm	Live Oak Slash Pine
Secondary	Ash Basswood Am. Beech Sugar Maple Aspen	Olive Monterey Pine White Alder Pistache	Canary Pine Arizona Ash Stone Pine Cypress	Tree Wax Myrtle Cabbage Palm Mahogany
Supplementary	Shadblow White Birch Hemlock Am. Cedar Striped Maple Pin Cherry	Fl. Cherry Hawthorn Vine Maple Ironwood Plum	Fruitless Mulberry Sour Orange Evergreen Pear Crape Myrtle	Black Olive Weeping Fig Royal Poinciana Mangrove Silver Buttonwood

Native, or indigenous, plants are those growing naturally on the site and historically characteristic of the region.

Naturalized plants are those introduced accidentally or by intent that have accommodated themselves to the growing conditions and become part of the local scene.

Exotic plants are those foreign to the natural site and locality.

A similar listing is made for shrubs, vines, and ground covers. Together they should comprise a compatible family of plants expressive of the site character desired.

Use secondary species to complement the primary planting installation and to define the site spaces of lesser magnitude. Each secondary tree type will be chosen to harmonize with the theme tree and natural landscape character, while imbuing each space with its own special qualities.

Supplementary tree species are used as appropriate to demarcate or differentiate areas of unique landscape quality. The uniqueness may be that of *topography,* as ridge, hollow, upland, or marsh. It may be that of *use,* as a local street or court, a quiet garden space, or a bustling urban shopping mall. It may be that of *special need,* as dense windscreen, light shade, or seasonal color.

Exotic species are to be limited to areas of high refinement. They are best used only in those situations in which they may receive intensive care and will not detract from the natural scene.

Use trees to sheathe the trafficways. An effective design approach is to plant the arterial roads or circulation drives with random groupings of trees selected from the *secondary list.* Local streets, loop drives, and culs-de-sac are "transitioned in," but each is given its own particular character with *supplementary* trees (and other plants) best suited to the use, the topography, and the architecture.

Give emphasis to trafficway nodes. The intersections of circulation routes are often given added prominence by the use of modulated ground forms, walls, fences, signing, increased levels of lighting, and supplementary planting.

Keep the sight lines clear at roadway intersections. Avoid the use of shrubs and low-branching trees within the sighting zones.

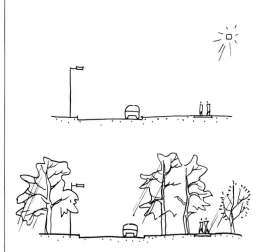

Trees along local streets are welcome attributes.

Create an attractive roadway portal to each neighborhood and activity center. The entrance planting should be arranged to provide a welcoming harbor quality.

Arrange the tree groupings to provide views and expansive open spaces. Plants are well used as enframers rather than fillers.

Close or compress the plantings where the ground forms or structures impinge. This sequential opening and closing and increasing or decreasing the height, density, and width of the planting along any route of movement give added richness and power to the landscape.

Expand the roadside plantings. Where space is limited, the initial landscape plantings and often site construction may occur outside the right-of-way. A landscape or planting easement may be required.

Use plantings to reinforce the alignment of paths and roadways. They can help to "explain" the plan layout and give clear direction.

Provide shade and interest along the paths and bikeways. If made attractive, they will be used.

Conceal parking, storage, and other service areas. Trees, hedges, or looser shrubs may be used alone or in combination with mounding, walls, or fencing to provide visual control.

Install screen plantings to hide unpleasant views, eliminate glare, and reduce noise levels. Their effectiveness in all seasons and stages of growth is a factor to be considered.

Provide evolving sequences of space to enclose and link the various site use areas. Each functional space has its own requirements of openness or containment as it relates to other spaces and the landscape environs.

Strengthen the protruding "points" of mass planting with dominant plants. Keep the bays recessive.

Establish vegetation along the swales and waterways. It helps to stabilize the banks, increases evapotranspiration, and adds landscape interest.

Avoid foundation plantings. Fine architecture can stand alone or in combination with one or more well-selected and well-placed accent plants.

Avoid the scatteration of multitudinous plant varieties. Horticultural zoos have little to commend them.

Keep the plantings simple. They are best composed of selected specimens, functional screen hedges, well-composed groupings, and massed tree enframement.

Consider climate control in all landscape planting. Plants can be used to block winter winds, channel the breeze, temper the heat of the sun, and otherwise improve the microclimate.

Complement the topographical forms. By skillful planting, the visual impact of the landscape can be greatly enhanced.

Use plants as space definers. They are admirably suited to enclose, subdivide, and otherwise articulate the various functional spaces of the site and the passageways that connect them. They convert use areas into use spaces. By their associative nature and their color, texture, and form, they can endow each space with qualities appropriate to the use or uses intended.

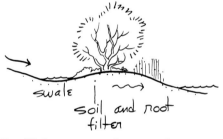

Establish vegetation between detention swales and water bodies to increase evapotranspiration and filtration.

PLANTS

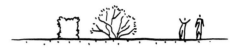

CANOPY TREES

These include the taller shade and forest species that, alone or together, form a high foliage crown.

Use indigenous canopy trees to:
- Filter the sun
- Soften architectural lines
- Set the landscape theme
- Unify the area
- Provide the spatial ceiling

Trees help establish pedestrian scale.

INTERMEDIATE TREES

Lower deciduous and coniferous species with foliage extending from near the ground plane to at least eye height.

Install intermediate trees in the open or understory for screening, backdrop, and visual interest.

SHRUBS

Shrubs are woody perennial plants, usually smaller than a tree, with multiple stems branching from or near the ground.

Utilize shrubs for supplementary low-level screening and for their interest of form, foliage, flowers, and fruit. They may also be used as natural and (sparingly) as trimmed hedges.

Plants and grasses may be augmented with mulches such as shredded bark, wood chips, or gravel.

VINES AND GROUND COVERS

Plants vary from woody to herbaceous, from deciduous to evergreen, from succulents to grasses.

Select those ground covers which will provide superior:
- Erosion control
- Soil moisture retention
- Naturalized foregrounds
- Lawns and playing surfaces
- Maintenance reduction

The illustrated principles are from a planting guideline prepared for Pelican Bay, a new Florida community.

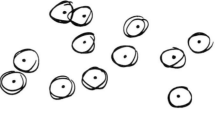

The random spacing of trees is suited to the naturalized landscape - as for park and recreation areas and reforestation. Often a blend of indigenous, nurse, and permanent species produces the best stand.

A sparse grove of well-placed trees can unify and give refreshing relief to a building group or compound.

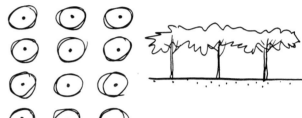

The geometric spacing of canopy trees creates spacious architectural rooms. This is more appropriate in level, geometric courtyards of civic-monumental character.

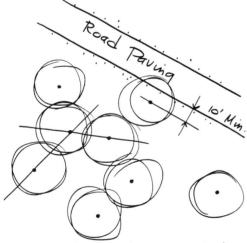

Group trees to simulate natural stands.

Avoid regular spacing — or the placement of more than two trees in a line. Distances depend upon tree types and whether free-standing specimens or any inter-laced canopy is desired.

NEW PLANTING INSTALLATIONS

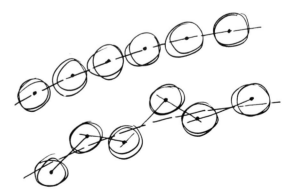

Trees in a single or double row have strong visual impact. This arrangement is therefore best reserved for the urban or built environment.

In the more natural landscape an off-set, irregular tree line is usually preferred.

PLANTS

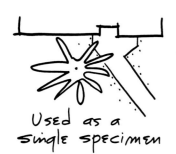

Used as a single specimen

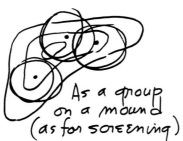

intermediate trees...

As a group on a mound (as for screening)

Plants combined with mounding can hide parking and service areas.

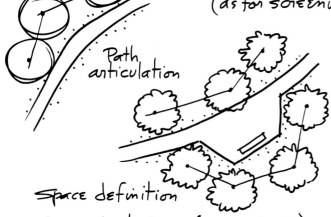

Path articulation

Space definition

Intermediate trees (and shrubs) are the place, plane, and alignment definers. Use them to reinforce the lines and forms of the plan.

Combine planting with earth shaping to create landscape interest.

Trees provide shade and interest along walks and bikeways.

Road R/W and Property line

Landscape Easement

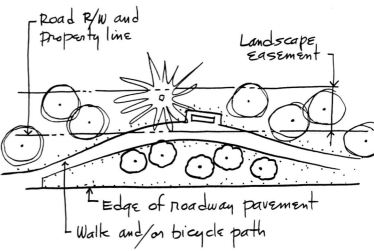

Edge of roadway pavement

Walk and/or bicycle path

Landscape construction and planting can occur outside of the street right-of-way (R/W) where space is limited and a "Landscape Easement" provided.

Install screen plantings adjacent to traffic-ways to reduce noise and glare.

FORM AND SPACE MODULATION

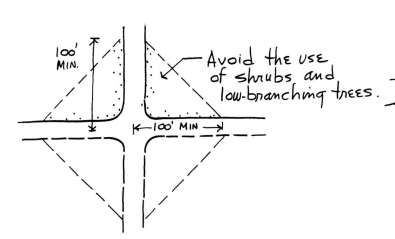

100' MIN.

← 100' MIN →

Avoid the use of shrubs and low-branching trees.

Keep the sight lines clear at traffic-way intersections.

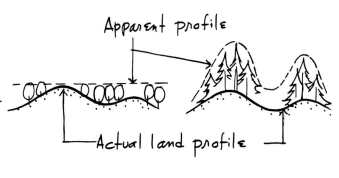

Apparent profile

Actual land profile

Plants are well used to accentuate land forms and intensify landscape power.

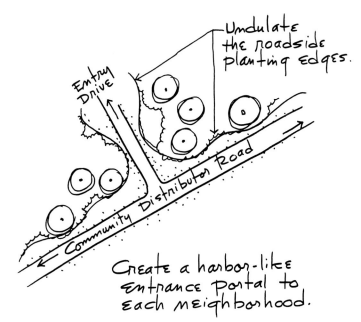

Undulate the roadside planting edges.

Entry Drive

Community Distributor Road

Create a harbor-like entrance portal to each neighborhood.

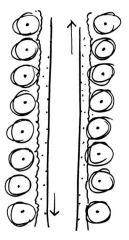

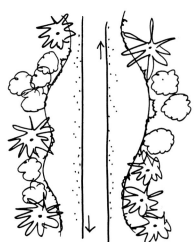

Avoid monotonous edges in road-side and other plantings.

Undulation in both the horizontal alignment and vertical profile add landscape appeal.

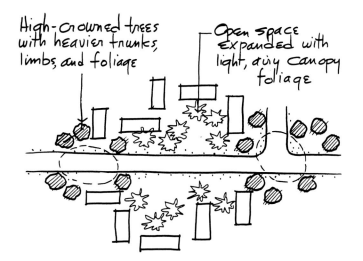

High-crowned trees with heavier trunks, limbs, and foliage

Open space expanded with light, airy canopy foliage

Strengthen the building closures and trafficway nodes with trees of more structural character.

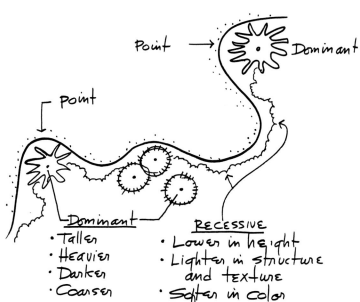

Point → ⊕ Dominant

Point

Dominant
• Taller
• Heavier
• Darker
• Coarser

RECESSIVE
• Lower in height
• Lighter in structure and texture
• Softer in color

In mass plantings emphasize the points with dominant plants and make the bays recede.

Climate

5

If a central purpose of planning is to create for any person or group of persons an environment suited to their needs, then *climate* must be a fundamental consideration. It is fundamental, first, in the selection of an appropriate region for the proposed activities and then, within that region, in the selection of the most appropriate property. Once a site has been chosen, two new considerations suggest themselves. How do we best respond to the climatic givens in terms of site and structural design, and by what means can we modify the effects of climate to improve the situation?

The planetary framework

As an introduction to a better understanding of climate it would be well to pause for a moment to contemplate the immensity of the universal framework that governs climatic and weather cycles.

The larger dimensions of world climate are determined and continually influenced by a number of imponderable factors, chief among which is the amount of solar radiation that the earth receives from the sun. This is the source of all terrestrial energy. It sets into motion and controls the thermal currents that sweep the oceans to their depths. It activates and determines the intensity of the sometimes mild, sometimes raging air currents of the troposphere. It sets the ponderous rhythm of glacial advances and retreats. Such phenomena are unalterable. We can only recognize the certainty of cause and effect and adapt our thinking accordingly.

77

Climate and response

There is little to be done about the world climate except to adjust to it. The most direct form of adjustment is to move to that region which has a climate best suited to one's needs or desires. Such migrations or attempted migrations are the basis of much of human history. The alternative approach, barring admission to a climatological Shangri-la, is to make the best of existing conditions wherever one may be.

In broad terms, the climatic regions of the earth are four: the *cold*, the *cool-temperate*, the *warm-humid*, and the *hot-dry*. North America provides examples of all four. While the boundaries of these regions or zones cannot be defined precisely and while there are within them considerable variations, each has its distinctive characteristics and its strong influences upon any site development or structures to be planned.

Literature, art, and music all give illuminating insights into the character of the various regions and their inhabitants. Travel and direct observation give even more vivid impressions, and if one is to work and plan for the people of any area, detailed on-site research is essential. As a guideline for the investigation of the nature of any climatological region or subregion, the following simplified checklist should be of help.

Physical characteristics Perhaps the most obvious facts of climate are the annual, seasonal, and daily ranges of temperature. These will vary with changing conditions of latitude, longitude, altitude, exposure, vegetation, and proximity to such weather modifiers as the Gulf Stream, water bodies, ice masses, or desert.

The amount of precipitation in the form of dew, rainfall, frost, or snow is to be recorded, as well as seasonal variations in humidity. The duration of sunlight in hours per day is of planning and design significance, as are the angles of incidence at prescribed times of day and year and the intensity of solar radiation. The direction and velocity of the winds and the date and path of violent storms are to be charted. The availability, quantity, and quality of potable water are to be noted, together with the depths at which it occurs. The geologic structure is to be described, together with soil types and depths and the existing vegetation and wildlife. Finally, the working together of all the physical elements as an ecological system is described to complete the story of regional climate.

Social characteristics The physical well-being and attitudes of people are directly affected by climate, and these in turn prescribe the planning needs. It is well, therefore, in the study of climatic regions to note behavioral reactions and patterns of community organization that are unique and attributable to the climate or the weather. The special foods and dishes, the manner of dress, and the traditional customs are indicative. And so it is with the favored types of recreation, the level of education, and cultural pursuits. Economic factors such as agricultural yields and the production of goods are to be noted. The forms of government and political trends are analyzed, as are the general state of public health and the incidence of particular health hazards and types of disease. A person's height, weight, circulation, respiration, perspiration, and dehydration have a direct relationship to climate, as do the factors of hardiness and acclimatization. It is no happenstance that the bird-like form of the maidens of the high Andes, with their thin ankles and capacious chests, differs from the squat and heavy build of Es-

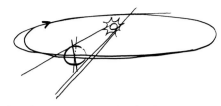

The planet Earth, with tilted axis, moves in its daily loop around the sun. The incidence of the sun's radiation is a function both of our sphere's elliptical orbit and of its oscillating axial tilt. This variance in radiation accounts for climatic differentials and seasonal temperature change.

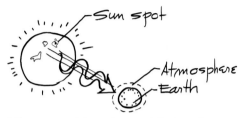

All terrestrial heat (energy) derives from the sun. The *amount* of energy received is related to the position of the earth in its elliptical orbit and in some yet inexplicable way to variations in the pattern of sunspots. In a lesser way energy reception is affected by conditions pertaining within the earth's intervening atmosphere.

The cyclic buildup and melt of polar ice are unpredictable. The periodic advance and retreat of the polar caps as they respond to solar forces in turn exert a massive influence on world weather conditions.

The ocean currents help to distribute the solar energy input to all areas of the globe. The thermal currents of the ocean, like the currents of the troposphere, are solar-generated. They sweep in counterrotary patterns and help to distribute the earth's store of sun-emitted heat.

Climate defines the type and range of human activities.

kimo women. There are sound climatological reasons. In short, what one eats, drinks, believes, and *is,* is climate-induced and characteristic of the region.

Planning considerations   Clearly, architectural or landscape planning for the well-being of a cultural group demands an understanding not only of the physical nature of the region and site but of the people as well. Then, given a specific location within the region and a well-defined program of needs, the two-dimensional plan forms can be developed to achieve a pattern of appropriate, functional, and agreeable relationships.

The plan layout of farms and homesteads within any region is a telling statement about the climate and the people's accommodation to it. Community plan organization, too, and the patterns of urban form respond directly to heat and cold, wind direction, the frequency and intensity of storms, the annual fall of snow and rain, the availability of fresh water, or the need for irrigation. Modes and routes of transportation and even trip lengths are functions of weather and climate also.

Sometimes the most important consideration in site selection or planning is a realization of the need and benefits of protecting the natural environment. The American Indians well understood that to preserve the integrity of their hunting grounds their nomadic villages must be widely dispersed and clustered. Contemporary Americans have yet to understand the timeliness and wisdom of this lesson.

Design response   As in the two-dimensional plan layout of farm, home, and community, so it is with the three-dimensional design of sites and structures within a region. Just as the use area or traffic-way is oriented "into the breeze," "away from the wind," or "toward the sun" in some instances, so are site and architectural *volumes* shaped to afford exposure to the sun's warmth and light summer airs or protection from glare, oppressive heat, or fierce winter winds. All site and architectural spaces of excellence are weather-responsive; their form, materials of construction, and even colors are all climate-related. A postcard received from any part of the world depicting people, their dress, or their buildings will convey at a glance an informative story of *region.*

It is proposed that within each region there is for a given climatological *condition,* a logical *planning-design response.* The accompanying examples show for various conditions an appropriate accommodation in the shaping of community patterns, site plans, or building designs.

Climate-conditioned spaces. Nationwide Plaza, Columbus, Ohio.

The cold region

Timberline and above.

Condition

1. Extreme winter cold.
2. Deep snow.
3. Strong winds.
4. High windchill factor.
5. Deep frost.
6. Scrub forest cover.
7. Short winter days.
8. Long winters.
9. Alternating freeze and thaw.
10. Rapid spring melt.

The cool-temperate region

Mild winters, agreeable summers.

Condition

1. Variable temperatures, ranging from warm to hot in the summer, cold in winter, and moderate in spring and fall.
2. Marked seasonal change.
3. Changing wind directions and velocities.
4. Violent storms occur infrequently.
5. Periods of drought, light to heavy rains, and frost and snow may be expected.
6. Soils are generally well drained and fertile.
7. Many streams, rivers, and freshwater lakes.
8. An abundant supply of water.
9. Land cover varies from open to forested, with rich vegetative variety.
10. Topographically scenic, including marine, plain, plateau, and mountainous areas.

Community

1. Orientation to warming sun.
2. Provision for snowplowing and snow storage.
3. Utilization of all protective ground forms and covers as windscreens and soil stabilizers.
4. Crosswind alignment of trafficways and linear site use areas.
5. Reduction in size of plan areas to minimize costly excavation and frostproof construction.
6. Preservation of all possible vegetation, with the strong wind-resistant edges left intact.
7. Grouping of activity areas to reduce travel time.
8. Provision of community recreation and cultural centers within or near concentrations of dwellings.
9. Alignment of trafficways to fall within shadow bands to preclude ice buildup.
10. Avoidance of low ground, natural drainageways, and floodplains.

Site

1. Creation of enclosed courts and sun traps; use of textured construction materials and warm, "primitive" colors.
2. Use of short accessways, grouped entries, raised platforms, and covered walks.
3. Preservation or planting of windscreens; installation of snow fencing; use of low, strong vertical enclosure to brace for the gale.
4. Provision of intermediate points of shelter on a long traverse; placement of structures to block or sideslip the wind.
5. Use of post, beam, and platform construction to avoid the need for extensive excavation and foundations. Move with the ground surface by the use of stepped horizontal planes.
6. Clearing of small and clustered use areas, or "rooms," and meandering paths of interconnection *within* the scrub and tree growth. Developed areas should be limited in size to leave natural growth undisturbed insofar as possible.
7. Maximum utilization of daylight; orientation of buildings toward sunlit spaces with views to the sky and sunlit hills.
8. Utilization of the clustered-compound plan approach, which tends to engender pleasant community life and close social ties.
9. Use of decks, raised walkways, and flexible ground surfacings to preclude frost heave and keep people out of the slush and mud.
10. Provision of positive surface drainage to the natural lines of storm-water flow, with the soils, grasses, and other covers left undisturbed to prevent soil erosion.

Building

1. Design of massive, low-profile, well-insulated structures, with maximum exposure of walls and roof areas to the sun and minimum exposure to the wind; heat loss to be reduced in all ways possible, including limitation of the window area.
2. Protection of approaches from snow drift; the raising of entrance platforms above anticipated levels. The hazard of roof collapse may be reduced by steep-roof-and-storage-loft architecture.
3. Placement of windows away from prevailing winds; orientation of the long building axis into the wind and utilization of all possible topographic shielding and tree screens.
4. Location of entrances in the lee of the structure, with short protected passageways to limit the time of exposure.
5. Reduction of building perimeter and ground contact to reduce foundation problems and heat loss.
6. Forest cover preserved and buildings nestled against the protective slopes and tree masses.
7. Design of windows and living areas to exact the full contribution of the sun.
8. Attention lavished on comfort, architectural interest, and detail. In frigid climates particularly the "home is a castle."
9. With condensation and ice formation a problem, elimination of vulnerable joints and hazardous surfaces insofar as possible.
10. Use of steep roof pitches, deep overhangs, and exaggerated storm drainage gradients and capacities to facilitate rapid runoff.

Community

1. Definition of land use and trafficway patterns to reflect local temperature ranges and other climatic conditions. Extremes suggest compact plan arrangements; more moderate conditions permit dispersal.
2. Accommodation. Community plans must stand the test of function in all seasons.
3. Alignment of streets and open spaces to block cold winter winds and admit welcome summer breezes.
4. Design of streets, utility systems, and drainage channels to meet extreme conditions.
5. Consideration of high winds, flooding, and occasional snowstorms as important design factors.
6. Provision of extensive park and open-space systems as distinguishing attributes.
7. Incorporation of the natural waterways into the community plan for the use and enjoyment of the public.
8. Widespread installation of private and public gardens as regional features.
9. Preservation of indigenous vegetation within the open-space framework.
10. Planning of each community as a unique expression of its setting.

Site

1. Possibility of, and necessity for, wide variety in the type and size of outdoor activity areas.
2. Dramatization of the seasonal variations; consideration of spaces for winter, spring, summer, and fall activities.
3. Design recognition of the prevailing wind and breeze patterns.
4. Construction to withstand the worst of the storms.
5. Provision for all-weather durability and maintenance.
6. Protection of prime regional forest and agricultural lands.
7. Sensitive planning and zoning of all water-related lands to preserve their scenic and ecological values.
8. Use of pools and fountains to enhance community parks and gathering places.
9. Adaptation of community plan forms to provide the best possible integration with the natural-landscape features.
10. Full utilization of scenic possibilities.

Building

1. Elimination, by design, of extremes of demands for cooling, heating, and ventilating.
2. Consideration of the special design requirements and possibilities suggested by each season in turn.
3. Architectural plan organization and detailing in response to the cooling and chilling effects of local breezes and winds.
4. Structural design to meet the most severe storm conditions.
5. Consideration of shrinkage, swelling, condensation, freezing, and snow loadings.
6. Expansion and extension of plan forms when desirable, since excavation and foundation construction are not generally a problem.
7. Full utilization of the recreation values of each site.
8. Water catchment and storage is not a prime consideration.
9. Design of building areas and form in response to the topography.
10. Treatment of each building site to realize the full landscape potential.

The warm-humid region

High temperatures and humidity.

Condition

1. Temperatures high and relatively constant.
2. High humidity.
3. Torrential rainfall.
4. Storm winds of typhoon and hurricane force.
5. Breeze often constant in the daylight hours.
6. Vegetative covers from sparse to luxuriant and sometimes junglelike.
7. The sun's heat is enervating.
8. Sky glare and sea glare can be distressing.
9. Climatic conditions breed insects in profusion.
10. Fungi are a persistent problem.

The hot-dry (desertlike) region

Desert.

Condition

1. Intense heat in the daytime.
2. Often intense cold at night.
3. Expanses are vast.
4. Sunlight and glare are penetrating.
5. Drying winds are prevalent and often raise devastating dust storms.
6. Annual rainfall is minimal. Vegetation is sparse to nonexistent except along watercourses.
7. Spring rains come as a cloudburst, with rapid runoff and heavy erosion.
8. Water supply is extremely limited.
9. Limited agricultural productivity necessitates the importation of food and other goods.
10. Irrigation is a fact of life.

Community

1. Spacing of habitations in the dispersed "hunter" tradition.
2. Adjustment of community patterns to channels or areas of air movement.
3. Avoidance of floodplains and drainageways. Disturbed areas are subject to heavy erosion.
4. Location of settlements in the lee of protective land masses and forest and above the level of storm-driven tides.
5. Alignment of streets and placement of gathering places to capture all possible air currents.
6. Avoidance of natural growth insofar as feasible. Disturbance of the ground cover subjects soils to erosion.
7. Use of existing tree masses and promontories to provide a sunscreen to public ways and places. Supplementary planting of shade trees is often desirable.
8. Planned location of settlements with the arc of the sun to the *rear*, not *seaward*, of the building sites.
9. Location of settlements upwind of insect-breeding areas.
10. Admittance of sun and breeze to building areas to reduce fungi and mildew.

Site

1. Design of site spaces to provide shade, ventilation, and the cooling effects of foliage and water.
2. Provision for air circulation and evaporation.
3. Protection against driving rains and adequate runoff capacity.
4. Location of critical use areas and routes in unexposed places, above the reach of tides and flooding.
5. Maximization, by exposure, channeling, and funneling, of the favorable effects of the breeze.
6. Use of lush foliage masses and specimen plants as backdrop and enframement and for the interest of form, foliage, or floral display.
7. Planning of outdoor activity areas for use in the cooler morning and evening hours. Heat-of-the-day gathering places should be roofed or tree-shaded.
8. Reduction or elimination of glare by plan location and well-placed tree plantings.
9. Elevation of use areas and walkways by deck and platform construction to open them to the breeze and reduce annoyance by insects.
10. Use of stone, concrete, metals, and treated wood only in contact with the ground.

Building

1. Induction of cooling by all feasible means, including the use of open building plans, high ceilings, broad overhangs, louvered openings, and air conditioning of local areas.
2. Provision of air circulation; periodic exposure to sunlight and artificial drying where required.
3. Architectural use of the colonnade, arcade, pavilion, covered passageway, and veranda; orientation of entranceways and windows away from the path of the storm track.
4. Design of wind-resistant structures or lighter temporary and expendable shelters.
5. Design of rooms, corridors, balconies, and patios as an interconnected system of breezeways.
6. Utilization, indoors and out, of indigenous plant materials for the cooling effect of their foliage.
7. Provision of shade, shade, shade.
8. Positioning of viewing points away from the glare and provision of well-designed screening.
9. Elevation of structures above the ground, facing into the breeze, and insectproofing of critical points and areas.
10. Provision of open, well-ventilated storage areas; use of fungus-resistant materials and drying devices as needed.

Community

1. Creation of cool and refreshing islands of use within the parched surroundings.
2. Provision of opportunities for group activity. Chill evenings in the desert, as on the tundra, suggest the need.
3. Adaptation of "outpost," "fort," and "ranch" plan patterns.
4. Within the dispersed compounds the planning of compact spaces with narrow passageways and colonnades to provide relief from the sun.
5. Location of homesteads and trade centers in areas of established ground covers; use of shelterbelt tree plantations.
6. Protection of all possible natural growth surrounding the development.
7. Avoidance of flood-prone areas. Those who have experienced desert freshets will keep well out of their way.
8. Minimization of irrigation requirements by compact planning and multiple use of planted and seeded spaces.
9. Location of settlements and community centers close to transportation and distribution nodes.
10. Coordination of land use and traffic patterns with existing and projected irrigation canal routes and reservoir locations.

Site

1. Amelioration of heat and glare by orientation away from the sun, by shading, by screening, and by the cast-shadow patterns of well-placed building components.
2. Adoption of the corral-compound (herder) arrangement of homesteads and neighborhood clusters.
3. Recognition of the automobile as the crucial means of daily transport and a dominant site-planning factor.
4. Screening of use areas and paths of movement from the direct blast of the sun.
5. Protection of outdoor activity spaces from exposure.
6. Preservation of native plant materials as self-sustaining and handsome components of the desert landscape.
7. Avoidance of arroyos and floodplains as development routes and sites.
8. Limitation in the size of parks, gardens, and seeded areas.
9. Use of tubbed and container-grown plants, drip irrigation, and hydroponic gardening.
10. Incorporation of irrigation canals, ponds, and structures as attractive site features.

Building

1. Architectural use of thick walls, high ceilings, wide roof overhangs, limited fenestration, light-reflective colors, and a precise design response to the angles and arcs of the sun.
2. Exclusion of the chill night air by insulation, reduction of heat loss, and use of localized radiant heat. The open fireplace is a desert tradition for good reason.
3. Low ranch-type spreads are a logical architectural expression of the hot-dry climate and desert topography.
4. Provision of cool, compact, and dim interior spaces in contrast to the stifling heat and brilliance of the great outdoors.
5. Sealing of all buildings against dust and wind. Airtight openings and skillful architectural detailing are required.
6. Grouping of rooms or structures around planted and irrigated courts and patios.
7. Provision of spring rainfall catchment and storage. Water from roofs, courts, and paved areas can be directed to cisterns.
8. Recycling of wastewater is prescribed. The type of use will determine the degree of treatment and purification required.
9. The provision of food and fodder storage is an important consideration in desert building design.
10. Adaptation of irrigation to interior courts and garden spaces. The evaporation of moisture from paved surfaces, fountains, spray heads, mulches, or foliage provides welcome relief from the heat.

Microclimatology

Microclimatology is the study of climatic conditions within a limited area. It is sometimes referred to as the "science of small-scale weather." It may be inferred that the purpose of the scientific study is to discover facts and principles which may be applied to improve the human condition. This is precisely the case.

An example As a hypothetical example let us consider a small walled courtyard in a hot-dry (desert) setting. It is proposed that by the application of well-known principles of microclimatic design the ambient air temperature at a point 3 feet above the ground surface could be reduced by as much as 30 to 40°F. This could well improve the existing condition from an intolerable situation to one of comfort and delight—all in all, a worthy enterprise.

As a base condition, let us assume the worst. Let us assume that the enclosing walls are solid, admit no breeze, are high enough to provide an extensive sun-receiving, heat-radiating area, and are black in color to maximize their heat absorption. Let us then compound the disaster by flooring the empty courtyard space with solid concrete, thick enough for massive heat buildup and radiation and colored in a dark-red hue. To complete our experimental volume let us imagine the courtyard to be so oriented as to receive the full force of the burning midday sun. It can be seen that a subject seated on a metal chair in the center of this unfortunate cube would be properly grilled, and that shortly.

In contrast, wishing to create a cool and refreshing courtyard in the same locality, let us "wing out" the side walls to catch the slightest breeze that might be channeled through the space. The walls themselves could be formed of light-gray textured concrete or stone rough enough to be heat-refractive and to receive several clumps of vines. A pool, a brimming basin, or a splashing fountain installed on the base plane would introduce water. Water would also be used as a spray to moisten low mounded beds of planting edged with gravel mulch for rapid evaporation. From the irrigated planting bed a multistemmed shade tree might support a canopy of foliage and flowers, to cast patterns of shadow across the walls and paving. Additional shade could be provided on the overhead plane by light sails or panels of cool-colored nylon fabric. Tubbed and potted plants would add green relief and decorative interest. With webbed rattan furniture, iced drinks, and the sound of wafting music, the oasis would be complete.

The example is extreme, but it serves to illustrate the possibilities of small-scale climate improvement.

A garden corner oasis.

The common denominators Whatever the climate or weather, when it comes to planning an agreeable living environment there are many microclimatic principles that can be applied to advantage. Among them are these:

Eliminate the extremes of heat, cold, humidity, air movement,

Climate and weather amelioration

Site planning for outdoor comfort

and exposure. This can be achieved by intelligent site selection, plan layout, building orientation, and creation of climate-responsive spaces.

Provide direct structural protection against the discomfort of solar radiation, precipitation, wind, storm, and cold.

Respond to the seasons. Each presents its problems; each provides its opportunities for more fully attuned adaptation and enjoyment.

Adjust community, site, and building plans to the movement of the sun. The design of living areas, indoors and out, should ensure that the favored type and amount of light are received at the favored time.

Use the sun's radiation and solar panels to provide supplementary heat and energy for cooling.

Consider the wind also as a time-tested source of energy.

Utilize the evaporation of moisture as a primary method of cooling. Air moving across any moist surface, be it masonry, fabric, or foliage, is thereby made cooler.

Maximize the beneficial effects of adjacent water bodies. These temper the atmosphere of the warmer or cooler adjacent lands.

Introduce water. The presence of water in any form, from film to waterfall, has a cooling effect both physically and psychologically.

Preserve the existing vegetative cover. It ameliorates climatic problems in many ways:

It shades the ground surface.

It retains the cooling moisture of precipitation.

It protects the soils and environs from the freezing winds.

It cools and refreshes heated air by evapotranspiration.

It provides sunscreen, shade, and shadow.

It helps to prevent rapid runoff and to recharge the water-bearing soil strata.

It checks the wind.

Install new plantings where needed. They may be utilized for various types of climate control. Windscreens, shade trees, and heat-absorptive ground covers are examples.

Consider the effects of altitude. The higher the altitude and

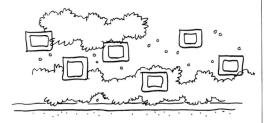

Trickle wall, for hot-weather cooling and plant irrigation.

Pattern of stone, concrete, or metal pans, with spray heads, set in planting border or mulch and allowed to overflow, for cooling and irrigation.

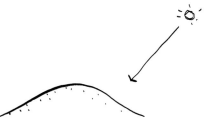

Slopes with southerly exposure receive the most hours and greatest intensity of solar heat each day. Spring can come weeks earlier on the sunny side of a hill.

Topographical forms, tall buildings, trees, or other objects may reduce the total hours of daylight. Depending upon the climatic situation, full sun all day may or may not be desirable.

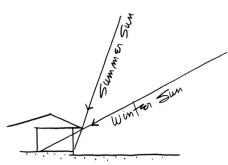

The sun's orbit and angle of incidence vary with the seasons. By orientation, screening, and overhang the amount of sunlight admitted to the interior can be precisely controlled.

The glare from water, sand, or other reflective surfaces can increase heat loads.

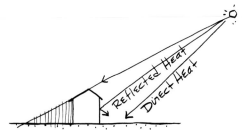

Buildings are temperature modifiers. By their positioning as well as by their form and character they suggest related uses.

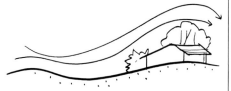

Abrupt forms cause unpleasant air turbulence.

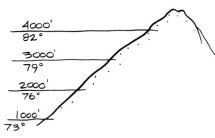

Smooth forms induce the smooth flow of air.

Temperatures vary with elevation—by about 3°F for each 1000 feet in the daytime. Nighttime differentials are greater.

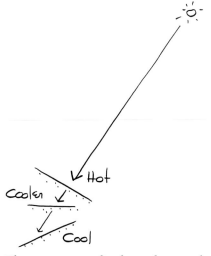

The more perpendicular a slope to the rays of the sun, the warmer the surface temperature.

A mild summer breeze can be amplified by the venturi effect of well-placed buildings, walls, hedges, or mass plantings.

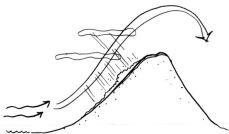

A breeze may be channeled and directed from space to space.

An air mass cools as it is driven up a mountain slope by prevailing winds, often to the point of precipitating its moisture content before reaching the crest. The windward slopes therefore tend to be humid and heavily vegetated, while the lee slopes, robbed of rainfall and subjected to the downdraft that warms as it falls, tend to be hot and arid. To a lesser extent any landform, such as a hill, island, or forest, can have the same effect.

latitude (in the northern hemisphere), the cooler or colder the climate.

Reduce the humidity. Generally speaking, a decrease in humidity effects an increase in bodily comfort. Dry cold is less chilling than wet cold. Dry heat is less enervating than wet heat. Humidity can be decreased by induced air circulation and the drying effects of the sun.

Avoid undrained air catchment areas and frost pockets.

Avoid winter winds, floods, and the paths of crippling storms. All can be charted.

Explore and apply all natural forms of heating and cooling before turning to mechanical (energy-consuming) devices.

The temperature advantage gained by alert siting and landscape improvement may sometimes be measured by no more than a few degrees. But aside from the increased comfort and pleasure derived, the savings of energy in cooling and heating can be significant.

Site planning for energy conservation includes the following possibilities.

Reduction of heat loss

- Avoid exposure to prevailing winds and cold downdrafts from upper slopes.
- Avoid extremes in elevation.
- Avoid also site areas with wet, impervious soils, dead-air basins, and frost pockets.
- Provide wind shielding by ground forms and existing tree cover (preferably evergreen).
- If exposure cannot be precluded, plan compactly and for a slipstream effect, with narrow and solid building walls facing into the winter winds.
- Protect the dwelling entrances.
- Orient building facades to the east, southeast, and south and to the high arc of the sun.
- In cold climates locate use areas and structures in the lee of windbreaks to utilize snow outfall for ground and building insulation.
- Provide open space around buildings for air circulation and the play of the winter sun.
- Deciduous tree cover provides summer shade and cast shadows while admitting winter sunlight.
- Dig in. Partially buried structures receive insulation from the earth and present a lower profile.
- Select construction materials, surface treatments, and colors that absorb and radiate solar heat.

Reduction of cooling requirements

- Face use areas and buildings into the natural airstreams.
- Provide an overhead tree canopy.
- Utilize structural sunshields. Colonnades, arbors, wide overhangs, and recessed openings are familiar in hot climates.
- Compose buildings, ground forms, walls, fencing, and planting to channelize summer breezes through exterior and interior spaces. A broad, dispersed plan arrangement is indicated.
- Excavate for foundations. Structures built into well-drained slopes are warmer in winter and cooler in the summertime.
- Reach for the breeze. Utilize open planning, flying decks, and balconies.
- Promote ventilation by the use of breezeways, screened patios, louvered walls, and fans.
- Feature the use of water for its cooling effects.
- Utilize porous soils, mulches, ground covers, and irrigation to promote evapotranspiration.
- Use heat-reflective materials, rough textures, and cool colors.

Utilization of natural thermodynamics

- Consider energy generation by such sources as wind power, falling and flowing water, and solar panels.
- Maximize the warming effects of the sun and the cooling effects of shade, air currents, and moisture.

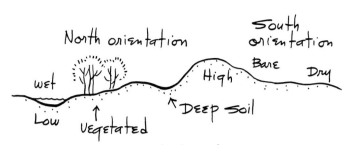

North orientation — South orientation

wet — Low — Vegetated — Deep Soil — High — Bare — Dry

Every property has to some degree a variety of microclimates. These are dependent upon orientation, wind and breeze direction, land conformation, vegetation, soil depth and types, moisture content — and even colors. Such off-site conditions as hills, forests, rivers, waterbodies, and urbanization make a difference too.

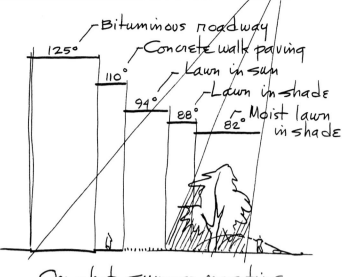

125° — Bituminous roadway
110° — Concrete walk paving
94° — Lawn in sun
88° — Lawn in shade
82° — Moist lawn in shade

On a hot summer noontime the temperatures may vary widely on any given site.

RELATIVE SURFACE TEMPERATURES

As the daytime sun heats the land surface and warm air rises, the cool moist air from adjacent waterbodies moves landward to fill the void.

At night the cooler air from the vegetated land mass flows toward the waterbodies.

THE DAILY LAND-WATER AIR EXCHANGE

Note: The temperature advantage gained by alert siting and landscape improvement may sometimes be measured in no more than a few degrees. But aside from the factor of increased comfort the savings of energy required in cooling and heating can be significant.

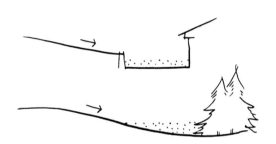

Since cool air flows downhill, local depressions or obstructions can form welcome "pools of cool" — or unwelcome frost pockets.

Relative humidity 74%
Cold air
50°
45°
40°
Cold air and fog collect
Temp. 36°
R.H. 92%

In colder climates the favored site is usually the upper slope below an exposed crest. Slopes facing south are warmer.

But exposure to cold winds at the crest may offset the temperature advantage.

TOPOGRAPHY AFFECTS THE MICROCLIMATE

Note: A number of the thoughts expressed in these pages were suggested by an early writing on microclimatology by Leavitt Dudley, published in *House Beautiful* in May 1954.

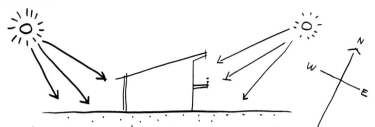

Full Exposure to winter wind

The sun's intensity increases from hour to daylight hour. The early morning (easterly) sun is mild and usually welcome. The late afternoon (westerly) sun is hot and penetrating. A home or office with morning sun enjoys an earlier morning warm-up and a cooler evening. A western exposure increases afternoon heat. Ground heat continues to radiate after the sun has set.

Wind deflected by ground Conformation

Wind deflected by trees

BUILDING SITING AND WINTER WINDS

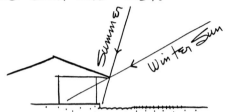

The sun's orbit and angle of incidence vary with the season. By orientation, screening, and overhang the amount of sunlight admitted to interior and exterior spaces can be precisely controlled.

Where possible avoid the sun's heat and glare and exposure to storm winds. In cold climates frost pockets and drifting snow are to be avoided also.

Late afternoon sun is hot and glaring.

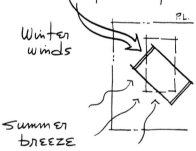

Winter winds

Summer breeze

Often the rotation of a proposed building on the site can improve its relation to breeze and wind and to the sweep of the sun...

Winter winds

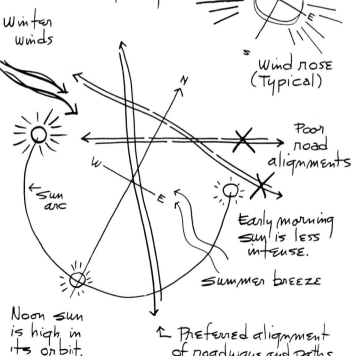

Wind rose (Typical)

Poor road alignments

Early morning sun is less intense.

Summer breeze

Noon sun is high in its orbit.

Preferred alignment of roadways and paths

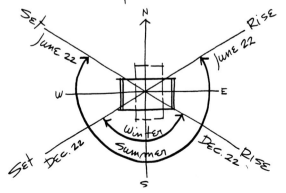

WARMER IN WINTER, COOLER IN SUMMER

PATHS OF MOVEMENT, TOO, SHOULD BE ALIGNED IN RESPONSE TO THE WIND AND SUN

Site

For every site there is an ideal use. For every use there is an ideal site.

Site selection

If we as planners are concerned with wedding a proposed function to a site, let us first be sure that the parties are compatible. We have all seen structures or groups of structures that seem foreign to their location. No matter how excellent these structures or how well contrived their plan, the total result is disturbing and unpleasant.

It would seem obviously foolish, for instance, to situate:

A school fronting on an arterial trafficway

A roadside restaurant with zero approach-sight distance

A shopping center without sufficient parking space

A farm without a source of water

A tavern near a city church

A fabricating plant with room for neither storage yard nor expansion

A new home at the end of a jet landing strip

A meat-packing plant upwind of a suburb

An apartment building 30 feet above a mined-out seam of coal

Each would seem, on the face of it, doomed to failure. Yet each, to the author's knowledge, has been attempted. It is reassuring to those of logical mind to note that in the due course of events each enterprise has been subjected to disrupting strains, scathing antipathies, bankruptcy, or collapse—all rooted in the choice of an inappropriate site for the given use.

In far too many cases, a project has started with the unquestioned acceptance of an unsuitable location. This is a cardinal planning error. An important, if not the most important, function of a planner is the sometimes delicate, sometimes forceful task of guiding an entrepreneur to the selection of the best possible place for a project.

Alternative sites   As advisers, we should be capable of determining the requisite requirements for any given venture and be able to weigh the relative merits of alternative situations. First, clearly we must know what we are looking for. We must thoughtfully, perhaps even tediously, list those site features that we consider necessary or useful for our proposed project, be it a power dam, a new town, or a frozen-custard stand. Next we should reconnoiter and scout out the territory for likely locations. For this task we have a number of helpful tools, such as aerial and remote-sensing photography, U.S. Geological Survey (USGS) maps, road maps, transportation maps, planning commission data, zoning maps, chamber of commerce publications, plat books, and city, county, township, and borough plans.

Of these, the USGS maps warrant special mention. They may often be purchased locally at map or stationery stores or may be ordered directly from the USGS. An index that shows which map

Our primary work as planners is to help fit human activities to the "want to be" of the land.

If a client makes the wrong planning decision in site acquisition or otherwise and has first advised the planner, the fault lies not so much with the client as with the planner, who has failed to present a persuasive case.

Given the facts and a full understanding of the alternatives, reason tends to prevail.

U.S. Geological Survey.

LOCATION APPRAISAL CHECKLIST

A Comparative Analysis of Alternative Residential Sites

Legend:

- ■ Severe limitation
- □ Moderate constraint
- ○ Condition good
- ● Condition excellent

Suggested procedure:

A visit to each site and locale is essential. Photographs help — as do notes describing in more detail the key features rated by symbol on the appraisal checksheet.

Note:

By substituting numbers for symbols (from 10 to 1 for positive values and from −1 to −10 for negative values) the arithmetic sum for each column would give a general indication of its relative overall rating. It is to be realized, however, that in some cases a single severe constraint or superlative feature might well overwhelm the statistics and become the deciding factor.

(1)Social mix and concerns
  Architectual quality
  Level of maintenance
  Freedom from pollution
  Parks, recreation and
    open space
  Landmarks
  General tone

CRITERIA	1	2	3	4	5
REGIONAL					
Climate (Temperature, rainfall, storms, etc.)	■	○	○	□	○
Soils (Stability, fertility, depths)	○	●	□	■	○
Water supply and quality	□	●	□	■	○
Economy (Rising, stable, declining)	○	○	□	□	○
Transportation (Highways and transit)	■	○	○	■	●
Energy (Availability and relative cost)	□	○	○	□	○
Landscape character	●	●	○	□	○
Cultural opportunities	○	○	○	□	□
Recreational opportunities	●	●	○	○	●
Employment opportunities	□	□	■	□	○
Health care facilities	○	□	□	○	□
Major detractions (List and describe)	□	○	○	■	●
Exceptional features (List and describe)	□	●	●	□	○
COMMUNITY					
Travel (Time-distance to work, shopping, etc.)	■	□	○	○	■
Travel experience (Pleasant or unpleasant)	○	○	○	□	○
Community ambience(1)	○	●	□	■	○
Schools	○	○	□	□	○
Shopping	○	●	○	□	○
Churches	○	○	○	□	□
Cultural opportunities (Library, auditorium)	○	○	○	□	○
Public services (Fire, police, etc.)	○	○	○	■	○
Safety and security	■	○	○	■	○
Medical facilities	○	□	■	□	○
Governance	○	○	○	■	○
Taxes	○	□	○	○	○
Major detractions (List and describe)	○	○	□	□	○
Exceptional features (List and describe)	○	●	○	□	○
NEIGHBORHOOD					
Landscape character	○	●	●	□	○
Life style	□	●	○	■	○
Compatibility of proposed uses	○	●	○	■	●
Trafficways (Access, hazard, attractiveness)	○	○	○	□	○
Schools	□	○	○	□	□
Conveniences (Schools, service, etc.)	□	○	□	□	●

Preliminary finding:

A broad item by item comparison would indicate that sites 2 and 5 are prime contenders, while site 4 and probably sites 1 and 3 should be dropped from further consideration.

(2) Rapid transit
    Highways
    Pedestrian
    Riding trails
    Jogging paths
    Bikeways

Note:
A comparable (but modified) checklist could well be compiled in considering alternative sites for a school, church, shopping center, industrial park, or project of any type and magnitude.

CRITERIA	1	2	3	4	5
Parks, recreation and open space	○	●	○	□	○
Exposure (sun, wind, storms, flooding)	○	○	□	■	○
Freedom from noise, fumes, etc.	○	●	○	□	○
Utilities (Availability and cost)	■	●	■	■	●
Major detractions (List and describe)	○	○	□	□	□
Exceptional features (List and describe)	○	●	○	□	○
PROPERTY					
Size and shape (suitability)	○	●	○	■	○
Aspect from approaches	□	●	●	○	○
Safe entrance and egress	□	○	○	□	●
On-site "feel"	○	●	●	□	●
Permanent trees and cover	○	●	○	■	○
Need for clearing, weed eradication	○	■	□	○	○
Ground forms and gradients	○	○	□	●	○
Soils (Quality and depth)	○	○	□	□	○
Relative cost of earthwork and foundations	□	□	■	□	○
Site drainage	□	●	○	●	○
Adjacent structures (or lack of)	○	○	□	■	○
Neighbors	○	○	□	■	○
Relationship to circulation patterns(2)	□	●	■	□	○
Relative cost of land and development	●	□	○	○	○
Major detractions (List and describe)	○	○	○	■	○
Exceptional features (List and describe)	○	●	○	■	■
BUILDING SITE					
Topographic "fit" of programmed uses	○	○	□	□	○
Gradient of approaches	○	○	□	□	□
Sight distance at entrance drive	■	○	○	■	○
Orientation to sun, wind and breeze	○	●	○	○	○
Views	○	●	□	○	●
Privacy	○	●	○	○	○
Freedom from noise and glare	●	●	□	□	○
Visual impact of neighboring uses	○	○	□	□	○
Visual impact upon neighboring uses	●	●	○	○	○
Proximity to utility leads	○	○	□	■	●

should be ordered for a given location may be obtained. Several series are available, at different scales, but the one most often useful to the planner is the 7.5-minute series, in which each map (or quadrangle, as it is called) covers an area of about 68 square miles at a scale of 1 to 24,000, or 1 inch to 2000 feet. These survey maps show most of the pertinent topography of the area, including relief, wooded areas, all bodies of water, transportation routes, and major buildings.

With such a map or other materials as a guide, we will visit the most likely places and explore them. Such scouting parties may be launched by automobile or plane or, even better, by helicopter. The last-named method not only makes one immune to barbed-wire fences, cockleburs, and no-trespassing signs but also gives an ideal overall perspective of likely properties. Much can be noted from an automobile, especially the relation of proposed sites to adjacent development patterns and approaches. But sooner or later, to be effective, we must get up off the seat cushions and cruise about the property on foot.

Having narrowed our choice to several alternative tracts of land, we will then analyze them in detail. The favorable and unfavorable aspects of each will be carefully noted and assayed. Sometimes we will discuss the comparative analysis of the various properties informally with the client. Again, we may prepare a well-documented report for presentation, as to a board of directors, an authority, or a city council. Such a report, oral or printed, may list the sites in order of suitability. Often, however, it is better to present only the relative merits of the alternative sites, in clear, concise terms, and leave to the decision makers the business of discussing pros and cons and making the selection.

A "leisure house" perched amid the treetops.

The ideal site   We all know planned developments that seem to be natural outgrowths of their sites: a subdivision artfully fitted to the contours, trees, and other topographical features of a pleasant valley; a school with its playground in a parklike setting placed at the community center and approached along safe and inviting pedestrian paths; a factory with ordered production units, tanks, storage areas, and shaded parking space all planned in admirable relationship to approach roads, trackage, or piers.

We must determine those landscape features, natural and built, best suited to our needs and then search for a site that provides them. The ideal situation is the one that, with least modification, most fully meets the project requirements.

Site analysis

Now that we have selected the location, what is our next concern? At this stage we have, in fact, two concerns, which may be dealt with simultaneously: the formulation of a detailed program and an analysis of the site.

Program development   Many a completed installation functions poorly, or actually precludes the very uses for which it was planned. Perhaps it was doomed because it was forced upon an unsuitable site or because it was not well designed, not clearly expressive of its purpose. Or its operation may be hampered by the frictions it generates. Most often, however, the root of failure lies in the fact that a program was never fully considered; the complete project with all its essential relationships and impacts was never envisioned or thoughtfully conceived.

It is our tacit responsibility as planners to carry each work to successful conclusion. To accomplish this aim, to plan a project intelligently, we must first understand its nature. It is essential that we develop a comprehensive *program*. By research and investigation we must organize a precise and detailed listing of requirements on which we may base our design. To this end we might well consult with all interested persons and draw freely upon their knowledge and views—with the owners, with potential users, with maintenance personnel, with planners of similar undertakings, with our collaborators, with anyone who can contribute constructive thought. We will look to history for applicable principles, for as Santayana has concluded, "Those who cannot remember the past

In defining the program for a project we are at this point less concerned about *what it will look like* and more concerned about *what it will be.*

To dream soaring dreams is not enough. To have value, dreams and ideas must be translated into the hard reality of feasible proposals.

The responsibility of the planner is to guide those involved to the best solution and to help ensure in all ways possible the project's success.

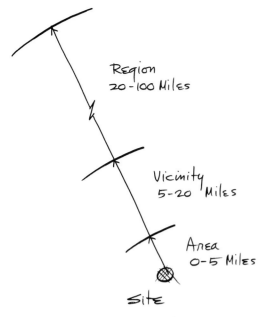

Region
20-100 Miles

Vicinity
5-20 Miles

Area
0-5 Miles

Site

The site and its extensional environs.

are condemned to repeat it.'' We will look ahead to envision possible improvements based on newly developing techniques, new materials, and new concepts of planning. We will try to combine the best of the old with the best of the new. Since the completed work will be the physical manifestation of this theoretical program, the program itself must be designed thoroughly, imaginatively, and completely.

Survey   At the same time that the program requirements are being studied, we must investigate and analyze the selected location: not only the specific area contained within the property boundaries but the total site, which includes the environs to the horizon and beyond.

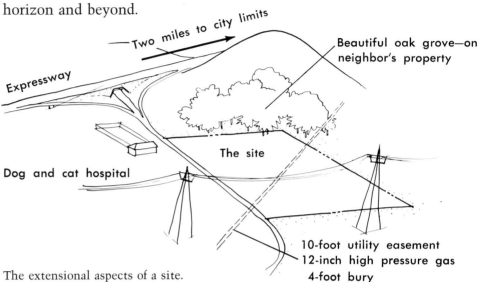

The extensional aspects of a site.

It is usually necessary to obtain a survey for the specific property. Just what do we mean by a *survey* and how is one procured?

The licensed surveyor is professionally trained to produce survey information of a wide range of types and of varying degrees of accuracy. If we ask for a *property survey*, we may very well get no more than a plan showing the boundary lines with their bearings and distances. If we ask for a *topographic survey,* we may expect, in addition to the property *metes and bounds,* contour lines indicating the relative height of various points of the ground surface above a point of known or assumed elevation. It would seem that to be sure of getting any particular information we must request it. The best way of indicating to the surveyor the particular information required is to provide a survey specification outlining all information needed but no more. While the following hypothetical survey specification may be too general for some planning needs and too detailed for others, it will serve as a guide.

Specification for topographic survey

Property: Lawson farm and portion of Beeler Mill property (marked location map attached).

General: Surveyor shall do all work necessary to determine accurately the physical conditions existing on the site. Surveyor shall prepare a map of the given area in ink on plastic drafting film at scale of 1 inch to _____ feet. Four black-line prints of the survey map shall be furnished.

Datum: Elevations shall be referenced to any convenient and permanent bench mark with an assumed elevation of 100.0 feet. The bench-mark location shall be shown on the map.

Information required:
1. Title of survey, property location, scale, north point, certification, and date.

2. Tract boundary lines, courses, and distances. Error of traverse closure shall not exceed 1:10,000. Calculate and show acreage.

3. Building setback lines, easements, and rights-of-way.

4. Names of on-site and abutting parcel owners.

5. Names and locations of existing streets on or abutting the tract. Show right-of-way, type and width of surfacing, and centerline of gutters.

6. Position of buildings and other structures, including foundations, piers, bridges, culverts, wells, and cisterns.

7. Location of all site construction, including walls, fences, roads, drives, curbs, gutters, steps, walks, trails, paved areas, etc., indicating types of materials or surfacing.

8. Locations, types, sizes, and direction of flow of existing storm and sanitary sewers on or contiguous to the tract, giving top and invert elevations of manholes and inlet and invert elevations of other drainage structures; location, ownership, type, and size of water and gas mains, manholes, valve boxes, meter boxes, hydrants, and other appurtenances; locations of utility poles and telephone lines and fire-alarm boxes. For utilities not traversing the site indicate, by key plan if necessary, the nearest off-site leads, giving all pertinent information on types, sizes, inverts, and ownership.

9. Location of water bodies, streams, springs, swamps, or boggy areas and drainage ditches or swales.

10. Outline of wooded areas. Within areas so noted, show all trees that have a trunk diameter of 4 inches or greater at waist height, giving approximate trunk diameters and common names of the trees.

11. Road elevations. Elevations shall be taken at 50-foot intervals along centerlines of roads, flow line of gutter on property side, and tops and bottoms of curbs. The pertinent grades of abutting street and road intersections shall also be shown.

12. Ground surface elevations shall be taken and shown on a 50-foot grid system as well as at the top and bottom of all considerable breaks in grade, whether vertical as in walls or sloping as in banks. Show all floor elevations for buildings. Spot elevations shall also be indicated at the finished grade of building corners, building entrance platforms, and all walk intersections. In addition to the elevations required, the map shall show contours at 2-foot vertical intervals. All elevations shall be to the nearest tenth of a foot. Permissible tolerance shall be 0.1 foot for spot elevations and one-half of the contour interval for contours.

Environmental impact assessment

Most site-planning considerations extend well beyond the property lines and often beyond the horizon. They deal with such regional influences as topography, land use and trafficway patterns, activity centers, and destinations. These set the broad framework within which each project must find its fit. Each specific site too has its physical characteristics and givens to which all lines and forms must relate and upon which they will exert a negative or a positive impact. Such off-site and on-site background factors are investigated to the extent deemed necessary and recorded on a set of reference maps for use throughout the planning process.

Once the topographic survey has been obtained, it is often useful to prepare a series of keyed overlays at the same scale. Each overlay may display information on one particular aspect of the site. The titles of such overlay sheets might be, for example, "Soils," "Slopes" (by range of gradients), "Vegetation," "Traffic," "Hydrology," "Utilities," etc. The sheets might simply indicate in a sharper focus the information recorded on the engineering survey. Or each might include, in addition to topographic data, pertinent notations from many other sources.

Eco-environs plan set (background planning—design data)   On projects of larger scope or greater complexity or on those requiring a lengthy planning process, the list of such reference and overlay sheets may be long. The sheets are often bound as a permanent set, constantly updated, and backed by files or shelves of supporting correspondence and reports. Such clearly displayed and well-organized background material is useful not only in conceptualizing and checking the studies as they progress but also in giving depth and strength to the plan presentations.

Further, since most extensive development proposals and all federally aided construction projects require the submission of an environmental impact assessment in some form, these sets may be considered a graphic checklist of environmental concerns.

When such environmental considerations are defined and explored early, they become not only a useful *test* but also a sound *basis* for the evolving studies and resulting plan solution. The negative impacts of the project can thus be reduced and the attributes significantly increased during the planning process. The many benefits of such a systematic approach cannot be overemphasized.

The feel of the land   Graphic survey information and supporting reference data are essential, but they must be supplemented by at least one and preferably repeated visits to the site. Only by actual site observation can we get the "feel" of the property, sense its relationship to the surrounding areas, and become fully aware of the lay of the land. Only in the field can we sense the dynamic lines that are the site's bounding roads, the insistent lines of pedestrian approach, the arc of the sun, the prevailing breeze, the good views, the ugly views, the sculptural landforms, the springs, the trees, the rock outcrops, the usable areas, those features to be preserved if possible, and those to be eliminated—in short, the character of the site. We must climb from hollow to hill, kick at the sod, dig into the soil. We must look and listen and fully sense those qualities that are peculiar to this specific landscape area.

Whatever we can see along the lines of approach is an extensional aspect of the site. Whatever we can see from the site (or will see in the probable future) is part of the site. Anything that can be heard, smelled, or felt from the property is part of the property. Any topographical feature, natural or built, that has any effect on the property or its use must be considered as a planning factor.

In our present power-happy and schedule-conscious era, this vitally important aspect of developing a *simpatico* feeling for the land and of learning to know and understand the land—learning to analyze the total project site—is too often overlooked. And too often our completed work gives tragic evidence of our haste and neglect.

In Japan, historically, this keen awareness of the site has been of great significance in landscape planning. Each structure has seemed a natural outgrowth of its site, preserving, accentuating, and extending its best features. Studying in Japan, the author was struck by this consistent quality and once asked an architect how he achieved it in his work.

Design excellence is most often achieved by the application of reasoned improvements in the conditions that obtain.

Environmental impact assessment checklist

1. Identify all proposed uses or actions that would have a significant impact upon the environment.
2. In the appropriate frame of the matrix place a square for a negative impact and a circle for one that is seen to be beneficial.
3. Within each square or circle place a number, from 1 to 10, to represent the magnitude and importance (local to regional) of each impact: 10 represents the greatest effect, 1 the least. While the arithmetic sum is not to be considered an absolute indication of the project's worth, it is a telling decision factor.
4. In text to accompany the completed chart discuss any unusual, potent, hazardous, or lasting impact or impacts inherent in the project.
5. In separate sections describe those means by which in the project planning and design the negative consequences have been mitigated and the benefits increased.

Proposed land use, project, or action

Columns:
1. Destruction of habitat
2. Modification of habitat
3. Alteration of surface drainage
4. Change in stream or river flow
5. Effect on freshwater reserves
6. Excavation, filling, or grading
7. Dredging
8. Mining or extraction
9. Forestry
10. Agricultural uses
11. Home and garden
12. Residential communities
13. Recreational uses
14. Institutional uses
15. Commercial uses
16. Industrial uses
17. Urbanization
18. Transportation; transit
19. Transmission
20. Utilities
21. Impoundments
22. Harbors, piers, or marinas
23. Blasting, drilling, and explosions
24. Energy generation
25. Other (list)

Earth
- Landform
- Soils
- Mineral resources
- Geologic features

Water
- Surface conformation
- Visual appeal
- Quality
- Supply

Atmosphere
- Quality (gases; particulates)
- Climate (macro; micro)
- Temperature

Processes
- Flooding
- Erosion
- Sedimentation
- Stability (slides and slumps)
- Air movement
- Solar penetration (sunlight; cast shadow)

Flora
- Ecological systems
- Visual continuity
- Trees
- Shrubs
- Ground covers
- Crops
- Habitat
- Rare plant species

Fauna
- Birds
- Land animals and reptiles
- Fish and shellfish
- Rare or endangered species
- Food chains

Land use
- Wilderness
- Wetlands
- Forestry; grazing or agricultural uses
- Recreational uses
- Residential uses
- Institutional uses
- Commercial uses
- Industrial uses
- Urbanization
- Open-space preserve

Visual and human interest
- Scenic quality
- Landscape character
- Views and vistas
- Parks and recreation
- Conservation areas
- Archaeological or historical interest
- Unique physical features
- Inappropriate uses
- Pollution

Social factors
- Health
- Safety
- Cultural patterns (lifestyle)
- Employment
- Population density and distribution
- Public services
- Cultural amenities

Built environment
- Buildings
- Engineering structures
- Landscape development
- Community integrity
- Urbanization patterns
- Transportation network
- Utility systems
- Waste disposal facilities

Other
- List

"Quite simply," said the architect. "If designing, say, a residence, I go each day to the piece of land on which it is to be constructed. Sometimes for long hours with a mat and tea. Sometimes in the quiet of evening when the shadows are long. Sometimes in the busy part of the day when the streets are abustle and the sun is clear and bright. Sometimes in the snow and even in the rain, for much can be learned of a piece of ground by watching the rainfall play across it and the runoff take its course in rivulets along the natural drainageways.

"I go to the land, and stay, until I have come to know it. I learn to know its bad features—the jangling friction of the passing street, the awkward angles of a windblown oak, an unpleasant sector of the mountain view, the lack of moisture in the soil, the nearness of a neighbor's house to an angle of the property.

"I learn to know its good features—a glorious clump of maple trees, a broad ledge perching high in space above a gushing waterfall that spills into the deep ravine below. I come to know the cool and pleasant summer airs that rise from the falls and move across an open draw of the land. I sense, perhaps, the deliciously pungent fragrance of the deeply layered cedar fronds as the warm sun plays across them in the morning. This patch I know must be left undisturbed.

"I know where the sun will appear in the early morning, when its warmth will be most welcome. I have learned which areas will be struck by its harshly blinding light as it burns hot and penetrating in the late afternoon and from which spots the sunset seems to glow the richest in the dusky peace of evening. I have marveled at the changing dappled light and soft, fresh colors of the bamboo thicket and watched for hours the lemon-crested warblers that have built their nests and feed there.

"I come to sense with great pleasure the subtle relationship of a jutting granite boulder to the jutting granite profile of the mountainside across the way. Little things, one may think, but they tell one, 'Here is the essence of this fragment of land; here is its very spirit. Preserve this spirit, and it will pervade your gardens, your home, and your every day.'

"And so I come to understand this bit of land, its moods, its limitations, its possibilities. Only now can I take my ink and brush in hand and start to draw my plans. But in my mind the structure by now is fully planned, complete in every detail. It has taken its form and character from the site and the passing street and the fragment of rock and the wafting breeze and the arching sun and the sound of the falls and the distant view.

"Knowing the owner and his family and the things they like, I have found for them here a living environment that brings them into the best relationship with the landscape that surrounds them. This structure, this house that I have planned, is no more than an arrangement of spaces, open and closed, accommodating and expressing in stone, timber, and rice paper a delightful, fulfilling way of life. How else can one plan the best home for this site?"

There can be no other way! This, in Japan as elsewhere, is in simplest terms the planning process—for the home, the community, the city, the highway, or the national park.

In America we planners approach our problems in a less contemplative frame of mind. We are "less sensitive" (of which fact we are proud) and "more practical" (a pathetic misnomer). We are rushed by the pressures of time, economics, and public temperament. The planning process is accelerated, sometimes to the point of frenzy. But the principle remains the same: to realize a project

Therefore, let us build houses that restore to man the life-giving, life-enhancing elements of nature. This means an architecture that begins with the nature of the site. Which means taking the first great step toward assuring a worthy architecture, for in the rightness of a house on the land we sense a fitness we call beauty.

Frank Lloyd Wright

A study in fitting relationships.

on a site effectively, we must fully understand the program, and we must be fully aware of the physical properties of the site and of the total environs. Our planning then becomes the science and art of arranging the most fitting relationships.

Site analysis The process of site analysis is usually initiated with the investigation of the region embracing the project site. The immediate vicinity and its interrelationships with the property to be developed is given more thorough study. Finally, the project site itself is analyzed intensively to gain the full understanding so essential to landscape planning.

The following procedure is suggested as a guide to systematic site analysis.

1. *Regional influences.* The site analysis process most often begins with the location of the project site on a regional map and a cursory investigation of regional, vicinity, and area planning factors.

From such documents as U.S. Geological Survey maps, road maps, and various planning reports much useful insight can be gained as to the surrounding topographic features, land uses, roadway and transportation network, recreational opportunities, and employment, commercial, and cultural centers.

2. *The Project site.* Before studies can be initiated, the planner must have gained a full understanding of the specific site's nature, constraints, and possibilities. This is obtained from survey information, aerial photography, site visitation, and the detailed analysis of existing and proposed conditions as outlined in a variety of available publications and maps.

3. *Topographic survey.* This base map is customarily prepared by a registered surveyor at an engineering scale (as 1 inch = 20 feet, 50 feet, 100 feet, 500 feet, 1000 feet, etc.) predetermined as that being best for the base mapping and planning studies. A survey *specification* describing the information to be provided and the form of presentation is prepared by the planner.

4. *Base map.* This plan, usually prepared at the same scale as the topographic survey, is used as the background or base of many

overlays to follow. Drawn on plastic or drafting paper to give clear reproduction, it contains only information that is to be carried forward to all sheets. This may include:

Trim lines, with a widened border for possible binding

Title block, with project name and location, owner's and planner's identification, north point, scale, and date line

Property lines by metes and bounds or coordinates

Contiguous and on-site roads, rights-of-way, and easements to remain

On each succeeding sheet will be added the information particular to the subject covered.

5. *Overlays.* A reproducible print of the base map is used for each overlay. Each overlay will contain all information relating to one type of background information pertinent to the planning study. While the number and nature of the overlay sheets will depend upon the complexity of the planning project, the following are usually included:

Slopes and drainage: Existing contours (dashed) and drainageways, natural and constructed, together with inlet and invert elevations, gradients, and materials.

Soils: Soil types by classification and depths, with location and log of known core boring or test pits.

Water resources: The location of water bodies and waterways, on-site test or producing wells, off-site well fields, nearest potable water sources, data on geological strata, aquifers, water quantity, quality, and saltwater intrusion.

Vegetation: Plant communities and key specimens.

Structures: Existing buildings, bridges, culverts, walls, dams, and major embankments.

Circulation: Existing routes of vehicular and pedestrian movement, bridle paths, and established game trails, with notation as to off-site connections and destinations.

Utilities: Existing transmission lines, poles, towers, pipes, or conduits, communication or signal systems, gas mains, water mains, and sanitary sewers with related data.

Climate: An analysis of such general information as temperatures, precipitation, prevailing winds and breeze, storm tracks, tide and flood data, and solar diagrams, together with such site-specific information as exposed and sheltered areas, known frost pockets, etc.

Visual analysis: Scenic features and views with notes as to their nature and best points or sectors of observation; unsightly features that are in need of removal, modification, or screening.

Impact assessment: Constraints such as areas of ecological sensitivity, difficult terrain, hazards, etc.; planning possibilities inherent in the specific site and its environs.

Preservation and conservation: Notation as to areas and features to be preserved in their entirety or conserved with limited and compatible uses. The balance of the site will thus be delineated for appropriate development as required.

6. Site analysis map. One of the most effective means of developing a keen perception of the property and its nature is the preparation of a *site analysis map.* A print of the topographic survey furnished by the surveyor is taken into the field, and from actual site observation additional notes are jotted down upon it in the planner's own symbols. These amplify the survey notations and describe all conditions on or related to the site that are pertinent in its planning. Such supplementary information might describe or note:

a. Outstanding natural features such as springs, ponds, streams, rock outcrops, specimen trees, contributing shrub masses, and established ground covers, all to be preserved insofar as possible

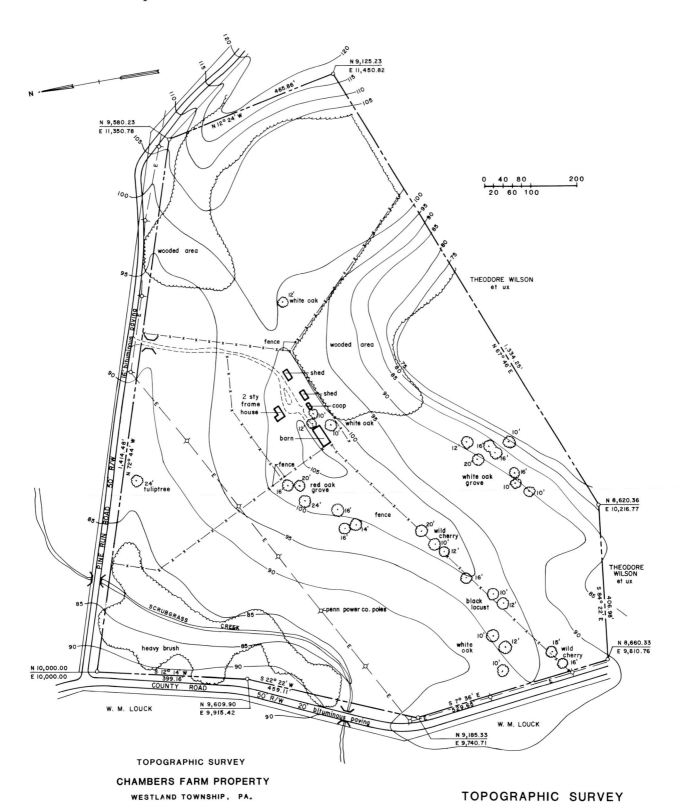

TOPOGRAPHIC SURVEY

CHAMBERS FARM PROPERTY

WESTLAND TOWNSHIP, PA.

TOPOGRAPHIC SURVEY

b. Negative site features or hazards such as obsolete structures or deleterious materials to be removed, dead or diseased vegetation, noxious weed infestation, lack of topsoil, or evidence of landslides, subsidence, or flooding

c. Directions and relative volumes of vehicular traffic flow on approach roads; points of connection to pedestrian routes, bikeways, and riding trails

d. Logical points of site ingress or egress

e. Potential building locations, use areas, or routes of movement

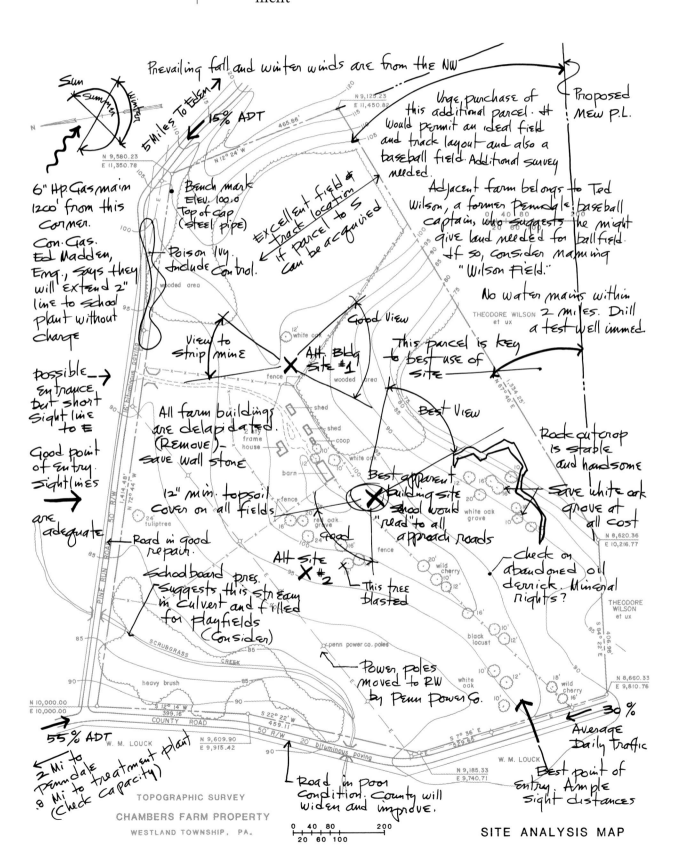

TOPOGRAPHIC SURVEY

CHAMBERS FARM PROPERTY

WESTLAND TOWNSHIP, PA.

SITE ANALYSIS MAP

f. Commanding observation points, overlook areas, and preferred viewing sectors

g. Best views, to be featured, and objectionable views, to be screened, together with a brief note describing each

h. Direction of prevailing winter winds and summer breezes

i. Exposed, windswept areas and those protected by nearby topographical forms or trees

j. Off-site attractions and nuisances

k. An ecological and microclimatic analysis of the property and its environs

l. Other factors of special significance in the project planning

In addition to such information observed in the field, further data gleaned from research may be noted on the site analysis map or included separately in the survey file. Such information might include:

a. Abutting landownerships

b. Names of utility companies whose lines are shown, company addresses, phone numbers, engineers

c. Routes and data on projected utility lines

d. Energy source, availability, and lines of distribution

e. Approach patterns of existing roads, drives, and walks

f. Traffic counts

g. Projected roadway network

h. Easements, rights-of-way

i. Zoning restrictions, building lines

j. Mineral rights, depth of coal, mined-out areas

k. Water quality and supply

l. Core-boring logs and data

7. *Plan set and reference file.* As the surveys, base sheets, overlays, and site analysis map are developed, they are assembled as a bound and coordinated set, together with a supporting file of referenced plans, reports, and correspondence. All are kept complete and updated throughout the planning process.

The material in the reference file will vary with each project but will often include information on:

a. Regional and area master plans

b. Zoning and subdivision regulations

c. Highway capacities and improvements

d. Water management

e. Airfields and flight zones

f. Transmission lines and stations

g. Utility systems

h. Fire, police, and ambulance services

i. Flood and storm records

There is little mystery to the art and science of site planning. Those whose professional work it is have developed it into a systematic process. Its purpose is to best arrange the elements of any planned development in relation to the natural and constructed features of a site and its environs. Whether for a home garden, university campus, or military installation, the approach is essentially the same.

The site-planning procedure normally involves the following ten steps, several of which may take place concurrently:

1. Definition of intent (scope, goal, and objectives)
2. Procurement of topographical survey
3. Program development
4. Data gathering and analysis
5. Site reconnaissance
6. Organization of reference plan set and file
7. Preparation of exploratory studies
8. Comparative analysis and revision of studies, leading to an approved conceptual plan
9. Development of preliminary development plans and estimate of costs
10. Preparation of construction plans, specifications, and bidding documents

There is an area of the conceptual and forming process that is common to the four major physical planning disciplines and often to others as well. This is the formulation of the basic *plan concept* by which in sketch or diagram the use areas and plan forms are conceived in harmony with the natural and constructed forms, forces, and features of the total project site. Usually the plan concept is best arrived at through a collaborative effort in which all participants contribute freely of their experience and ideas.

Thus we seek two values in every landscape: one, the expression of the native quality of the landscape, the other, the development of maximum human livability. . . .

Site planning must be thought of as the organization of the total land area and air space of the site for best use by the people who will occupy it. This means an integrated concept in which buildings, engineering construction, open space and natural materials are planned together at one time. . . .

Garrett Eckbo

j. Air and water pollution
k. Demographic data and user profiles
l. Schools
m. Recreation facilities
n. Cultural amenities
o. Economic statistics and trends
p. Tax rates and assessments
q. Governance

The conceptual plan

A seed of use—a cell of function—wisely applied to a receptive site will be allowed to develop organically, in harmonious adaptation to the natural and the planned environment.

We have by now developed a comprehensive program defining the proposed nature of our project. We have become fully aware of all features of the total environs. Up to this point, the planning effort has been one of research and analysis. It has been painstaking and perhaps tedious, but this phase is of vital importance because it is the only means by which we can achieve full command of the data on which our design will be based. From this point on, the planning process becomes one of integration of proposed uses, structures, and site.

Plan concepts If structure and landscape development are contemplated, it is impossible to conceive one without the other, for it is the relationship of structure to site and site to structure that gives meaning to each and to both.

This point perhaps raises the question of who on the planning team—architect, landscape architect, engineer, or others—is to do

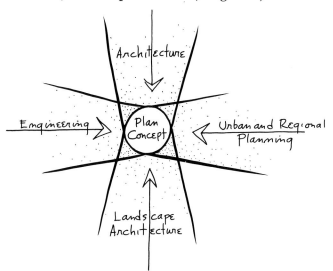

the "conceiving." Strangely, this problem, which might seemingly lead to warm debate, seldom arises, for an effective collaboration brings together experts in various fields of knowledge who, in a free interchange of ideas, develop a climate of perceptive awareness and know-how. In such a climate, plan concepts usually evolve more or less spontaneously. Since the collaboration is arranged and administered by one of the principals (who presumably holds the commission), it is usually this team leader who coordinates the planning in all its aspects and gives it expressive unity. It is the work of the collaborators to advance their assigned planning tasks and to aid in the articulation of the main design idea in all ways possible.

The planning-design process

Architecture, landscape architecture, engineering

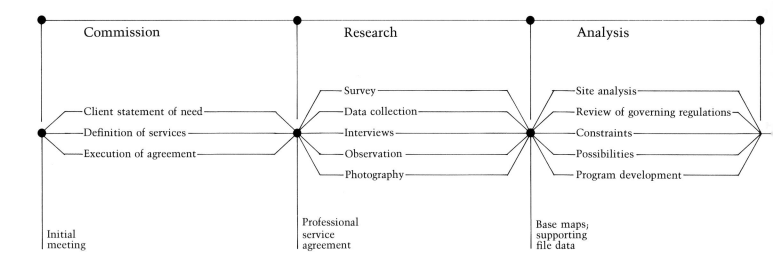

Commission	Research	Analysis
Client statement of need	Survey	Site analysis
Definition of services	Data collection	Review of governing regulations
Execution of agreement	Interviews	Constraints
	Observation	Possibilities
	Photography	Program development
Initial meeting	Professional service agreement	Base maps; supporting file data

Commission

Most planning-design interviews and commission awards are based upon experience and reputation.

Experience is gained by education and training, acceptance of increasingly demanding assignments, engaging consultants as required, and doing all necessary research.

Reputation is gained by full, prompt, and excellent performance. The successful professional has a widening coterie of pleased and vocal clients.

Effective professional service agreements embody a clear, simple statement of intent—who does what, how, when, and for how much compensation.

Remuneration for services is usually arranged in one of the following forms:
Lump sum, with phased payments
Time, plus reimbursement for travel, materials and related expenses
A percentage fee based on construction costs

Consultation is normally provided on a per diem plus reimbursement basis.

Form of agreement.
A verbal agreement is often enough.
A letter of confirmation is better.
A standard professional agreement is better yet.
With large, complex, or long-term projects, as with many public agencies, a detailed legal instrument of agreement is prescribed.

Research
(an exercise in gaining awareness)

The basic tool in land planning is a topographic survey, meeting a specification to provide all, and only, the information needed.

Data collection begins with a listing of all materials required together with a notation of the most likely source.

Maps, reports, and other useful data are available in public agencies and planning offices, often without charge.

Interviews with potential users, agency staff members, and public officials not only yield helpful information but also build in an understanding of the project and a sense of contribution.

Research includes the study of past and present examples and a knowledge of innovative trends. It is a continuing process of travel, observation, reading, and experimentation.

Visits to the site are essential. A photographic record keyed to a location map is always beneficial.

Surveys, base maps, and all related information are to be organized into a convenient project reference file kept complete and updated.

Analysis

Supplementary planning information, observations, and notes can be recorded on prints of the topographical survey and overlays.

Constraints such as land use and density limitations, easements, areas of ecological sensitivity, hazards, and difficult terrain or subsurface conditions are noted.

Favorable site aspects and features are also described.

Governmental regulations, standards, and requirements are reviewed and underlined.

Finally, in the analysis phase, a comprehensive development program is formulated. This will respond to the stated intent as modified in the light of the survey information and data obtained. It will include:

A statement of goals and objectives*
A summary of preliminary findings
A description of the project components and their interrelationship
Proposals as to conceptual alternatives
An outline of performance standards

*A *goal* is a generalized statement of the result to be achieved.
An *objective* is a means of attaining the desired result.

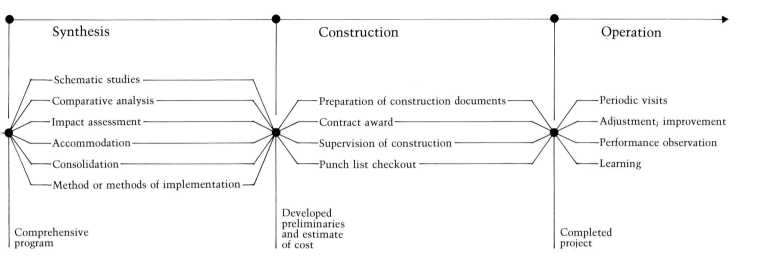

Synthesis	Construction	Operation

Synthesis
- Schematic studies
- Comparative analysis
- Impact assessment
- Accommodation
- Consolidation
- Method or methods of implementation

Comprehensive program

Construction
- Preparation of construction documents
- Contract award
- Supervision of construction
- Punch list checkout

Developed preliminaries and estimate of cost

Operation
- Periodic visits
- Adjustment; improvement
- Performance observation
- Learning

Completed project

Synthesis

Schematic studies are prepared to explore the plan alternatives. These are kept simple and diagrammatic to explain as directly as possible the conceptual idea as it relates to the givens of the site.

As the schematics evolve, they are subjected to a comparative analysis of their positive and negative values and net yields.

Unsuitable schemes are rejected or modified, promising concepts are improved, and other schematic approaches suggested by the reviews are added to the array of contenders.

Insofar as feasible, all constructive ideas and recommendations are accommodated, negative environmental impacts ameliorated, and benefits increased.

When the most likely plan approaches have been delineated and compared, the best is selected for conversion into a *developed preliminary plan* and an *estimate of cost*.

Construction

Upon approval of the developed preliminary plan and estimate detailed construction documents are prepared. These comprise plans, details, specifications, and bidding forms to be issued as a package. A final estimate of cost and a cash-flow analysis are also in order.

In form, bids are invited on the basis of either a *cost-plus proposal* (when top quality is a prerequisite and when conditions are uncertain or changes anticipated) or the *lowest responsible bid* (when economy and budget limitations are the decisive factors).

Professional services normally include supervision, "observation," or consultation during the bidding, contract award, and construction process.

Supervision is to be firm, fair, and expeditious. Field adjustments are to be welcomed if the project is thereby improved and if all parties have a clear understanding of the nature of the change and its cost implications.

During construction it is well to have the ongoing maintenance superintendent present to gain an understanding of the project installation and conditions.

In advance of construction completion a *punch list* is provided by the supervisor as the basis for final inspection and acceptance.

Operation

Prior to project completion the thoughtful planner will provide the owner with a sheet of instructions or, on larger projects, a concise manual to govern continuing operation and maintenance.

Many professional service agreements provide for continuing consultation. In any event, the conscientious planner will return for periodic visits to observe, learn, and advise as to suggested improvements.

There is no better lead to future commissions than a demonstration of continued interest in the project's success and the client's satisfaction.

Excel, and exceed expectations.

The site-structure diagram   When planning a project or a structure in relation to a land area, we first consider all the various uses to be fitted together and accommodated.   For a high school, for instance, we would determine the approximate architectural plan areas and their shapes—the general plan areas required for service, parking, outdoor classrooms, gardens, game courts, football fields, track, bleachers, and perhaps future school expansion.   Over a print of the topographic survey (or site analysis map) we would then indicate, in freehand line, use areas of logical size and shape in studied relation to each other and to the natural and built landscape features.   Having thus roughed in the site use areas, we may at last

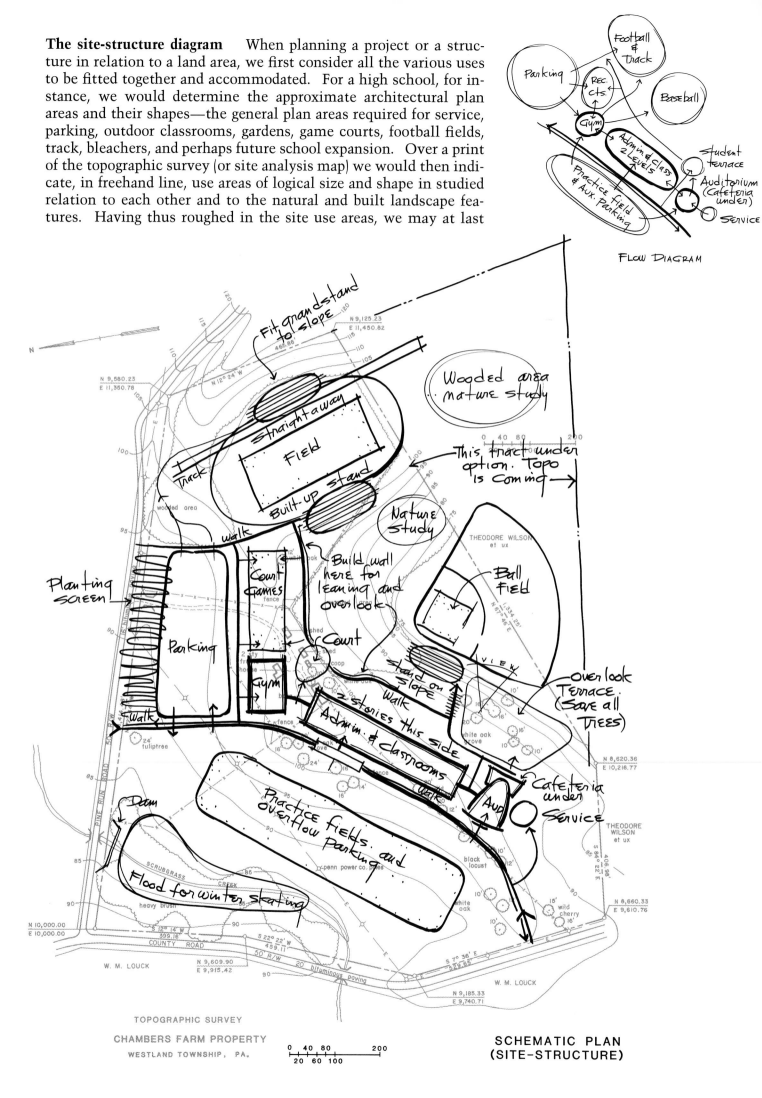

FLOW DIAGRAM

SCHEMATIC PLAN
(SITE-STRUCTURE)

block in the architectural elements of the project. The result is the *site-structure diagram.*

The balance of the planning process is a matter of comparative analysis and refinement of detail—a process of creative synthesis.

A good plan, reduced to essentials, is no more than a record of logical thought. A dull plan is a record of ineffectual thinking or of very little thinking at all. A brilliant plan gives evidence of response to all site factors, a clear perception of needs and relationships, and a sensitive expression of all components working well together.

The creative aspect of planning Planners may create in the mate-

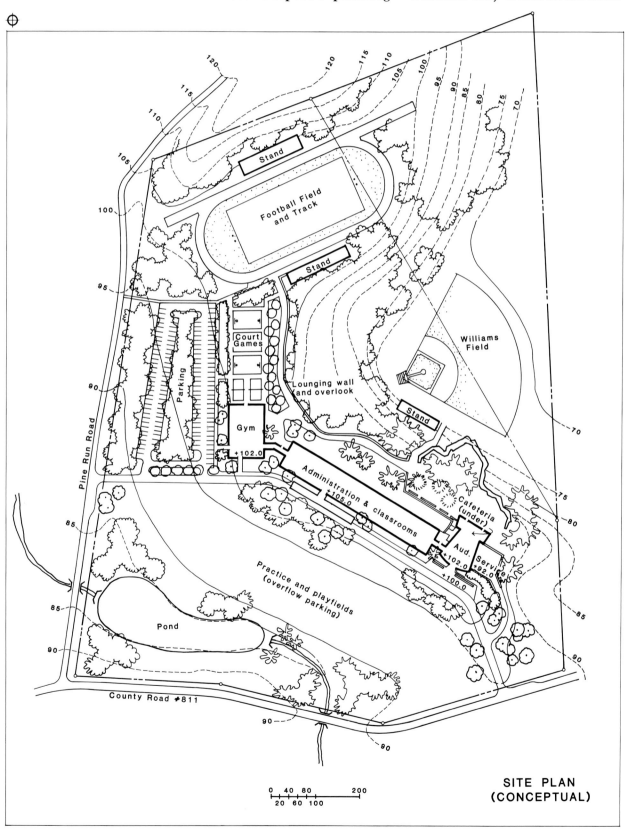

SITE PLAN
(CONCEPTUAL)

Footbridge and steps. Deere & Co. Administrative Center, Moline, Illinois.

Meaningful design is far from an exercise in graphic exposition. It is an empathetic process—a creative act of the intellect.

Design begins with a conceptual determination of the desired nature of space or object. This "what shall it be" aspect may be focalized by a flash of intuitive genius, by a methodical analysis of possibilities, or by logical extension and improvement upon past examples.

The visual aspects of superior design are marked by a clear and direct expression of idea, time, place, materials, and technology, coupled with a fine instinct for three-dimensional form.

It is not the thing done or made which is beautiful, but the doing. If we appreciate the thing, it is because we relive the heady freedom of making it. Beauty is the byproduct of interest and pleasure in the choice of action.

Jacob Bronowski

rials, forms, and symbols of their disciplines an object, space, or construction that they believe will engender in the users a certain predictable experience. In effect, users will *recreate* the planned elements through their perception of them and will thus be led to the desired experience. For when we perceive, we actually retrace through our senses the form-giving process. An understanding of this phenomenon leads us to a clearer concept of the creative function of design.

The planning attitude In his admirable treatise *On the Laws of Japanese Painting*, Henry P. Bowie has written, "One of the most important principles in the art of Japanese painting—indeed, a fundamental and entirely distinctive characteristic—is that of living movement, *sei do* . . . it being, so to say, the transfusion into the work of the felt nature of the thing to be painted by the artist. Whatever the subject to be translated—whether river or tree, rock or mountain, bird or flower, fish or animal—the artist at the moment of painting it must feel its very nature, which, by the magic of art, he transfers into his work to remain forever, affecting all who see it with the same sensations he experienced when executing it." And again, "Indeed, nothing is more constantly urged upon his attention than this great underlying principle, that it is impossible to express in art what one does not feel."

And so it is with planning. We can only create that for which we have first developed empathy and understanding. A shopping mall? As designers, we must *feel* the quickening tempo, the pull and attraction, the bustle, the excitement of the place. We must sense the chic boutique displays, the mouth-watering sights and smells of the bakery shop; we must see in our mind the jam-packed counters of the hardware store and the drugstore with its pyramids of mouthwash, perfume, nail polish, hot-water bottles, and jelly beans. We must see in the market the heaps of grapefruit, oranges, rhubarb, brussels sprouts, bananas; whiff the heady fragrance of the floral stalls; picture the shelf on shelf of bargain books, the bolts of cotton prints, the sloping trays of peppermints and chocolate creams. We must feel the brightness of the sunshine on the sidewalks and the coolness and protection of the shaded doorways and arcades. We must feel crowds and traffic and benches and trees and perhaps the sparkle and splash of a fountain or two. And then we can start planning.

A children's zoo? If we would design one, we must first feel like one of the flocking children, the gawking, clapping, squealing kids; we must appreciate the delight, the laughter, the chatter, the confusion, and the rollicking thrill of the place. We must feel the diminutive, squeaky "cuteness" of the mouse town, the bulk and immensity and cavelike hollowness of the spouting whale with its dimly illumined interior. We must know the preening strut of the elegantly wandering peacocks, the quack, quack, quacking of the waddling ducks, the soft furry whiteness of the lop-eared rabbits, and the clop, clop, clopping and creaking harness and the awed delight of the pony ride. We must, in our minds, be at the children's zoo, and we must see it, hear it, feel it, and love it as a child would love it as we make our plans.

Are we to design a parkway, hotel plaza, terminal, or bathing beach? If we would create them, we must first have a feeling for their nature. This self-induced sensitivity we might call the *planning attitude*. Before we mature as planners, it will be intuitive.

A Disney World parade.

A building is a thing in itself. It has a right to be there, as it is, and together with nature. I see it not as an isolated composition, but a composition related to nature, a composition of contrasts.

Marcel Breuer

Architecture subtly and eloquently inserts itself into the site, absorbing its power to move us and in return offering to it the symphonic elements of human geometry.

Le Corbusier

Site-structure expression

If to design a project or a structure in harmony with its total site is a valid objective, it follows that the *design expression* would vary from site to site in accordance with the variation in landscape character.

To illustrate, let us consider a summer weekend vacation lodge. If built on a sheltered, rock-rimmed inland lake in northern Maine, its abstract design form would vary greatly from the form it would have if located anywhere along the wind-whipped coast of Monterey, California, in the smoky Ozark Mountains, on Florida's shell-strewn Captiva Island, or along the lazily winding Mississinewa River in central Indiana. Forgetting for the moment the implications of a specific property, we can see that each of the varying locations suggests its own intrinsic design response.

It might therefore be helpful procedure to classify a site according to type and determine the design characteristics suggested. Let us consider four typical building sites and the design features that they elicit.

A city lot

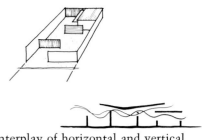

Area is at a premium. The plan will be compact, of necessity. To utilize the area fully, a maximum of the property may be included, by plan ingenuity, in the visual scheme.

Space is limited. Plan forms will probably be contrived to expand the apparent space by the multiple use of areas and the interplay of volumes.

Interplay of horizontal and vertical spaces.

The city environs impose a sense of confinement and oppression. Perhaps here embattled city dwellers will wish to entrench, dig their cave, or build their fort and feel secure. But more likely they will seek relief and release from pressure. If so, in their dwellings and gardens the hard, the rigid, the confining forms will give way to the light, the nebulous, the transparent, and the free.

Rigid property lines may be softened to relieve the sense of tight enclosure.

Areas and spaces are minute in scale. Scale, both induced and inductive, is an important design consideration. An object well suited to the open field could be overwhelming in the cityscape. A giant tree, for example, might dwarf an urban complex, while a dwarf tree could give it increased and more desirable visual dimension.

Consider carefully the scale of objects introduced.

City streets and pedestrian walks are major lines of approach, observation, and access. They are elements most strongly relating the dwelling to the community. The driveway throat and front entrance will normally be designed to convey a receptive cove quality. The relationship of the structure to the insistent lines of the city street becomes an important consideration.

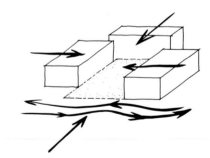

The feel of the city lot.

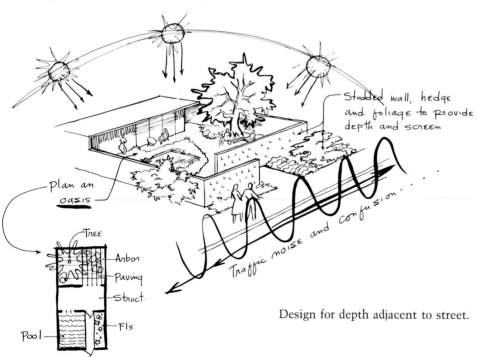

Design for depth adjacent to street.

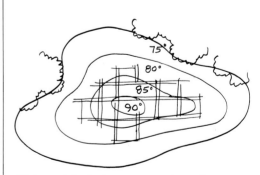

Cities, with their concentration of masonry and paving, are hotter in summer and colder in winter than the suburbs and countryside. The "desert" climate can be ameliorated by the provision of open-space preserves, parks, street planting, and private gardens.

The city street is a source of noise, fumes, and danger. Plan elements adjacent to the street may well be contrived to provide noise abatement, "depth," privacy, and security. Perforated screens or studded barriers have a useful application.

The city is, climatologically speaking, a desert of pavement and masonry. A city is often many degrees hotter in the summertime than the surrounding countryside. Design an oasis; make

In the city, a rock, a tree, or a single potted plant may represent all of nature.

maximum use of breeze, shade, shadow patterns, sunscreens, and the refreshing qualities of water in fountain, pool, or jet spray. The climate may be further modified by air movement fanned or directed through pierced or baffled screens or across moist fabric, gravel, or other evaporative surfaces. In cool weather, heat may be introduced in radiant elements or by warm water circulated in fountains or pools.

Natural features—trees, interesting ground forms, rocks, and water—are scarce and therefore have increased value and meaning. They are no longer part of the natural scene but are now isolated objects to be treated in a more stylized way. Utilize natural features to the full, design them into the scheme, orient to them. Earth, plants, and water in the city may well be treated as sculptural or architectural elements. Since in the city all materials appear to be introduced, exotic plants and materials are appropriate.

City materials and forms are, at their best, sophisticated. Because sizes and quantities are limited, richness of material and refinement of detail gain in importance. Sills of polished marble, handles of brass, or cases of hand-rubbed teak, as examples, would be particularly fitting.

Surrounded by neighbors, one becomes an integral part of the community, a unit in a group of related units, an important part of the whole. Neighborhood character cannnot be blithely violated without social repercussions. We are tacitly obliged to conform. To achieve a measure of conformity while designing a residential complex of individuality and distinction is a difficult art, mastered long ago by the Japanese. Their modular homes of stone, wood, tile, and woven mats are arranged tightly along their city streets with an artistry that produces patterns of infinite variety yet great harmony. Through ingenious plan arrangement even the smallest structures are made to feel spacious.

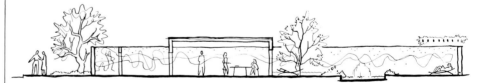

Living space in the city may extend from property line to property line.

From the street to the farthest limits of the city lot, there is little room for the necessary transitions from the compelling lines of traffic to areas for quiet family living. Designed transitions are a mark of the successful city house. The Japanese admire a quality called *wabi* that has application here. This quality may be exemplified by a black walnut with its rough, splotched, gray-green outer husk. With husk removed, the exposed walnut shell is seen to be a handsome rich brown case of hard ridges in structural pattern. Cracked open, the shell reveals the walnut kernels encased in a membrane of delicate veining and fitted to the smooth interior chambers. Finally, the ivory-white kernel itself is a marvel of beautiful sculptural form. We may see in this example an inward progression from the unostentatious to the highly refined.

A city property has a fishbowl quality resulting from the proximity of neighbors. Privacy is a basic design requirement in a city dwelling. A logical orientation of such structures is inward, to private gardens, patios, or courts.

Rural site

Land area is plentiful. The plan is more open, free, and "exploded." Although the specific site may be circumscribed by property boundaries, the visual limits may include extensive sweeps of the landscape. The scope of planning considerations is increased, since fence lines, orchards, paddocks, even a mountaintop miles away may become design factors and elements. Our scheme must be planned to the horizon.

Freedom, with open view of fields, woods, and sky, is the essential landscape quality. We may logically orient our plan outward to embrace the total site's best features and to command the best views.

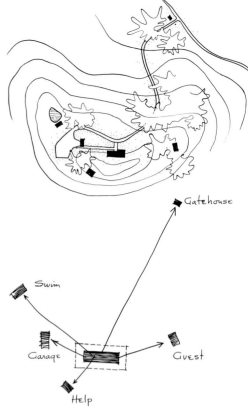

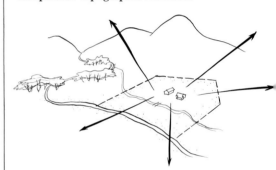

Ample area permits an exploded plan, each element being related to the most compatible topographic features.

Major landscape features are established; build to, around, and among them.

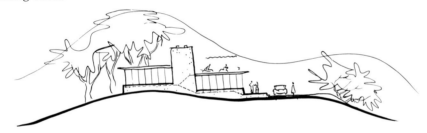

Structural forms conceived in sympathy with ground forms borrow power from and return power to the landscape.

Rural property has an expansive feel. Streams, groves, distant hills, all features of the landscape that can be seen or sensed, are a part of the extensional site.

The choice of a rural site would indicate a desire to be at one with nature. Make nature appreciation a design aim and theme. Insofar as possible, the natural environment will be disturbed or modified only to improve it.

The major landscape features are established. Build to them, feature the best, screen out and de-emphasize those that are less desirable, and contrive structural forms in best relation to the natural forms. Site use areas, sympathetically fitted to topographical features, may well dictate the architectural arrangement.

The landscape is dominant (in character and mood). Presumably the site was selected because of its qualities. If the existing landscape character is desirable, it may be preserved and accentuated by the site-structure diagram. If alterations are required, we may modify or completely change the site aspect, but only in such a way as to take fullest possible advantage of the existing features.

Earth and ground forms are strong visual elements. A structure conceived in studied relation to ground forms gains in architectural strength and in harmony with the site.

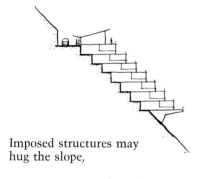

On a sloping site the level plane is achieved by terracing, retaining walls, the supported platform, or the cantilever.

Imposed structures may hug the slope,

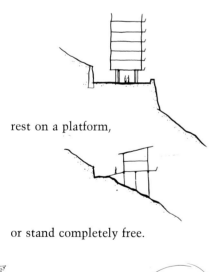

rest on a platform,

or stand completely free.

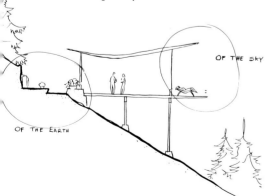

OF THE SKY

OF THE EARTH

A structure imposed on a sloping site belongs to the sky as well as to the earth.

The pleasant landscape is one of agreeable transitions. In the planning of transitions between structure and site, intermediate areas relating structure to the land are of key importance.

Structures become elements imposed on the landscape. Either structure or site must dominate. Either the site is considered basically a setting for a dominant structure, or the structure is conceived as subordinate to the landscape and designed to complement the natural contours and forms.

The rural landscape is a landscape of subtleties—of foliage shadings, sky tints, and cloud shadows. Our planning must recognize these qualities and treat them sympathetically, or they will be wasted.

In a rural site, one is more exposed to the elements and the weather—rain, storms, sun, wind, snow, frost, winter cold, and summer heat. The site-structure diagram and structural forms should reflect a thorough understanding of and adaptation to the climate.

A rural site implies increased land area and greater maneuverability. The automobile and pedestrian approaches, important elements in our design, may often be aligned within the property boundaries to reveal the best site and architectural features.

The indigenous materials of a rural site—ledge rock, fieldstone, slate, gravels, and timbers—contribute much to its landscape character. The use of such natural materials in buildings, fences, bridges, and walls helps relate structures to their surroundings.

The essential quality of the landscape is the natural and the unrefined. Our structural materials may well reflect this naturalness and forgo high refinement.

Steeply sloping site (unobstructed inclined plane)

Contours are major plan factors. Contour planning (the alignment of plan elements parallel with the contours) is generally indicated.

The areas of relatively equal elevation are narrow bands lying perpendicular to the axis of the slope. Narrow plan forms such as bars or ribbons are suggested.

Sizable level areas are nonexistent. Where required, they must be carved out of or projected from the slope. If they are shaped of earth, the earth must be retained by a wall or by a slope of increased inclination.

The essence of slope is rise and fall. A terraced scheme is suggested. Levels may separate functions, as in split-level or multideck structures.

The slope is a ramp. Ramps and steps are logical plan elements.

The slope grade is perhaps too steep for wheeled traffic. Access is easiest along contours. This fact dictates a normal approach from the sides.

The pull of gravity is down the slope. Our design forms not only must have stability, they must *express* stability to be pleasing. An exception, of course, would be those structures in which a feeling of daring or conditioned exhilaration is desired.

The sloping site has a dynamic landscape quality. The site lends itself to dynamic plan forms.

The dramatic quality of a slope is its apparent change in grade. Natural grade changes may be accentuated and dramatized through the use of terraces, overlook decks, and flying balconies.

A slope inherently emphasizes the meeting of earth and air. A level element imposed on a sloping plane often makes contact with the earth or rock at the inner side and is held free to the air at its outer extremity. Where the element makes contact with the earth, the jointure is to be clearly expressed. Where the leading edge flies free, this airy union of structure and sky should also be given design expression.

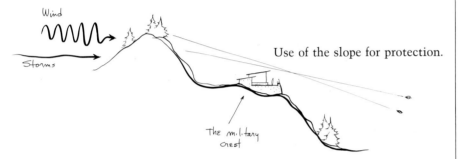

Use of the slope for protection.

The top of the slope is most exposed to the elements. The planner may exploit or create a land profile similar to the *military crest* of the artillery manual—an adaption or modification of the slope to preserve or enhance the view while affording increased protection.

A sloping site affords interest in views. Site development to create richness of landscape detail may be minimized, for when a sloping site commands a fine view, little else is required.

The slope is oriented outward. Plan orientation is normally outward and down. Since the view side is exposed, the plan relation to sun, wind, and storms is of increased concern.

A sloping site has drainage problems. Groundwater and surface runoff from above must be intercepted and diverted or allowed to pass freely under the structure.

A slope brings out many of the most desirable qualities of water. The play of water in falls, cascades, spouts, trickling rivulets, and films is an obvious plan opportunity.

Level site

A level site offers a minimum of plan restrictions. Of all site types, the level site best lends itself to the cell-bud, crystalline, or geometric plan pattern.

A level site has relatively minor landscape interest. Plan interest depends upon the relationship of space to space, object to space, and object to object.

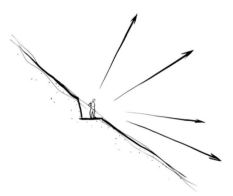

On the sloping plane, orientation is outward.

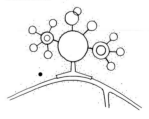

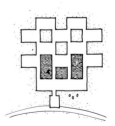

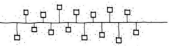

The level site adapts itself to the cell-bud, crystalline, or geometric plan.

The strong horizontality of the site evoked these sympathetic forms.

A flat site is essentially a broad-base plane. All elements set upon this plane are of strong visual importance, as is their relation one to the other. Each vertical plane established must be considered not only in terms of its own form but also as a background against which other objects may be seen or across which shadow patterns may be cast.

A flat site has no focal point. The most visually insistent element placed on this site will dominate the scene.

Lines of approach are not dictated by the topography. The possibility of approach from any side makes all elevations important. Lines of exterior and interior circulation are critical design elements since they control the visual unfolding of the plan.

The dome of the sky is a dominant landscape element of infinite change and beauty. We may well feature the sky through the use of reflecting basins, pools, courts, patios, and recessed openings.

The sun is a powerful design factor. We may use it as a sweeping beam or flood and design in terms of light and shade. We may explore the myriad qualities of light and utilize the most effective in relation to our forms, colors, textures, and materials. We may dramatize cast shadow—solid as from a wall, moving as from water, sculptural as from objects, dappled as from foliage, or as a dark background and foil for luminous objects displayed against it.

A level site has a neutral landscape quality. Site character is created by the elements introduced. Bold form, strong color, and often exotic materials may be used here without apparent violation of the native landscape.

Four studies of an exhibition group illustrating the free-plan arrangements made possible by a level site.

The site offers little privacy. The creation of privacy is a function of the plan orientation. Privacy may be attained by the focus of spaces toward screening elements, inward to enclosed courts, or outward to infinity from viewing points on the periphery.

Third dimension is lacking. Third dimension in the ground plane may be achieved through the creation of earth or architectural platforms or pits. Slight rises, drops, and steps assume exaggerated significance on the level site.

The flat site offers no obstruction to lateral planning. An expanded scheme with connective passageways or elements is a logical plan expression.

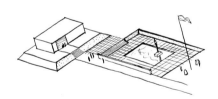

On the level site the pit, the mound, and the vertical assume telling significance.

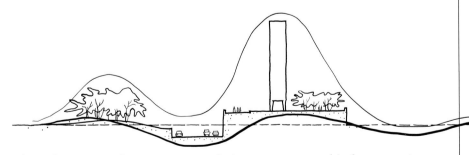

Where flatness equals monotony, maximize every topographical opportunity.

A flat site tends toward monotony. Since interest is in structure rather than in the natural landscape, the structure should be enhanced and dramatized in all ways possible.

The horizon is an insistent line. Striking effects may be achieved through the use of low, horizontal forms (complementary) or incisive verticals (contrasting).

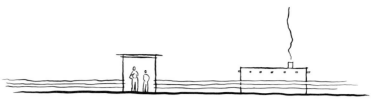

On the scaleless level plain, scale is what one makes it.

Flat landscape under the open sky is often oppressive and lacking in human scale. Scale is therefore easily controlled, from the intimate to the monumental. Human scale, if it is to exist, must be consciously created.

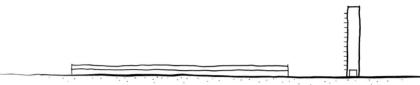

The monotony of the flat site is here relieved by the boldness of the structures and the forceful thrust of the jets in the water panel.

The horizontal in harmony, the vertical in dramatic contrast.

Other sites This same procedure of determining (by perception and deduction) the abstract design characteristics suggested by a given landscape type may, of course, be applied to sites of many varieties, including:

The mountainous	The lakeshore
The windswept	The island
The snow-covered	The estuarine
The forest	The oceanfront
The streamside	The resort
The boulder-strewn	The suburban
The pastoral	The institutional campus
The pond	The business district
The waterfall	The industrial park
The river edge	The heavy industrial

In planning any development or designing any structure in relation to a given site, it is helpful first to deduce the general design characteristics dictated by a thoroughgoing analysis of the existing landscape.

Site-structure plan development

It can be seen that the forces, forms, and features of the total site exert a powerful influence on the schematic plan arrangements and shapes. In the refinement of the plan and the design of each component their relationship to all aspects of the environs is to be further studied.

Outward and inward plan progression We must consider each function from the innermost point of generation to the off-site terminus. In the design of a home, for example, we would be concerned with the route of the small fry not only from bed to bathroom to breakfast table but also from breakfast table to the nearest door, to play areas, to pathway, to school—all in a natural and pleasant progression. Or, in more prosaic terms, we would plan the route of refuse from kitchen to service area to refuse truck to street—all with inconspicuous convenience. The relationship of dining table to window to view involves enframement and development of the view to the property limits and, in some cases, beyond to the far horizon.

Conversely, each element or area must be designed as the logical conclusion of a function originating at the extremities of the site environs. Anyone approaching your property to make a delivery is subtly directed to the service drive, the parking space for the delivery truck, the service walk, the service entrance, and the storage compartment. By design, guests arriving for the evening are alerted and invited in, welcomed to the approach court, directed to the parking bay, and guided to the entrance door, where they enter to the vestibule and the hospitality of the inner home. This same inward and outward progression is applicable to the planning of any project, be it a sawmill, a recreation park, or a world's fair exposition.

Expansion-contraction of plan concept Most site-planning problems can be fully solved only by expanding the areas of consideration to the farthest extensional aspect of the site and by contracting each problem to the minutiae of human experience and irreducible detail. For although it is true that an object or element must be judged in relation to all other elements with which it is allied, it is also true that objects can be fully appreciated only when they are experienced one at a time, in depth, and at the living moment.

Satellite plan As the total structure is conceived in harmony with the total site, so must each element or area of the structure be conceived in harmony with related site areas. In an elementary school, for instance, we would plan the kindergarten, its outdoor play lot, garden, and entrance gate all as one. The gymnasium we would coordinate with the game courts, equipment areas, and playfields. We would consider the boiler plant together with its service and storage areas. The auditorium with its approaches and parking compound, the classrooms with their related outdoor spaces, each element with its extensional site areas would be treated as an integrated plan complex. The overall scheme in diagram would thus resemble a solar system with sun, planets, and satellites.

Integral planning When a structure is imposed on a site, certain changes in landscape character are effected. It is important that these changes be controlled by the planner. Our elementary school is not just plunked down in a city block or in the midst of a suburban community. Rather, ideally, it is fitted to the property and conceived in harmony with the community with such skill that the new landscape created is an improvement over the original.

For a lesson in relating architecture to site we may well look to the planners of the Renaissance. In the building of the magnificent Piazza San Marco in Venice, the architect commissioned to design the cathedral, or the campanile, or the Doge's Palace, or the memorial columns at the water gate never conceived of his building or columns as design entities solely. Instead he instinctively considered his works as integral parts of the piazza in terms of his proposed structure, which he conceived, from broad plan to most minute detail, in terms of its impact on the piazza and vice versa. Each planner not only designed that for which he was commissioned but redesigned the entire piazza and, in doing so, his city of Venice. Thus, and only thus, was he fulfilling his obligation to his client and his city. The secret of much of the charm and great beauty of European towns and cities lies in the conscious application of this planning axiom. Much of the hodgepodge and helter-skelter appearance of the American scene results from planning with seeming ignorance of and indifference to the existing environs.

Proving the plan   How do we know if our proposed installation is well related to its site? There is one sure test we can apply. We can experience it vicariously through the senses of those who will see and use it. At any stage in the creative process, from rough sketches to final drawings or model, we can by our imagination lift ourselves up and look down at the project with a fresh perspective. We can bring it alive in our mind's eye. We can say, in effect, as we look down at the plans for a church:

"I am the minister. As I drive by my church or approach it, does it express those inspirational qualities to which I have dedicated my life? As I enter my study, do I sense that this space is remote enough to give me privacy for study and meditation, yet accessible enough to attract to its doors those who need help or counsel or those who come on church business? As an office is it so located that I can direct and oversee church activities? Does this church that I am to administer have an efficiently organized plan?"

"I am the janitor. As I come to work in the morning, where do I park my car? How do the barrels of cleaning compound get moved from the service dock to the storage area? Where do I store my ladders and snow removal equipment? Did someone in their planning think about me and my work?"

"I am a boy scout homing in to troop meeting. Are the walks planned to take me where I am going, or do I cut across the lawn? Some friends of mine are waiting outside. Do we have a place where we can rip around and blow off steam and maybe shoot a few baskets? Where do we put our bikes? Where do we set up practice tents? Where do we . . .?"

"I am a member of this church, and I am coming to worship. Does my church invite me in? Am I able to drive close to the entry on a cold, rainy day? Where do I park? Is there ample room? After service is there a pleasant space adjacent to the doors where we may linger and greet our friends and welcome visitors?"

All these things are a part of church life and are to be arranged for in its planning.

The function of any project and the relationship of building to site may thus be tested by an imaginary introduction to and through it of people typical of those who will see, service, or use it.

The process of site-structure plan development is a search for logical progressions and best relationships.

The best site plan is that which yields the greatest long-term benefit with the least total cost and stress.

Harbour Town, Hilton Head,
South Carolina

Site-structure unity

We have discussed the importance of developing responsive site-project relationships. Let us now consider other means by which we may achieve site-structure unity.

We may design the structural elements so as to utilize and accentuate landforms. A lighthouse, for example, is an extension of jutting promontory. The ancient fort or castle extended, architecturally, the craggy top of a hill or mountain. Our modern municipal water tanks and transmission or relay towers rise from and extend the height of a topographical eminence. These applications are obvious. Not so obvious is the location of a community swimming pool to utilize and accentuate the natural bowl configuration of a landscape basin or valley. More subtle yet may be the conscious planning of a yacht club to utilize and emphasize the structural protective shoulders of a point or the soft receptive forms of a quiet bay.

A terraced restaurant stepping down the naturally terraced banks of a river, floating structures on water, light, airy structures fixed against the sky, massive structures rooted in rock—each draws from its site a native power and returns to the site this power magnified. Whole cities have been imbued with this dynamic quality—Saigon overhanging its dark river and slow-flowing tributaries, Lhasa braced proudly against its mountain wall, Darjeeling extending its timbered mountain peaks and towers into the clouds.

A structure and its site may be strongly related by the architectural treatment of site areas or elements. Clipped allées and hedges, water panels, precise embankments and terraces, all extend the limits of design control. Many of the French and Italian villas of the Renaissance were so architectural in their treatment that the

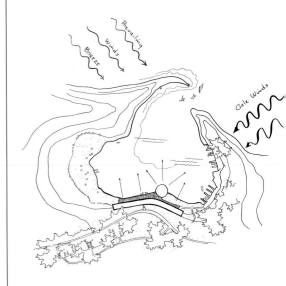

Site-structure unity: yacht club, terrace, and restaurant have been planned to the natural ground forms, which overhang and command the bay. Boat slips are fitted to the protective ridge. The beach area extends the soft receptive wash of the harbor. Cabanas follow the natural bowl. The breakwater and light extend the existing rocky shoulders of the point. The parking areas are "hidden" in the shade of the existing grove. Such a *simpatico* feeling for the existing topography ensures a plan development of fitness and pleasant harmonies of aesthetics and function.

Taliesin West emerges like boulder and cactus from the desert floor on which it lies. Low, horizontal, it spreads out into the landscape. Yet even in its melding it defines itself with forms as dynamic and sweeping as the desert wind and sun. There is complete integration of structure and site.

entire property from wall to wall became one grand composition of palatial indoor and outdoor rooms. These grandiose garden halls were demarcated by great planes or arches of sheared beech, of masonry and mosaic, rows of plinths, and elaborate balustraded walls. They embraced monumental sculptured fountains and parterre gardens of rich pattern or mazes of sharply trimmed box hedges. The integration of architecture and site thus became complete.

Unfortunately, the results were often vacuous: a meaningless exercise in applied geometry—the control of nature for no more reason than for the sake of exerting control. Many such villas, on the other hand, were and still remain notable for their great symphonic beauty. In these, without exception, the highest inherent

Villa d'Este at Tivoli, Italy.

qualities of the natural elements of the site—plants, topography, water—were fully appreciated by the planner and given design expression. Seldom, for instance, has water as a landscape element been treated with more imaginative control than at Villa d'Este in Tivoli, where a mountain torrent was diverted to spill down the steep villa slopes through the gardens, rushing, pouring, gushing, foaming, spurting, spewing, surging, gurgling, dripping, riffling, and finally shining deep and still in the stone reflecting basins. Here at Villa d'Este water, slopes, and plant materials were handled architecturally to enhance both the structure and the site and superbly unite the two.

Alternatively, the landscape features of the site may be embraced by the dispersion of structural or other planned elements into the landscape. The *satellite* plan, the *buckshot* plan, the *finger* plan, the *checkerboard* plan, the *ribbon* plan, and the *exploded* plan are typical examples.

Just as the early French and English explorers in North America controlled vast tracts of land by the strategic placement of a few forts, so can the well-placed elements of a scheme control a given landscape. Such is true of our national parks with their trails, lodges, and campgrounds so sited as to unfold to the user the most interesting features of the park. Such is true, in a *linear* plan expression, of any well-planned scenic drive or highway extended into the countryside. Our military installations are often, in plan, scattered over extensive land areas, each function—be it rifle range, officers' quarters, tank proving ground, tent sites, or artillery range—relating to those topographical features that seem most suitable. For this same purpose, many of our newer schools are exploded in plan. Unlike the old three-story monumental school set *on* the land, the newer schools of which we speak are planned *to* the landscape, embracing and revealing its more pleasant qualities with such success that school and landscape are one.

The site and the structure may be further related by the interlocking of common areas—patios, terraces, and courts, for example. A landscape feature displayed from or in such a court takes on a new aspect. It seems singled out. It becomes a specimen held up to close and frequent observation under varying conditions of position, weather, and light. A simple fragment of rock so featured acquires a modeling and a beauty of form and detail that would not be realized if it were seen in its natural state. As we watch it from

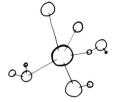
Satellite

Buckshot

Finger

Checkerboard

Ribbon

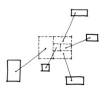
Exploded

Dispersion of plan elements.

This handsome residence is fitted into the natural forest, around the existing boulder, and to the view of the sea.

Rikiu was watching his son Shoan as he swept and watered the garden path. "Not clean enough," said Rikiu, when Shoan had finished his task, and bade him try again. After a weary hour the son turned to Rikiu: "Father, there is nothing more to be done. The steps have been washed for the third time; the stone lanterns and trees are well sprinkled with water; moss and lichens are shining with a fresh verdure; not a twig, not a leaf have I left on the ground." "Young fool," chided the teamaster, "that is not the way a garden path should be swept." Saying this, Rikiu stepped into the garden, shook a tree and scattered over the garden gold and crimson leaves, scraps of the brocade of autumn.

Kakuzo Okakura

day to day—streaming with rain, sparkling with hoarfrost or soft snow, glistening in the sharp sun and incised with shadow, or glowing in subdued evening light—we come to a fuller understanding of this landscape object and thus of the nature of the landscape from which it came.

The landscape may be even more strongly related to structure by the orientation of a room or an area to some feature of the landscape, as by a vista or a view. A view or a garden may be treated as a mural, a mural of constant change and variety of interest, extending the room area visually to the limits of the garden (or to infinity for a distant view). It can be seen that, to be pleasant, the scale, mood, and character of the landscape feature viewed must be suited to the function of the area from which it is observed.

To the foreign visitor in a traditional Japanese home, one of the most appealing features of many is the use of smoothly sliding screens of wood and paper by which the entire side of a room may be opened at will to bring into the space a cloudlike flowering plum tree, a vigorous composition of sand, stone, and sunlit pine, a view through tiered maple branches to the tiered roof of a distant pagoda, or a quiet pool edged with moss and rippled by a lazily fanning goldfish. Each feature viewed is treated with impeccable artistry as part of the room, to extend and unite it with the garden or landscape. The Japanese would tell us that they have a deeper purpose, that what they are really trying to do is to relate people and nature completely and make nature appreciation a part of their daily lives.

To this end they introduce into their dwellings the best of those objects of nature that they can find or afford. The posts and lintels of their rooms, for instance, are not squared and finished lumber but rather a trunk or limb of a favorite wood shaped, tooled, and finished to bring out its inherent form and pattern of grain and knotting. Each foundation stone, each section of bamboo, each tatami (woven grass mat) is so fashioned by the artisan as to discover, and reveal in the finished object, the highest natural quality of the material that is being used. In the Japanese home one finds plants and arrangements of twigs, leaves, and grasses that are startling in their beauty. Even in their art forms the Japanese consciously, almost reverently, bring nature into their homes.

In such ways we, too, may relate our projects and structures to their natural setting. We may use large areas of fenestration. We may so devise our approaches and paths of circulation as to achieve the most desirable relationships. We may recall and adapt from the landscape colors, shapes, and materials. We may make further ties by projecting into the landscape certain areas of interior paving and by extending structural walls or overhead planes. We may break down or vignette our structures from high refinement to a more rustic quality as we move from the interior outward. This is a reverse application of the quality *wabi* mentioned before. This controlled transition from the refined to the natural is a matter of great design significance. It is a matter of such high art that only rarely can outstanding examples be found. One such example is the temple of Tofukuji in Kyoto.

If a building or plan area of any predetermined character is to be imposed on a landscape of another character, transition from the one to the other will play an important role. If, for example, a civic plaza and art museum are to be built at the edge of a city park, all plan elements will become more "civic" and sophisticated as one leaves the park to approach the plaza. Lines will become more precise. Forms will become refined and architectural. Materials, colors, textures, and details will become richer. The natural park character will give way gradually, subtly, to an intensified urbane character consonant with the planned expression of the museum. Conversely, if a rolling, wooded public garden is to be built in a highly developed urban district, plan forms will relax and be freer and more "natural" as one approaches the garden preserve. Such controlled intensification, relaxation, or conversion of plan expression is the mark of skilled physical planning.

Yin and yang   The well-conceived plan involves far more than the application of a program to a plot of land: the fitting of the required use areas within the property boundaries. Planning that disregards the full array of landscape problems and possibilities can realize but a fraction of the site potential. Worse, it generates needless frictions. Often one or more of these frictions may become so insistent as to preclude the very uses for which the plans were made. Such a project fails.

Nor does a plan of excellence result often from the passive *adaptation* of designed components to the site as it exists. Such abject submission or attempt to blend into the scene usually produces an innocuous compromise.

The well-conceived project results instead from a design process of *integration* in which a new landscape is created. Components and site are consciously related and interrelated to yield the best that each can offer in dynamic interaction. Such unity is typified by the Chinese symbol yin and yang, evolved in the misty beginnings of time and representing the complete and balanced oneness of two opposing yet complementary elements—woman and man, earth and sea, and, in planning terms, the functions of the program and the functions of the site.

Site systems

As a logical extension of the principles of site-project unification the concept of *site systems* deserves special attention. The term implies simply that all site improvements are conceived to be constructed and function in a systematic way.

Natural systems   As a starter with such an approach, the natural systems are preserved insofar as feasible. It has been previously noted that every parcel of land is directly related to the surrounding

Transition from the constructed to the natural landscape.

Where site and structure meet we may well "structure" the site and at the same time "wash" the landscape over and into the structure.

Hideo Sasaki

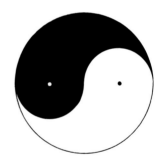

Philosophically, land planning requires an understanding of the two opposing life forces of *integration* and *dispersion*.

Closely related are the cyclical phenomena —the cycles of the constellations, seasons, day and night, and weather and of growth, decay, and regeneration.

landscape and may help to provide protection from the winds, storms, and erosion. It may contribute its share of surface and sub-surface water. It may help to ensure the continuity of vegetative growth and wildlife habitat. Its ground forms and cover may also give a visual continuity to the landscape. The evident continuation of these relationships helps to assure for the planned development a strong and satisfying tie to the surrounding environs.

Drainage   With few exceptions the natural site provides for storm runoff across its surface without causing erosion. The ground-sta-bilizing roots and tendrils of living plants knit the soils and absorb precipitation. The fallen twigs and leaves also form an absorptive mat to keep the soil moist and cool the air. The natural swales, streambeds, and river gorges of the undisturbed landscape provide for the most efficient storm-water flow, while marshes, ponds, and lakes provide the ultimate storage and recharge basins. Any altera-tion to this established network is both disruptive and costly. The movement of materials is required, new storm drainageways must be shaped, and often extensive artificial storm-sewer systems must be constructed. Usually, with the installation of roofs, paved areas, and sewer pipe, the amount and rate of runoff is increased, to the detriment of the project site and downstream landowners.

Experience would suggest that artificial drainage devices be minimized and that they and the natural drainageways be planned together as a balanced *system.*

Movement   Planned paths of pedestrian and vehicular movement that oppose the existing ground forms generate the problems and costs of earthwork, slope retention, interception gutters, storm-sewer connections, and the establishment of new ground covers. When such routes are aligned instead to rise and fall with the natu-ral grades, to follow the ridge lines and ravines, or to trace a cross-slope gradient that requires no heavy cuts or fills, they not only are more economical to build but are also better to look at and more pleasant to use.

Well-designed walks, bicycle trails, and roadways also provide interconnecting networks of movement that assure regional conti-nuity, are particularly suited to the type of traffic to be accommo-dated, and take into account all such factors as safety, efficiency, and landscape integrity. Materials, sections, profiles, lighting, sign-ing, and planting are coordinated and designed as an integrated *system.*

Lighting   Site illumination does many good things. It provides safety in traffic movement and crossings, it gives warning of haz-ards, and it serves to increase security and reduce vandalism. It interprets the plan arrangement by giving emphasis to focal points, gathering places, and building entrances. It demarcates and illumines paths of interconnection, serving as a guide-on. With accent light-ing, fine architecture or site areas of exceptional significance or beauty can be brought into visual prominence.

Well-conceived lighting gives clarity and unity to the overall site and to each subarea within it, especially if planned from the start as a coordinated *system.*

Signs   Graphic informational systems are closely allied with site illumination, since the two are usually interdependent and comple-mentary. Street and route lighting obviously must be planned to-gether with the positioning of related directional signs. Often light standards provide support for signs and informational symbols.

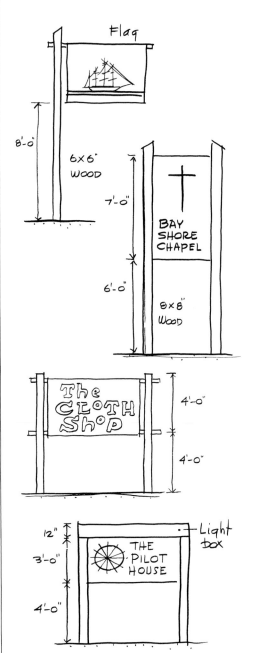

Signs, like lighting, are best developed as a hierarchy, each sign being designed in terms of its size, color, and placement to best serve its particular purpose and all existing together as a related family. When the system is kept simple and standardized, the signing gives its own sense of order and clarity to the trafficway pattern and the landscape plan.

Planting Planting of excellence is also systematic. It articulates and strengthens the site layout. It develops an interrelated pattern of open, closed, or semienclosed spaces, each shaped to suit its

Unity with diversity is the key to identification signs. Shapes, sizes, and letter forms may vary with the information to be conveyed. Materials, mountings, and colors are usually standardized.

planned function. Planting extends topographical forms, enframes views and vistas, anchors freestanding buildings, and provides visual transitions from object to object and place to place. It serves as backdrop, windscreen, and sunshield. It checks winter winds. It catches and channels the summer breeze. It casts shadow and shade. It absorbs precipitation, freshens the air, and modifies climatic extremes.

Aside from serving these "practical" functions, plants in their many forms and varieties are also decorative. But even their decorative quality is more pleasing if there is an evident reason behind their selection and use.

Fine plantings, like any other fine work of design, have a fundamental simplicity and a discernible order. Many experienced landscape designers limit their plant lists to a *primary* tree, shrub, and ground cover and one to three *secondary* trees, shrubs, and supplementary ground cover—grasses, herbs, or vines, with all other supporting and accent plants comprising no more than a small fraction of the total.

Except in urban settings, the large majority of all plants used will be native to the region and will therefore fit and thrive without special care.

Essentially, each plant used should serve a purpose, and all together should contribute to the function and expressiveness of the plan.

Materials   Just as the palette of plant materials is limited in the main to those which are indigenous, so it is also with the materials of construction. Wall stone from local quarries seems most appropriate. Crushed stone and gravels exposed as aggregate, bricks made of local clays, lumber from trees that grow in the vicinity, and mulches made of their chipped or shredded bark all seem right in the local scene. Even the architectural adaptation of the natural earth, foliage, and sky colors relates the constructions to the regional setting.

The reduction of the number of materials used to a small and selective list lends simplicity and unity to the planned development.

Operations   All projects must be planned to work, and work efficiently. Each building and each use area of the site must operate well as an entity, and all, together, as a well-organized complex. This can be achieved only if all components are planned together as an integrated *system.*

Maintenance   To be effective maintenance must be a consideration from the earliest planning stages. This presupposes that all maintenance operations have been programmed. It also assumes that storage for the required materials and equipment is provided, that access points and ways are strategically located, that convenient hydrants and electrical outlets are installed, and that maintenance needs are reduced insofar as practical.

It also means that the number of construction materials and components and thus the replacement inventory of items that must be kept stocked are reduced to a workable minimum. This requires standardization of light globes, bench slats, anchor bolts, sign blanks, curb templates, paint colors, and everything else. Usually a reduction in the quantity of items stocked can result in improved quality at significant savings. This is possible only if the maintenance operation is planned from the start as, or converted to, an efficient *system.*

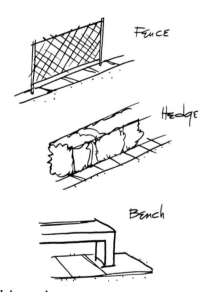

Edging strips
Paved mowing strips of concrete, set brick, or stone at lawn edges carry the wheel of an edger and eliminate hand trimming.

From small-home grounds to campus, to park, to large industrial complex, site installation and maintenance costs can be reduced and performance improved by the standardization of all possible components, materials, and equipment.

Use only the affordable best; therein lies quality and economy.

Site development guidelines:

A checklist of helpful considerations[1]

Excavation and grading

Keep to an absolute minimum.

Balance the on-site cut and fill. Off-site borrow or disposition is expensive.

Protect trees and established ground covers.

Remove and stockpile the topsoil.

Avoid working the soil when it is wet, powder-dry, or frozen.

Provide positive surface drainage away from buildings to swales, gutters, drain inlets, or outfalls.

Reestablish ground covers without delay. Unprotected soils cause erosion and siltation.

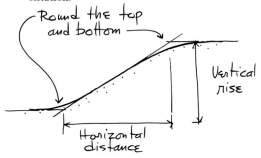

Most slopes are best blended into the natural landforms.

Slopes (earth cut or fill)

Do not exceed the angle of repose of the soils being cut or placed or a slope of 1 on 1½ maximum (1 foot of vertical rise for 1½ feet of horizontal distance).

A slope of 1 on 2 maximum is recommended for mulched or planted embankments.

A slope of 1 on 3 maximum is preferred for lawn areas to facilitate mowing.

Place fill material in uniform layers of 6 to 8 inches of loose material.

Allow for soil shrinkage (or swelling in some instances); 3 to 5 percent shrinkage is normal in compacted fills.

Provide mechanical compaction. Natural compaction by the eventual settlement of loosely placed soils is seldom uniform or complete.

All fills should be *compacted fills,* placed on prepared benches cut through topsoil and overburden.

Thrust benches and positive drainage must be provided at the base of major fills.

Steps

Avoid steps, if possible, except when they are used as a landscape feature.

Always consider the handicapped and provide alternate access ramps.

Avoid use of single steps. They are hazardous.

The risers in architectural flights of steps should be of uniform height. In free-form or naturalized flights of steps (where consistency is not anticipated), riser and tread dimensions may vary widely within a given flight.

Good footing is essential. On concrete steps a wood float or light broom finish or the use of abrasive fines is suggested.

In rough terrain particularly, perrons (as in a stepped ramp) may be desirable on slopes ranging in grade from 16 to 25 percent.

Lawn and seeded areas

Provide a 1 percent minimum gradient for lawn areas (a fall of 1 foot for each 100 feet).

A 1½ percent slope is preferred to ensure more positive surface drainage.

Swales should have a gradient of 1 percent minimum, 4 percent maximum. (On steeper grades a loose stone or paved gutter is required.)

Provide a 6-inch fall from buildings in the first 20 feet.

A 4-inch compacted topsoil section is considered the minimum for new lawn construction. A 6- to 8-inch section (or deeper) is recommended when soils are impervious or overly porous or when topsoil is abundant.

Walk paving

Provide a 1 percent minimum longitudinal or cross slope.

A slope of 1½ percent is recommended for terraces.

A pitch of 8 percent is considered maximum for walks if no handrail is provided.

With a handrail, the walk pitch can be steepened to 15 percent (for a short ramp distance only).

Width: a confined walkway requires a minimum width of 2 feet per person for comfortable passing. In the open, where people's shoulders can overhang the walk edge, the outer pedestrian lanes can be reduced by up to 6 inches. A width of 5 feet 0 inches for a typical low-volume community walk will allow three persons or one person and a baby carriage to pass. If bicycle use is anticipated (such a joint use is not generally recommended), a walk width of 6 feet 0 inches is required for a bicycle and two persons or for two bicycles to pass.

Capacity: each 2 feet of width will accommodate between *50 and 60 persons per minute,* or an average of *3300 persons per hour.* This holds as well for shuffling crowds, strolling window-shoppers, or students walking briskly across a campus, since as the rate of movement increases, the person-to-person spacing increases accordingly. Rates

and capacities vary with climatic conditions, surface textures, and gradients. They are to be adjusted for intermittent movement as at crossings, constrictions, and counter pedestrian flow, which can reduce capacities by up to 50 percent.

Roads and driveways

In planning the approach drive or roadway consider:

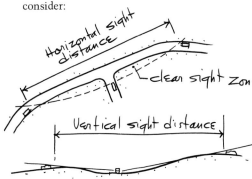

Sight distance: provide sufficient horizontal and vertical sight distance to give 10-second minimum observation time at permitted approach speeds.

> Adequate sight distances at intersections
> An attractive introduction and portal
> Sequential revealment of views, site features, and buildings
> All-weather drivability and safety
> Recognition of topography, sun angles, and storms
> Minimum length and minimum landscape disruption
> A pleasurable driving experience

Align roads and drives (and walkways) so that adjacent swales, gutters, and/or sewers will have continuous gravity flow, with minimum grading or depth of trenching.

A longitudinal gradient of 1½ percent is preferred; 1 percent is considered minimum.

When flatter grades are necessary, the road must be crowned or cross-sloped to drain, as:

> Concrete, ¼ inch per foot
> Bituminous, ⅜ inch per foot
> Gravel, ½ inch per foot

Use a dished (concave) section only in narrow lanes or minor service drives.

All road and drive intersections should be approximately perpendicular (90 degrees).

Horizontal and vertical curvature is subject to design speed and topography.

Horizontal curves are normally true arcs.

Vertical curves are parabolic. Radii vary from 30 feet at the entrance to public roads to 600 feet or more on private drives.

On private drives and in natural areas both the horizontal and the vertical curvature may follow the topography freely without need for geometric computation. In such

[1]These may vary in some instances with site or climatic conditions and material finishes.

cases the grading equipment is guided by prelocated field stakes or flags and responds with a light touch to the existing landforms.

Recommended private local street widths (on-street parking prohibited)

Dwellings served	Paving width
1–5	12 feet, single lane, optional to 500 feet
1–20	16 feet, two lanes
21–50	18 feet, two lanes
51 plus	20 feet, two lanes

For public roads, see local requirements:
18 feet minimum for two lanes
10 to 12 feet per lane normal

Parking

Allow a normal stall width of 8 feet 6 inches minimum to 12 feet maximum; 10 feet 0 inches is a comfortable average.

Stall marking: while a single divider stripe will suffice, a double 3-inch line, 12 to 16 inches on center with a half circle at the aisle end, is recommended.

Parking compound (two or more courts); for area-capacity calculation (approximate) allow 300 square feet of paved parking area per standard car, plus approach ramps, distributor loops, planting medians, turnabouts, collector walks, and buffer areas.

Site drainage

Preserve the natural drainageways insofar as feasible.

Preclude concentrated surface runoff to downgrade properties.

Avoid trapped water pockets.

Provide underdrains at road edges and low points.

Conduct surface water by swale, gutter, or buried pipe to storm-sewer mains or outfall.

If storm inlets and lateral sewers are needed, compute the required capacity and then use the next larger size.

Keep the site drainage system unobtrusive.

Site furnishings

In the selection and placement of lighting standards and fixtures, recreational equipment, informational signs, benches, movable tables, seating, etc., consider:
Functional suitability.
Compatibility of form, material, and finish.
Durability.

Long-term cost: a higher initial expense that yields longer life with less required maintenance is usually good economics.

Durability is to be stressed. Site equipment and furniture must be designed to withstand the effects of the elements, including sun, expansion-contraction, wind stress, moisture, and sometimes salt spray, frost, or ice.

Plan a coordinated *family* of shapes, materials, and finishes.

Generally, use strong, simple shapes, native materials, and natural finishes. Black, grays, and earth tones are basic, with bright colors reserved for accent.

Standardize components such as lighting globes, signposts and blanks, bench slats, bolts, and stains.

Invest in the best.

Landscape planting

Strive always for utmost simplicity.

Stress quality, not quantity. One well-selected, well-placed plant can be more effective than 100 plants scattered at random.

When budgets are limited, economize on the extent of the lawn and planted areas, but invest in soil quality and depth, larger plant pits, soil preparation, and provision for irrigation.

Lawn areas are best given a well-defined and pleasant shape and (in an architectural context particularly) edged with paving, curb, or mowing strip.

Install no lawn area or plant without a predetermined purpose.

Select each plant to best serve the purpose intended.

In the use of plant materials consider:
Need
Suitability
Appearance in all seasons
Appearance in all stages of growth
Compatibility of form, texture, color, and association in the total building and site composition
Hardiness, cultural requirements, and degree of maintenance needed

As a rule, use only indigenous or naturalized materials except for bedding plants and container-grown exotics.

Plants used for backdrop, screening, shade, or space definition are generally selected for strength and cleanliness of form, richness of texture, and subtlety of color.

Plants to be featured are selected for their sculptural qualities and for ornamental twigging, budding, foliage, flowers, and fruit.
They are to be placed strategically for optimum display.

Ground covers and mulches do much to enrich a fine planting.

In landscape planting of excellence *restraint* is the key.

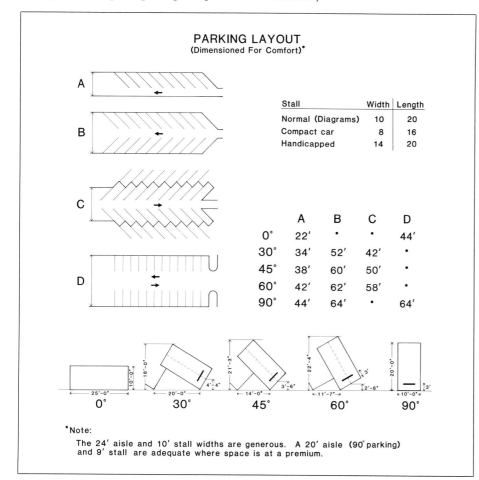

PARKING LAYOUT
(Dimensioned For Comfort)*

Stall	Width	Length
Normal (Diagrams)	10	20
Compact car	8	16
Handicapped	14	20

	A	B	C	D
0°	22'	•	•	44'
30°	34'	52'	42'	•
45°	38'	60'	50'	•
60°	42'	62'	58'	•
90°	44'	64'	•	64'

0° 30° 45° 60° 90°

*Note:
The 24' aisle and 10' stall widths are generous. A 20' aisle (90° parking) and 9' stall are adequate where space is at a premium.

A superior information system is designed as a <u>family</u> of coordinated and complementary signs. Locations, shapes, sizes, materials, and graphics are to be consistent.

The following sign types are basic for a community, campus, park, or business office center.

- Trail-blazer
- Entrance sign
- Arterial directory
- Internal directory
- Street signs
- Pathway guides
- Place identification

Entrance signs are placed inside the property lines to announce arrival and help to create an attractive portal.

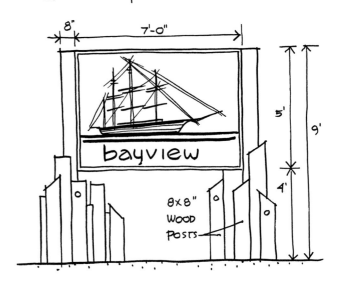

ENTRANCE SIGN

Trail-blazers are located on the major approach roads to alert and guide the visitor.

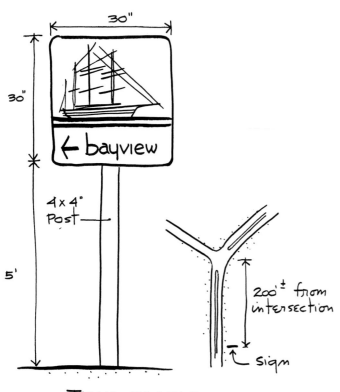

TRAIL-BLAZER

Directories are located on the arterial approaches to every major intersection, and list the chief community destinations.

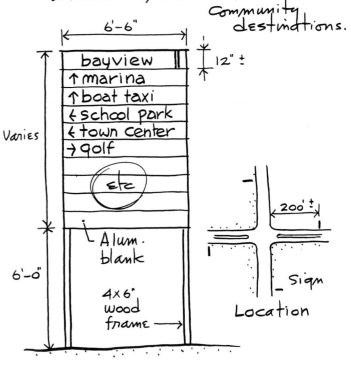

ARTERIAL DIRECTORY

At Each intersection within a sub-community neighborhood or activity center (area) a directory of lesser magnitude provides the essential guidance.

Place and way information is to be provided at the main intersections of pedestrian walks and bicycle paths.

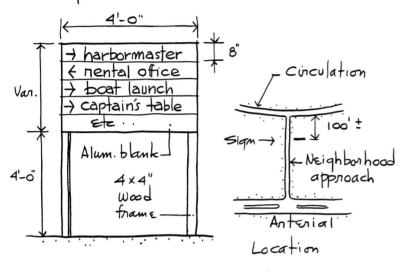

INTERNAL DIRECTORY

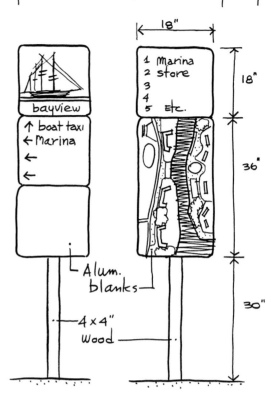

PATHWAY GUIDES

Street signs are to be located, with consistent setbacks, at every intersection — preferably in combination with lighting.

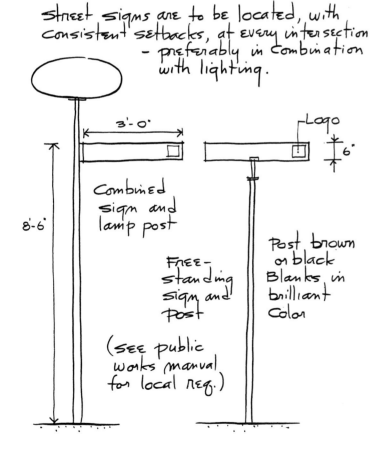

STREET SIGNS

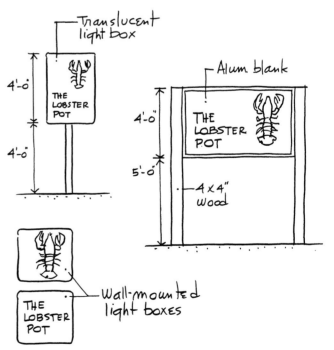

PLACE IDENTIFICATION

Spaces

7

In site-structure plan development we were concerned with defining *use areas* and their relationship to one another and to the total site. Now we are concerned chiefly with the translation of these areas into *use volumes,* or spaces, each volume having a shape, size, material, color, texture, and other qualities that best express and accommodate the function for which the space is intended. It can be said that *planning* is two-dimensional; three-dimensional thinking takes us into the realm of *design.*

Site volumes

Much of the art and science of land planning is revealed to the planner when it is first realized that one is dealing not with *areas* but with *spaces.* As an example, a playground composed of play equipment set about on a dull base plane has little child appeal, while the same apparatus arranged within a grouping of imaginative play *spaces* can provide endless hours of delight. It is a matter of designing the volumetric enclosure and spatial interconnections to suit the use.

In the same vein, a highway is not to be considered as just a ribbon of pavement on the base plane. A properly designed highway must be conceived also in terms of volumes—open where safe vision and pleasant views so dictate, closed for screening, varied in its spatial conformation to provide interest and relief from fatigue, and modulated to reveal the landscape traversed in the best possible way. The superior highway will be a scientifically contrived, expanding and contracting, variformed volume through which motorists may move speedily, safely, and freely, enjoying a highwayscape

135

designed to keep them relaxed and happy and, at the same time, alert.

A city is not at best a heterogeneous conglomeration of buildings lined out in rigid patterns; a well-planned city is perceived as an evolving composition of structures and interrelated *spaces*. More than the buildings, it is the form and character of the open spaces they define that give a city its essential quality. Perhaps the most disturbing fact about our disturbing American cities is that most structures are ranged as in a wall along constricted city streets rather than grouped around traffic-free courts, squares, and plazas.

The creation of well-organized interior and exterior *spaces* for uses of any type and scope is our goal as environmental designers.

Spatial impact Volumes have been designed for the intended purpose of torturing the occupants. It has been said that during the Spanish Civil War an architect was ordered to devise such a chamber. He developed a translucent, multicolored polyhedron of sharply intersecting planes—an insidious enclosure in which a locked-in victim found himself unable to lie, sit, stoop, or kneel without tilting or tumbling the cubicle. The surfaces were slippery, burning hot in the sun, and frigid in the night cold. In any light, the colors were distressing if seen alone; seen together, in their discordant clashing, they soon became maddening.

A site volume that clearly expresses its use.

If it is possible to devise distressing volumes, then it should also be possible to create volumes that yield an experience of pleasure. We may recall a favorite golf course fairway as such an agreeable space. Expansive, free, and undulating, it is open to the sky, enclosed with foliage, and carpeted with turf. An outdoor space of far different mien is the cascade approach and plaza of New York's Rockefeller Center. It is walled by a canyon of metal, masonry, and glass and has a base of cut stone and terrazzo; its overhead plane is a tower-framed segment of sky, relieved by the tracery of foliage and the moving color of waving flags. Here is a space artfully planned to attract, refresh, and excite us and condition us for entry into the elegant restaurants, shops, and offices at its sides. Not far away, we can find yet another outdoor space of high design refinement. The

People live on the earth, on the land, but in the three-dimensional air-space, the atmospheric volume, immediately above this land surface. Plans and land-use maps may be measured diagrammatically and abstractly in square footage and acreage, but space for living is measured in cubage, in volumes of air-space enclosed or organized with tangible physical elements. . . .

The experience of being within fine three-dimensional spatial volumes is one of the great experiences of life.

Garrett Eckbo

Site volumes: degrees of vertical enclosure.

Three moods of the Lower Plaza in Rockefeller Center: in the summertime with tables set out beside the Prometheus Fountain, during the Christmas holidays, and converted to a skating rink. This is an urbane space laced with music, motion, and kaleidoscopic color.

Designed for relaxation. The Landings on Skidaway Island, Georgia.

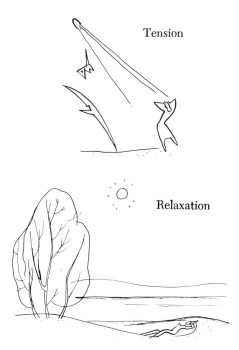

Tension

Relaxation

garden of the Museum of Modern Art is an urbane volume eminently suited as a backdrop and visual extension of the adjacent galleries or as a place in which to wander through sunlight and dappled shade, viewing the pools and sculpture. There will come to mind, upon reflection, many other similarly pleasant site spaces—a picnic spot on some lakeshore, a stadium, a public square, a residential swimming pool and garden. By analysis, we find that all are pleasant because, and only because, in size, shape, and character they are manifestly suited to the purposes for which they were intended.

As an instructive exercise, we might list the abstract qualities or spatial characteristics of a series of varying volumes, each designed to induce a predetermined response.

Tension. Unstable forms. Split composition. Illogical complexities. Wide range of values. Clash of colors. Intense colors without relief. Visual imbalance about a line or a point. No point at which the eye can rest. Hard, polished, or jagged surfaces. Unfamiliar elements. Harsh, blinding, or quavering light. Uncomfortable temperatures in any range. Piercing, jangling, jittery sound.

Relaxation. Simplicity. Volumes varying in size from the intimate to the infinite. Fitness. Familiar objects and materials.

Flowing lines. Curvilinear forms and spaces. Evident structural stability. Horizontality. Agreeable textures. Pleasant and comfortable shapes. Soft light. Soothing sound. Volume infused with quiet colors—whites, grays, blues, greens. "Think round thoughts."

Fright. Sensed confinement. A quality of compression and bearing. An apparent trap. No points of orientation. No means by which to judge position or scale. Hidden areas and spaces. Possibilities for surprise. Sloping, twisted, or broken planes. Illogical, unstable forms. Slippery, hazardous base plane. Danger. Unprotected voids. Sharp, protruding elements. Contorted spaces. The

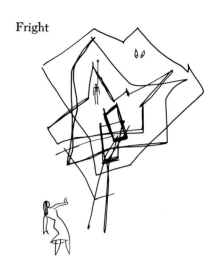

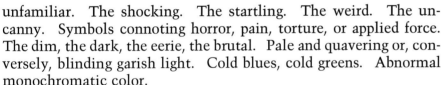

unfamiliar. The shocking. The startling. The weird. The uncanny. Symbols connoting horror, pain, torture, or applied force. The dim, the dark, the eerie, the brutal. Pale and quavering or, conversely, blinding garish light. Cold blues, cold greens. Abnormal monochromatic color.

Gaiety. Free spaces. Smooth, flowing forms and patterns. Looping, tumbling, swirling motion accommodated. Movement and rhythm expressed in structure. Lack of restrictions. Forms, colors, and symbols that appeal to the emotions rather than the intellect. Temporal. Casual. Lack of restraint. Pretense acceptable. The fanciful applauded. Often the light, bright, and spontaneous in contrast to the ponderous, dark, and timeless. Warm, bright colors. Sparkling, shimmering, shooting, or glowing light. Exuberant or lilting sound.

Gaiety

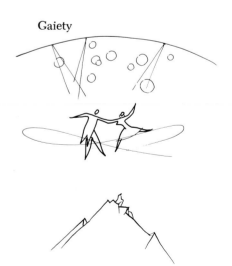

Contemplation. Scale not important since subjects will withdraw into their own sensed well of consciousness. Total space mild and unpretentious or immense and richly ornate, as long as the structural forms are not insistent. No insinuating elements. No distractions of sharp contrast. Symbols, if used, related to subject of contemplation. Space providing a sense of isolation, privacy, detachment, security, and peace. Soft, diffused light. Tranquil and recessive colors. If sound, a low muted stream of sound to be perceived subconsciously.

Contemplation

Dynamic action. Bold forms. Heavy, structural cadence. Angular planes. Diagonals. Solid materials such as stone, concrete, wood, or steel. Rough, natural textures. The pitched verti-

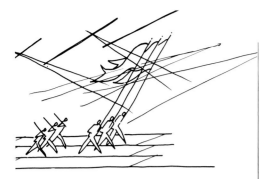

Dynamic action

Sensuous love

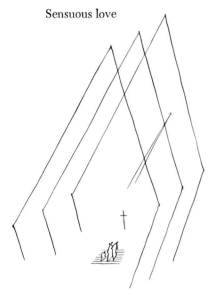

Sublime, spiritual awe

cal. Directional compositional focus. Concentration of interest on focal point of action, as to rostrum, rallying point, or exit gate through which the volume impels one. Motion induced by sweeping lines, shooting lights, and climatic sequences of form, pattern, and sound. Strong, primitive colors—crimson, scarlet, and yellow-orange. Billowing banners. Burnished standards. Martial music. Rush of sound. Ringing crescendos. Crash of brass. Blare of trumpets. The roll and boom of drums.

Sensuous love. Complete privacy. Inward orientation of room. Subject the focal point. Intimate scale. Low ceiling. Horizontal planes. Fluid lines. Soft, rounded forms. Juxtaposition of angles and curves. Delicate fabrics. Voluptuous and yielding surfaces. Exotic elements and scent. Soft, rosy pink to golden light. Pulsating, titillating music.

Sublime spiritual awe. Overwhelming scale that transcends normal human experience. Soaring forms in contrast with low horizontal forms. A volume so contrived as to hold one transfixed on a broad base plane and lift one's eyes and mind high along the vertical. Orientation upward to or beyond some symbol of the infinite. Complete compositional order, often symmetry. Highly developed sequences. Use of costly and permanent materials. Connotation of the eternal. Use of chaste white. If color is used, the cool detached colors, such as blue-greens, blue, and violet. Diffused glow with shafts of light. Deep, full, swelling music with lofty passages.

Displeasure.[1] Frustrating sequences of movement or revelation. Areas and spaces unsuitable to anticipated use. Obstacles. Excesses. Undue friction. Discomfort. Annoying textures. Improper use of materials. The illogical. The false. The insecure. The tedious. The blatant. The dull. The disorderly. Disagreeable colors. Discordant sounds. Uncomfortable temperature or humidity. Annoying lights. That which is ugly.

Pleasure.[2] Spaces, forms, textures, colors, symbols, sounds, light quality, and odors all suited to the use, whatever it may be. Satisfaction of anticipations, requirements, or desires. Sequences developed and fulfilled. Unity with variety. Harmonious relationships. A resultant quality of beauty.

If we were to list the requisites of the ideal space for each of a series of varying *uses,* we might be amazed at the variety of suggested spatial characteristics and at the degree of precision with which the characteristics can be defined. A child's play lot, for example, would be designed as a lilliputian wonderland of induced action, shrieks, and squeals. Intriguing forms, a rich variety of textures, and bright splashes of color would be right, for children have an acutely developed tactile sense and a love of shapes and primitive hues. Their play space might well be variformed with tunnels, obstacles, baffles, movable objects, and things to climb over, under, and through. It should be a place of strong contrasts: sun to shadow, smooth to rough, bright to dull, open to closed, and high to low. A well-designed play lot for a child is in itself a plaything, conducive to excitement and rollicking delight.

A space for private outdoor dining would have an entirely dif-

The marketplace, Long Beach, California.

[1]It is to be noted that *displeasure* and *pleasure* are general categories, whereas *tension, relaxation, fright,* and the others mentioned are more specific. With these more specific responses we can list in more specific detail the characteristics of the volumes designed to induce them. The degree of *pleasure* or its opposite, *displeasure,* would seem to depend on the degree of sensed fitness or unfitness of the volume for its function. It can be seen that one could experience pleasure and fright simultaneously (as in a fun house) or pleasure and sublime spiritual awe simultaneously (as in a cathedral), and so forth.
[2]Ibid.

Induced activity.

Induced serenity.

ferent set of criteria. As a volume it should be simple in shape, intimate in size, and refined in texture and detail. It should be shaped to invite repose. It should create a serene and pleasant atmosphere conducive to conversation. For the point of highest interest, it might well focus on the surface of the table and the faces of the diners poised above it. It should be a casual, light, and airy space of studied subleties. As can be imagined, if the child's play activities were to be transposed to a space such as we have described for dining, the child would soon become restive. If, on the other hand, the diners were moved to the space designed as a play lot, we could in time expect no less than chronic indigestion or nervous collapse.

Spatial qualities   The essence of a volume is its quality of implied containment.

A confined space may be static. It may hold interest, induce repose. It may direct and concentrate interest and vision inward. The whole spatial shell may be made seemingly to contract and bear down, to engender a feeling of intensity or compression.

Alternatively, a space may open out. It may direct attention to its frame and beyond. It may fall away or seem to expand. It may seem fairly to burst outward. It may impel outward motion to its perimeter and to more distant limits.

A space may be flowing and undulating, suggesting directional movement.

A space may be so developed as to have its own sufficient, satisfying qualities. It may appear complete within itself or incomplete, a setting for persons or objects.

A space may be in effect a vacuum.

A space may have expulsive pressure.

A space may be developed as an optimum environment for an object or a use.

A space may be so designed as to stimulate a prescribed emotional reaction or to produce a predetermined sequence of such responses.

A space may dominate an object, imbuing the object with its particular spatial qualities. Or it may be dominated by the object, drawing from it something of its nature.

A space may have orientation inward, outward, upward, downward, radial, or tangential.

A space may relate to a force, an object, or another space and may gain its very meaning from the relationship.

From its hollowness arises the reality of the vessel; from its empty space arises the reality of the building.

Lao-tse

A creation in space is an interweaving of parts of space. . . .

László Moholy-Nagy

Architecture . . . is the beautiful and serious game of space.

Willem Dudok

A space may be dominated by an object. This classic site volume was an early work of Mies van der Rohe.

A complex space assumes to a degree the qualities of its component volumes and should relate them into a unified entity.

Spaces may vary from the vast to the minute, from the light and ethereal to the heavy and ponderous, from the dynamic to the calm, from the crude to the refined, from the simple to the elaborate, and from the somber to the dazzling. In their size, shape, and character they may vary endlessly. Clearly, in designing a space for any given function, we would do well first to determine the essential qualities desired and then to do our best to provide them.

Spatial size   Planned spaces are usually considered only as they relate to humans. Paddocks, corrals, dog runs, canary cages, and elephant traps are exceptions, but even these are best conceived with more than fleeting attention to the habits, responses, and requirements of the proposed occupants. Take the elephant trap, for instance. Few architects approach their planning with a keener awareness of their client's traits than the native builder who directs the construction of the stout timber and rattan enclosure for the trapping and training of wild elephants. The canary cage, too, with its light enframement, seed cups, swinging perches, and cuttlebone, is a volume contrived with much thought for the well-being of the canary. In planning spaces for people, it seems plausible that their accommodation and happiness should be of as great concern to the planner as those designed for the bird and the pachyderm.

It is well known that the size of an interior space in relation to people has a strong effect on their feelings and behavior. This fact may be illustrated graphically in the accompanying diagrams.

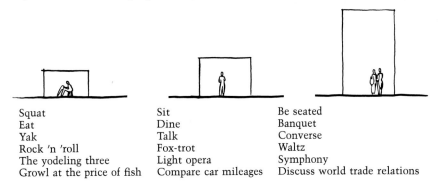

Squat	Sit	Be seated
Eat	Dine	Banquet
Yak	Talk	Converse
Rock 'n 'roll	Fox-trot	Waltz
The yodeling three	Light opera	Symphony
Growl at the price of fish	Compare car mileages	Discuss world trade relations

Exterior spaces have similar psychological attributes. On an open plain timid persons feel overwhelmed, lonesome, and unprotected; left to their own devices, they soon take off in the direction of shelter or kindred spirits. Yet, on this same plain, bolder persons feel challenged and impelled to action; with freedom and room for movement they are prone to dashing, leaping, yahooing. The level base plane not only accommodates but also induces mass action, as on the polo field, the football field, the soccer field, and the racetrack.

If, upon this unobstructed surface, we set an upright object, it becomes an element of high interest and a point of orientation for the visible field. We are drawn to it, cluster about it, and come to rest at its base. No small factor in this natural phenomenon is the human atavistic tendency to keep one's flanks protected. A vertical plane or wall gives this protection and suggests shelter. Increased protection is afforded by two intersecting upright planes. They provide a corner into which our subject may back and from which he or she can survey the field for either attacker or quarry. Additional vertical planes define spaces that are further controlled by the introduction of overhead planes. Such spaces derive their size and shape and degee of enclosure from the defining planes, act-

On the horizontal one orients to the vertical.

Residential spaces.

Space at exposition scale.

ing together and counteracting. A volume may be stimulating, or it may be relaxing. It may be immense, suggesting certain uses, or it may be confining, suggesting others. In any event, we are attracted to those spaces suited to our purpose, be it hiking, target shooting, eating grapes, or making love. We are repelled by, or at least have little interest in, those spaces that appear to be unsuited to the use we have in mind.

The Japanese, in their landscape design, have learned to develop spatial volumes of such intrinsic human scale and personalized character that the spaces can be satisfied only by the presence of the person or persons for whom they were conceived. The Abbot's Garden of Nikko, for instance, is complete only when the abbot and his followers are seated sedately on the low, broad terraces or are wandering contemplatively among the gnarled pine trees or beside the quiet ponds. The imperial Shinjuku Gardens, once sublimely beautiful and faultlessly groomed, seemed somehow incomplete except in the emperor's presence. The contemporary American family home and garden, planned together as one unit, provide a balanced composition of interior and exterior spaces so designed as to call for and need for fulfillment the family members and friends for whom they were created.

Some spaces are person-dominated, controlled in size by such factors as the reach of one's arm or the turning radius of one's car. Other spaces are intentionally planned to dominate us. The visitor to the Grand Canyon is brought into relation to the dizzying heights and yawning depths in such a way as to thrill at their maximum impact. On the Blue Ridge Parkway in Virginia we are intentionally brought to the precipice edge. Again, on some narrow rock one is thrust like an ant against the vast, empty dome of the sky. Mysterious Stonehenge in England, a great circle of space carved out of

Stonehenge.

the moors with massive stone posts and lintels, is a dramatic reminder that even neolithic people knew the power of the space to inspire and humble humans. It would seem that they must have sensed that one's soul is stretched by the feeling of awe and one's heart revitalized by the experience of abject humility.

Between the micro and macro spaces we may plan spaces of an infinite range in size. The volumetric dimensions should never be incidental.

Spatial form   It has been said that, ideally, in design *form must follow function*. This statement is more profound than it seems. It is open to some argument unless we assume that aesthetic and intellectual considerations are an inherent aspect of function. What all this means is that any object, space, or thing should be designed as the most effective mechanism for doing the job at hand; moreover, it should look it. If the designer can achieve an actual and *apparent* harmony of form, material, finish, and use, the object not only should work well but also should be pleasant to see. Let us take a simple example. An ax handle has for its purpose the transmission of the full power of the wielder's stroke to the cutting edge of the blade. A superior handle is made of selected straight-grained, seasoned ash with just the right degree of toughness and flexibility. It is shaped to the grip and butted to prevent slipping. From the grip it swells in a strong force-delivering, shatter-resistant curve of studied thickness and length. When the tapered helve is

It is an unfortunate roaming of theory that favors a separation, even an antithesis, of beauty and utility, and places an accent of additive extravagance and uselessness on the first of this pair. . . .

Whatever we perceive as "beauty" in nature is never, and in no way, an addition to what we perceive as "utility." All organic shape and detail depend clearly upon structure itself, and never can they be looked upon as decorative adjunct.

Richard J. Neutra

The man was perceived to be a fool who . . . seriously inclines to weigh the beautiful by any other standard but that of good. . . .

The useful is the noble and the hurtful is the base.

Plato

I shall define beauty to be a harmony of all the parts, in whatsoever subject it appears, fitted together with such proportion and connection, that nothing could be added, diminished or altered, but for the worse.

Leon Battista Alberti

Site-volume definition

Examples from Pedregal, Mexico

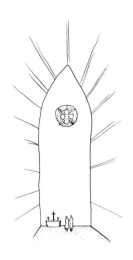

The qualities of space.

fitted and wedged at precisely the right angle to the head, the ax is in perfect balance, lies well in the hands, and is good to use. It is also good to look at. To the experienced user it is an object of true beauty.

If shown a new ax with a handle made of plastic, the user would probably be incredulous: a handle that had no grain and looked like glass surely couldn't be trusted. It would appear incongruous and ugly. If, however, one came to learn by experience that the new handle was in all ways superior, it would come in time to be admired, and no ax with a wooden handle could ever seem as beautiful again.

A sloop is designed to utilize the driving force of the wind in propelling a floating object. In the superior sloop the hull is fastidiously shaped to cleave the waves, slide buoyantly through the water, and leave a smoothly swelling wake; the deep keel extends the conformation of the hull as a streamlined stabilizer; the spars are so fashioned and bent as to carry the optimum areas of sail; the humming stays are of finest stainless-steel cable; the halyards and sheet are of nylon; the sails, of laminated fabric and Mylar; the cleats are so formed as fairly to reach for the lines; tiller and rudder are precisely fitted and balanced to sweep and bear. Such a sloop, heeled and scudding, is a miracle of shapes, materials, and forces working together in harmony. Here again form is designed for function, and the form is a beautiful thing. For, as the poet Keats has aptly proposed, "Beauty is truth, truth beauty."

Not only things but spaces as well are to be given their form with high regard for function. We have seen this to be true of the child's play lot, of the planned highway, and of the hypothetically ideal city. Without doubt the most frequent common denominator of pleasant site and architectural volumes is this very quality.

Indoor-outdoor volumes.

Having allocated and organized the required *use areas*, the planner proceeds to develop these areas into *use volumes*, each being designed to accommodate and express its predetermined use.

Spatial color   In passing, it is of interest to note an early Chinese theory of volumetric color design.   According to this theory, we have become so accustomed to the color arrangements of nature that we have an aversion to any violation of the accepted rule.   It follows that in selecting colors for any space, interior or exterior, the base plane is treated in earthy colors—the hues and values of clays, loams, stones, gravels, sands, forest duff, and moss.   The light blues and blue-greens of water, recalling its unstable surface, are used but rarely on base planes or floors, and then only in those areas where walking is to be discouraged.   The structural elements of wall and overhead are given the colors of the tree trunk and limb— blacks, browns, deep grays, red, and ochers.   The receding wall surfaces adapt their hue from the wall of the bamboo thicket, the hanging wisteria vines, the streaming sunlight of the glade, the pine bough, and the interlacing branches of the maple.   The ceiling colors recall the airiness of the sky and range from deep cerulean blue or aqueous greens to misty cloud whites or soft grays.   The author has found that this tested theory of nature adaptation applies as well to the use of materials, textures, and forms.

There are, of course, many other theories and systems of color application.   One would keep the volumetric enclosure neutral, in shades of gray, white, or black, and let the objects or persons within the space thus "glow" with their own subtle or vivid colors.   Another calls for infusing a space or coloring a form with those hues and values that, alone or in combination, produce a prescribed intellectual-emotional response.   Given a basic color theme or melody, it modulates harmonious overtones to soothe, contrasting ones to give interest and emphasis.   Another system manipulates spaces and objects within those spaces by the studied application of recessive and dominant values and hues.

Yet another would determine for any given area or structure one appropriate color which, running through the whole, could be used as a unifying trunk.   All other colors would be, to this trunk, its branches, twigs, leaves, flowers, and fruit.   In such a scheme can be sensed a cohesive *system* of color like that of the willow, the sassafras, the mountainside, the river valley, or any other element or feature of nature.   Still another theory proposes that hues and values gain their maximum impact in combination and through carefully devised relationships.   All approaches attest to the truth that spaces or things within the spaces have meaning only as they are experienced and that, in creating fulfilling spatial experiences, the knowledgeable handling of color is essential.

Abstract spatial expression   We have learned that just as abstract design characteristics may be suggested by a given *landscape type,* so may they be suggested by a proposed *use* as well.   The spatial requirements of a cemetery, for instance, would hardly resemble those of an amusement park.   We come to the amusement park for a laugh, for a shock, for a change, for relief and escape from ordered routine.   We want to be fooled, and we delight in confusion and

Beauty may be called "eternal" only when the form—whether in the Gothic cathedral, the Doric temple, or the Ise Shrine and the Palace of Katsura—has fulfilled to its utmost the demands made upon it by the environment and culture of the country: in short, when it is a successful realization of the entirety of things.   Eternal beauty no longer means today what it did only a short time ago. It does not mean an admonition to imitate outer appearance, or to copy with more or less virtuosity, but to take the spirit of beautiful works as a model, and to bring present conditions to the clearest and most perfect form, as was done in them.

Bruno Taut

Every field of design today—architecture, industrial, graphic, landscape and urban— operates on the common basic premise of functionalism; i.e., that the ultimate form of the object designated must flow from an objective analysis of its function.

James Fitch

Blue and green are the colors of the heavens, the sea, the fruitful plain, the shadow of the Southern noon, the evening, the remote mountains.   They are essentially atmospheric and not substantial colors. They are cold, they disembody, and they evoke impressions of expanse and distance and boundlessness.   Blue . . . always stands in relation to the dark, the unillumined, the unactual.   It does not press in on us, it pulls us out into the remote.   An "enchanting nothingness" Goethe calls it in his Farbenlehre.

Blue and green are transcendent, spiritual, nonsensuous colors . . . yellow and red, the classical colors, are the colors of the material, the near, the full-blooded. Red is the characteristic color of sexuality —hence it is the only color that works upon the beasts.   It matches best the phallus symbol—and therefore the statue and the Doric column—but it is pure blue that etherealizes the Madonna's mantle. This relation of the colors has established itself in every great school as a deepfelt necessity.   Violet, a red succumbing to blue, is the color of women no longer fruitful and of priests living in celibacy.

Yellow and red are the popular colors, *the colors of the crowd, of children, of women, and of savages.   Among the Venetians and the Spaniards high personages affected a splendid black or blue, with an unconscious sense of the aloofness inherent in these colors. . . .*

Oswald Spengler

The design characteristics of the successful trade fair are reminiscent of the carnival.

distorted, contorted, ridiculous shapes. We seek the spectacular, the spinning, tumbling, looping, erratic motion. We love the roller coaster's flash and roaring crescendo, the brassy clash of cymbals, the jarring sock-ring-a-ling-ting of the tambourines, the rap of the barker's hammer, and the raucous honky-tonk. We thrill to color as gaudy as greasepaint, as garish as scarlet and orange tinsel, as raffish as dyed feathers, gold sequins, and rainbow-hued glitter. We expect the scare, the boff, the flirt, the come-on, the tease, and the taunt. All is gay tumult; all is for the moment; all is happy illusion. We accept materials as cheap and as temporary as bunting and whitewashed two-by-fours. Everything is surprising, attracting, diverting, winding, expanding, contracting, arresting, amusing, tumultuous carnival atmosphere. If we want a successful amusement park, this atmosphere must be made inherent. We must create it with all the planned whoop-de-doo and spatial zis-boom-bah that we can conjure into being. This is not only desirable; it is, clearly, essential. Here, order and regimentation are wrong, and the stately avenue or the handsome mall would be in fatal error.

How different are the spatial requirements of a cemetery! Here we would expect the volumes to be serenely monumental, spacious, and beautiful. We would expect enveloping enclosure, to provide protection and imply detached seclusion. The entrance gates, like the prelude to an anthem, would give theme to the spaces within, for these are the earthly gates to paradise. We enter here in our moments of most poignant sorrow, to bury the dead in solemn ceremony, as from time's beginning.

We come in grief, seeking that which will give solace and comfort. The spatial character might well suggest peaceful quietude in terms of subtle harmonies of form and texture.

Troubled and questioning, we seek here reassurance and order. Order as a spatial quality is affected by evidence of logical progressions, visual balance, and a regular cadence of plan or sequential revelation.

Humbled and distraught by the presence of death, we would orient ourselves to some superior power. The presence of divine power may be suggested in plan form and by symbol. A sensitive variation of the classic axial treatment that so compellingly relates humans to a concept has no better application than here. There may also be breathtaking vistas and sweeping views, as long as vistas and views are in keeping with the sacred and the sublime. At those thoughtfully selected plan areas where an inspirational quality is to be concentrated or brought to culmination we might use the soaring verticals that effect an uplift of the spirit. A simple cross of white marble lifted against the clouds may evoke in the viewer an emotional response of great satisfaction and meaning.

We seek here a fitting and final resting place for those whom we have loved. In design, this concept is translated into terms of the eternal and the ideal. The eternal may be suggested by the timeless features of the landscape—the moss, the fern, the lichened rock, the sun, the grove of gnarled and venerable oaks, the gently sloping summit of a hill. Materials such as marble, granite, and bronze will be selected to endure.

Idealism may be expressed through the creation of those spaces and those high art forms that will instill the conviction that here in this sacred place the living and the dead are truly in the presence of their God.

Many will note that these spatial requirements are similar to those of a church chapel or sanctuary; and just to the extent that they are similar, will the church forms and spaces resemble architecturally their cemetery counterparts. These qualities refer to no one particular cemetery more than to any other. They are, rather, the abstract spatial qualities suggested by the function of all cemeteries.

In like manner, any such functional places and spaces we may name—the shopping center, the summer camp, the theater—will immediately bring to mind desirable spatial characteristics. These, it should be apparent, are fundamental to the design.

The elements of containment   In a large measure all spaces acquire their being and character from the elements that contain them. Because each element so used will imbue the space in some degree with its own qualities, it must be well related not only to all

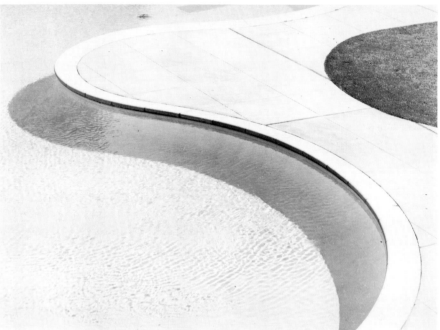

Abstract line expression is structural, solid, and strong. Commercial Place, Norfolk, Virginia.

Detail of pool edging. Abstract line expression is fluid.

other such elements but also to the essential resultant character desired for the space.

Lines, forms, colors, textures, sounds, and odors all have certain predictable impacts on the human intellectual-emotional responses. If, for example, a certain form of color *says* or *does* things to the observer, this is reason enough to employ such a form or color in the shaping of those structures, objects, or spaces that are to convey this message. Surely, if the *abstract* expression of a given line violates the proposed expression of structure, object, or space, it should be used only with studied intent. Every line evident in the form or planes has its own abstract design connotation. This must be in keeping with the intended nature of the space. There follows a graphic demonstration of variations in abstract line expression.

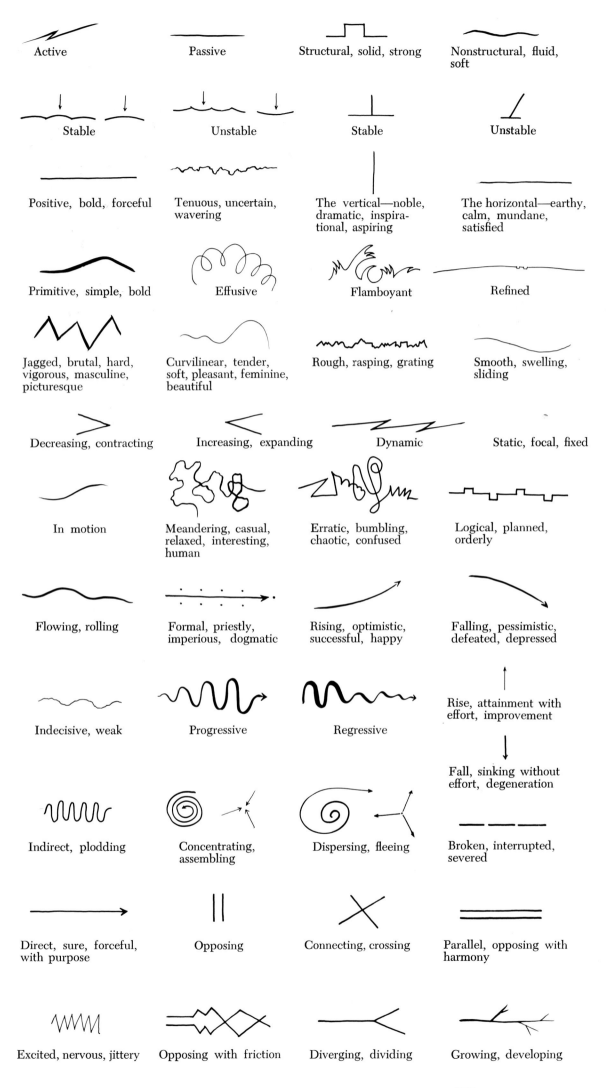

Active

Passive

Structural, solid, strong

Nonstructural, fluid, soft

Stable

Unstable

Stable

Unstable

Positive, bold, forceful

Tenuous, uncertain, wavering

The vertical—noble, dramatic, inspirational, aspiring

The horizontal—earthy, calm, mundane, satisfied

Primitive, simple, bold

Effusive

Flamboyant

Refined

Jagged, brutal, hard, vigorous, masculine, picturesque

Curvilinear, tender, soft, pleasant, feminine, beautiful

Rough, rasping, grating

Smooth, swelling, sliding

Decreasing, contracting

Increasing, expanding

Dynamic

Static, focal, fixed

In motion

Meandering, casual, relaxed, interesting, human

Erratic, bumbling, chaotic, confused

Logical, planned, orderly

Flowing, rolling

Formal, priestly, imperious, dogmatic

Rising, optimistic, successful, happy

Falling, pessimistic, defeated, depressed

Indecisive, weak

Progressive

Regressive

Rise, attainment with effort, improvement

Fall, sinking without effort, degeneration

Indirect, plodding

Concentrating, assembling

Dispersing, fleeing

Broken, interrupted, severed

Direct, sure, forceful, with purpose

Opposing

Connecting, crossing

Parallel, opposing with harmony

Excited, nervous, jittery

Opposing with friction

Diverging, dividing

Growing, developing

150 SPACES

Functions of vertical enclosure. Induced human responses vary with the type and degree of enclosure.

Complex for excitement, diversion, curiosity, surprise, induced movement.

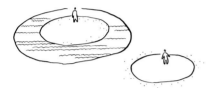

Enclosure may be effectively *implied* by strong demarcation of the base plane.

Simple enclosure for concentration on idea, form, and detail.

Confined for relaxation and induced repose.

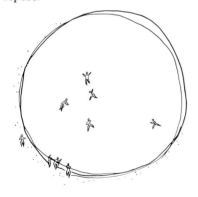

Open and free for induced action and exuberance.

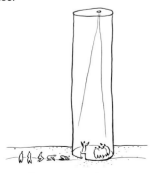

Volumes may be contrived to impart specific predetermined emotional and intellectual impacts.

Space unlimited.

An outdoor volume on a grand scale, delimited on the ground plane by rolling wooded pastureland, on the vertical plane by mountain slopes, and overhead by lowering clouds.

Definition of volumes   The orientals have long understood that to have significant spaces you must have definitive enclosure and that the size, shape, and character of the enclosure determine the quality of the space. Openness, void, and mere expanse are not enough; they may be only emptiness.

Outdoor volumes may be of infinite scope, limited only by the horizon, or they may be as finite as the space between two cedar fronds. In shaping outdoor volumes the designer is not as limited as in architectural or engineering construction by materials, forms, or sizes. One may employ not only the full range of fabricated materials but also all the materials of nature. A seaside volume may be formed naturally of shell-strewn beach, pounding surf, luminous sky, and a wind-battered wild sea grape. A sophisticated city park volume may be further defined by a pavement of sawed slate in pattern, clipped yew, tubbed oleanders, spun-brass fountain bowls, glazed tiles, and illuminated water.

An exterior space may be as loosely defined as one with sand for a floor, blue sky and quaking-aspen foliage overhead, and walls demarcated only by the aspen trunks and scattered junipers. Or an outdoor space may be tightly controlled by terrazzo mosaic pavement, polished marble walls, carved mahogany panels, fluted glass in burnished frames, ceramic murals in rich patterns, and gaily colored canopies of fabric. All exterior volumes, controlled or free, are formed of three volumetric elements: the *base plane,* the *overhead plane,* and the *vertical space dividers.*

An architectural volume focused upon a three-dimensional base-plane design.

The base plane

The base plane is closely related to the arrangement of use areas, for it is on this volumetric floor that we are most concerned with *use.* What we see when we look at a project *plan* is what will be laid out on the base plane. It will establish not only the kinds of use but also the plan relationship of each use to all others.

The base-plane surface is often the natural surface of the earth. With its topsoil strata, ranging from thin to deep, its soil moisture and fertility, and its cover of plants, this plane is veritably the base of all life. The wise planner will never disturb or modify the natural ground surface without reason. Any modifications made will be those that implement the proposed use while protecting the quality of the landscape.

More than two-thirds of the earth's surface is submerged in water. The balance of surface area is generally underlaid with a freshwater aquifer that fluctuates slowly in elevation and through which sometimes imperceptible currents flow. This water rises continually by capillary action, keeping the soil layers moist and the adjacent air layers cool. From this subsurface reservoir fresh water may be tapped and used as long as the local supply is not

On the base plane we are most concerned with use.

An American home rooted in the soil and rock of the earth's base plane.

depleted. Such depletion is caused not only by overuse but also, and more often, by the destruction of the natural ground covers—topsoil, duff, low plants, and trees—which would otherwise absorb precipitation and store it in the soils.

The general composition of the earth plane is mineral, ranging in hardness from granite, limestone, and shale to the clays, sands, and loams. The supporting strength and stability of the soil strata depend not only on the nature of each but also on its angle of inclination, the presence of water, and its relation to the other strata and the surface. Appearances are deceptive; deceptions are often disastrous. When the degree of support and stability are of consequence, the soil types and load-bearing capacities are to be determined by test pits or core borings.

Soils and the moisture and frost they retain are powerful eroders and corroders. From the structural point of view, extreme care must be taken in the selection of materials that are placed on or make contact with the earth. In considering outdoor spaces, we associate with the ground plane such natural construction materials as rock, gravel, and sand and such constructed materials as brick, concrete, asphalt, and ceramic tile. These seem compatible. Most other materials, including untreated wood or uncoated metals, are subject to rust and rapid decay.

It is on the base plane that we establish our trafficways. They are best aligned in compliance with the earth's natural conforma-

Topsoil conservation by the planting of windscreens.

Topsoil conservation by contour plowing.

A highway planned to flow in harmony with the natural conformation of this beautiful valley floor.

tion. To buck the land is to incur expensive cuts and fills and require costly drainage structures. Moreover, on the disturbed surface areas a tight-knit cover must be reestablished for the sake of appearance and to preclude devastating erosion. The most stable and beautiful drives and highways of the world are those that follow the ridges and the valley floors and rise or fall across the side slopes where the cross gradient is most suitable. Perhaps such drives are pleasant because they are basically lines of dynamic force flowing in harmony with the natural forms and forces of the earth. Our friend Plato, if we could question him on this point, would nod in sage agreement.

Every object existing on the base plane has plan significance. If the object is to be preserved, its relation to other elements of the plan must be thoughtfully considered. If the object is to be moved,

Skilled handling of the base plane. Brick, redwood, gravel, and foliage suggest patterns of movement and repose.

the ease and means of moving warrant careful study. If the object is to be modified, the degree and type of modification must be analyzed.

The base plane, in a world governed by the law of gravity, gets the most use and wear. It requires the most care and maintenance. The planner must recognize, as does the caretaker, that all materials and textures applied to this plane should be selected with concern for their permanence and appearance during all phases of their projected use.

The earth plane—level, warped, sloped, or terraced—is the base for all construction. This is the plane *on* which, *in* which, and *around* which all things are placed. On this plane are established the primary plan forms of the project.

The treatment of the ground plane is important to the accomplishment of proper transitions. The shapes and patterns of the base, if well handled, may subtly or powerfully relate a structural element to the site and to all other components. Through the sensitive design treatment of the ground surface we may coordinate, accentuate, and integrate all elements placed thereon.

The art of manipulating levels is a large part of the art of townscape.
Gordon Cullen

Masterfully related to its ground plane, this superb structure reveals a studied transition from the mineral and moisture of the earth to the lightness and airiness of the sky. Note the posts on stone, the platform, the lightly framed balcony, the upcurved straw roof, and the phoenix poised on the roof cap.

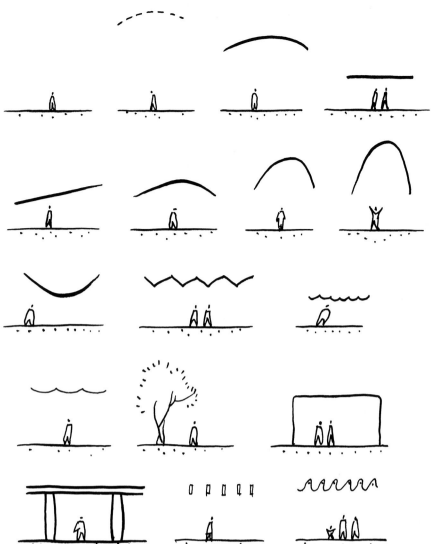

Overhead space definition

The form, height, pattern, density, solidity, translucence, reflectivity, sound absorbence, texture, color, symbolism, and degree of overhead enclosure all have a telling effect on the spatial quality.

The overhead plane

In the shaping of outdoor spaces we come to think of the overhead plane as being free, extending to the tree canopy or the sky. Seldom, if ever, have the most accomplished designers been able to devise anything as beautiful. Even the open sky, however, has its limitations. We sometimes require shelter; and further, we know that our site spaces and volumes must have height control. To realize this we need only hold one hand palm upward and the other palm downward over it, and slowly bring the two together. We can at once, by this exercise, sense the spatial importance of the overhead plane. We will remember, as children, our pleasure in crawling under a porch floor or, as adults, sitting under a low porch roof or an arbor. Even in a large open area, a suspended or supported overhead surface may provide this psychological, and perhaps physiological, function.

When open blue infinity is appropriate as a ceiling, we accept it and perhaps rack our powers of ingenuity to best feature the sky with its moving cloud forms and opalescent colors by day and its glorious show of constellations in the night. It has been said that if we were permitted to view the sky but one day and night of our life, we would count it our most memorable earthly experience.

When the sky is not suitable as a ceiling, we contrive overhead controls. The form, character, height, and extent of overhead enclosure will have a telling effect on the character of the volumes they help to define.

The new overhead plane may be as light as nylon fabric or a

A circular sunshade provides the overhead definition of this intriguing space.

Light fabric on the overhead plane.

Overhead space frame.

tracery of leaves; it may be as solid as beams, plank, or reinforced concrete. It may be perforated, pierced, or louvered. If solid, it controls not only the sun and rain but also, by its degree of translucence or limit of overhang, the amount and quality of light. To appreciate the effect of light on a given space we need consider but a few of its unlimited qualities. In color, light may be pearly, milky, amber, cobalt, lemony, aqueous, inky, sulfurous, or silvery. In intensity, it may range from pale, soft, or limpid to brilliant, blazing, dazzling, or blinding. Light has motion—as shooting, piercing, quivering, dancing, scintillating, creeping, flooding, or streaming light. It has distinctive character—as dappled, splotched, or mottled light; as subdued, harsh, or glaring light; as searching, glinting, shadowy, gleaming, or glowing light. Light has mood—as gloomy, haunting, or mysterious light; as cozy, inviting, or exciting light; as relaxing, refreshing, or cheering light. These are but a few of its qualities and effects that have design application. The solid overhead plane may serve as a shield or modifier of natural light, or it may act as a source of direct or reflected illumination.

If pierced or partially open, the overhead cover may not be in itself as important visually as are the shade and shadows it casts. We may consider such a plane as a disk, or film, or patterned screen held up between the sweeping orbit of the sun and the textured surfaces upon which its shadows fall and over which they move. Generally the spatial ceiling is kept simple because it is to be sensed more often than seen.

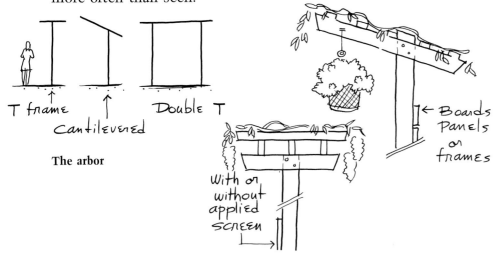

The arbor

With or without applied screen →

← Boards Panels or frames

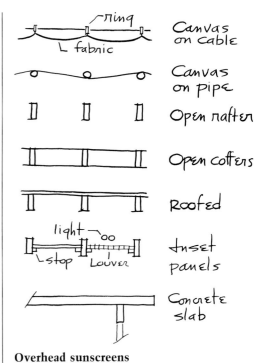

Overhead sunscreens

Canvas on cable — ring — fabric

Canvas on pipe

Open rafter

Open coffers

Roofed

Inset panels — light — stop — Louver

Concrete slab

The verticals

The vertical elements are the space dividers, screens, baffles, and backdrops. Of the three volumetric planes, the vertical is the most apparent and the easiest to control. It also has the most important function in the creation of outdoor spaces. The verticals contain and articulate the use areas and may tightly control and enclose them, as with masonry walls, or more loosely define them, as with vegetation.

By plan manipulation, the vertical elements may extend and expand the use areas to apparent infinity, by screening out the near or obtrusive features of the landscape and by revealing such receding or expansive features as the distant view, the horizon, or the limitless spaciousness of the open sky.

Enclosure for Privacy   Neither enclosure nor openness is of value in itself. The degree and quality of enclosure has meaning only in relation to the function of a given space. Enclosure is desirable when privacy is desired. The orientals have a faculty for creating their own privacy by mentally blocking out those things they find to be distracting or disturbing. They seem able to bring into sensed focus a volume suited to their pleasure or their needs. This ability enables them to enjoy a degree of privacy even in a crowded marketplace. For occidentals this is more difficult, and such privacy as we may require must usually be sought out or achieved by design.

It has been said that, in our contemporary civilization, privacy

The articulating power of the vertical. Without the upright posts, the low rock masses, or the enclosing wall of foliage, the charm of this space would be lost.

Vertical definition

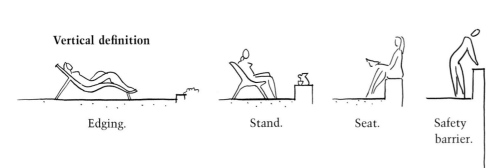

Edging.   Stand.   Seat.   Safety barrier.

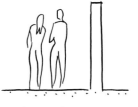

Enclosure for privacy. Wall height is determined by function.

is at once one of the most valuable and rarest of commodities. We may readily observe this lack of privacy by walking down almost any city street.

We are only now beginning to realize again the advantages of private living and working areas that are screened from the public view and focused upon the enclosed court or garden. In Egypt, Pompeii, Spain, Japan, and all mature cultures, such walled residences, palace courts, and temple grounds were, and still are, the most functional and pleasurable of all planned spaces. Privacy has

A pleasant outdoor volume that provides both shelter and privacy.

long been recognized as essential to the cultivation and appreciation of those things of highest human value.

Enclosure for privacy need not be complete. It may be achieved by no more than a strategically placed screen or by the dispersed arrangement of standing elements.

Qualities of enclosure   Vertical enclosure may be as rugged as the rocky face of a cliff or a wall of piled-up fieldstone. It may be as sophisticated as a panel of etched glass or rich ceramic mosaic. The range of form and materials is limitless. But whether the enclosure is massive or delicate, crude or refined, the essential business is to suit the enclosure to the use of the space or the use of the space to the predetermined enclosure.

Visual control   All things seen from a space are a visual function of the space. Not only the extent and nature of the enclosure but also the nature of the revealment must be in keeping with the use. Anything that can be seen from a space is visually *in* the space and must be taken into account. Often an object far removed may be introduced to the space by opening to, enframing, and focusing on the object. A far-off mountain peak or a nearby tree may thus be "brought into" a garden. The bustle and clamor of a sprawling city and its harbor may, for its interest and therapeutic value, be brought into the convalescent spaces of a military hospital grounds. A dis-

Post and rail

Three-rail   Two-rail

Painted board   Inset panel

Barbed wire   Chain link

Vertical boards.

Chestnut, cypress, or cedar poles on frame.

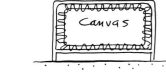

Pipe frame with canvas and grommets.

Fences

Vertical entrance court definition.

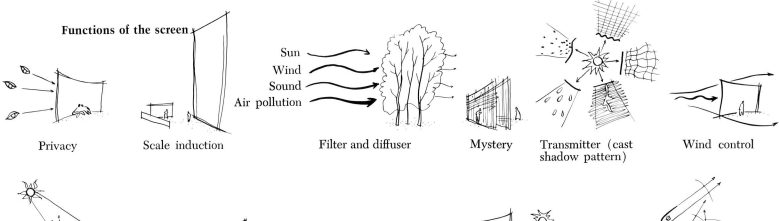

Functions of the screen

Privacy   Scale induction   Filter and diffuser   Mystery   Transmitter (cast shadow pattern)   Wind control

Sun / Wind / Sound / Air pollution

Receiver (shadow plane)   Decorative surface   Proper background   Background should not compete in interest   Sun control   Visual control

Neither size nor the seasons limit the pleasure derived from these enclosed garden spaces.

tant cathedral campanile may thus be "transported" to a churchyard, or a quiet pond to a garden terrace.

The verticals may direct attention inward or outward. Enclosure is desirable for those spaces in which an internal object is to be featured. It is evident in such cases that distractions should be eliminated and interest concentrated on the object to be viewed. It would be difficult, for instance, in viewing a piece of sculpture to appreciate those subtle nuances of light and shade that reveal the modeling of a torso if the sculpture were to be seen against a line of flapping laundry or a stream of moving traffic. Even against a vista of regal magnificence much of the loveliness of an individual rose, for instance, would be lost to the observer. The backdrop of anything to be observed in detail should rarely compete in interest. Spatial enclosure, when doubling as a backdrop, should be so devised as to bring out the highest qualities of the object seen against it.

In general, it may be stated that when interest is to be directed to an object within a given area, the elements of containment must focus attention inward. When interest is to be directed outward to object or view, the enclosure is pierced or opened to accentuate and frame that which is to hold our attention.

We must create pools of stillness, areas of entrancement; and the purpose of these is not to escape from life—even the vibrant life created by the new sources of energy that characterize our modern civilization—but to enjoy life in its profoundest essence.

Sir Herbert Read

A vertical element as the focal point of a volume. The spirit of the figure and the spirit of the space are one. Note how the heavy structuring and deep shadows of the volume give emphasis to the airy, luminous quality of the moving sky.

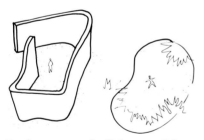

Enclosure may be light to solid.

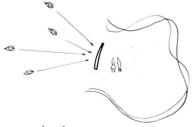

An arc of enframement may give adequate privacy.

Enclosure by dispersed plan elements.

Elements within a volume   Vertical planes not only provide containment, screen, and backdrop but often become the dominant spatial feature as well.   Other vertical elements may include furniture set about on the base plane, a specimen magnolia of striking branching habits and flower, a cool jet of rising and falling water, or a children's slide or climbing structure of welded metal tubing.   Such freestanding objects assume a sculptural quality.   In scale and form they must satisfy the hollowness of the square, enrich it, and pick up and accentuate its character.   The shape and color of freestanding objects may counterplay with the shape and color of the space, may "read" against the backdrop.   If the object is to dominate, the plane is subdued to serve as a foil.   If the spatial plane is to dominate, as in a mural or a building facade, the standing object is so placed or designed as to heighten the visual impact.

When an object is placed within a space, the object *and* enclosure may read, but often more important is the expanding, contracting, evolving relationship of the spaces between the two.   As an example, the roundness or squareness of an object may best be accentuated by placing it off-center in a variformed volume, so as to develop dynamic spatial relationships between it and the enclosing planes.

An object that of itself has complex form or intricate lines is usually best displayed in a volume of simple shape so that the spatial relationships enhance the object rather than confuse or detract.

When several objects are placed in a volume, the interacting spaces between objects, as well as between objects and the enclosing planes, are of design importance.

Structures as vertical elements   Often buildings are the dominant features within or surrounding a space.   If within, they may be treated as sculptural elements to be experienced in the round.

The vertical elements of the house are used to define, enframe, and interplay with the richly composed interior-exterior volumes.

Within or without, the space is so developed as to focalize attention on the major facades or components and to impel movement toward the entrances.

The external spaces may be designed to serve as foreground or setting, as an anteroom, or as an external building compartment. The function of the building may even be concentrated in the related space and the building itself be incidental. Such structures may serve primarily as spatial enclosers, dividers, and backdrops.

Public squares, courts, or plazas flanked by structures pose a complex problem in design, for they and the people who use them must all be in scale. Which has priority? St. Peter's clearly dominates its piazza and the assembled crowds. New York's Central Park rules as verdant queen over the edifices at her sides. The tiny town squares of Capri, Italy, and Taxco, Mexico, on the other hand, are in effect no more than charming stage sets for the lounging, dining, parading townsfolk and tourists who gather there from early sunup to the late, cool hours of the evening. People, spaces, or structures—which? There is no rule except that each, in turn and together, must be taken into full account and all relationships made pleasant through a sense of fitness.

The vertical as a point of reference   In planning an area for any purpose, except when mystery, bewilderment, or confusion might be intended, it is well to set up enough visual "guide-ons" to give orientation to the users. Often such points of reference serve also to provide the theme for their related spaces. A revolving ferris wheel, for example, draws one to, and becomes the symbol of, the amusement park. A venerable beech tree on a rise, the library campanile, or the ceremonial flagstaff of the parade ground may so "explain" and guide one through a campus, just as one is led around the golf course from green to numbered green.

Functions of enclosure

Concentration of interest.

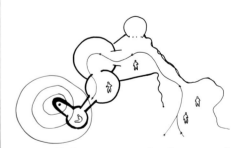

Controlled progressive development of a concept

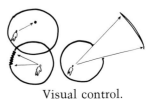

Visual control.

This village center at Reston is a favorite
gathering place.

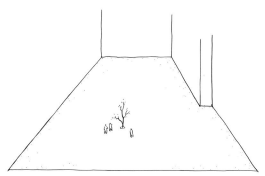

An object introduced within a large space
may impart, within the area of its
influence, its own lesser scale.

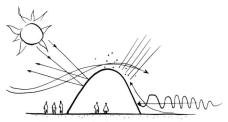

Privacy, shelter, protection.

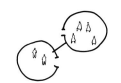

Classification of interest.

In the treatment of sizable areas, the author has discovered an intriguing planning phenomenon that has many useful applications. He has found that a freestanding vertical element or panel brought near a small use area within the larger space may have such a strong visual relationship to the user that it imparts its own scale. A great plaza, for example, may be overwhelming to a person who enters or wanders through. If, say, a small bench were to be placed within the space, the volume by contrast would seem even more overpowering. A person seated on the bench would sense only the relationship to the total plaza. If however, near the bench, we were to place a honey locust tree, a stone fountain, or a decorative screen, our intimidated friend would first sense being seated under the tree, beside the fountain, or near the screen and only incidentally would sense the dimensions of the greater volume. One would relate oneself to the scale of the introduced objects.

Within a large space many such human reference points may be placed, and, indeed, these must be furnished if pleasure is intended. (We recognize, of course, that historically the primary objective of many great public spaces has been to humble and sometimes even humiliate the crowds that mill about within them.) When awe, wonder, or humility is to be instilled by spatial impact, the human reference points are removed or distorted. When comfort and assurance are desirable, a human scale must be made evident. Generally, the steps, doorways, or windows of adjacent buildings suffice to establish a sense of scale; if not, such human reference points must be otherwise provided.

The vertical in relation to pix   In spatial design, the verticals generally have the greatest visual interest. Since, either moving about or seated within a volume, we are face to face with the verticals, we are usually more conscious of them than of either the base or the

Precise control of form, materials, light, acoustics, temperature.

Elimination of distractions.

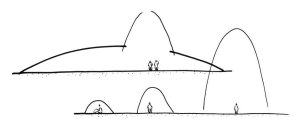

Emotional implications of varying spatial volumes.

No spatial variety—static.

Variety—dynamic.

Increased spatial variety and interest.

Form clarity lost by improper enframement.

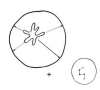

Complex form interest heightened by simple enframement.

Several objects placed in a volume relate to the enclosure not only singly but also as a group.

overhead plane. We may rightly assume, therefore, that such standing surfaces or objects present the most telling design possibilities. Features of greatest interest or refinement are normally placed or incorporated on the verticals and at eye height—*pix*. It would seem obvious that pix for a seated person is lower than pix for a person who is standing, but because this critical design factor is too often ignored, the point is emphasized.

One of the most distressing of all visual experiences is to have a vertical plane terminate at or near eye level, particularly in the case of a fence or a wall. The top of such a wall or screen seems to do violence to the eyes of those who pass or see it.

One of the most pleasant of visual treats, on the other hand, is to have the eye come comfortably to rest upon an object or plane so placed that it falls into pleasing perspective and focus. If, moreover, in the thing observed the viewer discovers subtle and fitting relationships to the space, the use, and the user, the pleasure is intensified. Such relationships may sometimes be accidental, but more often they must be consciously planned.

Verticals as articulators   Verticals reinforce and "explain" the traffic and use patterns of the base plane. Just as the gate piers of a driveway say "Enter," the sweeping curbline says "Follow me," and the entrance platform says "Come to rest and alight here," so must the verticals of any space elucidate the plan. They must attract, deflect, direct, detain, receive, and accommodate the planned use as the area demands. The plan pattern of the base plane most often sets the theme of a space, and the verticals most often modulate this theme and produce those variations that develop the rich harmonies.

Verticals as controlling elements   The verticals, providing as they do the degree and kind of spatial enclosure, are important in the control of wind, breeze, sunlight, shadow, temperature, and sound. The wind may be diverted, checked, and to a large extent eliminated. Desirable breezes may be directed to play across moist cooling surfaces or used to give motion and sound by activating flags, foliage, mobiles, or those delightful oriental divertissements, wind-flutes or wind-bells. Sunlight may be blocked, filtered, diffused, or admitted in its full glorious, healing, life-giving splendor.

Like the overhead, the verticals may serve an important function in casting shadows to wash across a paving, dapple a wall, dance, creep, flicker, tremble, stretch, blank out a space in dim coolness, or incise a bold architectural pattern onto a receiving plane.

Plant materials   Much of the earth's land surface, as it were, is subdivided into variformed volumes by trees—freestanding, in rows, in clumps, or in masses. Often proposed use areas may be sited to take advantage of spaces already tree-enframed. Again, partial tree or shrub enclosure may be supplemented by additional planting or by grading and construction. In such cases the native growth provides the ideal transition from development to the natural scene and ensures landscape continuity. If we cannot use existing trees for full or partial volume control, in most localities we may draw upon an extensive palette of plant materials that range from the wildly free to the stiffly architectonic in their native or manicured forms.

Effective enclosure   It must be remembered that the vertical space enframers are not usually seen from within the volume alone but in the round as well. They, together with the spaces they enclose, become in total a unified landscape element to be related to all other landscape features.

An axiom   Lack of effective enclosure is the key to most unsatisfactory spaces or places. We cannot stress too strongly the need for the proper type and degree of vertical definition. All good site development is marked by the organization of vertical (and overhead) planes to provide both optimum enclosure and optimum revealment. By such means, it can be seen, we must synthesize not only the microlandscape but the extensional landscape as well.

Deere & Company Administrative Center, Moline, Illinois.

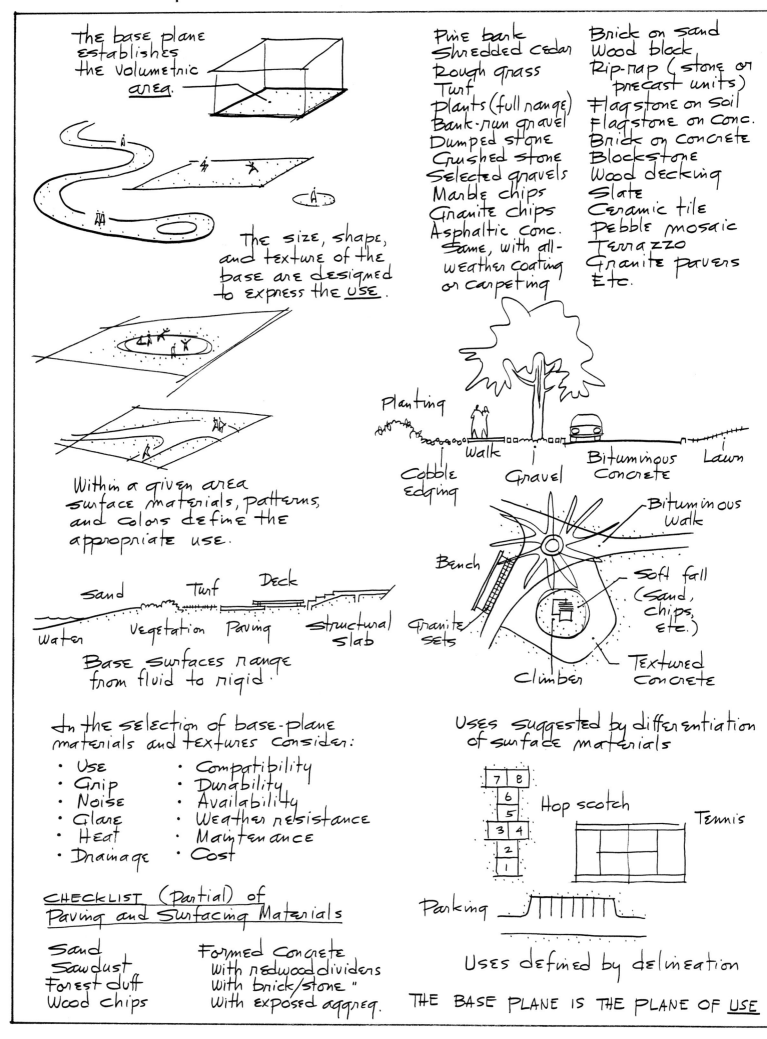

The base plane establishes the volumetric area.

The size, shape, and texture of the base are designed to express the USE.

Pine bark
Shredded cedar
Rough grass
Turf
Plants (full range)
Bank-run gravel
Dumped stone
Crushed stone
Selected gravels
Marble chips
Granite chips
Asphaltic Conc.
Same, with all-weather coating or carpeting

Brick on sand
Wood block
Rip-rap (stone or precast units)
Flagstone on soil
Flagstone on conc.
Brick on concrete
Blockstone
Wood decking
Slate
Ceramic tile
Pebble mosaic
Terrazzo
Granite pavers
Etc.

Within a given area surface materials, patterns, and colors define the appropriate use.

Planting
Walk
Cobble Edging
Gravel
Bituminous Concrete
Lawn

Sand   Turf   Deck
Water   Vegetation   Paving   Structural Slab

Base surfaces range from fluid to rigid.

Bench
Granite Sets
Climber
Bituminous Walk
Soft fall (Sand, chips, etc.)
Textured Concrete

In the selection of base-plane materials and textures consider:

- Use
- Grip
- Noise
- Glare
- Heat
- Drainage
- Compatibility
- Durability
- Availability
- Weather resistance
- Maintenance
- Cost

Uses suggested by differentiation of surface materials

7	8
6	
5	
3	4
2	
1	

Hop scotch

Tennis

CHECKLIST (Partial) of Paving and Surfacing Materials

Sand
Sawdust
Forest duff
Wood chips

Formed Concrete
with redwood dividers
with brick/stone "
with exposed aggreg.

Parking

Uses defined by delineation

THE BASE PLANE IS THE PLANE OF USE

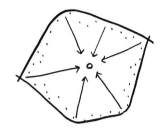

Where flows are light, absorption by lawn, planting, or mulches may be sufficient.

Where areas are drained to a central inlet, the fall is computed from the farthest points.

Walk with Positive longitudinal flow

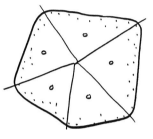

Drives, walks, and bicycle paths are often used as drainageways.

If smaller sub-area drain inlets are used, consider the patterned placement of the inlets and construction joints.

If flows are to be heavy, the paving is made concave in section.

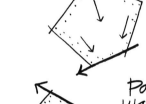

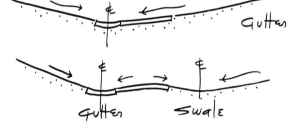

Swales

Gutter

Gutter   Swale

Paved surfaces may be warped or tilted to conduct runoff to a gutter or outfall at one or more sides.

Or better, where width permits, the paving is crowned with drainage to a swale or gutter at the side.

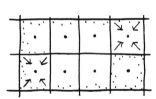

In modular areas a coffered grid can relate drainage and paving patterns.

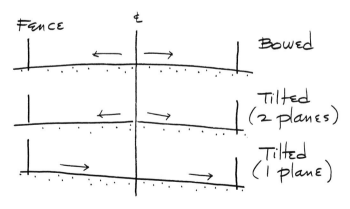

Fence   ₵

Bowed

Tilted (2 planes)

Tilted (1 plane)

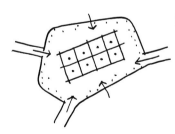

Or the geometric drainage grids can be incorporated in irregular paving shapes.

In recreation courts, as elsewhere, the drainage planes are related to the overall design.

BASE-PLANE SURFACE DRAINAGE

THE BASE PLANE

RAMPS, STEPS, AND PERRONS

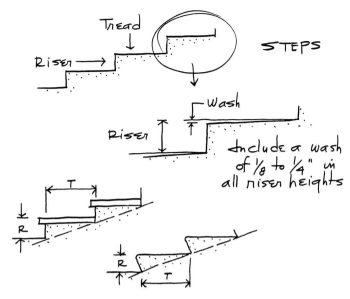

STEPS

Include a wash of 1/8 to 1/4" in all riser heights

_____ Site activities are generally associated with level planes. Except when porous, these must be tilted or shaped to provide for surface drainage.

In site usage the warped plane most often connotes passive areas or buffer zones.

Ramps, perrons, or steps are used to provide transition from level to level.

Terraces are designed to fit level use areas to sloping ground and to separate site functions.

THE BASE PLANE MAY BE LEVEL, WARPED, RAMPED, STEPPED, OR TERRACED

THE RAMP
(An inclined path or plane)

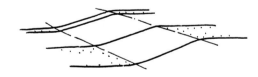

Provide a smooth transition

15% is the desirable max.
(5% is better)

As a connector of base planes, the <u>ramp</u> has several advantages over steps. A ramp is:
- Easier to ascend/descend
- Less formidable for wheeled vehicles
- More of a unifier than divider
- More economical to construct

TREAD-RISER RELATIONSHIPS

$$R + T + R = 26"$$

$$4 + 18 + 4 = 26"$$
$$4\tfrac{1}{2} + 17 + 4\tfrac{1}{2} = 26"$$
$$* \; 5 + 16 + 5 = 26"$$
$$5\tfrac{1}{2} + 15 + 5\tfrac{1}{2} = 26"$$
$$6 + 14 + 6 = 26"$$

} Normal range

$$8" + 10 + 8 = 26"$$
(Maximum, for a short, steep climb, if required)

* Preferred

As a rule of thumb, for outdoor steps in regular (architectural) flights— the sum of the heights of two risers plus the depth of the tread will equal 26 inches.

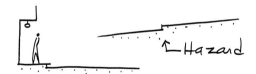

← Hazard

Never use a single riser except at a building platform.

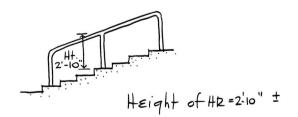

Height of HR = 2'-10" ±

In flights of 6 or more risers a handrail is recommended.

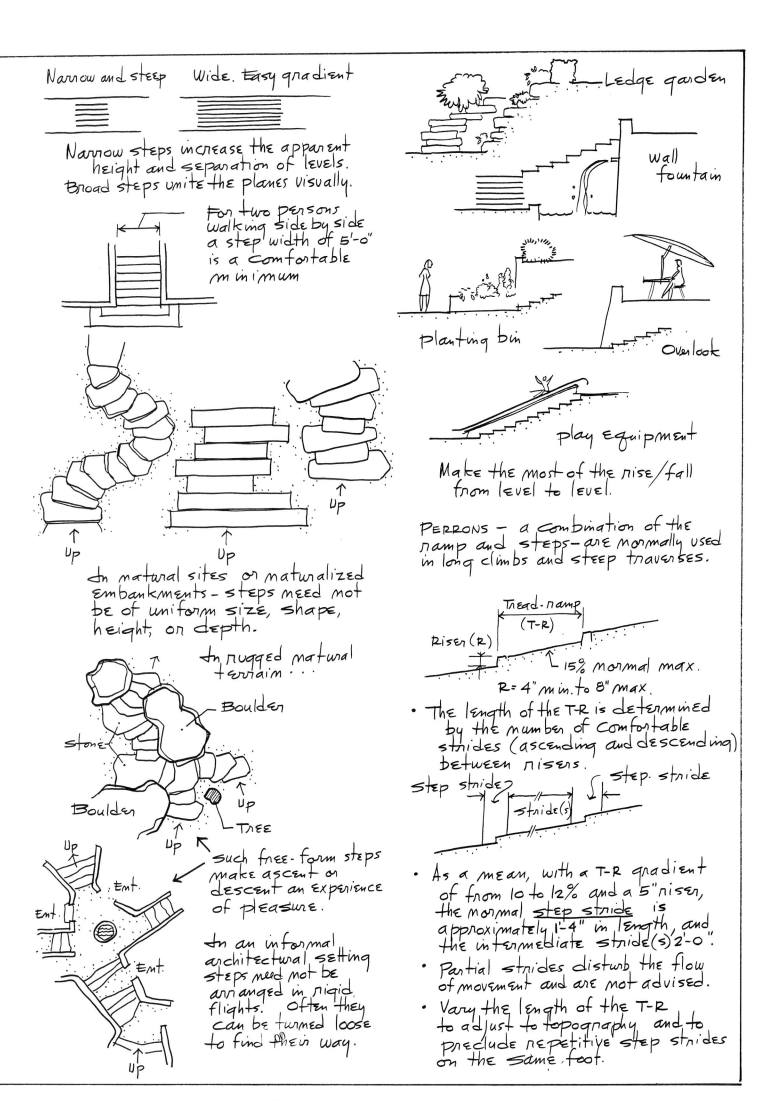

Narrow and steep   **Wide. Easy gradient**

Narrow steps increase the apparent height and separation of levels. Broad steps unite the planes visually.

For two persons walking side by side a step width of 5'-0" is a comfortable minimum

Up   Up   Up

In natural sites or naturalized embankments - steps need not be of uniform size, shape, height, or depth.

In rugged natural terraim . . .

Boulder
Stone
Boulder
Tree
Up   Up   Up

Such free-form steps make ascent or descent an experience of pleasure.

Ent.
Ent.
Ent.
Up

In an informal architectural setting steps need not be arranged in rigid flights. Often they can be turned loose to find their way.

Ledge garden

wall fountain

planting bin

Overlook

play equipment

Make the most of the rise/fall from level to level.

PERRONS - a combination of the ramp and steps - are normally used in long climbs and steep traverses.

Tread-ramp (T-R)
Riser (R)
15% normal max.
R = 4" min. to 8" max.

- The length of the T-R is determined by the number of comfortable strides (ascending and descending) between risers.

step stride   step. stride
stride(s)

- As a mean, with a T-R gradient of from 10 to 12% and a 5" riser, the normal <u>step stride</u> is approximately 1'-4" in length, and the intermediate stride(s) 2'-0".

- Partial strides disturb the flow of movement and are not advised.

- Vary the length of the T-R to adjust to topography and to preclude repetitive step strides on the same foot.

THE VERTICALS

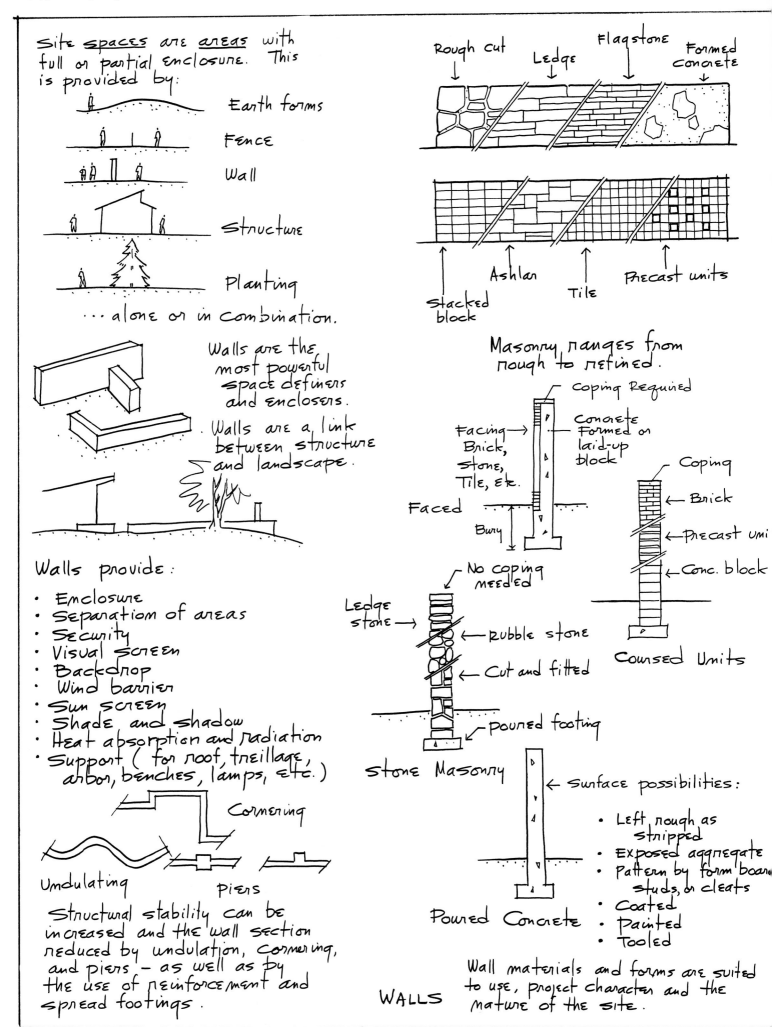

Site __spaces__ are __areas__ with full or partial enclosure. This is provided by:

Earth forms

Fence

Wall

Structure

Planting

...alone or in combination.

Walls are the most powerful space definers and enclosers.

Walls are a link between structure and landscape.

Walls provide:

- Enclosure
- Separation of areas
- Security
- Visual screen
- Backdrop
- Wind barrier
- Sun screen
- Shade and shadow
- Heat absorption and radiation
- Support (for roof, treillage, arbor, benches, lamps, etc.)

Cornering

Undulating   Piers

Structural stability can be increased and the wall section reduced by undulation, cornering, and piers — as well as by the use of reinforcement and spread footings.

Rough cut   Ledge   Flagstone   Formed Concrete

Stacked block   Ashlar   Tile   Precast units

Masonry ranges from rough to refined.

Coping Required

Facing → Brick, Stone, Tile, etc.

Concrete Formed or laid-up block

Faced

Bury

Coping

Brick

Precast unit

Conc. block

Coursed Units

No coping needed

Ledge stone →

Rubble stone

Cut and fitted

Poured footing

Stone Masonry

← Surface possibilities:

- Left rough as stripped
- Exposed aggregate
- Pattern by form board studs, or cleats
- Coated
- Painted
- Tooled

Poured Concrete

Wall materials and forms are suited to use, project character and the nature of the site.

WALLS

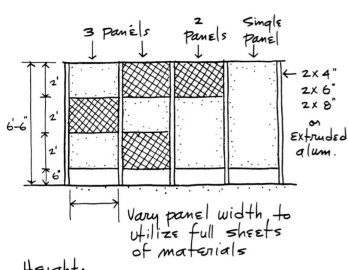

3 Panels   2 Panels   Single Panel

← 2×4"
2×6"
2×8"
or
Extruded alum.

6'-6"   2' 2' 2' 6"

Vary panel width to utilize full sheets of materials

Height:
6'-6"± → Privacy while standing
4'-6"± → Privacy while seated
2'-6"± → Low border edging

SPACE DIVIDERS

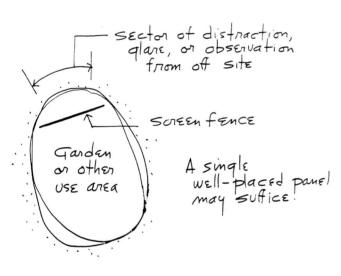

Sector of distraction, glare, or observation from off site

SCREEN FENCE

Garden or other use area

A single well-placed panel may suffice!

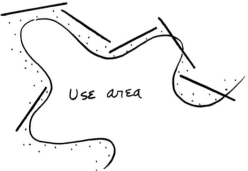

Use area

On panels may be freely grouped for visual control — while providing a pleasant backdrop and admitting the flow of air.

SCREENS

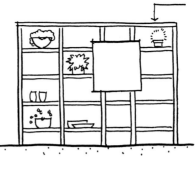

Frame of redwood or cedar. Open or with off-set panel at back and front.

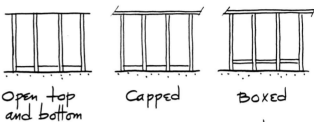

Open top and bottom   Capped   Boxed

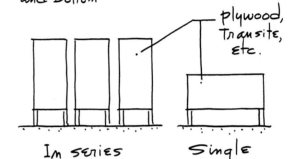

plywood, Transite, etc.

In series   Single

Panels may be linked or free-standing.

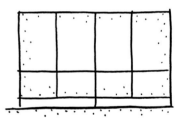

Open or closed

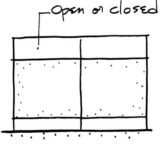

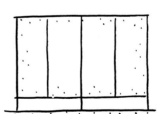

Use materials of standard dimensions

The basic frame of wood, pipe, or channel — to receive applied or inset:

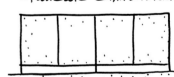

- Stained planking
- Boards and battens
- Painted boards (vert. or horizontal)
- Chestnut poles
- Grape stakes
- Rods
- Woven nylon cord

- Plywood panels
- Glass
- Aluminum mesh
- Transite
- Coated chain link
- Canvas
  Etc.

8

Visible landscape

The view

A view is a scene observed from a given vantage point. Often an outstanding view is reason enough for the selection of a property. Once the site has been attained, however, the view is seldom used to full advantage. Indeed, the proper treatment of a view is one of the least understood of all the planning arts. A view must be analyzed and composed with keenly perceptive artistry to utilize even a fraction of the full dramatic potential. Like other landscape features, the view by its handling may be preserved, neutralized, modified, or accentuated. But before we attempt to deal with the view, we must learn more of its nature.

A view is a picture to be framed, an evolving panorama of many blending facets.

A view is a theme. Its proper realization resembles the musical creation of variations on a theme.

A view is a constantly changing mood conveyed by association, light, and color.

A view is a limit of visual space. It transcends the boundaries of the site. It has directional pull. It may evoke a feeling of soaring freedom.

A view is a backdrop. It may serve as the wall of a garden or as a mural in a room.

A view is the setting for architecture.

Suitability as a factor   To be enjoyed, a view must be related to people and to those areas and spaces used by them. We must be sure, however, that the use and the view are compatible. A scene of

A view as a garden wall.

great activity or excitement, for instance, should hardly be introduced visually into an area of quiet repose. How could the pupil concentrate in a classroom facing a ball park or a river lock with its whistles, bells, shouting gatekeepers, and straining tugs and tows? Or how, cajoled by such a view, could the artist keep eyes on drawing or the librarian thoughts on card files? Again a scene of gentle pastoral tranquillity may negate the effectiveness of a space designed to exhort combatants to bold action or inspire one to lofty thought. For such a purpose, the view should be lofty and awe-inspiring, vast and grand, or there should be no view at all. The invigorating qualities of a rocky chasm scene with craggy fir and the thunderous roar of rushing, tumbling water might destroy the serenity or passive atmosphere intended for an introspective space. A dynamic industrial scene of belching smoke, leaping flame, and switching freight cars has its design applications and its limitations, too. Even a sweeping night scene of a sprawling river city with its jewel-like constellations and patterns of light, its cubes and prisms of shadow and illuminated surface, its luminous vapors of smoke and steam, its crawling, beetlelike traffic glows, its arching river wakes and shooting beams, its trembling cloud reflections—even such a wondrous view as this may be unsuited to a number of use areas, while for many others it would clearly be ideal.

Design treatment of a view A view has landscape character. This will of course determine those areas or functions with which it should be combined. If the view is a dominant landscape feature, the related use areas and spaces should be developed in harmony with the view as it exists or as it may be treated.

A view need not be seen full front or be approached from a fixed direction. It is a panorama or a segment of a panorama to be seen from any or all angles. It may be viewed on the oblique, on the sweep, or broadside.

A view is an impeller. A powerful magnet, it will draw one far, and from one position to another, for the opportunity of better commanding its limits or of seeing some part in a new and intriguing way. The skilled planner will let a view develop as the viewer

A view is a theme that may suggest and give added meaning to well-related functions.

The best view is not always or often the full view.

A view is usually better if enframed or seen through an appropriate screen.

moves across it, just as a mountain climber experiences more and more of a view in the ascent until it is seen in total.

A view may be subdivided. It may be appreciated facet by facet, with each bit treated as a separate picture and so displayed as to best capture its special qualities. By design, a view may be deftly modulated as one moves from area to area. Each area will, by direc-

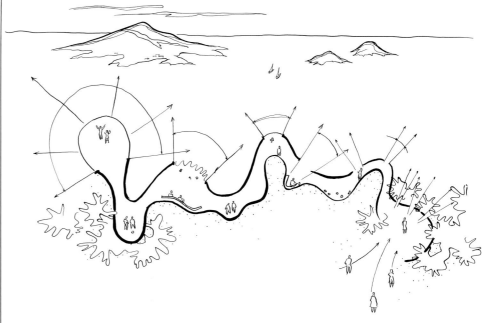

The modulation of a view. From a glimpse through loose foliage, to enframing slot, to wider sector, to reverse interest, to vista, to object seen against the view, to reverse interest, to objects placed against the view seen through a film of fabric, to concentration in a cavelike recess, to full, exuberant sweep.

tion, foreground, or framing or by the function of the space, relate one to some new aspect of the scene until, at last, it is fully revealed.

A view gains in effectiveness when certain plan areas are developed as a counterpoint or foil. If we stand for long at one vantage point comprehending a view in its entirety, it begins to lose its first fresh appeal and strikes the senses with less impact. The interest of the open view may be sustained and much accentuated when certain plan areas are developed in balanced opposition. Such an area might be enclosed, with a narrow slot or a constructed aperture opening on some absorbing detail of the scenery. It might be a chaste volume kept simple and severe in form and neutral in tone, so that the colorful sector of view might glow more vividly. It might be a recessive area, leading one away from the view into some cavelike interior space for contrast, so that, emerging to the expansiveness of the view, one senses an emotional response of great release and freedom. A designed space may incorporate some feature subtly or powerfully related to the view: a ship relic related to a

If the view is to serve as a backdrop, the object placed against it must be in character, and it must be dominant.

view of the ocean; black hammered iron to a spectacle of blazing furnaces; a fruit bowl to an orchard view; a trout etching to a scene of splashing brook; a drawing of fox, grouse, or wild turkey or hunting accoutrements to a panorama of rolling game land; or a candle to a distant cathedral spire.

Some areas, to give respite, might best be planned without apparent relationship. For a heady view, like a heady drink, should be absorbed slowly and in moderation.

Light or incongruous detail placed against a view may result in split interest and annoyance.

Split interest is a hazard in the treatment of a view. Light detail placed in front of a scene is usually lost or distracting—an element of annoyance. If the broad view is used as a backdrop, the object or objects placed before it must, singly or as a compositional group, either recede or dominate.

The power of suggestion   If a view or an object in the landscape is by design *suggested* only, the mind will multiply the possibilities of perception and thus expand the scope and richness of the suggested experience. The silhouette or shadow of a pine branch seen through a translucent panel or screen or projected upon it is often more effective than a direct view of the branch itself. The dim outline of an abstract form seen at a distance or in half-light is thus often of more interest than the same form seen fully and in detail. And so it is with the view.

It has long been the belief of the Zen Buddhists, writes Kakuzo Okakura in *A Book of Tea,* that "true beauty could be discovered only by one who mentally completed the incomplete. It was this love of the abstract that led the Zen to prefer black and white sketches to the elaborately colored paintings of the classic Buddhist School."

Concealment and revealment   A view should be totally revealed for fullest impact only from that position in the plan where this is most appropriate. It is not to be wasted in one first blast but conserved and displayed with perhaps more refinement, though certainly with no less feeling for suspense and timing, than shown by the striptease artist.

It has been told that, near the village of Tomo in Japan, a celebrated tea master planning to build a teahouse purchased, after much deliberation, a parcel of land with a startlingly beautiful view of the idyllic Inland Sea. His friends were most curious to learn how this great artist would exhibit his scenic prize, but during the time of construction they were, of course, too polite to investigate and waited to be invited.

On the day when the first guests arrived at the entrance gate, they could hardly contain their eagerness to see the fabulous ocean view as it must be so eloquently displayed. As they moved along the narrow stone pathway toward the teahouse, they were aware that the sea was teasingly hidden from sight by the alignment of the path through thin bamboo clumps. At the door of the teahouse, they reasoned, the view would be opened to them in some highly sensitive enframement. They were more than a little perplexed at finding the view there to be effectively *concealed* by a shoulder of lichened rock and a panel of woven straw fencing. As is the custom before entering a teahouse, they paused and bent over a stone basin brimming with water, to rinse their hands. As they raised their eyes from this bowed position they caught a glimpse, no more than a glimpse, between the great rock and a low, dark branch of ancient pine, of the shining sea below them. And as they looked, they sensed with tingling comprehension the relationship of the mother sea and the cool water at their fingertips.

Inside on the mats of the teahouse with the paper screens closed around them they performed the simple ritual of the tea ceremony, still mindful of the lesson of the sea. Relaxed and refreshed at the ceremony's conclusion, the guests were half surprised when their host rose quietly to slide back the screen walls of one side of the room, revealing in its perfect completeness the overwhelming beauty of a seascape that stretched from the edge of the grass floor mats to the farthest distant limits of the sky.

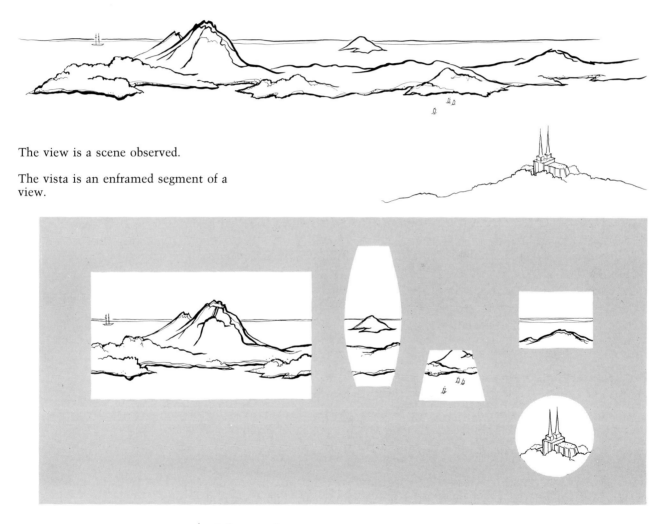

The view is a scene observed.

The vista is an enframed segment of a view.

The vista

A vista is a confined view, usually directed toward a terminal or dominant feature. It may be a natural vista, as an allée opened through a grove of Japanese maples to give a view of Fujiyama; or it may be architectural, as the majestic vista from the Palace of Versailles toward the lavish Neptune Fountain.

A vista, unlike most views, may be created in its entirety and is therefore subject to precise control. Each vista has, in simplest terms, a viewing station, an object or objects to be seen, and an intermediate ground. The three together should make a satisfactory visual unit and are usually conceived as an entity. If one or more of the elements already exist and are allowed to remain, then the others must, of course, be designed in conformity.

Again, vista and allied use areas must be compatible. If the vista is planned as an extension of a use area or space, the relationships of character and scale are important. For example, from the boardroom of a powerful bank the vista, if there is to be one, should hardly terminate at the roller coaster of an amusement park or the gates of the state penitentiary. Commanded by such a rarefied viewing box of marble, gilt, and paneled rosewood, the vista and its terminus should be equally impressive and richly conservative. The vista toward a national monument should hardly commence at a service station, drugstore, or factory. It might well be observed from another monument, a civic building, or a public gathering space. It is fundamental to the fine vista that the end justifies the beginning and the beginning justifies the end. And just as the beginning and the terminus of a vista are related in character, so must the middle ground and enframement of either be related to both.

The terminus   The terminal feature on which the vista is focused sets the theme to be developed. All other elements must fall into cadence, support the theme in harmony and counterpoint, and carry the work to a final satisfying crescendo. There is no room for discord, the superfluous, or the inappropriate. A well-conceived vista has the balance, rhythm, and polish of a symphony or perhaps of a string quartet.

For vistas are not always grandiose in scale, not even those that are most memorable. The world is, in fact, laced and interlaced with beautiful vistas and with vistas within vistas, some no longer than the length of one's arm. And these are often the more delightful ones, not necessarily consciously designed but always the right thing seen from the right place with just the right enframement.

If it is planned that the terminal feature shall also become a viewing station, then the reverse vista should provide a new and rewarding visual experience as well. A terminal feature may serve as a focal point for several vistas. The vistas need not, of course, be identical; the middle-ground treatment and enframement might well vary. If the same focal point is to be viewed from stations of varying character, each vista will of necessity vary also, since it is in essence a progressive visual transition from point to point.

A terminal feature may be seen in full or in part. It might be that a feature selected as a focal point is too large in mass or plan area for the suitable termination of the vista proposed. Some portion of the feature might in such a case be enframed because of its more suitable quality or scale. It is essential only that either the entire terminal feature *or a visually satisfying component* be brought into proper perspective.

Enframement   A vista has three planes of enframement, all of which are usually best kept simple in form, texture, and color. The vertical planes may be natural or architectural—as loose as unclipped foliage or as solid as masonry. The base plane or planes may be sloping, level, or terraced; they may be of turf, water, paving, or other surfacing. Often the overhead plane is open, or it may be lightly defined by the foliage arch provided by overhanging trees, or it may be roofed. By the manipulation of overhead planes at the viewing stations or elsewhere, we may exercise control over the quality and scale of the vista. In all cases distraction caused by

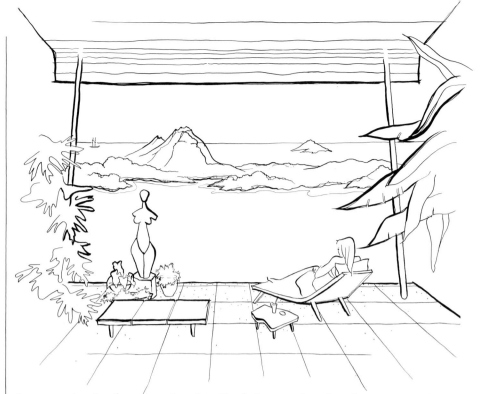

Enframement and vista must be compatible.

interest in the form or the detail of the overhead enframement is to be precluded.

A monumental vista, particularly, is often reflected in a water panel. If so, the water basin must reflect from the viewing station or stations a visually pleasant unit of the terminal feature. "Of course," we say, "of course."

In this regard, the author recalls a shattering experience during a visit to our national capital. Wishing to view the Washington Monument across the full sweep of the Mall, he assumed that the handsomest vista would be enjoyed from the raised entrance platform of the Lincoln Memorial. As he mounted the grand stairway to the monument and the impressive seated figure of Lincoln, he was astonished to find the line of the top step rising higher and higher in perspective on the figure of Lincoln until it cut him off at his chin. Here was an unbelievable error in sight-line design, a technique long ago perfected by the Egyptians and the Greeks. Flushed with embarrassment for the planner of this stairway, the author at last gained the main platform and turned to look back across the grand Mall to the towering shaft of marble at its far terminus. Surely, from here the viewing platform, reflecting panels, and shaft must have been coordinated into such a flawless vista as would be a marvel of civic art. Panels must have been thoughtfully shaped in materials and proportion to mirror the monumental image and hold it perfectly enframed in the long rectangle of water against the moving reflections of the background sky. But the image of the imposing shaft hardly reached the basin! From the platform at the base of the stairs the effect was equally disastrous. Crossing the avenue to the viewing stage at the basin's end, the author found the reflected image of the monument to be no more than an abortive stub projecting foolishly onto the far half of the panel's water surface. Nowhere along the Mall's entire length could viewer, panel, and terminus, let alone enframement, be brought into satisfying relationship. Shades of Le Nôtre, Amon-Ra, and wise old Pericles!

Progressive realization The terminal feature may be displayed in progressive stages. If a vista can be seen from several stations along the approaches, the section seen from each station is to be treated separately. Sometimes a terminus may be viewed along an entire approach. In such a case, it should be so revealed by its evolving spatial containment as to exact the full potential of its changing perspectives. If the approach is long, the vista becomes tiring and should be divided into segments by changing the level, by expanding or contracting the frame of reference, or by altering the character of the spaces through which and from which it is seen. Often, in moving toward a distant focal point, one can at first discern no more than the outline of the terminal feature. As one continues, the feature reveals itself progressively: the component masses, the sub-components, and finally the details.

Any vista may be satisfyingly staged in an infinite number of ways. It is only necessary that, from all viewing stations or lines of approach, there be developed a pleasing visual entity.

A vista may induce motion or repose. Some vistas are static, to be enjoyed from one fixed viewing station, and are seen in their completeness from this point. Others, by the interest of their unfolding revelation or by the attraction of the terminus, draw one from point to point. All vistas subject the observer to a compelling *line* of sight. A vista is insistent, a directional attraction to the eye. As such, a vista is a function of the *axis*.

The axis

Essentially, the axis is a linear plan element connecting two or more points. In use it may be a court, a mall, or a drill field. It may be a path, a drive, a city street, or a monumental parkway. Always it is to be regarded as an element of connection.

In land planning, the axis has important applications. It has limitations also, for once an axis has been introduced, it generally becomes the dominant landscape feature. Established in a plan complex, it becomes so insistent that all other elements must be related to it directly or tacitly. Any area or structure impinging upon the axis, adjacent to the axis, or leading toward the axis must draw much of its use, form, and character from this relationship. Any planned experience of view or movement from a peripheral point of origin toward the axis must be regarded as an experience of transition, culminating at the area of juncture.

In the garden of Versailles, for example, when we wander through the shady groves and diverting spaces far to the side of the axial canal, we are always aware that the canal is there and somehow subconsciously adjust to this relationship. We sense that a certain path, for instance, leads *away* from the canal, and thus we expect it to relax its discipline of form and finish and dwindle into gradual rustication. Should the same path moving *toward* the great canal grow thin and less well defined, we would be perturbed; for we would know that just ahead we should soon be surveying the full grandeur of the great axial sweep, and we would expect the path to be preparing us for the experience. Even if surprise were intended by the planner, the relationship of path to axis would be as significant, for in such a case the planner would, by spatial manipulation, soothe viewers into a state of pleasant complacency and then suddenly, around a seemingly casual turn, confront them abruptly with the most astonishing aspect of breathtaking axial splendor.

Because it is a powerful landscape element, the axis tends to subjugate other landscape features. This can happen in more ways than one. It has been told that, in building the Palace of Versailles, King Louis XIV questioned the fact that the three approach avenues were unequally spaced on the drawings. When he was advised that the offending avenue was so aligned to miss a nearby village, Louis

The axis

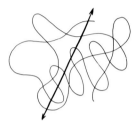

An axis imposed on a free plan area demands a new and related order.

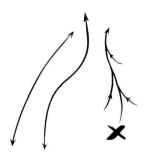

An axis may be bent or deflected but never divergent.

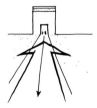

A powerful axis requires a powerful terminus.

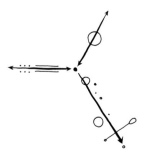

The axis is a unifying element.

replied that he failed to understand the point. The plans were revised. To preserve a perfect symmetry, one axial approach was of necessity driven through the hapless village. Demolition crews set to work, and the hamlet was neutralized.

Almost as effective would be the driving of an axis through any established landscape area. Because the existing order of things would be disrupted, a new order would have to be devised, and this in relation to the intruding axial line, for there is little of polite gentility to the axis. It is forceful; it is demanding; and, as a result, things usually go its way.

An axis is directional.

An axis is orderly.

An axis is dominating.

An axis is often monotonous.

This is not to say that the axis is always best avoided. It is only to suggest that none of these attributes are conducive to relaxation, pleasant confusion, nature appreciation, freedom of choice, or many other such experiences that we humans tend to enjoy.

Axial characteristics   From a given use area an axis is a dynamic plan line leading *out* and thus orienting the area outward. Such an area, both as a viewing point and as a source of axial movement, might well express this outward flow. How can this be accomplished? By shaping the space to induce movement outward. By constructing in effect a viewing box with its aperture well focused. By fanning the paving lines out and away or by sighting them accurately down the axial center line. By concentrating interest at the forward edge of the staging area, inducing flow to and past it. By directional forms. By use of concentric arcs circling outward, as from pebbles tossed into a pond.

Often, in an axial plan, the viewing stations and termini are interchangeable. It can be seen that the forms and lines and details that dispatch us from one station would, if we approached from the opposite direction, seem to beckon and receive us. This is fortunate, because most axial treatments allow for looking both up and down the line of sight and for moving from one end to the other and back again. We find that each transmitting area thus becomes, in turn, a receiving area. We may correctly conclude that when viewing points and terminal features are interchangeable, each must express the characteristics of the source as well as the terminus of axial view and movement.

An axis, being a line of *movement* and *use* as well as vision, must satisfy all three functions. The axis, like the vista it creates, combines primary, intermediate, and terminal spaces in the same volume. It would seem only reasonable that all three need to be planned as integral parts of the whole. If the axial plan area is intended as a boulevard, it should, from start to finish, look like a boulevard and function as a boulevard. Every building at its flanks should "belong" to the boulevard. Every space projected or leading into its central volume should partake of the boulevard character.

Much lyrical praise has been heaped upon that prototype of all grand boulevards, the Champs Élysées of Paris. Much criticism has also been leveled at its social and economic impact on the city at the time of its construction. But, for the moment, let us dismiss from our minds such weighty implications and let ourselves rise up in our imagination until we can gaze down upon the whole stirring expanse of this magnificent axis.

Below us we see the grand Étoile, a wide traffic circle with forcefully radiating streets that disappear in the distance. The circle is massively defined by the stately trees and severe gray buildings at its sides. Its glistening pavement of clipped granite blocks is precise in pattern. The whole martial space has about it a stiffly proud and solemn air, as well it might, for there at its center looms the Arc de Triomphe, and at the arch's wreath-lined base the Tomb

The Arc de Triomphe on the Étoile, at the head of the Champs Élysées.

of the Unknown Soldier, with its eternally glowing flame of tribute. The Étoile is a volume remarkably suited to its uses. A focal point, the arch is seen fittingly framed for miles in all directions. The circle is a marshaling space and point of generation, for, as well as being the powerful terminus, the Étoile is also the head of the Champs Élysées, and its archway commandingly rallies attention to the start of the wide boulevard.

The axial boulevard marches on, out to the east, still crisply military, progressing firmly in measured cadence of structures and trees until, almost imperceptibly, we note less of a military and more of a regal character, less of the coldly regimented, more of the ornately monumental; for now we approach the palace group. Here the royal Grand and Petit palaces flank the Esplanade des Invalides as it moves in grandeur across the Seine to join the boulevard. The transition is from palatial to civic as we continue along the Champs Élysées to the Place de la Concorde, with its pretentious ministries and secretariats.

In our journey eastward from the Étoile we have passed resplendent apartments with silver entablatures, elite shops with high velvet curtains, proud restaurants with glittering chandeliers, and, finally, small cafés with their trim green awnings and crowded sidewalk tables, between which bustle the white-aproned garçons with trays poised lightly on fingertips. Here the boulevard takes on a lively air. Colors are gay, spirits are light, the smile is quick, and the heart is glad on the boulevard in Paris.

Beyond the ordered spaces of the Place de la Concorde we come to the Tuileries, the magnificent public gardens and park. At the garden's end, and handsomely framed, we behold the Palace of the Louvre, with its warm stone walls and richly ornamented gables and turrets. Fronting the majestic Louvre we see the espaliered allées of sycamore, the gardens rolling with color, the screeching

The good life is not a matter of good gimmicks or of physical ease; it is a matter of things that uplift the spirit. High averages will not define it. The Arch of the Etoile and the tree-lined streets that come to it and depart are more important to the good life of the poorest Parisian than a tenth of one per cent improvement in his substandard dwelling. I mean this rejection of the high average to apply to all elements of the good life—to the poetic life, to the political life, to the visual life, to the spiritual life. It is a life which occasionally though not too often must reach to ecstasy. Not too often because ecstasy can not be prolonged, as the readers of Dante's Paradisio can discover. But a life without these high points is not the good life.

John Ely Burchard

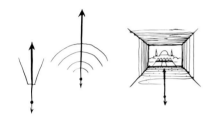

Terminus as a generator of axial movement.

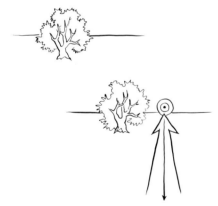

Often objects adjacent to a strong axis suffer in the relationship.

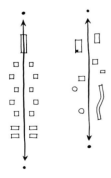

An axis may be symmetrical. But usually it is not.

traffic, trim nursemaids, perambulators, barking dogs and dodging children, the white-bearded, pink-cheeked old men in blue berets drowsing on benches in the sun, the well-scrubbed jaunty sailors and their *belles jeunes filles*. All that is in this whole exuberant space belongs to it—is of its very essence.

And where along the length of this great axis do we find the discrepancies in plan, the discordant notes? Some there must be, and many perhaps, but they are lost in the captivating and ringing experience of moving down through this evolving complex of boulevard volumes, the "elysian fields," from the hushed memorial solemnity of the arch at the Étoile to the palatial, then stately governmental core, to the splendid apartments, the chic shops, the lively café district, and on through the carefree expanse of the public gardens, to the grandiose museum of fine arts. We feel ourselves to be in turn, in one brief morning's stroll, the soldier, the courtier, the statesman, the man of wealth, the gay dilettante, the poet, the lover, the relaxed, free, and happy boulevardier, the stimulated observer, and finally the distinguished connoisseur.

If planned today, this Champs Élysées would have a different mien. And so it should, for since its conception times have changed and conditions have changed, and plan concepts and forms have changed with them. The new boulevard would have less of the old despotic formality, less unbending symmetry. Retaining its hallowed monuments, it would be less monumental. It would open out and free the teeming residential districts at its sides. It would be less of the classifier and more of the synthesizer. It would be more flexible and allow more flexibility. It would take its form from an empathetic understanding of individual Parisians and their emerging culture. It would express their new freedom, new ideas, new techniques, and new aspirations. But let those who will change the present Champs Élysées first study it long and thoughtfully because, in light of the times and the society for which it was built and of its masterful handling of forms and space, there is no boulevard of its equal.

An axis has sometimes a negative, sometimes a positive effect on landscape elements within its field of influence. We have said that areas and objects adjacent to an axis are perforce related to it. Sometimes they suffer from the relationship, because interest is less in the things themselves than in the thing-axis relationship. A fine sugar maple, for example, if standing alone, is observed in terms of trunk and limbing structure, twigging, burgeoning foliage, sunlight and shadow patterns, and the beauty of its broad outline and delicate detail. If related to an insistent axis, however, the same tree is noticed primarily in that context. The subtle, the natural, and the unique are lost to the axial line.

Sometimes, however, by the fact of their relationship, axial elements may gain in interest and value. If as units they are dull, in pattern they may be striking. If by position they are inconspicuous, by axial frame of reference they may gain in significance.

The axis as a unifying element A terminal or intermediate station of one axis may function also as the terminal or intermediate station of another. Thus two or more plan areas may be focalized on a common point. Washington, D.C., whose plan diagram exemplifies this principle, has thereby developed one of the most cohesive metropolitan plans yet devised. Its long, radial, tree-lined avenues, converging on park, circle, structure, or monument, enframe handsome vistas and bind the city's complex, extensive, and heterogeneous parts into coherent unity. If we distinguish in the plan arrangement the outline of monumentality, this seems preeminently fitting. Historically, in planning terms monumentality has been the *only* means of glorifying a concept. Certainly Washington, by monumental plan, spaces, and architecture as well as by sculpture, murals, and the enriching contributions of all the visual arts, should epitomize the glorious idea of democratic freedom.

An aerial view of Washington, D.C. The imposition of radial axes upon a rectilinear street pattern creates many awkward slices and undesirable properties. The freer urban street and land patterns of the future will eliminate this difficulty. Yet in our future urban planning we would do well to learn from Washington its lesson of the radial axis to organize and unify a vast and sprawling city.

Additional characteristics   A powerful axis requires a fitting terminus. Conversely, powerful design features are often, in the abstract, of such form or character as to require an axial approach. Such features are those best seen head on.

Or those seen on the oblique from a fixed direction

Or those best situated at the hub of converging plan lines

Or those to be revealed in stages along a given line of approach

Or those requiring controlled enframement and established viewing points

Or those that gain through a direct relationship to other lineal plan elements

The axis presents the most imposing approach to a structure or other plan feature. The key word in this axiom is *imposing,* for the axis imposes a discipline upon spaces and forms as well as upon the viewer. The movement, attention, and interest of the viewer are imposed upon by axial composition and induced to alignment with the direction of its strong polarizing forces. An impressive, dogmatic design form, the axis expresses the supremacy of the human will over nature. It denotes authority, the military, the civic, the religious, the imperial, the classic, and the monumental.

To understand the significance of the axis when properly applied, we may well look to the ancient city of Peking, the northern capital of the khans. Kublai Khan, its founder, and the great city builders who followed him understood the power of the axis as have few before or since. Centuries ago, in the building of their city, they scrupulously avoided the use of the axis in those areas where its insistent lines were unsuited. The refreshing parks, marketplaces, and winding residential streets were relaxed and free in their forms and spaces. In the whole fabulously delightful grounds of the

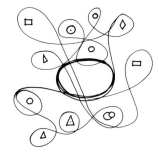

A small exhibit area may function well without a major vista or axis. Such a scheme permits a crowd to filter freely through the entire complex. In this case a powerful focal center is mandatory.

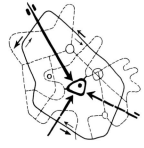

A diagrammatic and workable circulation plan for a large-scale exhibition area has the following features: main entrance, secondary entrances, major vista, minor vistas, strong focal point, major circulation loop, minor paths, and secondary focal areas and reference points for easy orientation.

Major and minor vistas need not be perpendicular.

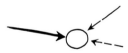

The terminus of a vista may be a space as well as an object.

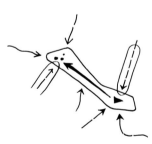

A major or a minor vista may be a function of an *area* or a *volume* as well as of a *line* of approach.

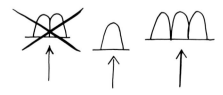

When the axis terminates in a structure that is to be entered, one or three openings are better than two since they provide a receptive element rather than an obstruction.

Summer Palace, planned for sumptuous divertissement, there is scarcely a conscious axis to be found.

But where the imperial presence was to be made manifest or the people were to be subjected to the concept of supreme deity, omnipotence, or military might, the axis was employed with sensitive understanding, as witness the military roads that stretch in broad grandeur from the city gates to the entrance of the once golden-roofed Forbidden City of the emperor or the tree-lined axial boulevard that sweeps southward from the shrine atop Coal Hill at the north, through parks, past temple groups, through bustling city centers, to the Forbidden City's imperial gateways and on beyond through parade grounds, fields, and forests—dynamic lines of force, subjecting the whole city and countryside to the will and authority of the all-powerful emperor, who sat astride it on his royal throne of jade.

Axial planning also highlights the Temple of Heaven, which now lies in ruin on the plain to the south of the Imperial City. Here, each year at the time of the vernal equinox, the great khan rode in magnificent pomp and ceremony to welcome the coming of spring. The approach to this sublimely beautiful temple was by a wide causeway of white marble that commenced at a circular platform of noble proportions, rising in balustraded tiers. The spacious causeway, elevated above the level plain, extended to the gilded and deep-red-lacquered gates of the temple. Spaced out along the causeway sides, at regular intervals, were sockets to hold the standards of hundreds of waving banners, and between the standards were carved fire pits, in which pitch faggots were burned to illumine the long processions that moved past them in the night.

In the dark hours before the great annual event, the people of Peking flocked through the streets of their city and out through the gates toward the temple, where they massed along the wooded edges of the plain to stand in watchful, wide-eyed wonder and respect. Then, through the gates, the foot soldiers came marching, division after bristling division of the khan's seasoned warriors, in dark helmets, chain breastplates, and padded felt boots, to mass in ordered formation along the causeway flanks. The courtiers and nobles followed in dazzling array, thousands upon thousands on horseback, each noble and mount in trappings of silk, gold, costly furs, and precious gems and each proudly taking his appointed place along the white marble pavement. The high priests, with smoldering incense pots, then moved in solemn procession, chanting, fur-capped, and in silken robes and gowns of unbelievable splendor. Slowly, with vast dignity, they took their august posts on the terraced platform, commanding the length of the ceremonial causeway.

Finally, as the first faint traces of light tinged the eastern sky with pink, the khan and his mounted retinue pranced through the golden gates of the Forbidden City and out through the throngs to the head of the causeway. There, to the cadenced booming of drums and the crashing of brass and silver gongs the khan rode imperiously past the blazing fire pits, down the avenue of floating banners, on through the massed troops and kowtowing nobles, to the resplendent temple and the gleaming altar seen through its opened doors. Precisely at that hushed moment when he reached the high altar and bowed his head in grave salutation, the blazing red orb of the rising sun arched above the purple hills to the east, and every face and every eye and every thought in all Peking were focused down the length of that great axis to the sacred place where the exalted khan, their emperor, knelt to greet the spring.

Court of the Lions, Alhambra Palace, Granada, Spain.

The symmetrical plan

The use of the axis does not necessarily dictate the development of a symmetrical plan.

The elements of a symmetrical plan are the same and are in equilibrium about a central point or opposite sides of an axial line. The central point may be an object or an area, such as a fountain or the plaza that contains it.

The axis may be a line or a plane of use, such as a path, a broad avenue, or a mall. It may be a powerfully induced line of sight or movement, as through a series of imposing arches or gates, or between rows of rhythmically spaced trees or pylons, or toward an object or space of high interest. It may be a quiet vista across an open panel of turf on either side of which things appear to be equally balanced.

Symmetry may be absolute, as in the pillared and carved and polished perfection of the Alhambra's Court of the Lions. Or it may be as loose and casually implied as in the balanced order of fence rows and haycocks along a country road.

Growing things, including humans, are often symmetrical, for the seed or the cell may be by nature symmetrical, and thus also are the shapes evolved through their development or growth. But in the natural landscape *plan symmetry* is a rarity. Where observed, therefore, symmetry generally indicates an imposed system of order.

It is revealing to note that in the western world the word *symmetrical* is synonymous with *beautiful* and has the connotation of pleasant and handsome form. Perhaps this is because it

Symmetry: plan elements in equilibrium

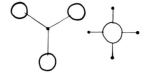

About a point or area

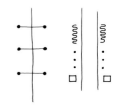

About an axis or plane

Bilateral — as the double wings of a maple seed

Trilateral — as the grappling hook

Multilateral — as the snowflake

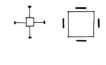

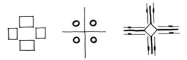

Quadrilateral — as by geometry

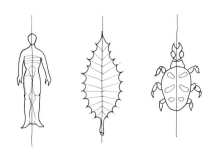

Symmetry in nature—growing objects in nature are often symmetrical because of the bilateral formation of their germ cell or seed; the natural landscape, a product of infinitely divergent forces, is rarely symmetrical.

We find from experience that the perception of repetition, sequence, and balance in landscape composition causes us an immediate pleasure, an amount of pleasure which seems insufficiently explained by the repetition, sequence, and balance of muscular motion or tendency to muscular motion involved in their perception. But we should remember that the emotions associated with repetition, sequence and balance are associated also with and often automatically expressed by repeated, sequential, or balanced muscular motions and positions of the whole body, and these in turn intensify the emotion that suggested them. The delicately balanced nervous and muscular machinery of the body is thus in a way a reverberator for the increasing of the effect of these experiences.

Henry V. Hubbard

implies an order to the scheme of things that is easily comprehended and thus enjoyed by humans. Perhaps it is because the word *symmetry* has come to be associated with plan clarity, balance, rhythm, stability, and unity, which are all positive qualities. Perhaps it is because we ourselves are symmetrical and take pleasure in the relationship.

Dynamic symmetry When, by symmetry, two opposing elements or structures are seemingly held apart, an apparent attraction and tension develop between them. The two are strongly related, to the point at which the opposing elements read as one, together with the intervening space and all that it contains.

The symmetrical plan has a quality of stability. Each pole generates its own field of force, and between these two fields is a field of dynamic tension. Each element within this field is at once in tension and in repose. By definition, every symmetrical composition must be in balance and, therefore, in repose. But the repose of symmetry is the more compelling for the fact that it bespeaks the resolution of myriad opposing forces held in equilibrium.

Each object in a symmetrical plan creates a need for fulfillment—a fulfillment that can be achieved only by its opposite number. This becomes apparent when in a symmetrical arrangement even the smallest element is removed. The equilibrium is lost at once, and the entire composition seems to strain at the gap.

When, in perceiving a plan, the eye discovers a rhythm of objects and intervals, it develops an anticipation of the next object and interval, and one is shocked if this anticipation is not satisfied. If the break in rhythm reveals only a void, one senses a plan imperfection, and the reaction is disappointment. If, however, the experience of shock coincides with the discovery of an interesting and appropriate plan feature, the reaction is that of pleasure, and the feature is thus emphasized.

The despotism of symmetry The symmetrical plan subjects plan elements to a rigid or formalized layout. Objects within a symmetrical frame of reference have meaning principally in their relation to the pattern of the whole. Each feature must always be considered, first and last, as a unit in the grand composition.

Sometimes a symmetrical plan may give added emphasis to objects. Such an object, for instance, might be featured as the terminus of a major or minor axis. Or it might be given greater importance through a progressively evolving sequence of approach or by its relationship to complimentary or complementary features. Usually, however, it may be said that the more powerful the total plan, the less potent the individual plan unit.

A symmetrical plan subjects a landscape to control. It systematizes the landscape. It organizes the landscape into rigid patterns. The natural environment is reduced to a setting or background for the plan composition. As a background it must be of suitable character and scale. By screening, enframing, or opening wide, the landscape environment may be neutralized, embraced, or modulated into views, vistas, or backdrops. But always the relationship of plan diagram, plan element, and natural landscape must be controlled—a study in harmonies. The landscape may be forced to compliance, its new symmetry achieved by extensive cutting, filling, and reshaping, or a complete new landscape may be deliberately devised.

When for any reason the eye is to be habitually directed to a single point—as to an altar, a throne, or a stage—there will be violence and distraction caused by the tendency to look aside in the recurring necessity of looking forward, if the object is not so arranged that the tensions of eye are balanced, and the center of gravity of vision lies in the point which one is obliged to keep in sight. In all such objects we therefore require bilateral symmetry.

George Santayana

Asymmetry prevails through the whole of this beautiful town on the Inland Sea, except at the central temple, where discipline, ceremony, and the implied presence of the supreme being demand symmetrical order.

A symmetrical plan subjects people to plan conformity. Not only are the landscape and all plan features subjugated to an organized plan of things, but so are we as well. We are held transfixed by a diagram of pattern. Our lines of movement are limited to the lines of the plan. The plan forms control our vision. We are consciously stirred or lulled by developing cadences, balanced repetitions, and the subjugation of all things to one concept. We are at-

The Louvre, Paris. Site and buildings are here combined in a grand plan of geometric symmetry. Such imperious and inhuman planning unfortunately characterized much of the work of the Renaissance.

tuned subconsciously, as if by hypnosis, to the rhythmic symmetrical order of things and find ourselves in all ways conforming to the order of the plan. This conformity induces a sense of harmony, but if overworked it may often produce monotony and boredom.

It can be realized, however, that symmetrical plan forms, if skillfully handled, may be used to dramatize a concept and to evoke a sense of discipline, high order, and even divine perfection.

The nature of symmetry Being precise and disciplined in plan, symmetry requires precision in detail.

Bold in concept, it demands bold forms.

The symmetrical plan becomes a structural framework, compartmentalizing site features and functions. To be successful, such an arrangement must be an expression of the logical relationship of the features or functions so grouped. The rhythmically recurring elements of a symmetrical scheme divide the plan field into units. All that occurs within the measured beat becomes in itself a unit and must be considered in all ways as a design entity. Each such unit, complete in itself, must still be related as a segment to the total plan.

Usually the symmetrical plan has a strong relationship to adjacent structures. Often it is designed to extend such structures or to relate two or more of them. Such a plan is the familiar campus quad, a sweep of greensward crisscrossed with walks, flanked by dormitories and classrooms, and perhaps featuring on its long axis the library or chapel at one end and, on the other, the administrative center. For this treatment to be effective, the buildings must be compatible with the physical expression of the symmetrical plan.

College buildings symmetrically placed on their quadrangle may express a closely knit and well-balanced community of learning. Such a grouping is better suited to buildings of classic context and to areas where a sense of established order is to be engendered.

Symmetry is unsuccessful if it obviously forces unsymmetrical functions to a symmetrical plan arrangement. This is a common error in plan organization. It is painful to discover an important function balanced against the trivial. It is pathetic to find a plan area contorted beyond workability in order to achieve a visual balance with an area of dissimilar use. It seems dishonest to disguise a function or falsify a form to comply with the dictates of symmetry. If Keats was right in his observation that truth and beauty are one and the same, then such symmetry can never be beautiful, for not only must a plan be truthful to be beautiful, its truth must be clearly evident.

Symmetry has little merit if its diagram cannot be realized from at least one point or line of observation. If this is not possible, we fail to comprehend the balanced composition. Again, the positive qualities to be gained from a symmetrical plan organization are lost if the plan is too large. This explains in part why, historically, few extensive symmetrical plan layouts have ever been coherent. There are symmetrical gardens, villas, and estates of great charm. There are symmetrical squares, circles, and parks. There are innumerable avenues, courts, and approaches of complex symmetry. Where successful, the symmetry of the plan or of a cohesive unit of the plan may be comprehended at a glance.

It can be seen that this same quality of symmetry which seems essential to its success may also be negative, for a plan that can be easily grasped *in toto* is generally static and, once seen, loses interest.

Symmetry is a coordinator. It has application whenever it

There is no such thing as "beauty of symmetry," with the exception of those cases where, because of the nature of the problem and its logical solution, the "balance" line of design happens to coincide with the middle line of symmetry. Only in such cases is symmetry logical and thus beautiful.

Eliel Saarinen

might be helpful in the comprehension of the whole of the plan or the relationship of the parts.

A symmetrical plan may be of crystalline form. This may be desirable if the function is by nature crystalline in its pattern of growth and expansion.

A symmetrical plan may be of geometric design. Such plan geometry may be excellent, but only if the function can be logically expressed in geometric line and form.

There are those who believe that geometry is the root of all beauty and that beauty of form and pattern can be consistently achieved by the application of mathematical formulas to the planning process. This thinking, they hold, gains support from the fact that people take pleasure in the comprehension of order. The writer contends, however, that the preference is generally for order over chaos rather that for symmetry over asymmetry.

A plan that imposes geometry without reason may destroy desirable landscape character or may neutralize the inherent qualities of the areas or objects affected.

A geometric plan, direct and obvious, is quickly comprehended. It thus has the advantage of clarity. It has also the disadvantage of monotony if seen often or for long.

A geometric plan is not valid in the context of that which is natural or when it is intended that the human eye and mind and spirit be set free.

In far too many cases, symmetrical plans are conceived as a design expedient, a sort of geometric doodling. Such plans are only repetitious and dreary, as uninspired as their authors. When geometric layouts are truly fitting, it is found that their symmetry is derived through clear logic and a conscious synthesis of all plan forms into symmetrical plan arrangement as the highest and best expression of the function. When appropriate and when intelligently applied in limited areas, symmetry is a plan form of compelling power.

The asymmetrical plan

In nature, we can seldom find the elements of a landscape symmetrically balanced on either side of a line of sight. Yet visual balance is fundamental to all satisfactory composition and to all art. It is generally conceded that any design, any picture, or any view or vista that lacks such balance is disturbing and unpleasant. Because we usually think of natural landscapes as being pleasant to look at, we might conclude that visual balance must somehow be inherent. This brings to mind two intriguing questions.

First, until an observer wanders along, how could there be visual balance? And then, does it not seem highly improbable that, from any given point of observation, the landscape should *happen* to balance visually on either side of a line of sight? Upon reflection it would seem, rather, that the eye must *find* in any landscape those vistas, views, or sight lines that *produce* a satisfactory visual balance. The trained eye is offended by the unbalanced and attracted to the balanced and tends constantly to seek out and bring into register those sections or portions of the visual landscape that provide a pleasant optical resolution of forces.

Visual balance   The human eye is constantly darting about, probing and exploring a vague and luminous flux of evolving visual impressions. These are sensed subconsciously. At intervals the mind permits or directs the eye to bring out of optical limbo and into

Confronted with a complex optical field, one will reduce it to basic interrelationships. Just as in nature there is a tendency to find the most economic surface unity in every formation, so in the visual organization there is a tendency to find the most economic spacial unity in the ordering of optical differences. . . .

We cannot bear chaos—the disturbance of equilibrium in the field of experience. Consequently, we must immediately form light-impacts into shapes and figures. Exposed to a visual field that in its light-quality is to the slightest degree heterogeneous, one organizes that field at once into two opposing elements; into a figure against a background. . . . Every image is based upon this dynamic dualism, the unity of opposites. Certain impulses are tied together in a stable visual whole, while other impulses are left in their unorganized fluid state and serve only as background and are perceived as intervals. This organization of figures and backgrounds is repeated progressively until the whole visual field is perceived as a formed, ordered unity—the plastic image. . . .

We live in the midst of a whirlwind of light qualities. From this whirling confusion we build unified entities, those forms of experience called visual images. To perceive an image is to participate in a forming process; it is a creative act.

Gyorgy Kepes

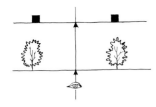

Symmetrical balance: equal and like masses balanced on either side of an optical axis or fulcrum.

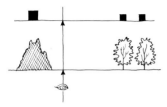

Asymmetrical occult balance: unequal and unlike masses balanced on either side of an optical axis.

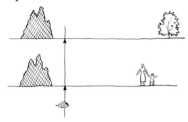

Asymmetrical occult balance: equilibrium achieved by mind-eye evaluation of form, mass, value, color, and association.

Occult balance

Balance may also consist in a disposition of objects not similar nor similarly placed, but still so chosen and arranged that the sum of the attractions on one side of the vertical axis is equalled by the sum of the attractions on the other side. This kind of balance is called unsymmetrical or occult balance.

Henry V. Hubbard

The natural landscape is an indeterminate object; it almost always contains enough diversity to allow the eye a great liberty in selecting, emphasizing and grouping its elements, and it is furthermore rich in suggestion and in vague emotional stimulus. A landscape to be seen has to be composed. . . .

George Santayana

The eye, especially, demands completeness.

Johann Wolfgang von Goethe

conscious focus certain visual images. This is a creative effort. For the mind demands that the eye ''compose'' a visual image that is complete and in equilibrium. This is a joint mind-eye effort, for the acceptable equilibrium is not one of form balance, value balance, or color balance alone but one of associative balance as well. The mind-eye team may give little weight to a massive object that has no associative value, but it may give much weight to that which has strong associative value or immediate interest. A ripe apple swaying on a branch may thus outweigh the tree itself, or a chunk of rose quartz outweigh the mountain from which it was broken, or a solitary sunbather outweigh the immensity of a seascape.

Thus no two mind-eye combinations scanning a scene could ever bring into register an identical visual image or combination of images. For a scene has no limits, and the possibilities of selective composition are endless. But, by a vastly complicated series of instantaneous subconscious adjustments, each individual ''creates'' out of optical impressions visual images that for that particular observer are in equilibrium and, therefore, complete. The more sensi-

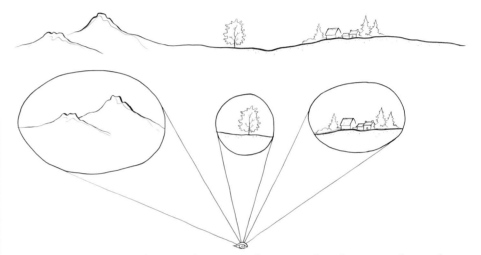

tive and perceptive the mind-eye combination has become through instinct or training, the richer, the more delightful, and the more wondrous is the visual world that it reveals.

The child or the primitive perceives only *objects* in space. A more highly developed mind and a more selective eye perceive *relationships*.

It can be seen that only rarely in nature would a sensed composition be balanced symmetrically on either side of a visual axis, but because equilibrium is required of all visual images, it must be possible to have balance without bilateral symmetry. This is indeed the case. Such asymmetrical, or ''occult,'' balance is the norm. Except in those cases in which bilateral symmetry has for some reason been contrived, it is by occult balance that we compose and comprehend the world about us.

Asymmetric planning   Asymmetric planning brings us into closest harmony with nature. Freed of the rigidity of the symmetrical plan, each area may be developed with a fuller regard for its natural landscape qualities. Circulation is more free. Views are of infinite variety. Each object in the landscape may be seen and enjoyed for itself or its relationship to other landscape elements rather than for its relationship to a prescribed plan diagram. Such plan asymmetry is more subtle, casual, refreshing, interesting, and human. We are not led step by step along or through a rigid composition. We are, rather, set free to explore for ourselves and to discover in the landscape that which we may find to be beautiful, pleasant, or useful.

Asymmetric planning requires less disturbance of the natural or built landscape. Because it is developed in sympathy with the site, it normally requires less grading, screening, and construction. It is therefore more economical.

Organic growth   The jack pine growing on the mountain slope sends out its probing roots in search of soil pockets and moisture. Its trunk and limbs are braced against the winds, its needle clusters are held up and extended as a living mesh, to best soak in the cool, drifting morning fogs and to absorb the utmost vitality from the light and warmth of the sun. It shapes itself to its patch of ground—the furrow and ridge, the rivulet, the stump, the fallen log, the boulder. It responds to the encroachment and to the protection of its neighbors. When a tip is bent or broken, a new tip is formed. When a branch is smashed or torn away, the wound is healed and the gaping void is filled with new wood or with fresh twigs and needles. All positive qualities of the environment are utilized. All negative factors are overcome to the limits of possibility. The form of the pine is expressive of its development in harmony with its environment. This age-old process we know to be the process of *organic growth*.

Organic planning   Organic planning, so widely touted and so seldom practiced, is fundamentally neither more nor less than the organic development of plan areas, volumes, and forms in response to all environmental constraints and opportunities.

Symmetrical plan form can never be organic in this sense, except in those rare instances in which the essential quality of the use is such that, given unrestrained freedom and developmental conditions, its most logical plan expression would be symmetrical. It can be seen that even in such a case the impact of natural landscape features would tend to disrupt the symmetry.

It is abundantly apparent that, in the great preponderance of cases, the logical site-structure or site-project diagram will be asymmetrical. If the diagram expresses a use or a complex of uses well suited to a site and if, in plan refinement, each function is developed in best relationship to other functions and to all positive and negative factors of the site, then such planning is truly organic.

Most things in nature, as well as most structures, are best appreciated when seen in the round. The asymmetric plan best provides such viewing. The approach of the observer to each plan element is meandering rather than fixed, giving a sense of modeling and third dimension. This plastic (sculptural) quality of an object, revealing its nature, shape, and detail, can be appreciated only if the observer moves around or past the object. Even the pictorial quality of a landscape is imbued with greater interest when observed from a constantly changing line of observation.

An axis may be developed asymmetrically. Such a treatment preserves the positive features of the axis while allowing greater plan flexibility. It does preclude the controlled, measured cadence and hypnotic induction of bilateral symmetry—qualities which, we have found, are in some few cases highly desirable. But the asymmetrically treated axis has much more universal application.

The use of asymmetry   Asymmetry is well suited to large-scale urban planning. The most pleasant squares of Europe are asymmetrical. What a sad day it would be for San Marco in Venice if the piazza were to be reconstructed in rigid symmetry. The wonder and charm of such towns as Siena, Verona, and Florence would be lost to a symmetrical handling of their streets and buildings and spaces.

The term "organic design" need not be an empty platitude. Biology has many valuable hints to offer the designer. . . . Indeed, there is much that could be said in support of a biological approach to the entire process of design, mainly in the sense that one broad biological field, known as ecology, *undertakes to investigate the dynamic relations of all the organisms—both fauna and flora— in natural association with each other and with the other forces of the total environment in a given area of the surface of the earth.*

Norman T. Newton

Architecture is not an art, it is a natural function. It grows on the soil like animals and plants. It is a function of the social order. Don't forget that.

Fernand Léger

The basic law—in all fields of creation workers are striving today to find purely functional solutions of a technological-biological kind: that is, to build up each piece of work solely from the elements which are required for its function. But "function" means here not a pure mechanical service. It includes also the psychological, social, and economical conditions of a given period. It might be better to use the term "organic [functional] design." Such design must even serve functions which could not be foreseen during the process of designing.

László Moholy-Nagy

Let me remind you of a famous passage in which Samuel Taylor Coleridge defined organic form. In a lecture on Shakespeare, given in 1818, he made a distinction between what he called mechanic form and organic form. "Form is mechanic," he said "when on any given material we impress a predetermined form, not necessarily arising out of the properties of the material." Organic form, on the other hand, is innate; shaping itself from within, as it develops, so that "the fullness of its development is one and the same with the perfection of its outward form."

Jacob Bronowski

I detest everything that is cold and academic. Only where the living purpose exists will new things be formed.

Eric Mendelsohn

In seeking now a reasonably solid grasp on the value of the word, organic, we should at the beginning fix in the mind the values of the correlated words, organism, structure, function, growth, development, form. All of these words imply the initiating pressure of a living force and a resultant structure or mechanism whereby such invisible force is made manifest and operative. The pressure, we call function—the resultant, form. Hence the law of form discernible throughout nature.

Louis H. Sullivan

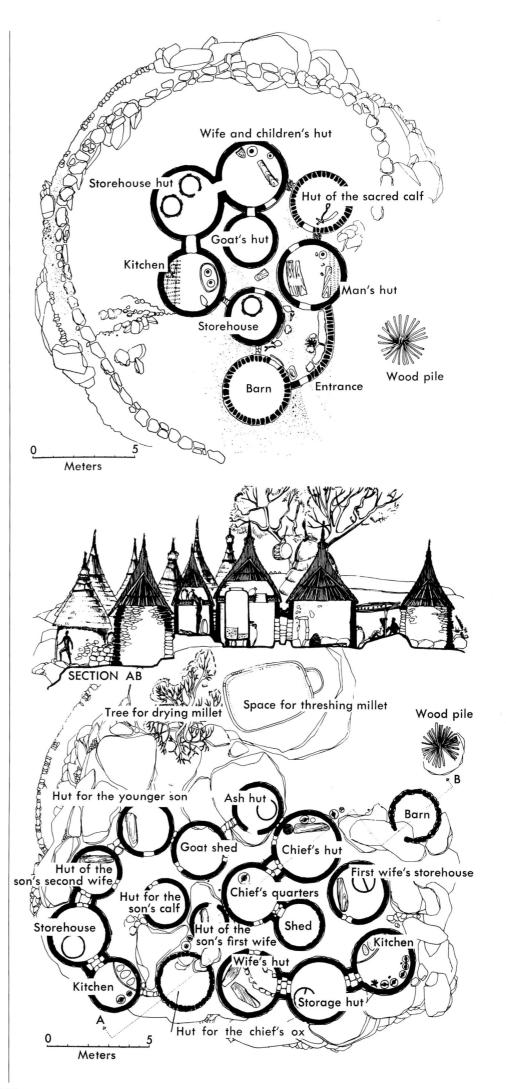

The notion of identical figures to the right and left of an axis was not the basis of any theory in ancient [European] times.

Camillo Sitte

The Greeks used symmetry when appropriate, they did not use symmetry when not appropriate, and they never used symmetry in their planning layouts. These layouts . . . were conceived in space. . . .

Eliel Saarinen

Organic planning: functional room arrangement of family dwelling. Cameroon.

Organic cell cluster arrangement of rooms: residence of Cameroon chief.

Wife and children's hut

Storehouse hut

Hut of the sacred calf

Goat's hut

Kitchen

Man's hut

Storehouse

Barn   Entrance

Wood pile

0   5
Meters

SECTION AB

Tree for drying millet   Space for threshing millet

Wood pile

B

Hut for the younger son   Ash hut   Barn

Goat shed   Chief's hut

Hut of the son's second wife   First wife's storehouse

Hut for the son's calf   Chief's quarters

Storehouse   Shed

Hut of the son's first wife   Kitchen

Wife's hut

Kitchen   Storage hut

A   Hut for the chief's ox

0   5
Meters

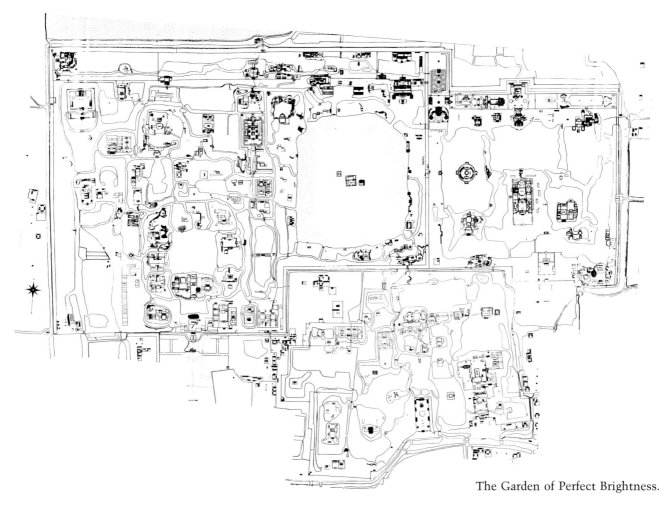

The Garden of Perfect Brightness.

The most magnificent garden of history, the Yuan Ming Yuan, or Garden of Perfect Brightness, which today lies in ruin to the west of Peking, was scrupulously asymmetric in plan, as attested to by Jean-Denis Attiret, a French priest who many years ago found his way to the court of Emperor Ch'ien Lung. In 1743, he wrote to a friend in France describing its wonders:

"One quits a valley, not by fine straight allées as in Europe, but by zigzag and circuitous routes—and on leaving one finds oneself in a second valley entirely different from the first as regards the form of the land and the structure of the buildings. All the mountains and hills are covered with trees, especially with flowering trees, which are very common here. It is a veritable paradise on earth.

"Each valley . . . has its pleasance, small in comparison with the whole enclosure, but in itself large enough to house the greatest of our European lords with all his retinue. But how many of these palaces would you think there are in the different valleys of this vast enclosure? There are more than two hundred.

"In Europe, uniformity and symmetry are desired everywhere. We wish that there should be nothing odd, nothing misplaced, that one part should correspond exactly with the part facing it; in China also they love this symmetry, this fine order. The palace in Peking . . . is in this style . . . but in the pleasances there reigns a graceful disorder, an anti-symmetry is desired almost everywhere. Everything is based on this principle. . . . When one hears this, one would think it to be ridiculous, that it must strike the eye disagreeably; but when one sees them one thinks differently and admires the art with which the irregularity is planned.

"I am tempted to believe that we [in eighteenth-century France] are poor and sterile in comparison."[1]

The rash of symmetrical planning that marked the Renaissance

---

[1]As quoted by Hope Danby in *The Garden of Perfect Brightness.*

in Europe had little reasonable basis. Far too often, it was symmetry solely for symmetry's sake, a senseless forcing of the natural and built landscape into geometric patterns. No wonder our friend Attiret, like many others to follow, found this planning, by comparison with the freedom and rich variety of asymmetry, to be but "poor and sterile."

Visual resource management

Visual resource management is a relatively new term being applied by several of the public agencies to the technique of preserving and enhancing the nation's scenery. Innovative approaches are outlined in a number of well-prepared manuals which demonstrate a promising new concern.

Essentially, for any area or corridor of proposed development or rehabilitation, the scenic or blighting landscape features are inventoried and recorded by various graphic means and given a rating as to their visual significance. Alternative proposals (for timber cutting, highway construction, extraction pits, reservoirs, or military installations, as examples) are then analyzed and evaluated as to their relative benefits and negative visual impacts upon existing conditions. In the decision as to the preferred route or course of action the scenic considerations are shown to be telling and often deciding factors.

The procedures developed by the U.S. Forest Service are particularly sound, easy to understand, and effective. They are based on the premise that visitors to the national forests have an image of what they expect to see and that, insofar as possible, this expectation should be fulfilled. They recognize and consider the numbers and types of viewers, the duration of viewing time, and the relative quality and intensity of the viewing experience. They assume that all lands are to be viewed on the ground, from passing roads or transitways, and from the air. They build upon the principle that all landscapes have a definable character and that those with the greatest variety have the greatest scenic value. They assess each potential view in terms of its foreground, midground, and background contribution. They give priority, in each scene, to the dominant elements in terms of line, form, color, and imagery. They consider the capacity of each landscape area to absorb alteration without loss of its visual character. Finally, they outline a systematic, step-by-step process of evaluation that makes good sense. Often in the recommended procedures of some agencies far too much emphasis is given to the numerical weighting and tabular mathematical rating of the various scenic elements. (How many points should be assigned, for instance, for a view of an historic church, an acre of mountain laurel, or a plummeting waterfall?)

It is suggested that in the assessment of scenic or any other values all *quantifiable* costs and benefits be computed and tabulated. Their relative weight can thus be established with a fair degree of accuracy. *Unquantifiable* values, such as those of aesthetic, historical, or educational significance, can be reasonably evaluated only on a broad relative scale or on the basis of expert testimony in the presence of those who are to decide upon the merits of the alternatives.

The recent manuals on visual resource management are especially helpful as aids to untrained technicians and decision makers. Some provide the trained professional with welcome new insights and advanced approaches to the design of the visible landscape and have wide application.

Eighty-five percent of perception is based on sight.

9

Circulation

Most constructions have meaning only to humans, and only as we experience them. They are revealed by lines or patterns of circulation that lead us to, through, over, under, or around them, on foot or on horseback, by plane, train, automobile, or any other means of locomotion or conveyance. We thus realize that the circulation pattern is a major function of any planned development because it establishes the rate, sequence, and nature of its sensed realization or visual unfolding.

Every object as a perceptible entity exists in time as well as in space. This is to say that an object cannot be comprehended in its entirety at any one instant or from any one point of observation. It is perceived, rather, through a flow of impressions. When in motion, one sees a series of images blending into an expanding visual realization of an object, space, or scene. Perception is not a matter of sight alone. All the senses may be involved—sight, taste, smell, touch, and hearing. The rate, order, type, and degree of perception are a matter of design control. Much of this control is effected by planned patterns of circulation.

Motion

Experience is rarely static; almost always is motion involved in the person or in the thing experienced. A structure is seldom seen from a fixed point of view or in direct elevation but usually by people on the move. Its three-dimensional form and modeling are therefore more important than its facade. The plan pattern of a site is also usually realized from an infinite number of viewing points by people moving through it. The more fluid the circulation pattern, the more points of view and, therefore, the more interest and enjoyment in viewing.

Motion impelled by form and concept

One afternoon, some time ago, the author entered the National Gallery in Washington to join a group of sightseers who were starting out with a guide. The group stood in the great rotunda, at the base of the towering black marble columns that support the lofty dome. "Do you know," asked the guide, "what the architect of this great edifice has planned as an introduction? He has directed you here to give you the theme—the magnificence of all history—to make you feel splinter-high and insignificant before all the greatness that lies behind and ahead. You are awed by new, strange shapes and sizes and the astonishing opulence. But the architect doesn't want to scare you away, as most of us are by strange and unfamiliar things. So, as we approach the Mercury Fountain at the rotunda's center, he wants to make us feel at ease. And how does he accomplish this? By the size of things, by scale.

"The figure of Mercury is less than life-size. The steps leading up to the fountain are broad and low rather than high and forbidding. The water play is subdued to a splash and trickle rather than a rush. The architect gives us also a concept with which we are familiar, not a terrible war god but one of the more kindly gods, Mercury, who speeds and flashes about on winged feet. We, who know the legends, want to walk closer to this figure. Here in this lofty dome of light and space is held out to us that which makes us want to come near, makes us feel pleased and relaxed.

"And so the architect has piqued our curiosity, impressed us, and humbled us. He has pleased us. Now he wants to get us moving out into the exhibit rooms. How is this accomplished? You will notice that he starts a centrifugal movement with a dominant spiral theme. The lines of the figure of Mercury are spiral in diagram. The subject of the sculpture, appropriately, is 'flight.' Motion is further suggested by the movement of the water as it ripples toward the fountain brim. All lines move outward. Above us, even the carved eagles on the architrave seem ready to soar away. Even the coffers of the tremendous dome sweep in a great spiral pattern. By sound, motion, and induced ideas, by strong urging of architectural form and line, we are compelled to outward motion."

The kinematics of motion

Without reference to the cause of movement, it is interesting to dwell for a few moments on the various characteristics of pure motion. By design, the line or trajectory of induced movement may be meandering, discursive, circuitous, looping, zigzagging, ricocheting, ascending, descending, hyperbolic, or centripetal; it may be an arc or a direct straight shot. In speed, the motion may range from the creeping-crawling to the whizzing-whistling. The nature of induced motion may be soothing, startling, shocking, baffling, confusing, exploratory, logical, sequential, progressive, hieratic, linear, wavelike, flowing, branching, diverging, converging, timorous, forceful, expanding, contracting, and so on, *ad infinitum*.

Obviously, the alignment, speed, and nature of motion produce in a moving subject a predictable emotional and intellectual response and must, therefore, be carefully considered. The abstract qualities of the path or line by which an object or space is approached must also be controlled with care. Motion that is induced must be accommodated and satisfactorily resolved. This fact is also obvious, but, like so many obvious things, it is too often overlooked in our planning.

We are living a mobile existence. The earth is rotating; the sun is moving; trees are growing; flowers are opening and closing; clouds are merging, dissolving, coming and going; light and shadow are hunting each other in an indefatigable play; forms are appearing and disappearing. . . . The perception of physical reality cannot escape the quality of movement. The very understanding of spatial facts, the meaning of extension or distances, involves the notion of time—a fusion of space-time which is movement. "Nobody has ever noticed a place except at a time or a time except at a place," said Minkowsky in his Principles of Relativity.

Gyorgy Kepes

The reorganization of our visual habits so that we perceive not isolated "things" in "space," but structure, order, and the relatedness of events in space-time, is perhaps the most profound kind of a revolution possible—a revolution that is long overdue not only in art, but in all our experience.

S. I. Hayakawa

The planner of an exhibition attempts to foresee people's behavior and predict where they will hurry, stop, look, or drift on. His aim is to control the flow and arrest it where he wants; but controlling the flow does not mean that people are to be moved along predestinate grooves like trams or shuffled around hurdles like sheep. Ideally the planner is aiming to direct people's movement in such a way that they see what there is to see with ease and in their own time. He must also ensure that the public does not get lost, tired, or bored with the whole affair.

James Gardner and Caroline Heller

Line of approach
Abstract variables in line of approach to a given point, area, or space.

Meandering

Direct

Curvilinear

Erratic

Looping

Passing

In-circling

Dispersing

Congregating

Rounding

Returning

Diverging

Homing

Converging

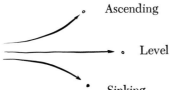
Ascending

Level

Sinking

With friction

Obscure

Massive

Tenuous

With interference

Concentration

Dilution

Interrupted

Conditional

With distraction

With diversion

Impelling factors. We tend to move:

In logical sequences of progression

In lines of least resistance

Along easiest grades

In lines suggested by directional forms, signs, or symbols

Toward that which pleases

Toward that which is fitting

Toward things wanted

Toward things that have use

Toward change, from cold to warm, from sun to shade, from shade to sun

Toward that which has interest

Toward that which excites curiosity

Toward points of entry

Toward the receptive

Toward points of highest contrast

Toward points of richest texture or color

To attain a goal

By pride of height attained, distance traveled, friction overcome

In haste, via the direct; with leisure, via the indirect

In harmony with circulation patterns

In harmony with abstract design forms

Toward the beautiful, the picturesque

For the pleasurable sensation of motion

For the experience of space modulation

Toward exposure, if adventurous

Toward protection, if threatened

Toward and through pleasant areas and spaces

Toward order, if tired of confusion

Toward confusion, if bored with order

Toward objects, areas, and spaces that suit our mood or needs

Repelling factors. We are repelled by:

Obstacles	The uninspiring
Steep grades	The forbidding
The unpleasant	The demanding
The monotonous	Danger
The uninteresting	Friction
The dull	Disorder
The obvious	The ugly
The undesirable	The unsuitable

Motion directors. We are directed or guided by:

Arrangement of natural or structural forms

Implied patterns of circulation

Baffles, screens, and space dividers

Dynamic plan lines

Signs

Symbols

Mechanical controls such as gates, curbs, and barriers

Spatial shapes

Suggested progressions such as from violet to red, from Hole Number 1 to Hole Number 2

Repose inducers. We are induced to repose by:

Conditions of comfort, enjoyment, or rest

Opportunity for privacy

Opportunity for fuller appreciation of view, object, or detail

Opportunity for concentration

Restriction of movement

Inability to proceed

Imposed indecision

Pleasant arrangements of forms and space

Functions related to rest and repose

Attainment of optimum position

Horizontal motion. We are affected by horizontal motion in the following ways:

Movement is easier, freer, and more efficient in horizontal planes.

Movement is safer.

Change of direction is easier.

Choice of direction is greater.

Most functions are better suited to horizontal surfaces.

Movement is easier to control.

Vision of moving object is easier to control.

Vision from moving object is easier to control.

Visual interest is in the vertical planes.

Downward motion or decline.

We are affected by downward motion in the following ways:

Effort is minimized, but elevation must be regained.

Safety depends on checks and on texture.

Downward motion gives a sense of refuge, hiding, digging in.

It gives a sense of regression, return to the primitive.

It gives a coasting, swooping sense of being in harmony with the forces of gravity.

It gives a sense of increased confinement, protection, and privacy.

It suggests the coalpit, the swamp, the fertile valley.

It embodies the rathskeller concept.

It embodies the bargain basement concept.

Downward movement and depth are accentuated by deep earth colors, solidity and simplicity of form, natural materials, and falling or quiet water.

Vision is oriented to the base plane.

Interest is increased in things of the earth—in plants, water, and minerals.

It offers relatively effortless movement, most welcome in the home stretch when energies flag.

Upward motion, rise, or climb.

We are affected by upward motion in the following ways:

Upward motion requires force of lift to overcome gravity.

It adds a new dimension to motion.

It is exhilarating.

It gives a sense of accomplishment, of conquest of gravity.

It gives a sense of going up in life.

It offers detachment from the things of the earth.

It imparts a moral implication of exaltation, of being close to God.

It gives a sense of being closer to the sun, of being rarefied.

It offers detachment from the crowd, supremacy, command.

It implies military advantage.

It means attainment of the pinnacle.

It offers expanding views and vistas.

It embodies the concept of man or woman against the sky.

It epitomizes increased concern for safety and stability and for texture of the base plane to provide necessary traction and grip.

It offers visual interest in the overhead plane, using sun and sky to full effect.

All the above are increased in proportion to the angle of inclination.

Induced response. We respond by:

Relaxing in the familiar, becoming aroused or excited by the unfamiliar

Finding pleasure in unity, variety, and that which is fitting

Finding security in order

Finding amusement and divertissement in the strange, in the lively, and in change

Ossifying and decaying physically, mentally, and spiritually amid the rigid and the fixed

We are attracted to:

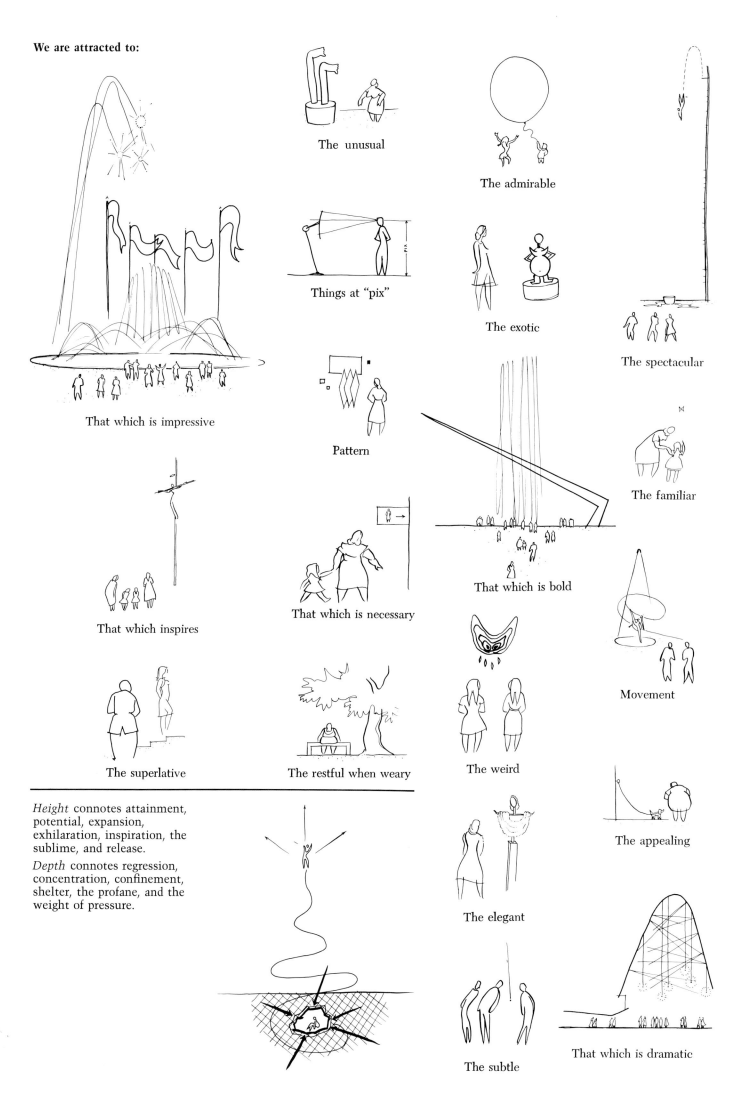

The unusual

The admirable

Things at "pix"

The exotic

The spectacular

That which is impressive

Pattern

The familiar

That which inspires

That which is necessary

That which is bold

Movement

The superlative

The restful when weary

The weird

The appealing

Height connotes attainment, potential, expansion, exhilaration, inspiration, the sublime, and release.

Depth connotes regression, concentration, confinement, shelter, the profane, and the weight of pressure.

The elegant

The subtle

That which is dramatic

On the street, in crowded shopping districts, and perhaps even more particularly in exhibition areas we are invited, cajoled, badgered, seduced, preached to, begged, teased, blasted at, or otherwise attracted by a constantly evolving, rolling barrage of visual persuaders. Sometimes falteringly, we follow our eye-mind impellers toward that which is:

Meaningful	Pleasantly shocking
Animated	Bright
Contrasting	Familiar, amid much that is
Unusual	strange
Beautiful	In motion against a fixed
Varied	background
Near pix, or eye level	Charming
Decorative	Subdued, when weary of the
Necessary	bright
Desirable	Abstract
Restful, when weary of tu-	Select
mult	Successful
Startling	Distinguished
Vigorous	Sophisticated
Bold	Comprehensible
Interesting	Superlative
Exciting	Supreme
Dominant	Impressive
Spectacular	Surprising
Subtle	Ingenious
Associative	Useful
Inspiring	Logical
Strange, amid the familiar	Sequential
New	Progressive
Pleasing in pattern	Human
Pleasing in form	Appealing
Pleasing in scale	Educational
Pleasing in texture	Curious
Pleasing in color	Exotic
Safe	Extraordinary
Stable	Appropriate
Suitable	Stimulating
Convenient	Admirable
On course	True
Dramatic	Diverting
Simple	Amusing
Clean	Suggestive
Natural	Satisfying
Weird	Awesome
Plausible	Symbolic
Colorful	Fresh
Lively	Excellent

Our senses of sight, hearing, taste, touch, and smell are often compelling factors in the subconscious plotting of our courses and the determination of our actions. Physical comfort is a powerful factor too.

Distance as friction In the various fields of transportation particularly, distance is considered an obstacle to be overcome, area that must be traversed and space that must be bridged, with energy expended. When speed and economy are factors, it is incumbent upon the planner to select or devise a route that is as direct as practicable and that provides a minimum of deterrent to smooth and rapid travel.

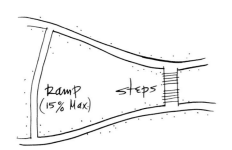

Often a ramp is planned as an alternative to nearby steps in order to accommodate the handicapped, wheeled vehicles, and equipment.

Such a route would be of suitable grade and alignment. The speed and volume of traffic would be accommodated. Traffic of various types and velocities would be classified and separated. All obstacles would be removed. Grade crossings would be eliminated. Safety would be assured in all ways possible. All objects and elements along the route would facilitate and express a freedom of movement because such trafficways must not only be direct and free but must also suggest efficiency.

Positive qualities of distance   Distance is a function of area, and area is a function of space. Both area and space are usually at a premium. In our world of expanding population and increasing pressures, we often yearn for more room and seek to extend our constricting boundaries. When boundaries are fixed, as is usually the case, we attempt to expand them by some plan device. We increase *perceived* distances. This high art was long ago mastered by the planners of those cultures that lived in compression—on the fortified island or hilltop or within the city wall. It is an art that we, in the increased planning concentrations and population densities of the near future, must relearn and develop.

Space modulation   It is an established planning fact that we seek in an area that quality of harmony, oneness, or unity that is the mark of any well-conceived work of science or art. We are attracted to such places and rebel at the intrusion of the incongruous element, for example, a claptrap hotdog stand in a beautiful natural gorge.

In addition, we seek a harmonious sequence of transition from one space to another. In going from club terrace to the swimming pool below, a detour through the parking lot would be disturbing. When driving the family from home to a picnic spot, we would avoid the business districts and prefer a parkway route, river road, or country lane, to sustain or heighten the anticipated mood and provide a pleasantly evolving transition. We seek, in all such cases, a unified sequential experience of *space modulation.*

People in motion take great pleasure in the sensation of change—change of texture, light, quality, temperature, scent, visual patterns, expanding or contracting vistas, and the fluid visual impressions of objects, spaces, and views.

We take pleasure in an area arranged in shape, line, color, and texture to accommodate and express the use for which it was planned. We have learned also that our pleasure is increased when the area is further developed into a volume or series of volumes that, by degree and type of enclosure, further articulate the planned use. We enjoy moving to and through a space and around or past an object. We also enjoy moving from one space to another, the experience of sequential space-to-space transition.

Sometimes the transition is subtle. One may be led through a sequence of varying spaces that provide a complete change in use and mood in such a way that the transition is almost imperceptible. Sometimes the transition is powerful. One may, by planned intent, be so compressed into a low, tight, dark space that release into a lofty, dazzling, free space is startling and dramatic. But, in any event, the skilled planner, by spatial manipulation, can play upon human emotions, reflexes, and responses as surely as does the skilled musician with the harp or flute or drum.

In one of the Summer Palace groups near the Jade Fountain to the west of Peking, there once existed a walled enclosure known as the Court of the Concubine. Here, many years ago, lived the favorite concubine of one of the imperial princes. At one end of the courtyard stood her handsome residence of lacquered wood, tile, soft mats, and woven screens, and at the other end a light, airy pavilion, where she and her maids whiled away the summer afternoons. By legend, she had been brought from the open plains of Szechwan (Sichuan) Province, and she longed for its lakes, woods, meadows, and far mountains and for the wide spaces and the freedoms she had known there. And here, in the Summer Palace, this confining courtyard had now become her world.

The prince and his planners, wishing to please her, set out to create, within the limits of this space, an expansive paradise of freedom and delight. From her residence, to give the illusion of distance, the walls of the courtyard were stepped both inward and down to increase vastly the apparent distance to the facing pavilion; furthermore, to reduce the effect of rigid enclosure, the far plantings extended on either side of, and beyond, the lines of the converging walls. Even the size of the paving slabs was reduced from near to far. Moving outward, all textures changed imperceptibly from the rough to the refined, and colors varied from the warm scarlets, reds, oranges, and yellows to the soft, cool, muted greens and lavenders and evanescent grays. Trees and plants in the foreground were bold in outline and foliage; those near the fragile pavilion were dwarfed and delicate. Water in the near fountain gurgled and splashed, while in the far ponds it lay mirrorlike and still. By such manipulations of perspective alone, the views from the concubine's quarters were made to seem expansive and the pavilion remote.

As the mistress left the terrace of her residence, to move out in the courtyard, she passed through a pungently aromatic clump of twisted junipers to come upon a curiously contorted "mountain stone" that rose serenely from a bed of moss. On the stone wall behind it was incised a pattern of stylized cloud forms with the poetic inscription "Above the plains of Szechwan the clouds rest lightly on the lofty mountain peaks." Here, ten steps from her terrace yet hidden from view, she could be, in her thoughts, again among her mountains.

Just beyond, and angling temptingly out of sight, was a wall of emerald tile with an embossed tile dragon that seemed to writhe in splendid fury toward an open gateway. Inside the gate was a low stone bin spilling over with blooming peonies that laced the sunlit space with their pastel colors and delicious spicy fragrance. The sound of trickling water was meant to lead her eye to a cool and shadowy recess where a teakwood bench was placed near the light spray of a waterfall. From overhead the branches of weeping willow cascaded down until the tips dipped into the water, where gold and silver fantails drifted languidly among the floating willow leaves. A meandering line of stepping-stones led across the pond to disappear into the tracery of a bamboo grove where swaying finches trilled and filled the light air with soft and tremulous melody. The thin pathway led out beyond to a ferny opening beside the farthermost lobe of the pool, which here lay deep and silent. At its edge, a carved soapstone table and cushioned seats were arranged in the shade of a feathery smoke pine near the steps of the pavilion.

From the raised pavilion platform, looking back, a surprising new vista met the eye. For, by forced perspective, the residence seemed startlingly near. The path that led from it was ingeniously concealed, and another route of return invited one to new garden features and spaces.

This masterful courtyard was designed as an evolving complex of spaces, each complete in itself. And each transition, space to space and element to element, was contrived, with a deft assurance born of long centuries of practice, as a harmonious progression.

Space modulation! We in America have yet to learn the meaning of the words. But we *will* learn it in the crowded years ahead, for indeed we *must;* and we will develop it, without a doubt, to new heights of artistry.

Conditioned perception   Experience has taught us that what a thing is, is often of less importance than how we relate to it. The tree unseen or unremembered for us does not exist. The tree on the distant hilltop may be for the moment only an object that marks our path. As we approach, we see it to be a pear tree with many pleasant connotations. Coming close, we may be tempted to pick its fruit. Or perhaps in the noontime heat of an August day we may welcome the chance to lie in its shade, hang a child's swing from one of its lower branches, or spread a picnic at its base. In every case the tree is the same, but our impression of it changes with our sensed relationship. This being so, it would seem that should we place a tree or any other object in a space, we must consider not only the relationship of the object to the space but also the relationship of the object to all who will use the space. We must program the user's perception of the object by a sequence of planned relationships that will reveal its most appealing qualities.

Our impressions of an object or a space are conditioned by those we have already experienced or those anticipated. A bright, sunlit court is the more pleasant because we have just left the leafy coolness of an arbor. The splash and spray of a fountain are the more appreciated when we have approached it by way of the hot, dry, sunbaked court. The birch clumps have more meaning when we sense that the river lies just ahead. The wide, free space is wider and freer to us when we realize that behind or beyond it we have known or will know the compression of confined spaces.

We plan, then, not a single experience alone but rather a series of conditioned experiences that will heighten the interacting pleasurable impact of each. The Chinese epicure would understand this procedure, for to him the well-conceived banquet is a balanced succession of sensory delights. The thin, bland shark-fin soup, the brittle wafer of salt seaweed, the glutinous pungency of jellied egg, mealy water chestnuts with almond bits, the sweet astringent bite of crabapple preserves, light, fluffy fried rice, steaming sweet-sour fish in persimmon sauce, bitter tea, crisp vegetables braised in light peanut oil, tender, chewy bits of mushroom and meat, soft noodles in broth with pigeon eggs, the rich custard of ripe durian, mouth-cleansing tea, the cool acidulous mango and more tea, and finally the lightest and driest of wines. Each such meal is designed as an artistically balanced sequence of gustatory, tactile, visual, and intellectual experiences. Should we be satisfied with less artistry in the planning of the places and spaces of our living environment?

Experience, we may see, is compounded of that which we have perceived, that which we are perceiving, and that which we expect to perceive.

As we move through a space or a complex of spaces, we subconsciously remember that which we have passed or sensed. We thus orient backward in time and space, as well as forward, and find that each orientation gives meaning to the other and to all.

Sequence   *Sequence,* in terms of planning, may be defined as a succession of perceptions having continuity. Sequences have no meaning except as we experience them. Conversely, all experience is sequential.

In nature, sequences are casual and free. Sometimes, but not always, they are progressive. Such a progression may be one of ascent, as in the experience of climbing from lowland to mountain peak; or one of direction, as westward from the central plains across the desert, over the mountains, through the valleys, and to the ocean; or one moving inward, from the sunlit edges of a forest to its deep, shadowy interior; or a progression of enclosure, complexity, intensity, convenience, or comprehension.

Sometimes the sequences of nature are revealed with no more order than in the haphazard impressions of an adult or a child wandering lackadaisically through the landscape, along a lonely stretch of seashore, or among the shallow pools of a tidal flat.

The planned sequence may be casual or disciplined. It may be rambling and intentionally devil-may-care, or it may, to achieve a purpose, be contrived with a high degree of order. The planned sequence is an extremely effective design device. It may induce motion, give direction, create cadence, instill a mood, reveal or "explain" an object or a series of objects in space, or even develop a philosophical concept.

A planned sequence is a conscious organization of elements in space. It has a beginning and an end that is usually, but not always, the climax. Indeed, there may be several or many climaxes, each of which must satisfy its supporting sequence. Through its suggestion of motion and momentum, one feels compelled to move from the start of a sequence to its completion. Once initiated, sequence and induced movement must be brought to a logical, or at least a satisfying, conclusion.

It can be seen that all planned spaces are experienced by a progressive order of perceptions or events. It can also be appreciated that such sequences are subject to precise design control. A well-conceived plan determines not only the nature of climaxes but also their timing, their intensity, and the transitions by which they are evolved.

A sequence may be simple, compound, or complicated. It may be sustained, interrupted, varied, or modulated. It may be focalizing or diversifying, minute or extensive; and it may be subtle or powerful.

A sequence should reveal, interpret, and feature the elements to be perceived and the spaces used or traversed. Each sequence, like a distinctive refrain, has its own character and evokes an emotional response that can be fairly well predetermined.

A sequence in its abstract beat or meter may, like the varied

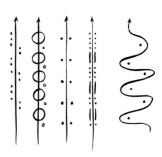

Development of cadence

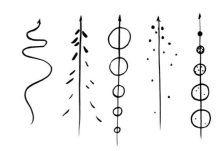

Sequence of intensification

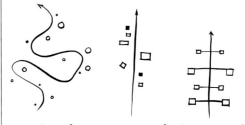

Casual   Asymmetrical   Symmetrical

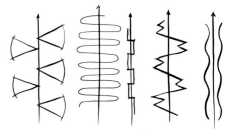

Sequence of alternation

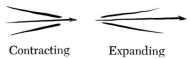

Contracting   Expanding

Sequence
Abstract representation of various types of plan sequence. Arrows indicate line of progression.

Stepping-stones in the Kiyozumi Garden, Tokyo, Japan: a planned sequence of high design quality.

rhythms of a jungle drum, instill a feeling of excitement, warning, fear, frenzy, mystery, wonder, awe, pleasure, happiness, exultation, power, anger, belligerence, challenge, temptation, regret, sadness, uncontrollable grief, or comfort.

Woe be to the designer who, by plan sequence, induces in the observer a mood or expectation not in keeping with the functions of the plan. In contrast, how superbly effective is that sequential order of spaces and form that develops and accentuates an induced response in consonance with the preconceived experience.

If a sequence is marked with a rhythmic recurrence of one or more spatial qualities—size, shape, color, lighting, or texture—a cadence soon becomes evident. Depending upon its nature, intensity, and rate of incidence, such a cadence has a slight to very considerable emotional impact upon the moving observer. Sometimes the effect is desirable, sometimes disastrous. Suffice it to note that, in the planning of any spaces through which people are to move on foot or by vehicle, an understanding of both spatial modulation and space cadence is essential.

The ordered approach   When in motion, we are acted upon by the physical environment through which we pass. It would seem, therefore, that when moving toward a goal we could be prepared, by design, for that goal, or when moving toward an anticipated experience, we could be prepared for that experience. This is, in fact, the case.

As an example of the reverse effect, let us consider the members of a family on their way to a city church that fronts upon a busy commercial highway. As they drive along, they feel hurried and then perhaps a little alarmed when they must swing sharply out of the rushing traffic into the tight entrance of the church drive. It is narrow and jammed with idling cars that are waiting to discharge passengers. After a lurching and nervous advance, the driver finally stops to let his wife and children out near the entrance door, only to find soon after that the church parking lot is filled. Frantically he crosses the highway to park in the lot of a nearby supermarket, then jogs back up the hill to the church, where he squeezes into the pew beside his family just as the service begins. He and his wife and children are ruffled and tense, and the service is over before they regain their composure. Obviously, for these people and for great multitudes like them, a pleasant experience of "going to church" has never been properly planned.

In the same community, let us say, another church has been sited to front on a quiet and beautiful residential parkway. On Sunday mornings, as the families make their way to church by car or along the pleasant approach walks, the church is seen set back, framed by trees, and serenely inviting. Driveways, entrance loop, and parking areas are easily reached and adequate. Connecting walks lead to a wide and spacious court, from which the entrance doors open. Here, pausing before entry, one is prepared by form, by symbol, by the very quality of the space, for the services inside. Here, after service, families and friends can meet and visit in appropriate surroundings. The approaching, attending, and leaving of this church are all planned as conducive, meaningful aspects of worship.

In the orient such approaches are designed with admirable sensitivity. As one moves, for example, down the roadway toward the entrance gate of temple grounds, the very street assumes an air of reverent dignity. By tradition, walls and gates close out the temporal world and enclose a garden space of tranquil peace, a symbolic paradise. From far down the road to the innermost altar, the ap-

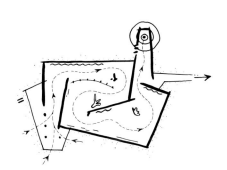

Planned sequential development of a predetermined experience.

proach is designed as a superbly modulated transition, from the crude to the refined, from the crass to the rich, from the distracting to the introspective, from the temporal to sublimity.

By similar means, we may be conditioned for any planned human experience. And, by all odds, we should be.

Pedestrian traffic

The characteristics of pedestrian traffic can best be understood by comparing them with those of a stream or river. Foot traffic, like flowing water, follows a course of least resistance. It tends toward the shortest distance, point to point. It has a pressure of momentum. It has force. It erodes. Swift movement requires a straight, smooth channel with increased width at the curves. If not provided, such a channel will be forced. As in the swift river jutting points are worn away, rock ledges are undercut, and the oxbow is "strung," just so does the force of pedestrian traffic grind away at impinging or constricting forms or leap the channel to shape a new and freer course.

Just as a canal establishes the route, rate, and maximum volume of its traffic, so constructed walks can fix the path and control the movement of pedestrian traffic. Again, as with the intermittent stream on a level plain, the course of such traffic may be governed by unpredictable variables. Sometimes, in campus planning particularly, where momentums and lines of pedestrian force are so difficult to predetermine, only the major walks are constructed with the buildings, and the crosswalks or meandering pathways are laid down later along those unconscious and natural lines of movement worn thin in the campus turf.

An obstacle in a traffic stream, as in a stream of water, produces turbulence. Turbulence is friction. Where directional traffic or rapid flow is desirable, islands in the path or walkway are best streamlined or shaped to divert and direct flowing traffic in a sweep or glide.

Intersections are points of maximum turbulence. In pedestrian trafficway planning, such turbulence is often a positive quality, as in those places where excitement, activity, or high interest is desirable, or where perforce the flow of traffic is to be decelerated, or where, by plan intent, people are made to mill and churn and jostle about. The degree and nature of such ebullient hurly-burly may be planned, as in the marketplace, the trade show, the amusement park, or the country fair. When two or more intersecting streams of traffic are to be merged into one fast, free-flowing stream, the area of juncture must be widened and shaped to provide a smoothly swelling transition and an uninterrupted flow.

An intersection must accommodate and express the functions induced by the fact of intersection. Geographically, the place of the

Progressive sequential realization of a concept or conditioned attainment of a goal.

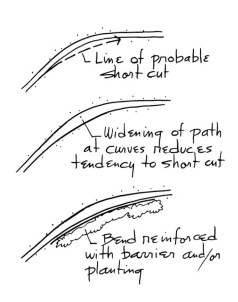

Line of probable short cut

Widening of path at curves reduces tendency to short cut

Bend reinforced with barrier and/or planting

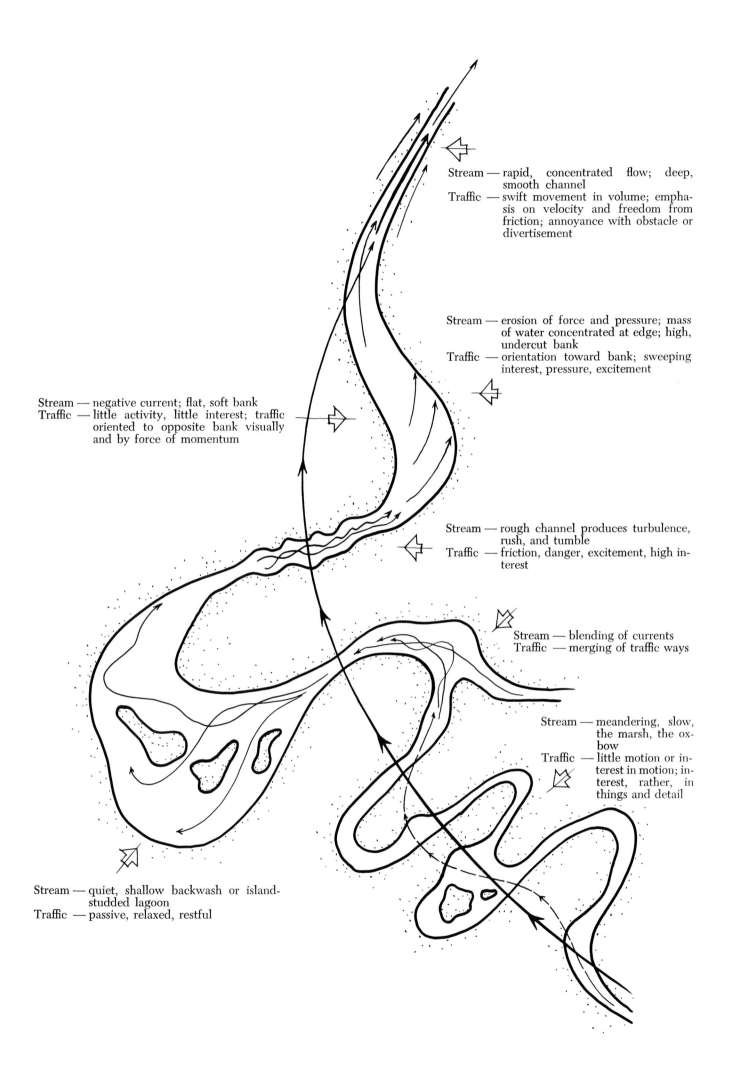

Stream — rapid, concentrated flow; deep, smooth channel
Traffic — swift movement in volume; emphasis on velocity and freedom from friction; annoyance with obstacle or divertisement

Stream — erosion of force and pressure; mass of water concentrated at edge; high, undercut bank
Traffic — orientation toward bank; sweeping interest, pressure, excitement

Stream — negative current; flat, soft bank
Traffic — little activity, little interest; traffic oriented to opposite bank visually and by force of momentum

Stream — rough channel produces turbulence, rush, and tumble
Traffic — friction, danger, excitement, high interest

Stream — blending of currents
Traffic — merging of traffic ways

Stream — meandering, slow, the marsh, the oxbow
Traffic — little motion or interest in motion; interest, rather, in things and detail

Stream — quiet, shallow backwash or island-studded lagoon
Traffic — passive, relaxed, restful

Pedestrian ways and places

Exploring the village of Ios, Greece

Steps are for more than up and down; they are a means of experiencing space and movement from one plane to another.

meeting of streams or rivers is strategically important. For here not only are the watersheds of two valley systems merged, but also the life and trade and culture that flow down with the streams. In Pittsburgh, for example, the Golden Triangle is centered for good reasons at the point where the Allegheny and Monongahela rivers meet to form the start of the Ohio. Here, as in most such instances, many interacting forces are engendered by the fact of convergence. The conjunction, whether of water, trade, culture, transportation, motor traffic, or pedestrian movement, introduces considerations that must be resolved or developed in the related land planning.

Casual foot traffic, like a quiet stream, takes a meandering course. Traffic that is passive by nature or preference is found where quiet water on a river would be found, in the lagoon or is-land-studded backwash and out of the mainstream or current. This sheltered lagoon character, with all its design implications, is ger-mane to those many plan functions that are related to, yet out of, main pedestrian traffic streams. In the same way, the swift free-dom of the channel or the sweeping interest of the bend is clearly analogous to many planned landscape areas.

Things seen   Since walking is still the most frequent means of locomotion, most places and spaces are seen by the circulating pe-destrian and from eye level. As we have learned, the line of move-ment may be fixed, or it may be undirected and free, allowing a number of alternative routes and a variety of viewing experiences. Slow movement engenders interest in detail. When we are in a hurry, we tolerate few delays, but if moving leisurely we welcome deflection and distraction. We have little interest in motion and take pleasure instead in things seen or experienced. We explore with our senses, delight in relationships, and are pleased by subtle transitions.

The base plane   Pedestrian traffic moving on the base plane is sensitive to its textures, which determine the type and speed of foot traffic. A given texture not only accommodates a certain classifica-tion of use but may attract it as well, as in the following examples:

Texture	Traffic
Natural granite, rough sandstone	The hobnailed boot
Packed earth, the field, the forest duff	The hiking shoe, the moccasin
Snow	The ski, the snowshoe
Ice	The skate, the crampon
Sand	The clog, the bare foot, the sandal
Turf	The spiked or crepe-soled sports shoe, the cleated football boot
Bituminous paving	The tennis sneaker
Flagstone	The loafer
Cut stone, concrete, paving brick	The business shoe
Polished marble	The dancing pump

Distance and grade   Moving under our own power, we are con-scious of distances to be overcome and the effort of climbing a grade. When these are negative factors, they are reduced insofar as possible by the arrangement of the plan. Apparent distances and grades can be reduced by route alignment, by screening, and by

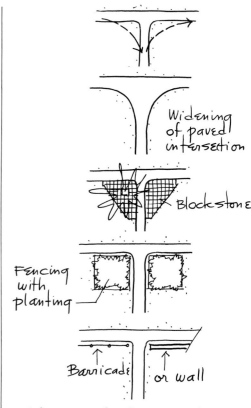

Widening of paved intersection

Blockstone

Fencing with planting

Barricade or wall

Reinforcement of walk curves and intersections
Short-cutting, with its consequent wear and erosion, can be precluded.

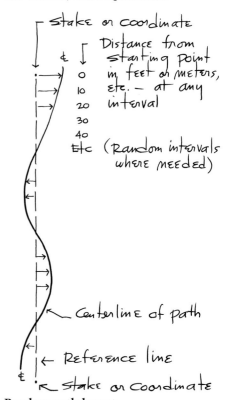

Stake or coordinate

Distance from starting point in feet or meters, etc. — at any interval

Etc (Random intervals where needed)

Centerline of path

Reference line

Stake or coordinate

Random path layout
To describe or field-stake meandering paths, measurements to the centerline can be made by offset distances along a reference line.

The best source of design criteria is *field observation,* in which materials and their treatment can be appraised firsthand and in which area capacities, rates of flow, or dimensions can be counted and measured under comparable conditions.

The best test of design is *performance.*

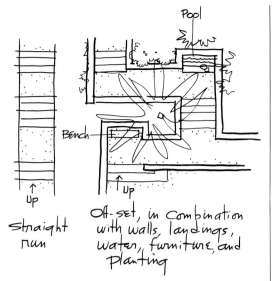

Straight run

Off-set, in combination with walls, landings, water, furniture, and planting

Changes of grade requiring steps provide design opportunities.

When the horse was discarded, the winding roads and streets over which he jogged were not discarded with him. The automobile inherited them. Some of them have been "improved" from time to time, but their basic features have remained unchanged. The result of pushing motor cars out over these old roads was at first simply a mild havoc and runaway horses, but later, "the traffic problem." Today we are still rebuilding old roads that were constructed for another vehicle, instead of special roads for the special needs of the automobile. This simple fact is the key to the whole present-day traffic problem.

Norman Bel Geddes

The street system of our cities and the road system of the region follow archaic patterns which go back to a time of beast drawn vehicles. The needs and practices that created the old thoroughfares are entirely alien to the auto. The old road necessarily ran through the villages, which provided resting places for passengers, a stage where horses could be fed and exchanged. Today those old regional routes—have become highways, and motor vehicles speeding along them carry traffic danger into every village and town.

Ludwig K. Hilberseimer

There will be in the future no roads or tracks which must be crossed at grade. Transportation and transit lines will be depressed or buried as free-flowing tubes—or lifted up above the earth that the goods or traffic they carry may glide along swiftly, safely, almost without friction.

Philip Douglas Simonds

Highways are best planned, as in this example, as free-flowing streams of vehicular traffic.

space modulation. Paths, for instance, can loop up or down a long, steep slope to reduce the apparent height, for the straight, unbroken climb to the top is in all ways more tiresome than gradual ascent from station to station along a path that angles up the contours.

Often, as we have noted, within a constricted complex it becomes desirable to *increase* apparent distances and heights. This again may be achieved in large measure by the manipulation of trafficways and sight lines or by the viewing of a peak from a pit, a pit from a peak, and a far corner from the longest diagonal.

Traffic flow   Pedestrian traffic, being earthbound, is more of a *flow* than a trajectory. This flow may be induced, arrested, divided, pooled, channeled, directed, diverted, or accelerated by skillful planning.

Automobile traffic

Highways, streets, and even driveways, as plan elements, must be considered as *lethal lines of force*. These lines and their intersections are lines and points of smashups, crippling accidents, and death. If a high-tension line crossed a community with its wires stretched low or sagging within reach of children, there would be a storm of citizen protest. Yet unprotected highways slice freely through the landscape, and our cities and our suburbs are cut into senseless squares by murderous boulevards and streets. Why? In the name of all reason, *why?*

There is, in the light of unprejudiced analysis, not one valid reason for our present checkerboard system of streets except for the obvious ease of laying them out. This seems a sorry excuse indeed. Our street and property patterns were, in fact, devised in the era of the horse and buggy and for the convenience of the surveyor. Because they so profoundly affect the patterns of movement, the quality, and very safety of our daily lives, it is high time for a change.

In our omnipresent automobiles we have found traffic friction increased from mere annoyance to a deadly phenomenon. In self-defense we have devised wider roads, separated roads, the overpass, the underpass, freeways, skyways, and multitiered interchanges. Engineers, in solving the very practical problem of moving people and automobiles through space, have created sweeping forms of awesome grandeur. Yet ever-new types of vehicles, trafficways,

and communities must be developed if we are to domesticate the roaring, fuming, four-wheeled monsters that we have created.

In the planning of our highways and streets, we must conceive them as *friction-free paths of vehicular movement.* This clearly is their primary purpose. Yet if we were to plot a typical street or highway as a force diagram, we would wonder how a more friction-studded, danger-loaded, chaotic trafficway could possibly be imagined. We know, for instance, that each point at which the paths of two vehicles merge is a point of potential conflict and that each point at which they cross is a point of hazard. Obviously, the fewer such points, the better. Yet, with rare exceptions, our present trafficways are so laced and interlaced with mergings and crossings that their very function is precluded. How blind we have become in our conditioned complacency!

In our trafficways of the future, the grade intersection will be eliminated in every possible instance. Roads will be planned for fast, safe, uninterrupted traffic *flow.* Turning radii will be greatly increased. Rights-of-way will be widened and shaped to accommodate and contain all foreseeable and compatible roadway functions. Vehicular traffic of various types and speeds will be segregated and given separate and specially planned routes. Marginal intrusions will be eliminated. Innovative safety controls and devices will be planned with and built into the highways. High-speed transconti-

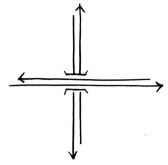

Grade separation without interconnection is often desirable.

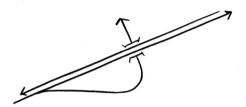

The left-turn underpass (or overpass)
Highway crossing provided without hazard or interruption of traffic flows.

The basic traffic interchanges (overpass with ramps)

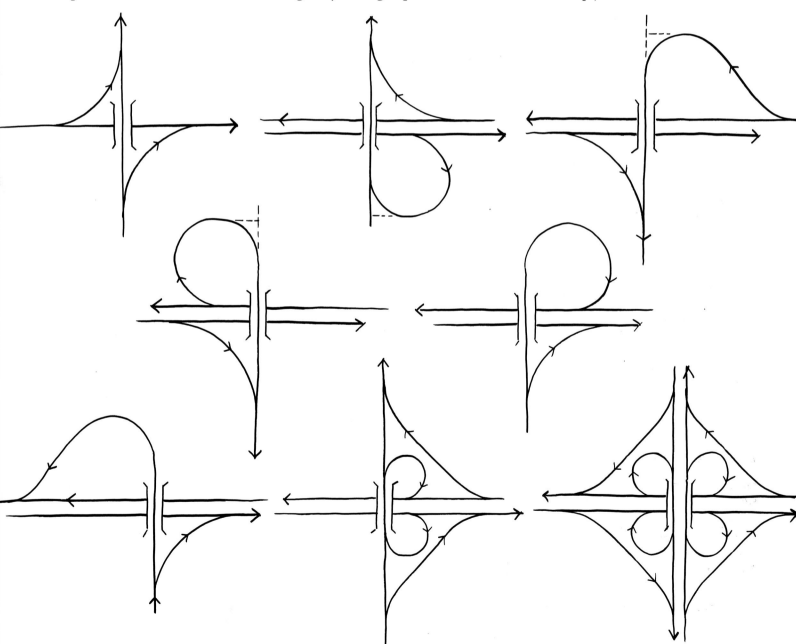

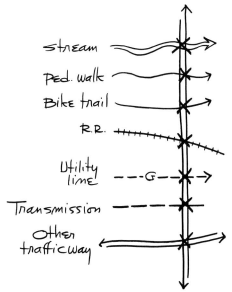

In the interest of safety, efficiency, and economy the crossing of transportation routes by any other line of flow or trafficway should be avoided insofar as feasible.

An early vehicular overpass, perhaps the first in America: Central Park, New York City.

This tiered urban highway, combined with park and overlook, is fitted to a steep, rocky slope across the river from Manhattan.

Have you ever conceived of a road which would allow no car to approach your own—which would hold you to your course without the danger of being struck or striking any object—where you could decide in advance how fast you would like to drive, and by maintaining that constant, effortless pace, arrive at your destination on scheduled time? It sounds impossible! But you can have such a road. The means of bringing it about are available. The idea is thoroughly practical. It can be built to work in conjunction with an automatic control installed in your car. The highway you use can be made as safe and pleasant at all times as it would be if your car were the only automobile upon it.

Norman Bel Geddes

nental motorways will weave through the open country *between* our towns and cities rather than threading them from center to center. Our residential, commercial, and industrial districts will be planned off to the side, protected and entered by widely spaced, free-flowing parkways or designated truckways. Multimodal systems of movement will be devised to interconnect polarized cities and new satellite communities.

A highway, road, or driveway is in itself a unified whole. It must be complete. It must be safe. It must be efficient. It must work well as a route of circulation and interconnection. It should also provide a pleasant experience of movement from point to point through the landscape. This useful and pleasurable quality is most evident when the right-of-way is aligned in harmony with the topography and is wide enough to accommodate all required physical and visual functions. How pleasant is the parkway with limits that extend to the rim of the valley through which it winds or with right-of-way widened to protect the sight lines from a sloping grade or ridge top!

It can be reasonably expected that highways, roads, and driveways will long continue to be designed as the major means of access to most project sites. Each landscape area will be considered in relation to its accessway, and, conversely, each line of access will be conceived as an integral part of the thing or place toward which or away from which it leads.

The contemporary highway with its adjunct approaches and structures is not only the most dominant feature of our landscape, it is also the most salient factor in our land and community planning. Once established in any landscape, a roadway becomes a potent feature and immediately changes the character of the land areas through which it makes its way. In most site-structure diagrams the roadway is the most dynamic line to which use areas can be related. Without doubt, the most telling advances in our future planning will be the diagraming of more reasonable relationships between our teeming trafficways, communities, cities, and the surrounding landscape. The automobile has rendered obsolete all prior concepts of land planning.

This much cannot be denied the automobile: it has given us exhilarating freedoms of distance and time. We move about more readily than ever before. The automobile has, however, invaded our living and working areas, disrupted cherished pedestrian ways and places, and imposed a distressing double visual scale.

Far too much of our landscape is presently viewed at the same time by persons in speeding automobiles and by people moving about on foot. These two experiences and the forced relationships are incompatible. This omnipresent dilemma has hardly as yet been generally recognized, let alone resolved. If ignoring it has caused us increasing and sometimes insurmountable problems, perhaps its study and resolution may bring the first plan forms and patterns fully expressive of our automotive age. In the new landscape for living all motor and pedestrian traffic will be segregated. Our living and working areas will be readily approached and serviced by the automobile, but they will be oriented to, and interspersed with, attractive, refreshing pedestrian spaces unpenetrated by roadways. Walking will again be a pleasure when it is freed from the sound, sight, fumes, and danger of rushing traffic and when it leads us through places and spaces designed for walking and congregating. And our motorways, designed solely and specifically for free vehicular movement and riding pleasure, will seem a dream on wheels.

The relationship of land use areas and buildings to trafficways is discussed in other sections of this book. In considering vehicular *circulation*, however, it should be instructive at this point to list the key principles to be applied in the location and design of roadways, approach drives, motor entrance courts, and parking compounds.

The roadway   Every roadway, be it a rural drive or an urban expressway, is a unique work of design and will have its own regional and functional characteristics. In planning trafficways of any type or magnitude, however, the following principles will pertain.

Determine the most rational alignment. This implies efficient point-to-point connection. The roadway will weave *between* and provide access *to* activity centers and areas of population concentration. It will follow existing boundary lines and borders insofar as feasible. It will respond to the topographical forms and vegetative growth and fit into the landscape.

Accommodate the traffic. The eventual carrying capacity is based on the best possible projection of development within the roadway corridor. If the full facility is not to be constructed initially, the right-of-way should be adequate for all future needs.

Preserve the natural systems and scenic superlatives. A first requisite in this regard is a right-of-way of ample and variable width. It will allow for all foreseeable lanes, shoulders, side slopes, and drainageways without crowding. It will expand in places to include such natural landscape features as streams, ponds, groves, and rock outcrops. It will also provide buffering to screen unsightly uses and to protect and enframe desirable views.

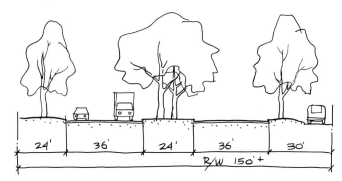

Arterial: six-lane divided
Six-lane divided arterials carry massive volumes of high-speed traffic. They interconnect and provide access to the large metropolitan communities and districts. While pedestrian walks are not compatible, minitransit and reserved bus lanes may share the right-of-way.

Most residential streets (forced to comply with rigid subdivision standards) are grossly oversized and by their width destroy the livability so much to be desired.

Increased street width means increased speed, hazard, cost, and disruption.

On-street parking is a principal cause of traffic-related accidents.

Provide the optimum cross section. Lane widths and their number will depend upon projected traffic types and volumes. When traffic volumes are high, the topography is rough, and existing conditions and land values permit, it is usually desirable to plan for separated roadways. Earthwork and construction costs can often thus be reduced to more than recoup the additional land taking. The advantages include the reduction of the roadway scale, the elimination of headlight glare, the reduction of side-slope height and width, and a more natural landscape fit.

Adjust the horizontal curvature. Major high-speed roads are designed with radius curves and interconnecting spirals. Lesser roads are often designed with tangents connected by radius curves at their points of intersection. Minor roads and woodland trails usually just feel their way along the land and between the trees and other obstacles without benefit of geometry.
   The important point is that in every case the planned centerline is to be field-staked and adjusted to avoid unforeseen obstructions and problem areas and to take full advantage of the topographical setting and views.

Slip lane in the arterial median.

Adjust the vertical profiles concurrently. The best vertical alignment rolls with the contours to require a minimum of clearing, grading, and erosion control. It must provide clear sighting of oncoming vehicles and points of roadway entry from the sides. It must also ensure the positive drainage of the roadbed and the adjacent swales or gutters. The degree of rise or fall is an important safety factor in inclement weather.

Design for stability. A well-built road like a well-built structure starts with a solid foundation. In the construction of any roadway it is essential that the base be stable and well drained and that the successive courses laid thereon be interlocked and well compacted. The total section, including slab or wearing course, is designed as a unit to best withstand the local climate and support the anticipated loadings.

Provide a suitable driving surface. In texture, the surface will give grip under adverse weather conditions. In color it will be at once heat-reflective, easy on the eyes, and differentiated from the hues of the road-edge soils and materials to give visual definition. On major roads this definition of the traveled roadway can also be achieved by edge and centerline striping. The use of native crushed stone, coral, or gravels as surface aggregate is always appropriate.

Build in the safety features. Reduced gradients, wider curves, controlled access, and elimination of on-grade crossings are all conducive to safety. Other protective features include guardrails, reflectors, and clear directional signage. At special nodes such as major off ramps or interchanges, roadway illumination by nonglaring light sources can be helpful.

Keep the structures simple. The best highway structures—bridges, overpasses, underpasses, retaining walls, and culverts—are usually direct expressions of their purpose, the locality, and the materials of construction. In some local situations, as in parks, rough-dressed native stone and rough-sawn timbers may be used effectively. Usually, and especially on highways, unadorned concrete and structural steel are more appropriate.

Coordinate the informational system. Good directional signage is easily visible and complete. It gives the right information at the right place and in a clearly comprehensible form consistent with the character and design speed of the roadway.

Use indigenous plant materials. The best planting of any roadway is achieved by the preservation of all possible existing native vegetation. Selective thinning is usually needed to articulate the road edges, enframe the views, and create a pleasantly modulated volumetric enclosure. Supplementary seeding and planting are in the main installed for slope protection and erosion control.

In the open, uncultivated countryside a highly effective procedure is to seed all disturbed roadside areas to a hardy strain of wild grass. An undulating border is then mowed with a sickle bar, while the naturalized area beyond is left uncut to receive a crop of wind-blown seeds from the adjacent meadows and woodlands. Trees, shrubs, vines, weeds, and wild flowers combine in time to produce a maintenance-free roadside of great indigenous beauty.

Maximize the landscape values. In every case a well-designed

Every highway is bordered by an idle strip as long as it is; keep cow, plow and mower out of these idle spots, and the full native flora, plus dozens of interesting stowaways from foreign parts, could be part of the normal environment of every citizen.

Aldo Leopold

roadway will be aligned through the landscape in such a way and be so constructed as to preserve and display the best features and views while attaining a harmonious fit. A good roadway provides comfort, interest, and pleasure to the traveler. A good roadway is also a good neighbor.

The approach drive   In locating a project on any site, the line of approach not only will influence or dictate the position of the structural elements but will probably also determine the relationships of the site use areas as well. Assuming that an approach drive is to be developed between an existing circulation drive or street and a proposed building, let us consider the design requirements. All else being equal, it should:

Announce itself at the passing roadway. The driveway entrance is best located where it *wants* to be. This is at the point of most logical penetration or highest visual interest along the fronting property line. The driveway should be well identified by street number or appropriate entrance sign. It should be considered in relationship to adjacent driveway entrances and nearby landscape

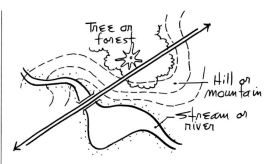

Whenever a roadway transects a natural landscape form, disruption and/or costly construction is the result.

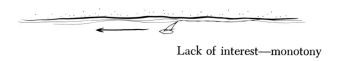

Lack of interest—monotony

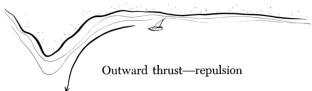

Outward thrust—repulsion

features. It will invite one in with recessive forms, as in a cove or harbor. In plan layout and site treatment it will set the theme for all that lies ahead. Often it will introduce at the gateway the materials and architectural theme that will be used throughout the site development.

Provide safe access and egress. The driveway entrance is set at a point which will assure safe sighting distance up and down the passing street or roadway. It is not to be located just below a steep crest or around a sharp curve. Abrupt turning movements are avoided, and, where possible, a glide-in entry with a generous turning radius is planned. On larger projects a deceleration lane is often provided if traffic volumes are heavy. A right-angle roadway entrance connection is best for two-way sighting.

Develop a pleasant transition. We design an attractive space and theme modulation from driveway throat to building entrance, to parking court, and return. The drive width may vary, swelling at the drive entry, at the curves, and at the forecourt and always suggesting traffic *flow*.

We devise a transition from the character of the highway to the character of the project and structure, be it a residence, an apartment tower, a business office, a shopping mall, or a school. We move from the scale of the passing road to the scale of the building entrance court, from high velocity to repose. At one instant, for example, a person may be whisking along the trafficway at whistling speed; 2 minutes later the same person may be standing contemplatively at the building entrance. Between the two conditions are telling changes in mental attitude that must somehow be agreeably resolved. By the design of the driveway, the visitor must be prepared for the experience of arrival.

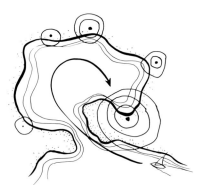

Inward pull—attraction

The pull of the harbor
The successful drive approach and forecourt will suggest a receptive cove. Usually the most attractive point on the cove periphery will be the entrance door or gate.

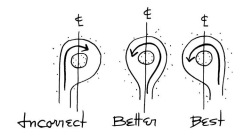

The approach loop Turn (*at left*) is contrary to normal flow. Approach from the center or right induces the correct turning movement.

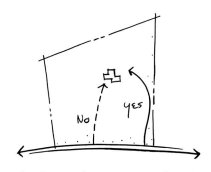

Avoid splitting the property in locating the entrance drive.

The psychology of arrival is more important than you think. If it is not obvious where to park, if there is no room to park when you get there, if you stumble into the back door looking for the front entrance, or if the entrance is badly lighted, you will have subjected your guests to a series of annoyances which will linger long in their subconscious. No matter how warm your hearth or how beautiful your view, the overall effect will be dimmed by these first irritations.

Thomas D. Church

Be logical. The approach should present the driver with a minimum number of decisions. It is to be remembered that traffic tends to the right but also to the easier fork and to the easier grade. The pathway should be obvious but restrained. This is to say that it must read clearly to the driver while intruding as little as possible on the natural landscape.

Take full advantage of the site. The alignment of the driveway presents an excellent opportunity to plan for the visual unfolding or realization of the site—its topography, cover, vistas, views, and better landscape features. It should be so aligned as to reveal the pleasantly undulating edge of a woodlot or planting, the modeling of ground forms, and the counterplay of tree trunk against tree trunk, mass against mass, texture against texture, and color against color as one sweeps along.

Move with the contours. To preclude unnecessary disruption the drive should flow with or angle easily across the contours. Often it may follow a broad ridgeline. Again, it may move up a drainageway to the side of and preserving the natural flow line, thus gaining positive drainage at one side while enjoying a degree of protection and concealment. Because a driveway and its gutters often provide for the storm-water flow from large areas of the property, the grades should be such as to permit surface flow without undue erosion and gravity flow of any contiguous storm or sanitary sewers.

Avoid splitting the property. The driveway alignment will be such as to reserve as much land as possible in an undisturbed condition. The planner will strive to retain the best landscape features while defining cohesive use areas.

Be economical in layout. The driveway will be kept short for economy of construction and ease of maintenance. Other considerations include the relative ease of excavation, a balance of cut-and-fill materials, and the alternative costs of drainage structures or bridges.

Be safe. Avoid the crossing of other drives, walks, bicycle trails, or active use areas.

Be consistent. The designer will strive to keep the quality of the approach drive consonant with that of the site, the proposed project uses, and the structures. Again, as with all project components, the driveway is to be considered a complete and unified work of design.

Reveal the structures gradually. We design the approach road to make the first impression of the property and buildings attractive. A building is usually more interesting if seen from a curving drive approach, to show its form and extent before attention is centered on detail. Much of the nature of a structure is thus revealed by a planned exposition of its sculptural qualities from a drive that leads past or around it. We open successive views to the structure, each from the optimum distance and position and with the best attainable enframement.

The entrance court The entrance court is an integral part of both the approach drive and the building. It terminates the one, introduces the other, and unifies the two.

The driveway should never appear to collide with a building but should rather sweep toward and past it.

Approach from the right. Since in the United States a car moves in the right lane of traffic, we have developed taxicab and private car conditioning that tells us, as we near a destination, to chart a course that will bring the right side of the vehicle toward the building entrance. This right-curb approach is valid mainly because of two-way streets, which make pulling to the left curb inconvenient, illegal, or dangerous and usually all three.

Where possible, plan a one-way loop. One-way traffic at a building entrance is always preferable. It is safer. There is also a psychological advantage, for a driver with right wheels to the curb feels superior and, for some reason, very clever.

Accommodate the left-hand approach where necessary. On some sites an approach from the left is the only way possible. If this is planned, we try to arrange sufficent depth to permit the drive to swing past the entrance and circle back to achieve the favored position. If, however, the drive must perforce lead in from the left, we do what we can to make this feasible by making the point of discharge obvious, by providing a landing platform opposite the building entrance, or by planning for discharge within a paved forecourt.

Consider the climatic conditions. The approach court and building entry are planned for all conditions of weather, darkness, and light. Visitors are to be protected from wind sweep, rain, and glaring sun. Since paving is hot in the summer and cold in the winter, the building is not to be planned as an island in a sea of paving. We avoid the long walk or the long view across paving toward the building entrance.

Avoid the need for backing. The backing of vehicles near entranceways, especially in areas where children may be congregated or playing, is to be scrupulously avoided.

The parking compound Parking compounds provide an essential link between vehicular circulation ways, approach drives, and their termini. They are designed for the safe and efficient storage of cars. When space and site conditions permit, they are usually located beyond the building entrance as one approaches by car. Sometimes, however, they may serve in themselves as the approach court to one or more buildings. Whatever the planned function, it is to be accommodated and clearly expressed.

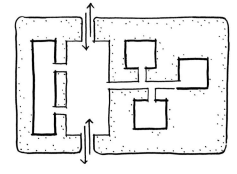

Single and clustered buildings are benefited by the provision of internal parking courts.
Provide off-street parking

Test all plan possibilities. The siting of parking areas is best achieved by the study of alternative shapes and flow lines in relation to the building and topographical features. The most prevalent parking layouts are easily diagramed for adaptation and testing.

Approach, pass, and park. Ideally a driver will approach with the building to his or her right, discharge the passengers, continue to the parking space, and return on foot by a pleasant and convenient route to the doorway. Ideally too, upon departing the driver would be able to pick up the car and circle back to passengers at the building entrance.

Screen the parking areas. A direct view from the entrance court into the parking area is not usually desirable. A well-placed parking or service compound is convenient but incidental to and secluded from the building.

Consider multiple use. A parking compound may be located for shared use by several buildings or activity areas concurrently. Or it may serve one purpose in daytime and another for evening or off-peak hours. Parking areas, when not in use for their primary purpose, may also serve other functions such as recreation, assembly, or temporary storage.

Accommodate the vehicle. Since the parking court is planned for the efficient storage of automobiles, it must be designed with full understanding of the maneuvering requirements of the car. These dictate gradients, turning radii, aisle and stall widths, and paving textures, which may well vary to differentiate lanes of movement and areas for parking storage.

Segregate service traffic. Service vehicles range in size from small motorized carts and pickups to larger delivery and refuse trucks. They require convenient access to building entrances, collection stations, mechanical rooms, utility vaults, and similar locations. When practical, service vehicle circulation and parking areas are separated from passenger automobiles and are designed to accommodate the larger turning radii, maneuvering space, and holding patterns required.

Plan for emergency access. Fire trucks, ambulances, police cars, and utility service vans require building access. The site plan must ensure that these vehicles can get where they need to go. If direct road access cannot be provided, walks and other paved areas may be utilized provided they are designed with this purpose in mind.

Consider the handicapped
Reserve stalls of extra width, with depressed curb, near the destination.

We spend more and more hundreds of millions of dollars to build more and more super highways to more and more remote distances so that more and more people may drive more and more rapidly until they come to the place where they must stop and wait and wait longer and longer—to get into the district where it is harder and harder and harder to move around at all!

Frederick Bigger

RESIDENTIAL STREETS

THE ORDER OF RESIDENTIAL STREETS

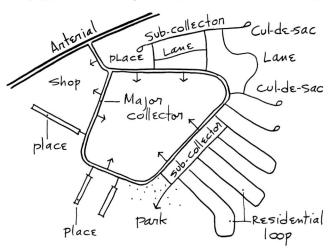

	R/W ±	Paved ±
Lane	36'	18'
Cul-de-sac	40-50	20
Residential loop	50	22
Sub-collector	60	24
Place (Motor court)	70-130	Varies
Major collector	80	24 + 24
Arterial	100' +	24 - 72

- Low-speed traffic on neighborhood loop and cul-de-sac streets and in residential motor courts (places) often permits sharing the paved way with bicycles and pedestrians.

- Sidewalks and/or bikeways are usually provided on one or both sides of sub-collector drives where required for pathway linkage.

- Separate walks and bicycle paths may also be prescribed along major collector streets, arterial parkways, and boulevards — except where pedestrians or bicycles are to be accommodated by paths through internal community greenways.

- Direct building frontage and/or driveway connections are best prohibited on arterials, collectors, and some sub-collectors.

- Parking is not to be permitted on any community street.

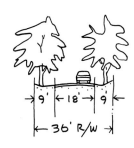

The lane is a narrow, often meandering, paved or unpaved frontage street for scattered single-family homes.

LANE

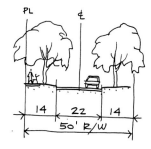

Bicycles use the roadway. Walks are optional. No on-street parking.

Along these frontage streets are grouped the single-family homes and residential clusters of most neighborhoods. Low traffic volumes, low speeds, and good visibility are the essentials.

RESIDENTIAL LOOP STREET

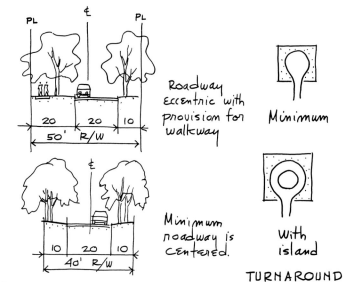

Roadway eccentric with provision for walkway

Minimum roadway is centered.

Minimum

With island

TURNAROUND

The cul-de-sac provides desirable residential frontage on a low-speed lineal accessway, with a sense of neighborhood. It should not exceed 1000' ± without intermediate turn-arounds.

THE CUL-DE-SAC

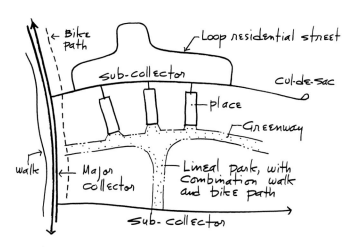

RESIDENTIAL STREETS AND WAYS

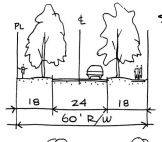

SUB-COLLECTOR STREET

Walks and/or bikeways installed as needed for safety and continuity

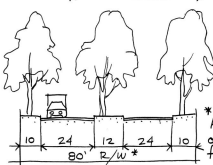

18 24 18
60' R/W

Sub-collector streets provide safe and pleasant low-speed connection between motor courts (places), culs-de-sac, residential frontage streets, and the major collectors. Entrance drives to the side should be limited to multi-family clusters.

MAJOR COLLECTOR

* Add 10' per side where walks or bikeways are required for access or system continuity

10 24 12 24 10
80' R/W *

This dominant form giver of the community plan visually serves as the portal as well and describes a modified loop from which the lesser streets branch. Intersections of streets or entrance drives serving residential courts, shopping malls, marinas, or other community centers should occur at intervals no closer than 660'.

Arterial roadways of several types provide rapid connection between the regional freeways and the community collector streets. All are to be designed as free-moving trafficways, without building frontage at the side.

Arterial parkways, ideally planned as one-way pairs, exclude trucks but with widened R/W may provide for a reserved bus lane or other forms of rapid transit.

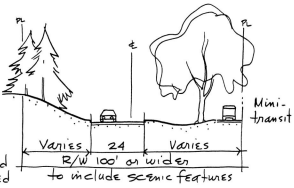

Varies 24 Varies
R/W 100' or wider
to include scenic features

ARTERIAL PARKWAY

Mini-transit

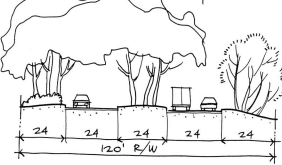

24 24 24 24 24
120' R/W

ARTERIAL-4-LANE DIVIDED

The 4-lane divided arterial, with a 24' median and slip lanes, provides for safe turning movements and entrance or egress on either side at intervals no closer than 660'.

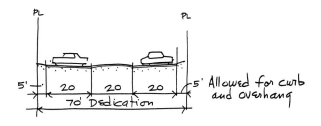

5' 20 20 20 5' Allowed for curb and overhang
70' Dedication

Motor courts (places) planned at the rear for parking and service, or as all-purpose entrance courts, provide off-street car storage and a planted open space around which dwellings may be grouped.

MOTOR COURTS (PLACES)

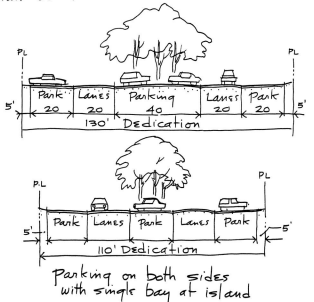

5' Park 20 Lanes 20 Parking 40 Lanes 20 Park 20 5'
130' Dedication

5' Park Lanes Park Lanes Park 5'
110' Dedication

Parking on both sides with single bay at island

PARKING

First determine the number and type of spaces required. (1)

As a rule of thumb: (2)

Single-family home	2 spaces/dwelling
Attached res. units	2 " "
Garden apts.	1.75 " "
Mid-rise "	1.5+ " "
High-rise "	1.5 " "
Hotels and motels	1 space/room
Restaurants	1 space/50 s.f. of patron area
Convenience shopping	1 space/250 s.f. of gross fl. area
Other commercial dept. stores, banks	1 space/300 g.f.a.
Bus. and prof. off.	1 space/400 g.f.a.
Churches, theatres, auditorium, etc.	1 space ±/3 seats
Schools (Jr.-Sr.)	1 space/200 g.fl.a. excluding gym.
Hospitals	1 space/bed
Industrial	1 space/2 employ
Parks/recreation	Varies

(1) Consider the parking of buses, service vehicles, compact cars, and cycles.

(2) To be modified to meet local zoning or other requirements. Staff parking is additional.

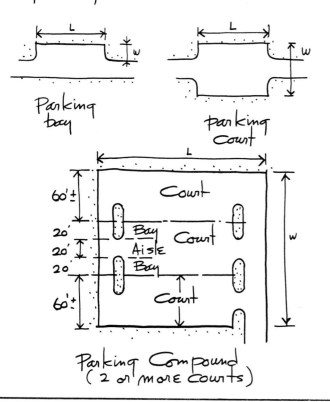

Parking bay

Parking court

Parking Compound
(2 or more courts)

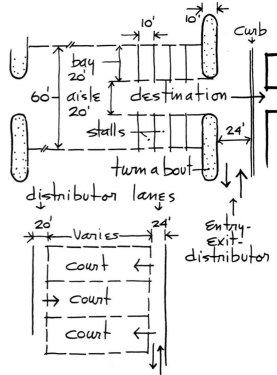

In the trial layout of large parking areas these approximate (rounded) dimensions are useful. Actual dimensions are later adjusted in the construction drawings.

Learn the Components.

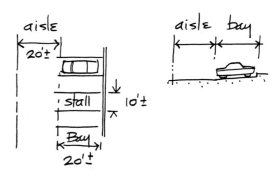

Perpendicular parking is standard for parking areas having two-way traffic in the aisles. It requires more space than angle parking and more difficult turning movements.

Perpendicular

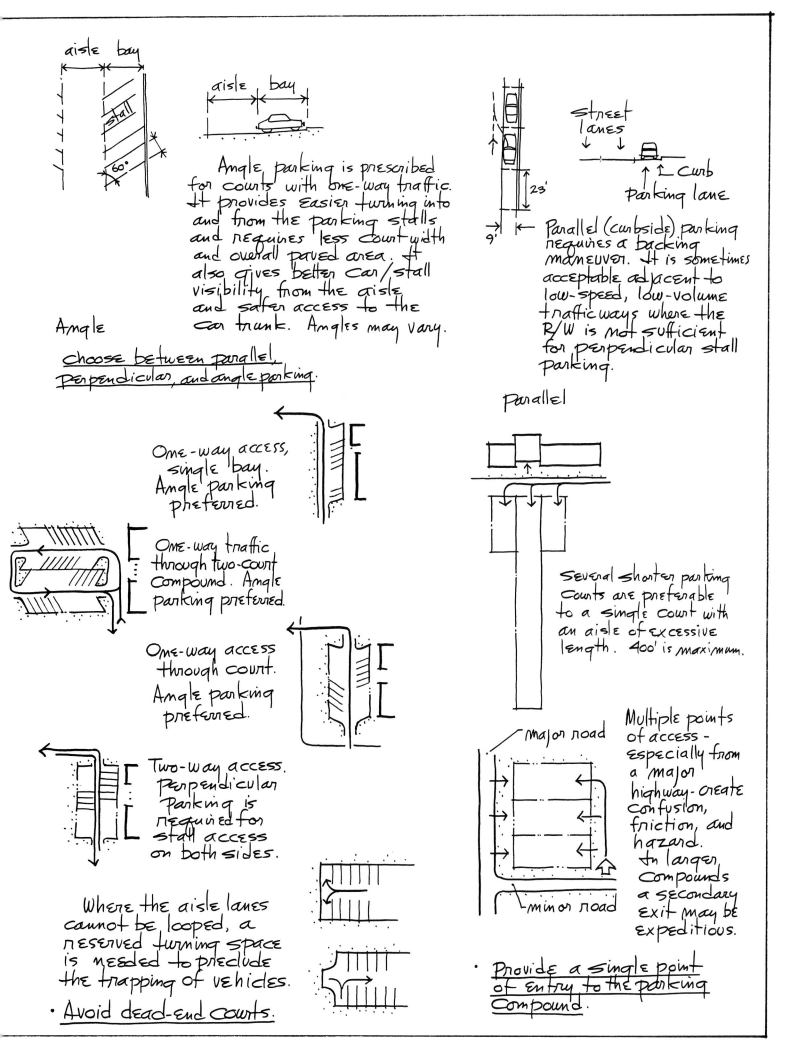

Angle parking is prescribed for courts with one-way traffic. It provides easier turning into and from the parking stalls and requires less court width and overall paved area. It also gives better car/stall visibility from the aisle and safer access to the car trunk. Angles may vary.

Angle

Choose between parallel, perpendicular, and angle parking.

Parallel (curbside) parking requires a backing maneuver. It is sometimes acceptable adjacent to low-speed, low-volume trafficways where the R/W is not sufficient for perpendicular stall parking.

Parallel

One-way access, single bay. Angle parking preferred.

One-way traffic through two-court compound. Angle parking preferred.

One-way access through court. Angle parking preferred.

Two-way access. Perpendicular parking is required for stall access on both sides.

Several shorter parking courts are preferable to a single court with an aisle of excessive length. 400' is maximum.

Multiple points of access - especially from a major highway - create confusion, friction, and hazard. In larger compounds a secondary exit may be expeditious.

Where the aisle lanes cannot be looped, a reserved turning space is needed to preclude the trapping of vehicles.

· Avoid dead-end courts.

· Provide a single point of entry to the parking compound.

PARKING

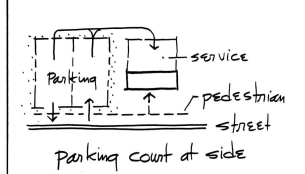

Parking court at side

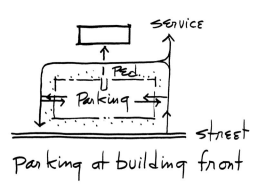

Parking at building front

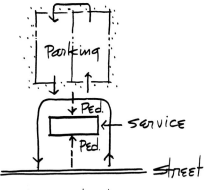

Parking at the rear

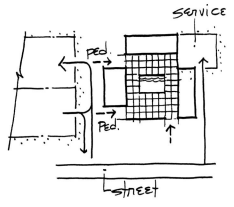

Buildings grouped around a pedestrian court with parking and service areas at the side.

- <u>Plan buildings, circulation, and parking together.</u>

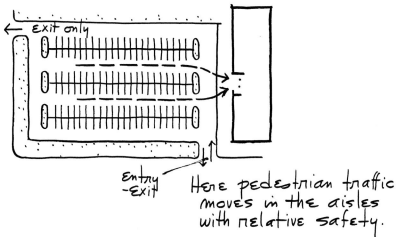

Here pedestrian traffic moves in the aisles with relative safety.

- <u>Align the parking aisles toward the major destination.</u>

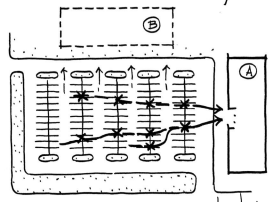

Pedestrians moving from their cars to building Ⓐ are induced to cross both the parking bays and aisle traffic. This layout favors pedestrian flow from cars to and from a building at position Ⓑ.

- <u>Avoid pedestrian movement through parked cars.</u>

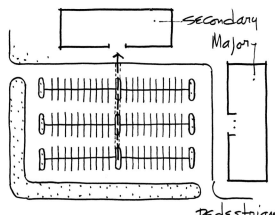

Pedestrians can move in aisles from their cars to a well-marked crosswalk.

- <u>Provide cross-compound walkways where needed.</u>

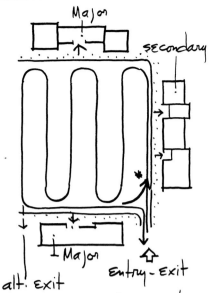

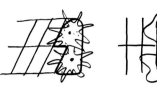

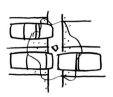

The turn abouts can also be utilized for planting.

For lesser widths plant the tree on the stall line.

alt. exit

Entry-Exit

Major

* Always provide a return loop for passenger pick-up in inclement weather.

- <u>Keep the courts rectilinear and the traffic pattern simple.</u>

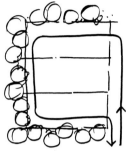

Peripheral shade and screen plantings are always desirable.

By depressing the parking Compound in combination with walls, fencing, mounding, and planting, cars and paving can be concealed.

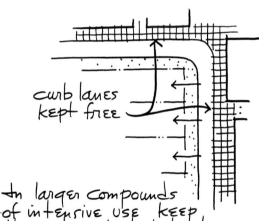

curb lanes kept free

In larger Compounds of intensive use keep the Entry-distributor lanes unimpeded for passenger let-off and pick-up.

- <u>Keep the curb lanes clear.</u>

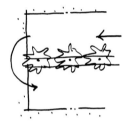

Where space permits, separate the courts with a planting strip.

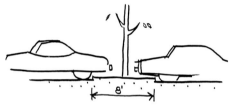

8' of width is recommended to allow for front and rear car overhang.

- <u>Plan to accommodate planting.</u>

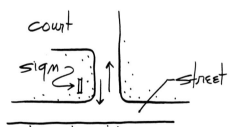

court

sign

street

Nighttime illumination of the entire Compound is essential to security and safety.

- <u>Mark the Entry-exit clearly with sign and illumination.</u>

canopy trees

As the vehicular portal, the Compound provides the introduction to the adjacent structures. Walls, paving, signing, lighting and planting are all to be kept "in character."

- <u>Make the parking Compound in all ways attractive.</u>

Rail, water, and air

Aside from the automobile, the traditional means of transporting people and goods have been railroads, boats, and airplanes. These in their early forms opened up the country. Their routes, crossings, and points of convergence set the locations of our towns and cities and provided their outlying regions with the essential outlets for agricultural products and manufactured goods.

The railroads, ships, and airlines served their purpose well. Recently, however, they have experienced increasing problems in their stubborn insistence, and sometimes forced requirement, that they maintain their original all-purpose role of moving goods and people concurrently. Except in rare cases the two functions are incompatible. As new forms of conveyance by rail, water, and air emerge, the carriers will be highly specialized, as will be their routes, equipment, and terminals. Improved means of transit, transportation, and distribution will change established concepts of *land use, community,* and *city* and require a whole new planning approach.

Travel by rail   Passenger travel by rail in its most recent forms is known as *rapid transit.* Some types are streamlined versions of the old interurban or commuter trains. They move on fixed rails on grade, underground, or elevated. Some vehicles are equipped with steel wheels; some, with wheels that are rubber-tired. All are highly automated and can be computer-controlled. Other types use

Rapid transit vehicle.

linked cars which are suspended from or propelled along a single or multiple guideway. All systems have been improved to a point at which they are light, bright, environmentally sound, and highly efficient. They can move people in groups from point to point within a region far more rapidly and at less total cost per passenger-mile than the passenger car or bus. Why then hasn't rapid transit been more widely accepted?

First, it carries many more people to more places each day than is generally realized. The advanced systems of San Francisco, Toronto, Montreal, and Washington are promising examples, as are the guided systems of Disneyland and Disney World. Where rapid transit has not succeeded or has failed to realize its full potential, there are common causes at the root of the failure.

The communities served are too widely dispersed. In the typical single-family-home suburb, it often takes longer to drive to or be driven to the station than to ride from station to destination.

The transit connections are not direct. At the downtown end of the line the station is often blocks away from the business, civic, shopping, or cultural centers.

The stations are inadequate. They are often grim. Old railway stations or other obsolete structures are sometimes converted to the new use without remodeling or thought for the convenience, comfort, or pleasant relaxation of the waiting passengers.

The passing scenery is ugly. Some routes, using the existing railroad trackage or right-of-way, provide the most extensive slumming excursions extant. By established railroad custom the public must ride the same route as the tank cars, flatcars, crated chickens, and bawling calves, past the rear doors of the soap factory, junkyard, and slaughterhouse. It is not a good way to attract or hold would-be commuters.

The transit potential The mass movement of people at high velocities between areas of residential concentration and regional activity centers has manifest advantages. Among these are predictability, safety, and savings in time, land area, and energy. The era of

Regional rapid transit
Energy conservation (economic necessity) may soon force us to do what reason so far has not.

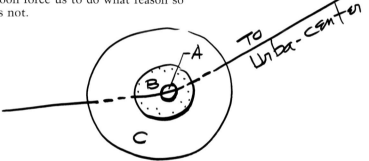

Transit node community *A*—Station with minicar storage and recharge. Multifamily dwellings and convenience center. *B*—Dwellings within walking distance. *C*—Minitransit access by all-weather golf carts or electric bus.

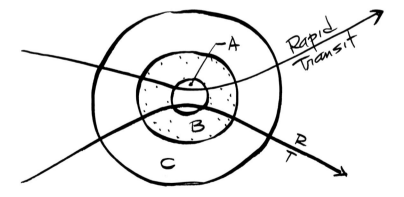

Urba-center *A*—Multilevel transit terminal. *B*—Primary urban activity zone. Terraced pedestrian domain. Movement by elevators, escalators, and moving walks. *C*—Supporting urban activities. Movement by minibus or minirail. Decked parking but no surface automobile traffic. Goods distributed by tubes and beltways from peripheral transport terminals.

transit is at hand, perhaps as much by necessity as by reason. It will come into its own as a flourishing travel mode when but only when:

> The transitway is planned as a means by which to structure or restructure the region and new types of residential communities and urban activity cores.

> The experience of travel by rapid transit is conceived in terms of safe, efficient, and pleasurable motion.

> The transit facility is programmed and planned as a complete, interrelated, and interrelating whole. In other words, communities, stations, vehicles, routes, and termini are planned together as a smoothly operating *system.*

The fleeting landscape   From the transit cars, as from the automobile, the passing scene is observed as a continuing flow of impressions. Just as in a static composition we take pleasure in harmonious relationships, so it is that in the blending compositions of the passing scene we seek harmonious transitions. That which is abrupt, chaotic, or inappropriate we find to be displeasing. That which is fitting and orderly and "evolves" we find agreeable.

Nearby objects streaking past have little meaning in themselves. They may effectively serve as screening, either as a blur of loose foliage or as a solid wall, earth bank, or building. They often develop cadences, sometimes pleasurable, sometimes annoying. They usually distract and disturb by their flicker and by the fact that one strains to distinguish and identify them. By their jittery insistence they often destroy the scenic qualities inherent in the landscape. Viewing in such cases would be made more pleasant if the foreground objects were removed or simplified.

As from the moving automobile, visual interest from a moving transit car is centered in the middle distance or on the distant view. The far view changes slowly and soon becomes monotonous unless given variety by things observed in the middle ground. To be enjoyable to the viewer, the midground interest or action must be consistent with the background and with the modulating foreground enframement. This is well known to the artist who draws the background scenes for animated cartoons. The artist is concerned with *producing* unfolding relationships of foreground, midground, and background that work agreeably together. The passenger in the speeding car is interested in *realizing* such relationships.

Travel by water   When we think of a boat in motion, we think of a smoothly gliding hull, a curving wake of tumbling water, and dancing light. The course of a boat, like the water through which it moves, is fluid and undulating. Having no fixed track or roadway, it curves in wide arcs and must be given ample space for maneuvering. Even at rest at its mooring, a proper boat seems mobile. All plan lines relating to boats at rest or in motion should suggest this streamlined fluid mobility. In every way possible, smooth flow should be encouraged and obstructions eliminated. The heavy, the rough, the jagged, the sharp are out of place. They are destructive and impeding in fact and disturbing by connotation.

Travel by boat seems almost frictionless. All things and places are left, passed, and approached on the glide. Movement is relatively slow. Except for the tacking sailboat, change of direction is seldom abrupt. The middle and far distances become, visually, a

The solution to public transit is planning activity centers to which people can ride together.

Community transit stations should have direct vertical access to the central convenience plaza around which multifamily units are clustered.

Proposal for a boating park.

A structure that dramatizes its relation to
the river.

panoramic background for the objects and details to be seen more
closely at hand. With the sky for the overhead plane and water for
the base, interest is centered on the vertical plane.

Being exposed to the elements and the tides, a boat requires for
its mooring a sheltered harbor or a protective pier. Harbor and pier
logically provide such shelter by topography, structure, or a combination of both. They are points of transition between the water and
the land, where the mobile and free meet the static. The fact of this
meeting might well be developed and expressed in all plan forms.
Indeed, no great stretch of the imagination is required to understand
that *any* structure related to water and boatways gains when the full
drama of the relationship is exploited.

A summer cottage on a lake or bay, for example, is best conceived as a planned transition from land to water. Together with its landscape forms it relates the solid to the fluid, the mineral to the aqueous, the confined to the expansive, and strong cast shadow to shimmering light. Often it provides also a transition from car to yacht, yawl, or rowboat. It is terraced down; it overhangs, overlooks; it screens off and then subtly or dramatically reveals; it embraces, ramps or steps into, invites view or movement from land to water and water to land. It accentuates, by lucid structural relationships, the highest qualities of land and water. At the land approach, it is of the land; at the water's edge, it is of the water.

A riverside restaurant, if worthy of its site, will orient to the river and its traffic and display it in all its motion and color. On the landward side, it will take its form from the features of the land and from the passing walk or street or highway. On the riverside, it will be shaped to the line of the river's flow and to the curve of approaching craft. It is a rewarding experience to dine in such a waterside restaurant, with its glass-walled dining room projected and elevated to catch the sweeping river view, or at shaded tables set on a terrace or deck beside the river wall, or at tables spaced out on the pier beside the bobbing boats and lapping water. In the same way, with the seaside hotel, the waterfront park, the bridge, the pier, the harbor, and the lighthouse, our plan forms and structures will express the land-and-water meeting.

Boatways and waterways, when well conceived, have few detrimental characteristics and many attractive features. Large bodies of water ameliorate the climate, enliven the landscape, and provide a direct and inexpensive means of travel and transportation. Rivers follow the valley floors. Usually their easy gradient encourages travel along their banks as well as upon their surface. They, together with their feeding streams and rivulets, promote a lush growth of vegetation and the most pleasing landscape environment of the regions through which they pass. All waterways attract industrial, commercial, and residential development. How can they all be accommodated? Which should have preference? The solution here is not usually one of blanket prohibition, for such prohibitions tend to dam up overriding pressures, but is rather one of planned relationships. Lucky the region or city that is empathetically related to its rivers, lakes, canals, or waterfront.

Travel by air The view from a plane unfolds a modeled and checkered landscape of towns, hills, lakes, rivers, valleys, farmland, field, and forest moving slowly under the wings. We are impressed with the continuity of the landscape. We sense, perhaps for the first time, that every object in the landscape is related to the whole. Sight distances are great. Visible areas are enormous. Objects, to be seen, must be simple, bold, and contrasting in colors or textures. They are most often read from the air by their shadows. All essential plan forms or objects requiring recognition from the air, and especially at the airports and their approaches, must be so emphasized.

Travel by plane is *flight* and is seemingly effortless while one is airborne. This smooth, flashing speed accentuates the frictions and delays of the airport and cross-country travel beyond it. The frictions of port transfer and of port-to-city distance must be drastically reduced by improved land and transportation planning. The competitive port of the future will have fast and easy access to other transportation centers and to central discharge points. There are other problems to be overcome. Among them, the deafening din at the airport aprons is mounting, decibel by decibel, to a point at which it will soon become unbearable. Sometime before that critical point or very shortly after, the pressure of economics and the advance of science will have reduced the ear-shattering roar to a pleasant whistling hum.

An airport should rightly be planned as a *port*. Here, again, in this *air* harbor the land meets an opposite. This meeting and all induced transitions are to be analyzed and expressed. All current or foreseeable requirements and characteristics of planes, at rest or in flight, are to be accommodated. Further, the joint use of airfields by cargo and passenger planes with their varying speeds, needs, and capabilities will no longer be tolerable. Transport planes will be related to industrial and distribution centers. Passenger planes and ports will be linked to centers of population and urban activity. From the surrounding towns and cities new exclusive or classified approach roads will be necessary, as will a system of strategically placed air taxi stations. In this light, we can consider an airport primarily in terms of a continuing and ultimate experience of travel in which passengers can arrive by car, park, check baggage, and enplane or arrive by plane, pick up baggage, and leave by car, limousine, or tramway in one swift, pleasant, uninterrupted swoop. There are, of course, many other considerations in the planning of an airport.

Airports require large areas of flat topography or land that can be readily modified to give long, level runways. Because such areas are often of necessity remote, the tendency of airports is to bring to the spot as many port facilities as possible. Hotel, theaters, conference rooms, libraries, and even recreation, amusement, and shopping centers have been planned into the airports as revenue producers. In the interest of increased efficiency all extraneous uses must be limited in the future.

A municipal airport is no longer a landing strip, a dollysock, and a ticket booth. The modern airport is an extremely intricate complex of myriad related functions. These must be studied as to their optimum relationship to the cities and the region that the airport serves. Like all projects planned in the landscape, the airport must be studied in terms of minimizing its negative impacts and increasing its benefits.

People movers

The need for increasing numbers of persons to get from here to there, usually in a hurry, has given rise to a whole new array of vehicles and devices that have been grouped together in the category of transportation and circulation systems. Without them many of our newer governmental, business office, and commercial centers and even zoos and botanic gardens could no longer function. In type and size they vary according to the distance and height to be traveled, the number of passengers to be carried, and the rate of speed required.

Moving walkways, chairways, and escalators. These are a low-speed, step-on-and-off means of movement that can be used alone or in combination, indoors or out.

Automated cars. Electronically controlled automated cars that move on rails or guideways are in effect horizontal elevators. Used singly or linked, they can transport groups of people at moderate speeds for distances ranging from several hundred yards to several miles. They are smaller campus and in-town adaptations of the longer-range and faster subway, guideway, and monorail transit vehicles.

Small bus trains. Jeeps with trailers may be open to the sky or provided with full, all-weather protection. Bus trains are used frequently in recreation or exhibition areas and are often equipped with public address systems.

Minibuses. Small buses of all sizes and shapes have longer ranges, higher speeds, and greater maneuverability than bus trains. Some minibuses, used to link airport waiting rooms with distant plane pods, are of "maxi" proportions, carrying many dozens of passengers and hoisting them by hydraulic lifts to the level of the plane door.

Long-range buses. Long-range buses on separate busway routes are an increasingly popular form of suburban-urban transportation. They make stops at strategically located community waiting shelters or at one or more peripheral parking fields and then provide express linkage on reserved lanes to downtown centers.

Cable cars. Traversing steep slopes or mountainsides (as in Bogotá and Caracas) or skimming high overhead on suspended aerial cables (as at Cologne in Germany), cable cars can leap chasms, rivers, and ranges with safety and ease.

The bikeway as a lineal park.

Bicycles, tricycles, and mopeds. While self-propelled, these vehicles are not to be overlooked as people movers. It is only recently that, for the first time in many decades, the annual sale of bicycles in the United States has exceeded that of automobiles. Where off-road, off-sidewalk paths and trails are provided, especially as lineal parklike connectors to community and regional centers of attraction, bicycles and electric carts blossom into use.

The electric cart. A modified golf cart on three to four wheels, with all-weather provision and carrying from one to a dozen passengers, is the electric cart, soon to come into its own. It will provide the ideal future link between home and transit station, where it can be easily stored and recharged while awaiting the transit rider's return. The use of such carts together with cycles for intracommunity travel would remove the need for internal roads and reduce reliance on the more costly, more space-demanding automobile.

Integrated systems

It might be thought that the proliferating assortment of people conveyers would lead to utter chaos in their weaving in and out, up and down, and back and forth on crisscrossing routes and trajectories. Far from it. These vehicles provide, at last, the components needed to fit together a rational *system* of multimodal transportation. They provide the key to the structuring or restructuring of the regions and metropolitan areas around intensive multilevel transit-transportation hubs. These concentrated activity centers, freed of automobile traffic and the divisive interchanges, streets, and desertlike parking lots, can become again urbane and delightful pedestrian domains.

The sterile vehicular trafficways will be replaced by terraced plazas, garden courts and malls, and refreshing in-city parks through which people can move about on foot or be transported from level to level and center to center in year-round comfort.

Automobiles will swoop through the open countryside on controlled-access parkways, freed of trucks and buses. They will provide safe and pleasant alternative means of connection between the urban and regional nodes, where they will be "stabled" at the periphery.

New integrated *systems* of circulation give promise of innovative and vastly superior concepts of land and community planning.

Urba-center: a prototype transit activity node.

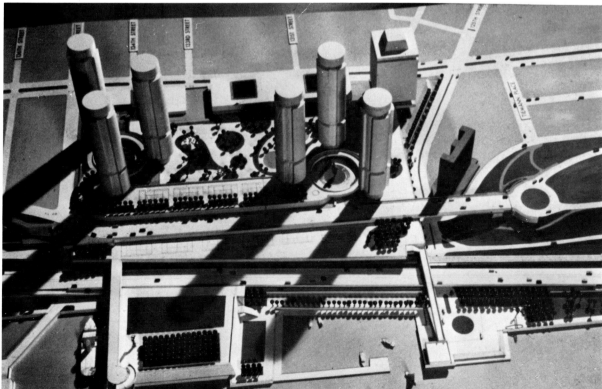

Structures 10

We physical planners like to think of ourselves as masters of space organization, yet in truth we are often baffled by the simplest problems of spatial arrangement and structural composition. What, for instance, are the design considerations in relating a building to its surrounding sea of space, or a building to its fronting approaches, or two buildings facing each other across an intervening mall, or a group of structures to each other and the spaces they enclose? Our predecessors had their theories on these matters and developed their sound principles. Many superb examples of their art are still to be seen: the Parthenon, Rome's Capitoline Piazza by Michelangelo, Villa Lante, the Alhambra. Yet we contemporaries proceed in blithe disregard of the truths and lessons of history. If we, proud spirits that we are, must learn our truth firsthand, there need be no problem, for we are surrounded by examples of the good and the bad and need only develop a discerning eye to distinguish art from error.

Composition

What can we say of the composition of structures and spaces? Let us start from the beginning.

Structures and spaces If we were to place a building or any other structure on a ground plane, for instance, how much space should we allow around it? First, we will want to see it well from its approaches. The spaces about it should not only be large enough or *small enough* but also of the right shape and spatial quality to compose with the structure and best display it. We want to be sure that

237

enough room is allowed to accommodate all the building's exterior functions, including approaches, parking and service areas, courts, patios, terraces, recreation areas, or gardens. Such spaces are volumetric expressions of the site-structure diagram. We want to be certain that the structure and its surrounding spaces are in toto a complete and balanced composition. Just as all buildings have purpose, so should the open spaces that they define or enclose. Such spaces must be clearly related to the character, mass, and purpose of the structures.

Often the form of a building itself is not as important as the exterior space patterns that it creates. The portrait painter knows that the outline of a figure or the profile of a head is sometimes secondary to the shape of the spaces created between figure or head and the surrounding pictorial enframement; it is the relationship of the figure to the surrounding shapes that gives the figure its essential meaning. So it is with buildings. Our buildings are to be spaced out in the landscape in such a way as to permit full and meaningful integration with other structures and spaces and with the natural landscape itself.

Groups of structures When two or more buildings are related, the buildings as a cluster, together with the interrelated spaces, become an architectural entity. In such a situation, each structure, aside from its primary function as a building, has many secondary functions in relation to the assemblage. The buildings as units are arranged to shape and define exterior volumes in the best way possible. They may be placed:

As enclosing elements

As screening elements

As backdrop elements

To dominate the landscape

To organize the landscape

To command the landscape

To embrace the landscape

To enframe the landscape

To create a new and controlled landscape

To orient the new landscape outward or inward

To dramatize a function

To dramatize the enclosing structures

To dramatize the enclosed space

To dramatize some feature or features within the space

They are placed, in short, to develop closed or semienclosed spaces that best express and accommodate their function, that best reveal the structural form, facade, or other features of the surrounding structures, and that best relate the group as a whole to the total extensional landscape.

We have seen too often in our day a building rising on its site in proud and utter disdain of its neighbors or its position. We search in vain for any of those relationships of form, material, or treatment that would bring it into consonance with the surrounding forms or spaces, that would compose it with the existing elements of the local scene. Such insensitive planning would have been incomprehensible to the ancient Greeks or Romans, who conceived each new

We need desperately to relearn the art of disposing of buildings to create different kinds of space: the quiet, enclosed, isolated, shaded space; the hustling, bustling space pungent with vitality; the paved, dignified, vast, sumptuous, even awe-inspiring space; the mysterious space; the transition space which defines, separates and yet joins juxtaposed spaces of contrasting character.

We need sequences of space which arouse one's curiosity, give a sense of anticipation, which beckon and impel us to rush forward to find that releasing space which dominates, which climaxes and acts as a magnet, and gives direction.

Paul Rudolph

This rage for isolating everything is truly a modern sickness.

Camillo Sitte

An isolated city dwelling, suspended as it were in space, is but a Utopian dream. City dwellings should always be considered as the component parts of groups of structures, or districts.

José Luis Sert

For as there cannot be a socially healthy population consisting only of egotistic individualists having no common spirit, so there cannot be an architecturally healthy community consisting of self-sufficient buildings.

Eliel Saarinen

Spatial penetration of structure.

This handsome cluster of street lights was designed, in the best tradition, as an integral part of the city and square.

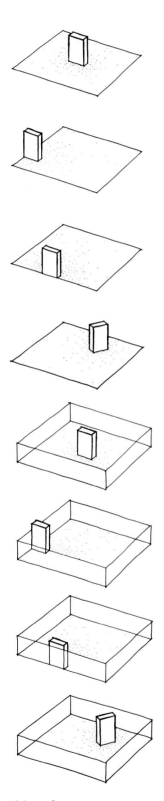

Composition of structures

When a structure is to be related to a given area or space, both the shape and the character of the area or space will be affected by the positioning of the structure.

structure as a compositional element of the street, forum, or square. They did not simply erect a new temple, a new fountain, or even a new lantern; they consciously redesigned the square or street. Each new structure and each new space were contrived as integral and balanced parts of the immediate and extensional environment. These planners knew no other way. And in truth, there can be no other way if our buildings and our cities are again to please and satisfy us.

We have said that each building or structure as a solid requires for its fullest expression a satisfying counterbalance of negative open space. This truth, of all planning truths, is perhaps the most difficult to comprehend. It has been comprehended and mastered in many periods and places—by the builders of the Karnak Temple, Kyoto's Katsura Palace, or the gardens of Soochow (Suzhou), for example. We still find their groupings of buildings and interrelated spaces to be of supremely satisfying harmony and balance; each solid has its void, each building has its satisfying measure of space, and each interior function has its exterior extension, generation, or resolution of that function.

What do we contemporary planners know of this art or its principles, which have been evolved through centuries of trial and error, modification, reappraisal, and patient refinement? The orientals have a highly developed planning discipline that deals with such matters in terms of *tension and repose.* Though its tenets are heavily veiled in religious mysticism, its plan applications are clear. It is a conscious effort in all systems of composition to attain a sense of repose through the occult balance of all plan elements, whether viewed as in a pictorial composition or experienced in three dimensions:

The near balanced against the far

The solid against the void

The light against the dark

The bright against the dull

The familiar against the strange

The dominant against the recessive

The active against the passive

The fluid against the fixed

In each instance, the most telling dynamic tensions are sought out or arranged to give maximum meaning to all opposing elements and the total scheme. Though repose through equilibrium must be the end result, it is the *relationship* of the plan elements through which repose is achieved that is of utmost interest. It is the contrived opposition of elements, the studied interplay of tensions, and the sensed resolution of these tensions that, when fully comprehended, are most keenly enjoyed.

A group of structures may be planned in opposition both to each other and to the landscape in which they rise, so that as one moves through or about them, one experiences an evolving composition of opposing elements, a resolution of tensions, and a sense of dynamic repose. A single tree may be so placed and trained as to hold a distant forest or group of smaller trees in balanced opposition and give them richer meaning. A lake shining deep and still in the natural bowl of a valley may, by its area, conformation, and other qualities, real or associative, hold in balanced repose the opposing hills that surround it. A plume of falling water at the lake's far end may balance its placid surface in the same way. And to achieve a satisfying equilibrium, the lake or falls may need to be modified or reinforced; perhaps other elements will have to be added.

Walter Beck, long a student of oriental art and composition, has said of the superb gardens that he planned at Innisfree: "On a wall, at the lake edge, is a rock which I call the dragon rock; it is the key in a grouping of stones whose function is to hold in balance the lake and nearby hills; whose function is to cope with the energies of the sky and the distant landscape."[1] It can be seen that tremendous compositional interest and power can be concentrated in such key objects—rocks, sculpture, structures, or whatever you will—that by design may hold a great system of elements in balanced tension and thus in dynamic repose.

It would seem, from a comparison of the European and oriental systems of planning, that the western mind is traditionally concerned primarily with the object or structure as it appears in space, while the eastern mind tends to think of structure primarily as a means of defining and articulating a space or a complex of spaces.

In this light, Steen Rasmussen, in his book *Towns and Build-*

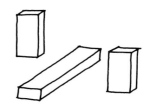

Composition of structures
Often the form of the structures themselves is not as important as that of the spaces they enclose. A single structure is perceived as an object in space. Two or more structures are perceived not alone as objects but also as related objects, and they gain or lose much of their significance in the relationship.

Static ▬

Dynamic

Opposing structures generate a field of dynamic tension.

[1]From *Painting with Starch.*

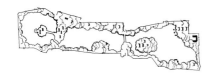

Peking, Sea Palace gardens

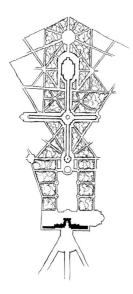

Versailles Park

A close study of the two diametrically opposed planning approaches here demonstrated will lead one to a fuller understanding of the philosophy of both occidental and oriental planning.

In designing a building, the architect is always led to imagine the work as it is intended to look when finished, placing himself mentally in the position of a visitor who is examining it carefully and critically. Thus it is that he feels the future impressions that his design may make, the surprises that certain new and original solutions may reserve, the architectonic subtleties that the most sensitive will seek out and comprehend. And in the course of this effort of the imagination, the architect reviews the architectonic elements that he considers essential, endeavoring to ascertain whether his reasoning is sound, whether the material he proposes to use is suitable, whether the colors are harmonious, and whether the forms created are handsome and true. For this purpose he takes up an imaginary position in places where drawings are liable to be inexpressive, and strives to feel the volumes he is designing, in all their grandeur and proportion.

Oscar Niemeyer

ings, has made a revealing graphic comparison of two imperial parks, that of King Louis XIV at Versailles and that of the Chinese emperor in Peking. Both were completed in the early 1700s, both made use of huge artificial bodies of water, and both were immense; but there the similarity ends. A close study of these two diametrically opposed planning approaches, illustrated here, will lead one to a fuller understanding of the philosophy of both occidental and oriental planning in this period of history.

Too often when placing or composing structures in space we revert to cold geometry. Our architectural libraries are bulging with building plans and diagrams laid out in crisp, abstract patterns of black and white that have little meaning except in the flat. It is small wonder that buildings that take their substance from such plans are destined to failure, for they were never conceived in terms of form in space or of spaces within form. The world is cluttered with such unfortunate travesties. The intelligent planning of buildings, parks, and cities is a far cry from such geometric doodling. A logical plan in two dimensions is a record of logical thinking in three dimensions. The enlightened planner is thinking always of space-structure composition. His or her concern is not with the plan forms and spaces as they appear on the drawings but rather with these forms and spaces as they will be experienced in actuality.

Many Renaissance squares, parks, and palaces are little more than dull geometry seen in the round. One clear, strong voice crying out against such puerile design was that of Camillo Sitte, a Viennese architect whose writings on city building first appeared in 1889 and whose ideas are still valid and compelling today.

It was Sitte who pointed out that pre-Renaissance people *used* their public spaces and that these spaces and the buildings around them were planned together to satisfy the use. There were market squares, religious squares, ducal squares, civic squares, and others of many varieties; and each, from inception through the numerous changes of time, maintained its own distinctive quality. These public places were never symmetrical, nor were they entered by wide, axial streets that would have destroyed their essential attribute of enclosure. Rather, they were asymmetrical; they were entered by narrow, winding ways that penetrated at or near the corners. Each building or object within the space was planned *to* and *for* the space and the streams of pedestrian traffic that would converge and merge there. The centers of such spaces were left open; the monuments, fountains, and sculpture that were so much a part of them were placed on islands in the traffic pattern, off building corners, against blank walls, and beside the entryways, each positioned with infinite care in relation to surfaces, masses, and *space.* Seldom were such objects set on axis with the approach to a building or its entrance, for it was felt that they would detract from the full appreciation of the architecture. Conversely, it was felt that the axis of a building was seldom a proper background for a work of art.

Sitte discovered that such important buildings as cathedrals were rarely placed at the center of an open space, as we almost invariably place them today. Instead, they were set back against other buildings or off to the side to give a better view of facade, spires, or portals and to give the best impression from within the square or from its meandering approaches.

Rules of composition Down through the centuries, much thought has been given to the establishment of fixed formulas or rules that might govern building proportions, or the relationship of

The location of the equestrian statue of Gattamelata by Donatello in front of Saint Anthony of Padua is most instructive. First we may be astonished at its great variance from our rigid modern system, but it is quickly and strikingly seen that the monument in this place produces a majestic effect. Finally we become convinced that removed to the center of the square its effect would be greatly diminished. We cease to wonder at its orientation and other locational advantages once this principle becomes familiar.

The ancient Egyptians understood this principle, for as Gattamelata and the little column stand beside the entrance to the Cathedral of Padua, the obelisks and the statues of the Pharaohs are aligned beside the temple doors. There is the entire secret that we refuse to decipher today.

Camillo Sitte

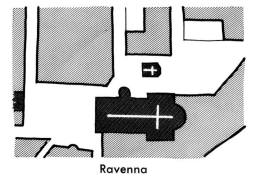
Ravenna

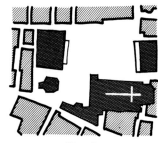
Pistoia

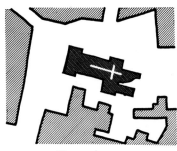
Nuremberg

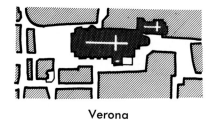
Verona

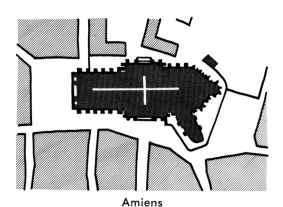
Amiens

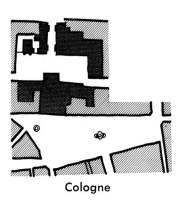
Cologne

one building to another, or the relationship of a building to its surrounding volumetric enclosure.

There have long been those who believe that mathematics is the all-pervading basis of our world of matter, growth, and order. To them it has followed naturally that order, beauty, and even truth are functions of mathematical law and proportion. The *golden rectangle*, for example, has long been a favorite of mathematicians, perhaps because of the fact that if a unit square is subtracted from each ever-diminishing rectangle, a golden rectangle each time remains. This "ideal" rectilinear shape (whose sides have a ratio of 1:1.618, or roughly 3:5) has appeared again and again, in plan and in elevation, in the structures and formed spaces of the western world.

Miloutine Borissavliévitch, in his absorbing work *The Golden Number*, has explored its application to architectural composition. He proposes that although the golden rectangle *considered by itself* is, both philosophically and aesthetically, the most beautiful among

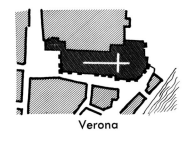

Verona

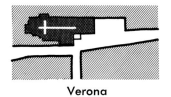

Verona

Padua

Geneva

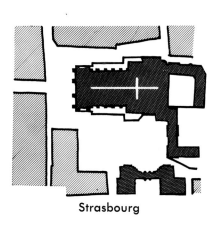

Strasbourg

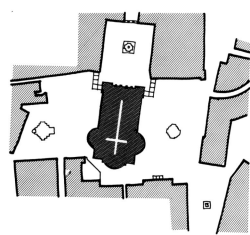

Salzburg

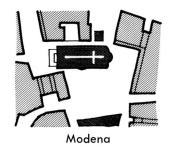

Modena

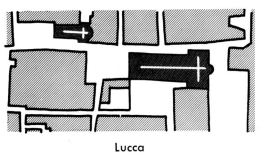

Lucca

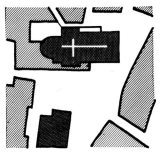

Perugia

all horizontal rectangles, "when considered *as a part of a whole*, it is neither more beautiful nor unattractive than any other rectangle. Because a whole is ruled by the laws of harmony, by the ratios between the parts and not by a single part considered by itself." He notes that "*Order* is indeed the greatest and most general of esthetic laws," and then suggests that there are only two laws of architectural harmony, the *law of the similar* and the *law of the same:*[2]

The law of the same. Architectural harmony may be perceived or created in a structure or composition of structures that attains order through the repetition of the *same* elements, forms, or spaces.

The law of the similar. Architectural harmony may be perceived or created in a composition that attains order through the repetition of *similar* elements, forms, or spaces.

---

[2]Though Borissavliévitch is speaking here only of *proportions,* it is to be noted that the laws of the *same* and the *similar* apply as well to materials, colors, textures, and symbols.

Architectural harmony created through the repetition of the *same* elements.

Architectural harmony created through the repetition of *similar* elements.

Borissavliévitch notes that "whilst the *Law of the Same* represents unity (or harmony) in uniformity, the *Law of the Similar* represents unity in variety." He wisely notes also that "an artist will create beautiful works only in obeying unconsciously one of these two laws, that is without even knowing them, otherwise they would not be true. Whilst we create, we do not think about them, and we follow only our imagination and our artistic feeling. But when our sketch is made, we look at it and examine it as if we were its first spectator and not its creator, and if it is successful we shall know, because of our knowledge of these laws *why* it is successful; if it is not, we shall know the reason of the failure."

"The beautiful," said Borissavliévitch, "is felt and not calculated."

Leonardo Fibonacci, an Italian mathematician of the thirteenth century, discovered a progression that was soon widely adapted to all phases of planning. He noted that starting with units 1 and 2, if each new digit is made the sum of the previous two, there results a progression of 1, 2, 3, 5, 8, 13, 21, 34, and so forth, which translated into plan forms and rhythms is visually pleasing. It was later discovered that the progression approximates the growth sequence of plants and other organisms; this, of course, added to its interest and confirmed in the minds of planners the notion that this progression is "natural" and "organic."

Marcus Vitruvius, a Roman architect and scholar who lived in the first century before Christ, set out to formulate a system of proportion that he could apply to his plans and structures. In his search he undertook an exhaustive study of the architecture and planning of ancient Greece. In the course of his work he produced a book setting forth his findings and expounding his theories on the anthropomorphic module, a unit of measurement based on the proportions of the human body. This was to have a profound effect on the thinking and planning of the Renaissance. In his treatise Vitruvius included the following passage, containing the crux of his proposition:

"The plan of a temple must have an exact proportion worked out after the fashion of the members of a finely proportioned human body. For nature has so planned the human body that the face from the chin to the top of the forehead and root of the hair is $1/10$ part; also the palm of the hand from the wrist to the top of the middle finger is as much; the head from the chin to the crown is $1/8$ part; from the top of the breast with the bottom of the neck to the roots, $1/6$ part; from the middle of the breast to the crown, $1/4$ part; $1/3$ part of the height of the face is from the bottom of chin to the bottom of the nostrils; the nose from the bottom of the nostrils to the line between the brows, as much; from that line to the roots of the hair, the forehead is given $1/3$ part. The foot is $1/6$ the height of the body; the cubit $1/4$; the breast also $1/4$. The other limbs also have their own proportionate measurements. By using these, ancient painters and famous sculptors have attained great and unbounded distinction.

"In like fashion the members of the temples ought to have dimensions of their several parts answering suitably to the general sum of their whole magnitude. Now the navel is naturally the exact center of the body. For if a man lies on his back with his hands and feet outspread, and the center of the circle is placed on his navel, his fingers and toes will be touched by the circumference. Also a square will be found described by the figure in the same way that a round figure is produced. For if we measure from the sole of the foot to the top of the head, and apply the measure to the outstretched hands, the breadth will be found equal to the height, just like sites which are squared by rule.

"Therefore if nature has planned the human body so that the members correspond in their proportions to its complete configuration, the ancients seem to have had reason in determining that in the execution of their works they should observe an exact adjustment of their several members to the general pattern of the plan."[3]

The Renaissance masters pored over these Vitruvian theories and developed them further in detail and depth. They revived the Greek mathematical interpretation of God and the world and adapted to their thinking the Christian belief that man, as the image of God, embodies the harmonies of the universe.

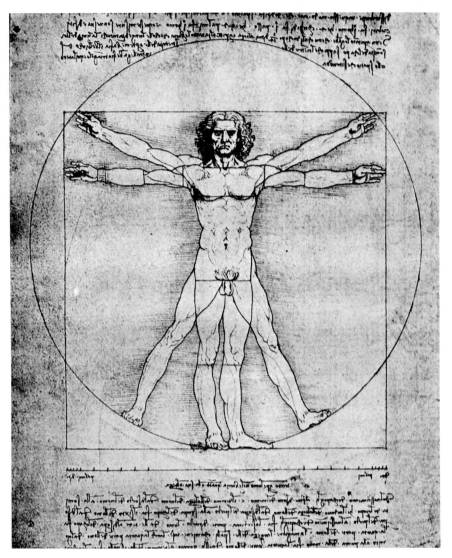

The Vitruvian figure inscribed in a circle and square became a symbol of the mathematical sympathy between macrocosm and microcosm.
Rudolph Wittkower

A study by Leonardo da Vinci from one of his notebooks illustrating his principle that "the span of a man's outstanding arms is equal to his height."

Leonardo da Vinci, the creative giant of his time, analyzed and tabulated his own system of mean proportions of the component parts of the human figure in relation to its total height and then derived a table of classic proportions and ratios from which he developed for each project a suitable modular system. As architect-engineer-sculptor-painter, he translated his findings into all his works and through them demonstrated to posterity his conviction that, to achieve order and beautiful proportion in any work, the major masses or lines and the smallest detail must have a consistent mathematical relationship.

"The conviction that architecture is a science and that each part of a building has to be integrated into one and the same system of mathematical ratios may be called the basic axiom of Renaissance architects," Granger tells us. Today we physical planners are still searching for the modular system most applicable to our work.

---

[3]From *Vitruvius on Architecture,* translated by Frank S. Granger.

It was long ago discovered that the ratio of height to width, structure to space, or element to element should not appear to be exactly 1 to 1, 1 to 2, 1 to 3, or 1 to 4. A proof of the general validity of this tacit rule was brought home to the author vividly on an occasion when he visited, with several friends, the studio of Hiroshi Yoshida, the late distinguished Japanese wood-block artist. The old master was leafing through a stack of prints he particularly liked, as in another pile he would put those that had for him less appeal. A philosopher who was present suggested that much could be learned if the artist told us what elements were common to those he preferred and those he had discarded. Yoshida thoughtfully noted the qualities of harmonious color, expressive form, and composition in what he termed his better work, but he was at a loss to discover the root of his displeasure in the lesser prints.

"I have noticed," said one of the other visitors, "that each of the compositions you dislike is split by some line or form into two, three, or four equal parts. In Western composition this is usually avoided."

"Ah so!" replied Yoshida after some moments of quiet reflection. "In Japan we have no such rule, but it must be, I perceive, a valid one." After a few moments he continued, "I shall not violate this rule again, at least without intention."

"Without intention?" someone queried.

"Yes," continued the artist, "we have seen that this compositional phenomenon has its unfortunate effects. It must also have its proper applications—and one might so split a composition if, by subject, one should wish to convey a subtle sense of schism or tension."

One of the distinguishing marks of Japanese planning and architecture is a fundamental order or mathematical relationship of the elements. This stems, at least in part, from the use of the *tatami*, or woven grass mat (approximately 3 by 6 feet), as a standardized unit of measurement. Traditionally, a modular grid system based upon this unit has been the foundation of most building plans and surrounding spaces. By this system doors are 3 by 6 feet, ceilings are 9 feet high, a room is a given number of mats in length and width, and a building plan is so many mats in area. In their planning the Japanese make use also of the 12-foot dimension, which is divisible by 1, 2, 3, 4, and 6.

If a unit such as a closet or a case requires less than the full module, it is not distorted to fill the module; rather it is set free within the module and *composed* within the modular framework. The fact that an object is smaller or larger than the module is not concealed but is artistically revealed and elucidated. This approach would seem to be clearly superior to our American modular systems by which components are designed to fit precisely within a given structural grid. The Japanese form order differs significantly also from the rigid geometric planning of Europe's Renaissance, which worshiped insistent symmetry rather than such a free and flexible system of modular organization.

Structures in the landscape

We have seen how the ancients struggled with the *visual* aspects of architectural composition, of trying to create a fairer world in their own rational image. They found within the mathematical context no universal rules excepting those of order, proportion, and scale. Could it be that in their compulsion to measure, compare, and debate they overlooked the ultimate truth so evident in all of nature's structures? This is the *law of fitness*. The law of fitness would reveal to us that the optimum structure, of any type, is that which for its time and place and with the most economical use of materials best fulfills its purpose.

Without exception nature has fashioned, in the mast-and-spar construction of each tree, the skeleton of each animal or bird, each eggshell, and each weed stalk, a structure of simplicity, strength, and resilience. Each as a form is eminently suited to its function. Each is "designed" and "engineered" without concern for aesthetics, yet each, in its absolute fitness, is intrinsically beautiful. Could it be that a dogma of rules and formulas could preclude rather than foster meaningful design? Could it be that a preconceived notion of plan form and structural shapes could produce archaic buildings? Could it be that, as in nature, our most ingenious and handsome structures will be derived in a forthright search for ever more *expressive* form? It could be. The unselfconscious architecture of the New England farm, the Greek hill town, and the African council house all share nature's direct approach, and all, in their ways, are eloquently expressive.

As with structural forms and objects, nature has much to teach us, as well, in the plan layout of our homes and cities. We have yet to see an axial anthill or a symmetrical plan arrangement of a beaver colony. The creatures of the wild have learned to fit their habitations to the natural land conformation, to established patterns of water flow, to the force and direction of the winds, and to the orbit of the sun. Should not we be as responsive?

Yet we have all seen towers with expanses of metal and heat-absorbing glass focused into the rays of the sun. We are all too familiar with broad avenues aligned to receive, unchecked, the full blast of prevailing winter winds. We recall groupings of campus buildings which have completely destroyed the natural character of the hills and ravines upon which they have been imposed. We know of checkerboard communities laid out in utter disdain of contours, watercourses, or wooded slopes, or geology, storm, or view.

If there be a lesson, it is this: *Architecture by formula and site planning by sterile geometry are equally doomed to failure.*

Individual buildings are sometimes spaced out as deployed units of a greater architectural composition. It can be seen that such structures and the spaces they define combine to give a more telling impact than would be possible for any single structure of the group. Sometimes this is desirable; sometimes it is not. Such an arrangement of structures seems most reasonable when each building not only *appears* but also *functions* as a part of the total complex. In every case in which a building serves as a unit of an architectural group, the entire group is treated as a cohesive and unified composition and each structure owes allegiance to the whole.

Buildings may be arranged freely in the landscape as individual units. In such cases, when they need not be planned as part of a complex, they and the spaces around them may be designed with much more freedom. Their relationship is not one of building to building but rather one of building to landscape, with all that this implies.

Buildings of similar character may be dispersed, even at great distances, in such a manner as to dominate a landscape and unify it. The arrangement may be architectonic, outpost to related outpost, or it may be casual. By such a treatment military, campus, or any other character may be given to an extensive landscape. Though a great variety of uses may be given to the intervening landscape areas, each element within the visual field must be compatible by association. A quiet chapel within the exuberant atmos-

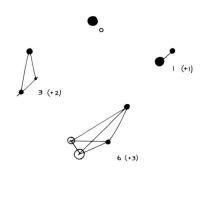

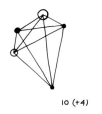

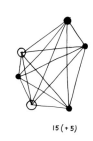

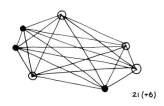

Composition of structures
The number of polar relationships increases arithmetically with the addition of each unit to a complex of structures. Since each new unit modifies the composition, its relationship to all other units is a matter of design and planning concern.

phere of Disneyland would lose much of its meaning, as would a faro casino within the visual limits of a theological seminary.

Structures are often composed in relation to natural or constructed elements of the landscape, such as a water body, a railroad siding, or a highway. In such cases, the buildings, singly or in composite, may be given their form and spacing to achieve the best possible relationships. A resort complex and its fronting lake are in effect composed as an interrelated unit, in which the lake adds much to the resort and the resort, in turn, adds to the ambience of the lake. A factory and its receiving and shipping yards are designed *to* and *with* the railroad. A roadside restaurant is planned as one with the highway in terms of landscape character, sight distances, approaches, resolution of momentums, and composition of spaces and forms.

It is to be remembered that a building complex, as much as a natural forest grove, has its own landscape character. This must be recognized if it is to be accentuated by the planned relationships and supporting site treatment.

Some buildings are static. They stand aloof and are complete in themselves. Such structures are no doubt valid when the intended architectural expression is that of detachment, grandeur, the austere, or the monumental. They require that setting and site development be in keeping.

Various compositional arrangements of apartment structures.

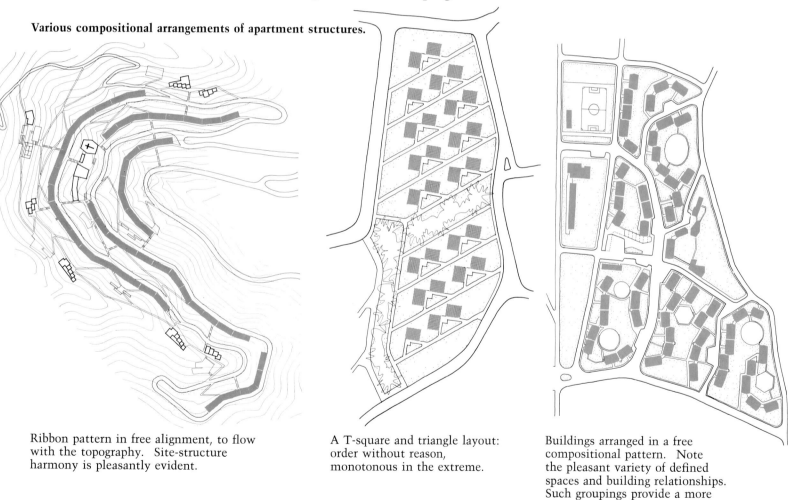

Ribbon pattern in free alignment, to flow with the topography. Site-structure harmony is pleasantly evident.

A T-square and triangle layout: order without reason, monotonous in the extreme.

Buildings arranged in a free compositional pattern. Note the pleasant variety of defined spaces and building relationships. Such groupings provide a more relaxed and pleasant environment for living.

Other building groupings by their very plan layout seem to express human freedom and interaction. They form a responsive relationship with nature and the constructed landscape. It can be seen that not only the structures themselves but also their abstract arrangement determine to a large degree their character and the character of the larger landscape area that they influence or embrace.

Often scattered buildings may be brought into a more workable and visually satisfying relationship by connecting them with paved areas or by well-defined lines of circulation. Again, this integration may be accomplished by the addition of structural elements such as walls or fences. Sometimes tree rows or even hedges may suffice to bind them together. The elements that unite such structures may at the same time define for each the most fitting volumes of related space.

Diverse plan elements related by circulation patterns.

Induced directional movement by volumetric shaping.

The defined open space

Open spaces assume an architectural character when they are enclosed in full or in part by structural elements. Such a space may be an extension of a building. Sometimes it is confined within the limits of a single building or enclosed by a building group. Sometimes such a space surrounds a structure or serves as its foreground, or as a foil, or as a focal point. Each such defined open space is an entity, complete within itself. But more, it is an inseparable part of each adjacent space or structure. It can be seen that such related spaces, structures, and the landscape that surrounds them must all be considered together in the process of design.

A defined outdoor volume is a well of space. Its very hollowness is its essential quality. Without the corresponding void a solid has no meaning. Is it not then quite evident that the size, shape, and quality of the negative space will have a powerful retroactive effect upon the adjacent positive masses? Each structure requires for its fullest effective expression a satisfying balance of mass and void. The same void may not only satisfy two or more solids and relate them to each other, it may also relate them as a group to some further structures or spaces beyond.

Whatever its function, when the hollowness of a volume is a

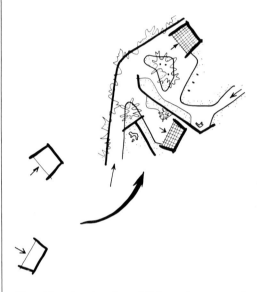

Classification by the addition of structural elements plus definitive circulation ways.

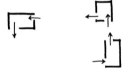

Three disconnected plan elements

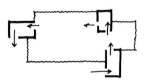

Addition of connective linkage

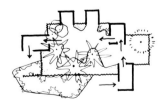

Further articulation
of plan circulation

Integration of structures

The garden of Ryōanji, Kyoto, surely one of the ten outstanding gardens of all time, is an abstract composition of raked gravel simulating the sea. This walled space expands the limits of the related monastery refectory and terrace. Designed as a garden for contemplation, it owes its distinction to its simplicity, its perfection of detail, its suggestion of vast spaces, and its power to set free the human mind and spirit.

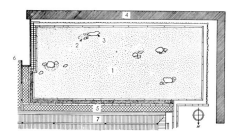

(1) Sanded ground, (2) moss, (3) stone, (4) earth wall, (5) tile pavement, (6) ornamental gate, and (7) veranda.

quality to be desired, this concavity is to be meticulously preserved and emphasized by letting the shell read clearly, by revealing enclosing members and planes, by incurving, by belling out the sides, by the use of recessive colors and forms, by letting the bottom fall away visually, by terracing or sloping down into and up out of the base, by digging the pit, or by depressing a water basin or reflective pool and thus extending the apparent depth of the space to infinity. A cleanly shaped space is not to be choked or clogged with plants or other standing objects. This is not to imply that the volume should be kept empty, but rather that its *hollowness* should be in all ways maintained. A well-placed arrangement of elements or even a clump or grove of high-crowned trees might well increase this sense of shell-like hollowness.

The defined space, open to the sky, has the obvious advantages of flooding sunlight, shadow patterns, airiness, sky color, and the beauty of moving clouds. It has disadvantages, too, but we need only plan to minimize these and to capitalize on every beneficial aspect of the openness. Let us not waste one precious yard of azure blue, one glorious burst of sunshine, or one puff of welcome summer breeze that can be caught and made to animate, illuminate, or aerate this outdoor volume that we plan.

If the volume defined by a structure is open to the side, it becomes the focal transition between the structure and the landscape. If open to the view, it is usually developed as the best possible viewing station and the best possible enframement for the view seen from the various points of observation.

The defined open space is normally developed for some use. It may extend the function of a structure, as the motor court extends the entrance hall or as the dining court extends the dining room or kitchen. It may serve a separate function in itself, as does a recreation court in a dormitory grouping or a military parade ground flanked by barracks. But whether or not it is directly related to its structure in *use*, it must be in *character*. Such spaces, be they patios, courts, or public squares, become so dominant and focal in most architectural groupings that the very essence of the adjacent structures is distilled and captured there.

(above) This magnificent urban space was designed to complement the Museum of Modern Art and serve in all seasons as an exhilarating exhibition area. *(left)* A winter scene in the Abby Aldrich Rockefeller Sculpture Garden.

11

Habitations

What does a dwelling want to be? Shelter? Family activity center? Base of operations? All three, no doubt, and each of these functions is to be expressed and facilitated. But in its fullest sense a *habitation* is much more. It is our human fix on the planet Earth, our earthly abode. Once accepted, this simple philosophic concept has far-reaching implications.

In the planning of their homes and gardens the orientals not only adapt them with great artistry to the natural landscape but also consciously *root* them in nature. Constructed of materials derived from the earth (with varying degrees of tooling and refinement), these homes and gardens are humanized extensions of earth form and structure and are fully attuned to the natural processes. Like the nest of the bird or the beaver's lodge, they are nature particularized.

Dwelling-nature relationships

It is proposed that each human habitation is best conceived as an integral component of the natural site and landscape environs. The extent to which this can be accomplished is a measure of the dwelling's success and the occupant's sense of fitness and well-being. This integration of habitation with nature is an exacting enterprise. How is it to be achieved? As a beginning:

Explore and analyze the site. Just as the bird or the animal scouts the territory for the optimum situation, just as the farmer surveys the holding and lays out fields and buildings to conform to the lay of the land, just so must the planner of each home and garden come to know and respond to the unique and compelling conditions of the selected site.

Adapt to the geological structure. The conformation of every land area is determined largely by its geologic formation—the convolutions, layering, upheavals, erosion, and weathering of the underlying strata. These establish the stability and load-bearing capacity of the various site areas and the ease or difficulty of excavation and grading. They determine as well the structure, porosity, and fertility of the subsoil and topsoil, the presence of groundwater, and the availability of freshwater reserves. Only with the knowledge of subsurface conditions, gained by test holes or drilling, can one plan to the site with assurance.

Preserve the natural systems. Topography, drainageways, waterways, vegetative covers, bird and wildlife trails and habitat, all have continuity. One test of good land planning is that it minimizes disruption to established patterns and flows.

Adjust the plan to fit the land. In the recomposition of solids and voids the structural elements are usually designed to extend the hill or ridge and overlook the valley. Well-conceived plan forms honor and articulate the basic land contours and water edges. The prominence is made more dominant; the hollow and cove, more recessive.

Reflect the climatic condition. Cold, temperate, hot-dry, or warm-humid, each broad climatic range brings to mind at once planning problems and possibilities. Within each range, however, there are many subarea variations of climate or site-specific microclimate that have direct planning implications.

All landscape design of distinction embodies to some extent an abstract and idealized representation of nature.

When the area to be developed is small, the design will take into account all positive qualities of the site—the ground forms, cover, exposures, views, and all other natural or architectural features—and bring them into harmony.

When the area to be considered is large or complex, each *segment* is to be developed as an entity and all segments brought together into a unified whole.

The spirit of a garden is its power to charm the heart.
Kanto Shigemori

Indoor-outdoor living

Contemporary homes and gardens

Design in response to the elements. Protect from the wind. Invite the breeze. Accommodate the rain or snow. Avoid the flood. Brace for the storm. Trace the sun's orbit.

Consider the human factors. On- and off-site structures, trafficways, utility installations, easements, and even such givens as social characteristics, political jurisdictions, zoning, covenants, restrictions, and regulations may have a telling influence.

Eliminate the negatives. Insofar as possible, all undesirable features are to be removed or their impacts abated. These undesirable aspects include pollution in its many aspects, hazards, and visual detractions. When they cannot be eliminated, they are mitigated by ground forms, vegetation, or distance or by visual screening.

Accentuate the best features. Fit the paths of movement, use areas, and structures around and between the landscape superlatives. Protect them, face toward them, focus upon them, enframe them, and enjoy them in all conditions of light and in all seasons.

Let the native character set the theme. Every landscape area has its own mood and character. Presumably these were among the chief reasons for the site selection. Only if the indigenous quality is not desirable or suited to the project use should it be significantly altered. Otherwise, design in harmony with the theme, devising pleasant modulations, light counterpoint, and resonant overtones.

Integrate. Bring all the elements together in the best possible dynamic relationships. This is the lesson of nature. This is the primary objective of all planning and design.

The most obvious place to put the house is not always the right one. If there is only a small area of flat land, you'll be tempted to use it for the house. It probably should be saved for arrival, parking or garden. . . .

Is there one particular spot on the property that seems just right in every way? Have you picnicked there and found it idyllic? Have you spent long winter evenings planning a house there? Has it occurred to you that if you build your house there the spot will be gone? Maybe that's where your garden should be.

Thomas D. Church

Whatever the type of dwelling, be it a single-family home, a townhouse unit with garden court, or a tower apartment . . .

Wherever the location, be the site urban or rural, mountain or plain, desert or lakeside . . .

The planning approach is the same.

Human needs and habitat

What would the ideal garden home be like? As a clue, observation will teach us that at least the following requirements of most home dwellers should be satisfied:

Shelter   The contemporary home, like all before it, is first of all a refuge from the storm. With the advent of sophisticated heating devices, climate controls, diversified construction materials, and ingenious structural systems, the concept of shelter has been brought to a new high level of refinement. But architecturally this basic function of shelter is to be served and given clear expression.

Protection   This implies safety from all forms of danger, not only from the elements but from fire, flood, and intruders as well. Although the nature of potential threats has changed through the centuries, our instincts have not. Safety must be implicit.

Today an ever-present hazard is that of the moving vehicle with its backings and turnings. It does not belong within our living area and should not be admitted. The automobile should be "stabled" within its own service area or compound.

Utility   Each dwelling should be a lucid statement of the various purposes to be served. Not only is each use to be accommodated, it

Borrowed scenery (an oriental term for visual volumetric expansion) is accomplished by the inclusion of objects, spaces, or views from beyond the site or garden wall. We in America have much to learn about such spatial expansion techniques, long applied in the diminutive living spaces of Europe and the orient.

The earth is our home and the ways of nature our paths to understanding.

A garden should have no beginning and no end.

Thomas D. Church

is to be conveniently related to all others. And what are these uses? They are those of food preparation, dining, entertaining, sleeping, and (perhaps) child rearing. These uses are supplemented by the library, correspondence corner, workshop, and laundry and supported by storage spaces, mechanical equipment, and waste disposal systems. Often much of the home entertainment and relaxation takes place on the balcony or terrace. The outdoor spaces also provide healthful exercise and satisfy our agricultural yearnings. Even the pot of chives or the parsley bed has its important symbolic meaning.

Utility connotes "a place for everything, and everything in its place," all working well together. While a home is far more than a machine for living, it must function efficiently.

Amenity It is not enough that a dwelling works well. It must also be attractive and pleasant. It must satisfy the human bent for display and our love of beautiful objects. Beauty is not, however, to be confused with decoration, ornamentation, or the elaborate. True beauty is most often discerned in that which is utterly simple and unpretentious—a well-formed clay pot, a simple carpet of blended wools, handsomely fitted and finished wood, cut slate, hand-crafted silver—always just the right form, material, and finish to serve the specific purpose; always the understatement, for *less* is truly *more.*

In considering dwellings and display, mention should be made of the *tokonoma* of the traditional Japanese home. Constructed of natural materials of elegant simplicity, the *tokonoma* is a place reserved for the sharing of beautiful objects. These objets d'art are selected from storage cabinets or gathered from the garden or site and brought out, a few at most at one time, to mark the season or a special occasion. They may include hangings, paintings, a bowl, sculpture, or a vase or tray to receive a floral arrangement. Our

western homes and gardens and their displays could well be distinguished by such artistry and restraint.

Privacy　In a world of hustle and hassle we all need, sometimes desperately, a place of quiet retreat. It need not be large—a space in the home or garden set apart from normal activities, where one can share the enjoyment of reading, music, or conversation or turn for quiet introspection. It is very human to feel the need for one's own private space.

A sense of spaciousness　Just as we feel the need to retreat, we feel also upon occasion the need for expansive freedom. With dwellings and neighborhoods becoming more and more constricted, such spaciousness inside property limits is almost a rarity. But we can learn from those cultures in which people have lived for centuries in forced compression that space can be "borrowed."

Living spaces may be so arranged and interrelated that common areas may be shared to make each component space seem larger. Apparent spatial size may be increased also by the subtle use of forced perspective and by miniaturization. Again, by the studied arrangement of walls and openings views can be designed to include attractive features of the site or neighboring properties or extended to the distant hill or horizon. Even within the walled garden or court the ultimate spaciousness can be experienced by the featured viewing of the sky and clouds and the evening constellations. It is no happenstance that in crowded Japan a favorite spot on the garden terrace is that reserved for the viewing of the moon.

Nature appreciation　Deeply ingrained in all of us is an instinctive feeling for the outdoors—for soil, stone, water, and the living things of the earth. We need to be near them, to observe and to

Evolution of a way of life

Primitive
Shelter is main consideration.

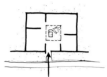

Greco-Roman
Protection and privacy are of prime value.

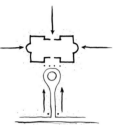

Renaissance
Each structure an idealized object in space.

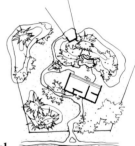

Oriental
Nature revered, privacy demanded; structures related to lot and total landscape.

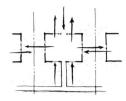

Present American showcase (vestigial renaissance)

Nature ignored. Outward orientation. Privacy is lost. Little use of property. A product of side-yard, setback, and no-fence restrictions.

Future American-trend home

Total use of site as living space. Privacy regained. Indoor-outdoor integration. Natural elements introduced. Compact home-garden units grouped amid open park and recreation areas which preserve natural-landscape features.

touch them. We need to maintain a close relationship with nature, to dwell amid natural features and surroundings, and to bring nature into our homes and lives.

A distinguishing mark of the recent American dwelling is the trend toward indoor-outdoor living. Most interior use areas now have their outdoor extensions—entryway to entrance court, kitchen to service area, dining space to patio, living space to atrium, bedroom to pool, game room to recreation court, and storage room to garden. In the well-planned habitation, especially in milder climes, it is often difficult to differentiate between indoors and outdoors.

It has been theorized that ideally each home and garden should be conceived as the universe in microcosm. If this idea seems abstruse, let it pass. Perhaps in time, upon further reflection, you may find it to have deep meaning.

Variations on a theme

The accompanying photographic examples have been selected to illustrate the means by which homes and gardens may be planned together, in harmony with their site and landscape environs.

When in our planning we ignore the natural processes or violate the land, we must live with the distressing consequences. When, however, we truly design our structures and living spaces in response to the forces, forms, and features of the host landscape, the lives of the occupants will be infused with a sense of well-being and pleasure.

OUTDOOR LIVING SPACES

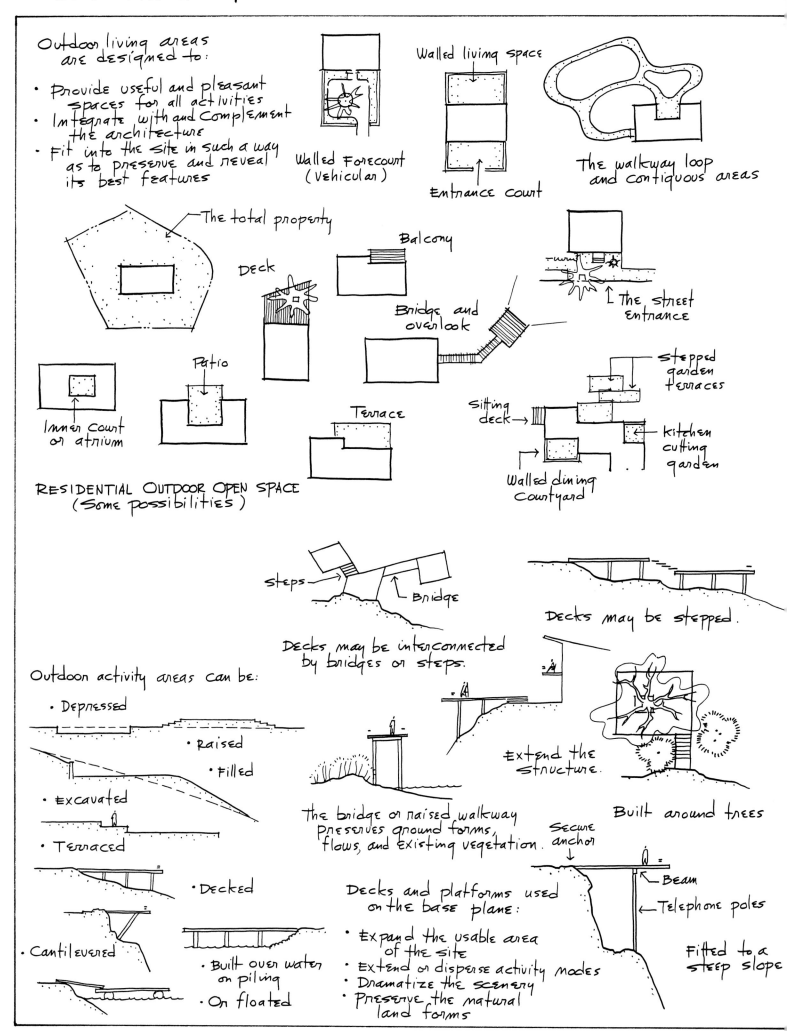

Outdoor living areas are designed to:

- Provide useful and pleasant spaces for all activities
- Integrate with and complement the architecture
- Fit into the site in such a way as to preserve and reveal its best features

Walled Forecourt (Vehicular)

Walled living space

Entrance court

The walkway loop and contiguous areas

The total property

Deck

Balcony

Bridge and overlook

The street Entrance

Patio

Inner court or atrium

Terrace

Sitting deck

Stepped garden terraces

kitchen cutting garden

Walled dining Courtyard

RESIDENTIAL OUTDOOR OPEN SPACE (Some possibilities)

steps

Bridge

Decks may be stepped.

Decks may be interconnected by bridges or steps.

Extend the Structure.

Built around trees

Outdoor activity areas can be:

- Depressed
- Raised
- Filled
- Excavated
- Terraced
- Decked
- Cantilevered
- Built over water on piling
- On floated

The bridge or raised walkway preserves ground forms, flows, and existing vegetation.

Secure anchor

Beam

Telephone poles

Fitted to a steep slope

Decks and platforms used on the base plane:

- Expand the usable area of the site
- Extend or disperse activity modes
- Dramatize the scenery
- Preserve the natural land forms

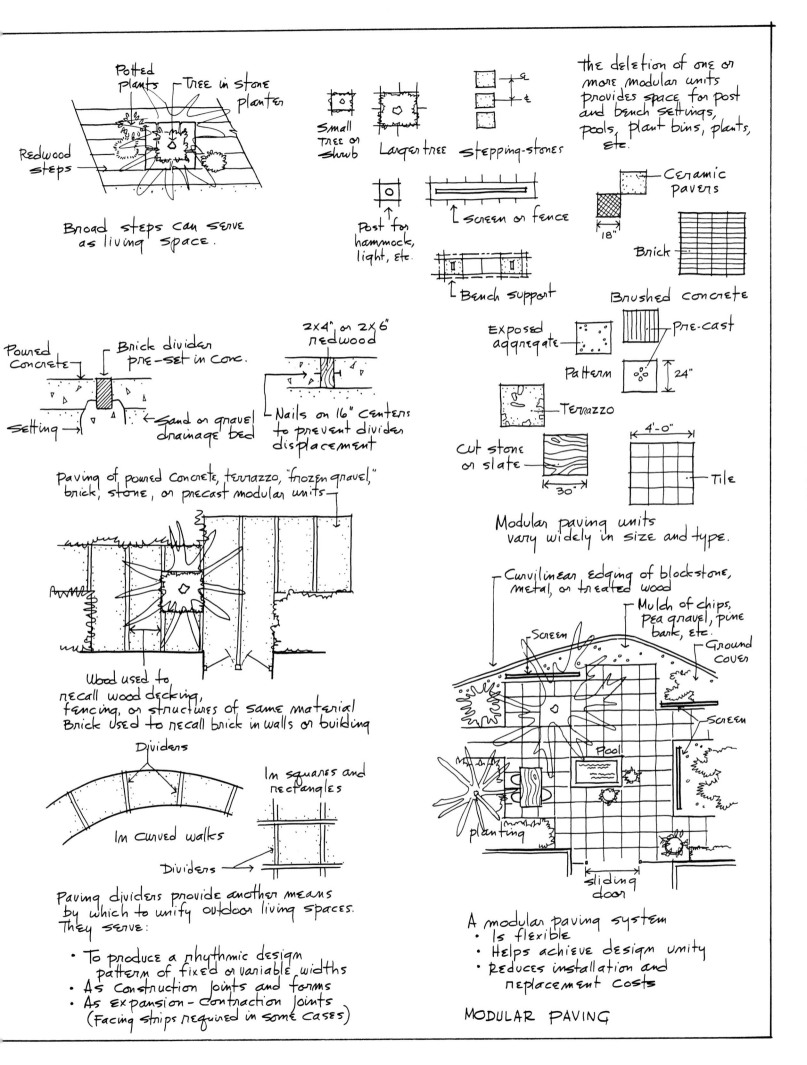

Potted plants — TREE in stone planter

Redwood steps

Broad steps can serve as living space.

Small tree or shrub

Larger tree

Stepping-stones

Post for hammock, light, etc.

Screen or fence

Bench support

the deletion of one or more modular units provides space for post and bench settings, pools, plant bins, plants, etc.

Ceramic pavers

18"

Brick

Brushed concrete

Exposed aggregate

Pre-cast

Pattern

24"

Terrazzo

Cut stone or slate

30"

4'-0"

Tile

Modular paving units vary widely in size and type.

Poured Concrete

Brick divider pre-set in conc.

2×4" or 2×6" redwood

Setting

Sand or gravel drainage bed

Nails on 16" centers to prevent divider displacement

Paving of poured concrete, terrazzo, "frozen gravel," brick, stone, or precast modular units.

Wood used to recall wood decking, fencing, or structures of same material
Brick used to recall brick in walls or building

Dividers

In squares and rectangles

In curved walks

Dividers

Paving dividers provide another means by which to unify outdoor living spaces. They serve:

- To produce a rhythmic design pattern of fixed or variable widths
- As construction joints and forms
- As expansion-contraction joints (Facing strips required in some cases)

Curvilinear edging of blockstone, metal, or treated wood

Mulch of chips, pea gravel, pine bark, etc.

Screen

Ground cover

Screen

Pool

planting

sliding door

A modular paving system
- Is flexible
- Helps achieve design unity
- Reduces installation and replacement costs

MODULAR PAVING

12

Community

The word *community* has many connotations, most of them favorable. For people, like plants and animals, seem to flourish in shared and supportive groupings. What is the nature of such community groupings, and how are they best formed?

The group imperative

Historically, people have banded together for some compelling reason, as for protection within the gated walls of the medieval city or the palisade of the fort. They have formed communities to engage in farming, commerce, or industry or to pursue their religious beliefs. In the opening up of America other settlements grew spontaneously around harbors and river landings, at the crossings of transportation routes, and wherever natural resources were concentrated or abundant.

Within communal aggregations friendships have been made mainly on the basis of propinquity. Dwellings were built in the most favorable and affordable locations, and then families moved in to make friends or sometimes to feud with the folks next door. Social groupings and working alliances were accidental and seldom consciously contrived. Homes were permanent, and neighborhoods were relatively stable. Towns and cities proliferated—too often in patterns of squared-off streets. Residential districts became impacted, often without schools, conveniences, or open-space relief. As densities and traffic increased, time-distances became greater, pollution often became intolerable, and surrounding fields and woodlands melted inexorably away.

With the coming of the twentieth century and the advent of the automobile the farm-to-city movement was suddenly reversed. Initially a few of the wealthy fled the industrial city to build romanticized farmsteads and rusticated villas such as those along the Hudson River. They were soon joined by many members of the middle class, to whom social reform was bringing an improving standard of living and newfound mobility. These families shared the beckoning dream of a better, more fulfilling life out beyond the city outskirts, where they could live amid forest, fields, and gardens in communion with nature. As they surged outward in ever-increasing numbers, the new suburbia was born. It was to become an American phenomenon.

The subdivision as we know it is a typical United States invention, with few counterparts in Europe or the orient.

Radburn, New Jersey, 1928. This revolutionary concept of community living was devised by its planners, Henry Wright and Clarence Stein, as an answer to living with the automobile. Homes were grouped in superblocks with automobile access from cul-de-sac streets, precluding high-speed through traffic. Pedestrian walkways, free of automobile crossings, provided access to large central park areas in which and around which were grouped the community social, recreational, and shopping centers.

In this plan concept were sown the seeds of ideas that have sprouted in most of the superior neighborhood and community plans of succeeding years.

New types of dwellings would be designed, and innovative community patterns were to be created. The subdivision tracts, planned communities, and new towns gradually evolved and are still evolving. If they fall somewhat short of the vision, it is because they have destroyed too much of the nature that they sought to embrace. It is because they have carried along with them from the city too many of the urban foibles—the bad habit of facing homes upon traffic-laden streets instead of pleasant courts or open-space preserves, of inexplicably lining schools, churches, and factories haunch to haunch along the roaring highways. It is because we have allowed the interconnecting roadways to become teeming thoroughfares along which has coalesced mile after mile of brash, traffic-clogging strip commercial development. It is because we still have much to learn about the basics and intricacies of group living, of land use, and of transportation planning.

This is not to aver that the back-to-nature movement has been a failure. On the contrary, it has produced many delightful homes and neighborhoods. It has raised hopes and expectations. It has provided exciting glimpses of what a more healthful and satisfying living environment can be. It will leave an indelible mark on all future community planning.

Meanwhile, back in the city those left behind found deteriorating conditions. The exodus of upper- and middle-class families exacerbated the problems. Not only did a large percentage of the more substantial homeowners seek refuge and a new start in the suburbs and countryside, but in turn the supporting shops, stores, banks, and businesses were soon to follow. The tax yields on all forms of urban property declined, provoking serious economic ills in most municipalities. Sagging cities required shoring up by increasing state and federal subsidies.

The quality of public services worsened. The central business districts rattled. As stores were demolished, the empty lots were preempted for parking, and the waning urban vitality was further sapped by the widening gaps that destroyed the essential compression. Vacated homes in obsolescent neighborhoods invited insurgence by minority families, many living on public assistance. Parks, poorly maintained and underpoliced, became hazardous. Crime and pollution increased to critical levels. Clearly, the cities were—and for the most part still are—in trouble.

They have fought back. In the early 1930s the first of many extensive public housing projects were built, although without lasting success. Cheap in construction and planned "by the manual" with its rigid minimum standards, they provided some of the most sterile dwellings and vacuous neighborhoods imaginable. Gradually these dreary look-alike tenements have given way to urban housing programs demonstrating new insights into individual and family housing needs and group behavior.

Other restorative devices and programs have helped the sick and sundered cities to regain their strength. The emergence of zoning and the powers of eminent domain as legalized planning tools have provided the means for reassembling buildable parcels and realigning the trafficways. The creation of urban redevelopment authorities and parking authorities has given the cities new mechanisms for receiving and disbursing grants-in-aid and guiding renewal programs. Rehabilitation techniques have been refined and improved. Transit and transportation have assumed new forms and dimensions. New types of parks, recreation, shopping, and community centers have come into being. Open-space structuring and waterfront improvements have given breathing space and invited nature back into the cities. Their revitalization has now progressed to a point at which in many cases the outward flow of émigrés has been reversed. People are attracted back when the advantages of urban living and working outweigh the negative aspects.

Form order

The early American subdivisions and new-town developments borrowed from the "garden city" theories of England's Ebenezer Howard. They applied the creative thinking of such native pioneers as the Olmsteds, Warren Manning, Henry Wright, and Clarence Stein to become pace-setting prototypes.

Soon, however, in Europe and especially in the devastated wake of World War II, new communities blossomed everywhere. Many extended the American techniques and theories and contributed their own fresh thinking. Such planned communities as Vällingby and Farsta in Sweden, Tapiola in Finland, and the more recent Milton Keynes and Thamesmead in England are exemplary. In the United States, too, the evolution continues.

New directions

In appraising the better examples of recently planned communities we find many new features. Some planning concepts, like the *transfer of development rights* and *flexibility zoning,* were unheard of even a few years ago. Some have met with immediate acceptance, others have not, and still others have yet to be adequately tested. While some approaches have failed in their initial application, they may have in them the seeds of ideas that will flower in the communities of the future.

Fine communities seldom if ever just happen. They must be thoughtfully and painstakingly brought into being. Improved approaches are continually emerging and give new meaning to such words as *housing, health, education, recreation,* and *community.* In the shaping of our more advanced residential areas the following principles are being successfully applied.

Apply the PCD approach. Planned community development (PCD), or PUD as it is sometimes called, is a rational framework for the phased development of community plans. Essentially it establishes at the start the types of uses to be included, the total number of dwellings, and a conceptual plan diagram. The traditional restrictive regulations are waived, and each successive phase as it is brought on in detail is checked against the conceptual plan and judged solely on the basis of foreseeable performance.

Request flexibility zoning. For larger tracts, this permits within the zone boundaries the free arrangement and progressive restudy of the land use and traffic-flow diagrams as long as the established caps are rebalanced and not exceeded and as long as the plan remains consistent with community goals.

Consider the transfer of development rights (TDR). In recognition of the fact that for reasons of their ecologic, scenic, or other values certain areas of land and water should be preserved in their natural state, TDR provisons allow and encourage a developer to transfer from the sensitive area those uses originally permitted by zoning. Although the relocation of the uses or dwelling units to another property is sometimes provided, TDR is most effective when the densities of contiguous building sites in the same ownership are increased to absorb the relocated units.

Relate all studies to water resource management. The fourfold purpose is to prevent flooding, protect water quality, replenish freshwater reserves, and provide for wastewater disposal.

Provide perimeter buffering. As supplementary or alternative open space, a band of land in its natural state may well be left around the borders of larger development sites. This provides a screen against adjacent trafficways or other abutting uses and a welcome backdrop for building construction.

Create a community portal. One of the best ways in which to engender a sense of neighborhood or community is by the provision of a cohesive circulation system and an attractive gateway.

Assure regional access. Thriving communities need connection to the shopping, cultural, and recreation centers and the open spaces of the regions which surround them. Aside from paths and controlled-access roadways, linkage may be attained by bikeways, by boat if on water, and by rapid transit in one or more of its many forms.

Preclude through-community trucking. Although local streets must be used on occasion by heavy trucks (by permit) and for daily deliveries by smaller vehicles, a direct truckway link to a community storage and distribution center has many advantages. Here heavy loads may be broken down for home or commercial delivery and bulk and private storage space provided for seasonal equipment, boats, and recreation vehicles.

Plan an open-space framework. As an alternative to facing homes and other development directly upon trafficways, many communities now wisely provide for the reservation of variformed swaths of land, in public or private ownership, as preferred building frontage. Vehicular approach to buildings, parking, and service areas is from the rear. The open-space system, which usually follows streams and drainageways, may also include walks, bicycle and jogging paths, and wider recreation areas.

Community open space, Kiawah, South Carolina.

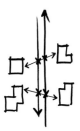

Home-to-home relationships across a busy street or highway . . .

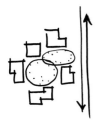

should give way to roadside clusters around a shared court.

Plan a hierarchy of trafficways. Even in smaller communities a clear differentiation between arterial, circulation, and local-frontage streets ensures more efficient traffic movement and safer, more agreeable living areas.

Limit roadside frontage. Insofar as possible, the facing of buildings upon arterials and circulation streets is to be precluded, with intersections to local-frontage streets spaced no closer than 660 feet.

Make use of three-way street intersections. They reduce through traffic, increase visibility, and make pedestrian crossings much safer.

Provide for rapid transit. Sheltered bus and minitransit stops and attractive community rapid transit stations, where appropriate, do much to stimulate transit use and reduce vehicular traffic.

Integrate paths of movement. Only when streets, walkways, bicycle trails, and other routes of movement are planned together can their full possibilities and optimum interrelationships be realized.

Attached and clustered dwellings yield shared open space.

Vary the housing types.   A well-balanced community provides not only a variety of dwellings, from single-family to multifamily, but also accommodates residents of differing lifestyles and a broad income range.

Cluster the buildings.   The more compact grouping of individual dwellings and the inclusion of patio and zero-lotline homes yield welcome additional open space for neighborhood definition and recreation use.

Feature the school-park campus.   The combining of schools with neighborhood and community parks permits much fuller use of each at substantial savings.

Include convenience shopping.   While regional shopping centers fill the largest share of family marketing needs, they usually require travel by automobile.   Neighborhood and community centers, with access by walks and bikeways, are needed to provide for a lesser scale of convenience shopping and service.

Provide employment opportunities.   Bedroom communities—those planned for residential living only—require the expenditure of time, income, and energy just to get to work.   Integral or closely related employment centers add vitality and convenience.

Relate to the regional centers. The larger business office campus, industrial park, or regional commercial mall is best kept outside, but convenient to, the residental groupings. Such centers are logically located near the regional freeway interchanges and accessible to the interconnecting circulation roads.

Plan for transient accommodations. When highway-related motel, hotel, or boatel accommodations do not otherwise fulfill the traveler's needs, a community inn is a welcome addition.

Consider a conference center. In addition to the auditorium and meeting rooms of the school-park community centers, a conference facility related to the commercial mall, business office park, cultural core, marina, golf course, tennis club, or inn is a popular amenity and asset.

Make recreation a way of life. Aside from private recreation opportunities and those provided at the neighborhood and community school parks, there is usually need for swimming, golf, and racquet clubs, a marina and beach club if the community is on water, a youth center, and access to hiking, jogging, and bicycle trails. The broader the range of available recreation, the more fulfilling is community living.

Encourage community programs, activities, and events. Although many do not require special space or site areas, no development program could be complete without consideration of all those social activities that contribute so much to community life. These include worship, contining education and health care programs, children's day care, a craft center and workshop, a little theater, game and meeting rooms, a newspaper, service clubs, Little League, dances, contests, and parades. Some start spontaneously; others may require encouragement and guidance.

Build out as you go. Scattered or partially finished building areas are uneconomical and disruptive. In the better communities construction proceeds by the phased *extension* of trafficways, utilities, and development areas. They are *completed* as examples. Construction materials and equipment are brought in from the rear, and the prearranged staging areas and access roads retreat as the work advances.

Assure a high level of maintenance. A maintenance center and enclosed yard, perhaps combined with a water storage or treatment plant, is best located inconspicuously at the periphery, with ready access to trucking and the areas to be served. It is to be well equipped and phased in advance of development to provide complete maintenance from the very start.

Honor the historic landmarks. When features of archaeological or historical significance exist, they are to be cherished. Their presence extends knowledge of the locality, its beginnings, and traditions and gives depth of meaning to life within the community.

Establish nature preserves. Every locality or site has in some degree its prized natural features. Be they subtle or dramatic, they add richness and interest and are to be protected, interpreted, and admired.

Name a scientist advisory council. In both initial and ongoing planning much can be gained by the naming of a team of scientist advisers. Convened periodically to bring their expertise to bear on the evolving plans and proposals, they are especially helpful in the study of large, complex, or ecologically sensitive holdings.

Appoint an environmental control officer. In the phased construction of each new parcel the responsibility for environmental protection is best centralized in one trained person who is present during all phases of planning, design review, and field installation.

Form a design review board. The plans for all buildings and major site improvements are best subjected from the start to a panel of qualified designers for review and recommendation as to acceptance, rejection, or modification. An architect, a landscape architect, and the environmental control officer would be appropriate members.

Prepare a development guideline manual. As the basic reference document for all planning, design, and continuing operation of the community an expanding loose-leaf manual is essential. As it evolves, it will contain:

The community goals and objectives

The conceptual community plan

Each phased neighborhood or parcel plan as it is brought into detailed study

A section and flowchart describing plan review procedures

Plan submission requirements and forms

Architectural design guidelines

Site design guidelines

The master planting plan and policy and recommended plant lists

A section on environmental quality control

A section on energy conservation

A section on solid waste disposal and recycling

Homeowners' association covenants

As the need arises or is foreseen, supplementary sections will be added and the manual kept updated and complete. To be fully effective its provisions must be equitably and uniformly enforced.

Establish a means of governance. It is important from the start of planning to have in mind the type of political entity that the community is to be or to become a part of. This will be a key factor in the determination of the type and level of public services to be provided and of responsibilities for planning reviews and permitting, for the installation of utilities, streets, and other improvements, and for taxation and decision making.

Create a homeowners' association. The developer, builders, and final homeowners all benefit by the early formation of a permanent organization in which the owner of each lot or home has a pro rata responsibility and vote and to which assessments are paid. The purpose of the association is to provide the mechanism for the formulation and implementation of continuing community maintenance and improvement policies.

Ensure flexibility with control. The most successful American communities have been guided in their development by policies that

1. Established the broad outlines of compatible land use and routes of movement

2. Provided the guidelines required to ensure flexibility, design quality, and environmental protection

3. Encouraged individuality and creativity

Systematize the site installations. All physical elements of a community—buildings, roadways, walks, utilities, lighting, signing, and planting—are best planned as working and interrelated *systems*.

Pelican Bay, Florida
1. *Beach in public use*
2. *Dunes protected*
3. *Tidal-bay system preserved as wildlife sanctuary*
4. *Conservation, with limited use*
5. *Storm-water retention dike*
6. *Water management recharge ponds*
7. *Clustered upland development*

The new ethic in community planning

Preserve the best of the natural features.
Conserve, with limited use, an extended open-space framework.
Develop selected upland areas with site-responsive building clusters.

STREET LIGHTING

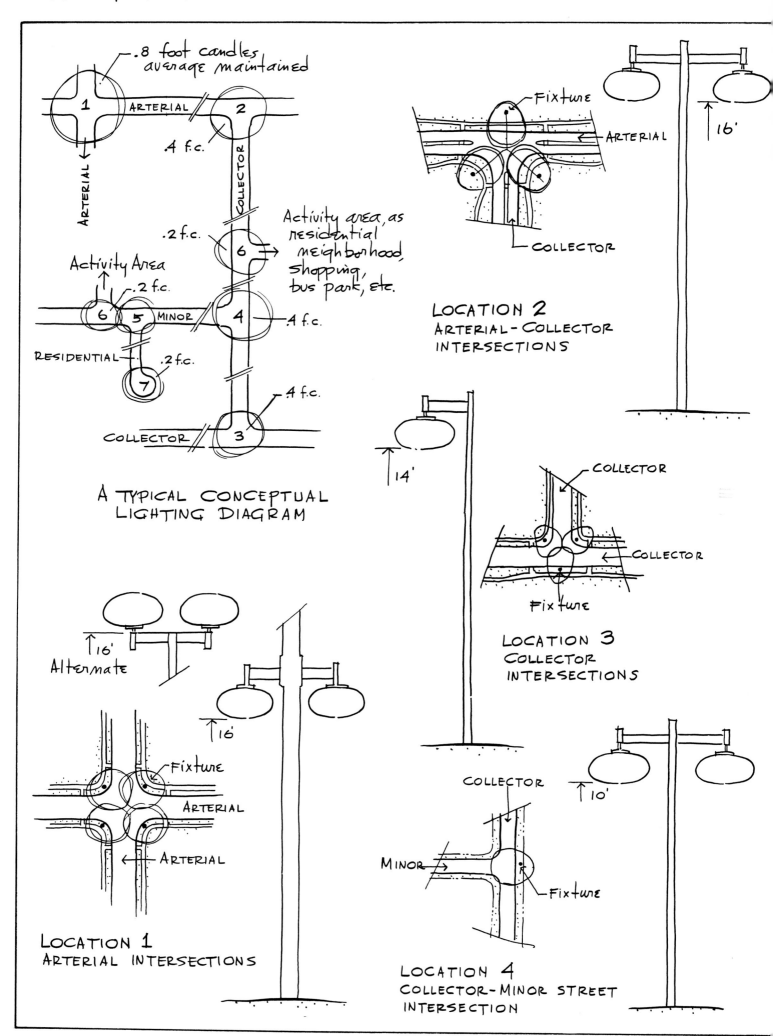

.8 foot candles average maintained

ARTERIAL

1   ARTERIAL   2

.4 f.c.

COLLECTOR

Activity area, as residential neighborhood, shopping, bus park, etc.

.2 f.c.   6

Activity Area

.2 f.c.

6   5   MINOR   4   .4 f.c.

RESIDENTIAL   .2 f.c.

7

COLLECTOR   3   .4 f.c.

A TYPICAL CONCEPTUAL LIGHTING DIAGRAM

Fixture

ARTERIAL

COLLECTOR

16'

LOCATION 2
ARTERIAL-COLLECTOR INTERSECTIONS

14'

COLLECTOR

COLLECTOR

Fixture

LOCATION 3
COLLECTOR INTERSECTIONS

16'

Alternate

16'

Fixture

ARTERIAL

ARTERIAL

LOCATION 1
ARTERIAL INTERSECTIONS

COLLECTOR

10'

MINOR

Fixture

LOCATION 4
COLLECTOR-MINOR STREET INTERSECTION

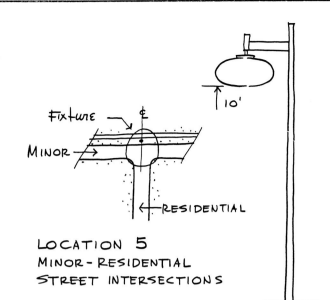

LOCATION 5
MINOR - RESIDENTIAL
STREET INTERSECTIONS

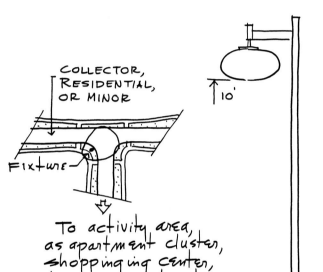

LOCATION 6
ENTRANCE TO COMMUNITY
ACTIVITY NODE

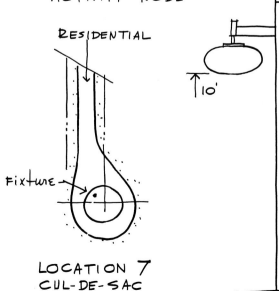

LOCATION 7
CUL-DE-SAC

PEDESTRIAN LIGHTING
IN PUBLIC EASEMENT

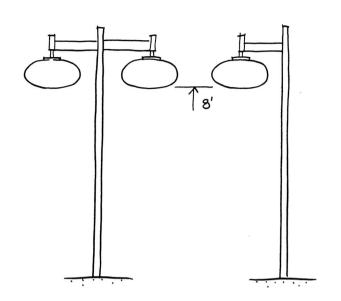

Note: All dimensions
are approximate.

A STREET-LIGHTING SYSTEM

A well-conceived lighting
system will:

- Mark the points of decision
- Define the <u>way</u> and the <u>place</u> —
  the <u>way</u> with "guide-on" illumination,
  the <u>place</u> with increased intensity
  and expressive lighting patterns
- Differentiate between roadway
  and walkway lighting
- Provide ample light at pedestrian
  crossings
- Couple site lighting with the
  informational and directional signs
- Highlight the more attractive
  structures and site features
- Borrow light from adjacent areas
  and buildings
- Eliminate all sources of glare
- Provide consistent light standard
  locations in relation to intersections
  and turning points
- Use standardized fixtures,
  globes, and fittings

13

The city

It sometimes seems that our contemporary planning is an unholy game of piling as much structure or as much city as possible in one spot. The urban areas to which we point with pride are often merely the highest, widest, and densest piles of brick, stone, and mortar. Where, in these heaps and stacks of masonry, are the forgotten, stifled people? Are they refreshed, inspired, and stimulated by their urban environment? Hardly, for in our times, too often a city is a desert.

Cityscape

To be bluntly truthful, our burgeoning American cities, squared off and cut into uncompromising geometric blocks by unrelieved, unterminated trafficways, have had more of this arid desert quality than the mature cities of either Europe or the orient.

If we compare a map of Rome as it was in 1748 with an aerial photograph of New York as it is today, we marvel at the infinite variety of pleasant spaces that occurred throughout the Eternal City. Of course, as Rasmussen has pointed out in *Towns and Buildings*, "Great artists formed the city, and the inhabitants, themselves, were artists enough to know how to live in it." We wonder why such spaces are for the most part missing in our contemporary city plans.

Traditionally, the urban spaces of America have been mainly corridors. Our streets, boulevards, and sidewalks have led past or through to something or somewhere beyond. Our cities, our suburbs, and our homesites are laced and interlaced with these corridors, and we often seek in vain to find those places or spaces that

Urban redevelopment, Baltimore.

The corridor-canyons that are New York City's streets stretch on interminably without relief, without focal point, or without the welcome interruption of useful or meaningful space.

attract and hold us and satisfy. We do not like to live in corridors; we like to live in rooms. The cities of history are full of such rooms, planned and furnished with as much concern as were the surrounding structures. If we would have such appealing outdoor places, we must plan our corridors not as channels trying to be places as well but as free-flowing channelized trafficways. And we must plan our places for the use and enjoyment of people.

The old cities had, and still have to their credit and memorable

According to a recent poll most Americans (56 percent), if given the choice, would now prefer a rural life; 25 percent would opt for the suburbs, and only 19 percent for an urban living environment.

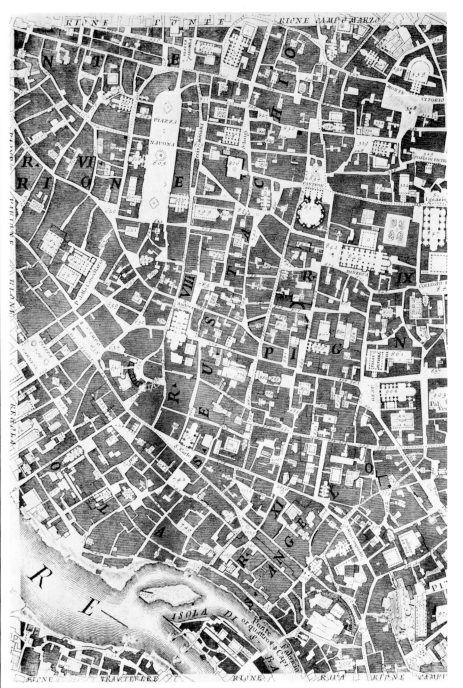

From Giovanni Battista Nolli's map of Rome.

Large cities seen from an altitude of several hundred feet do not present, as a whole, an orderly facade. Their vastness is their most striking feature; whatever quality they possess is lost in sheer quantity. Areas that give evidence of planning occupy but a small surface. Disorder predominates. Buildings are piled up near the center and scattered haphazardly toward the outskirts. The few green spots and other places of beauty known to the tourist, seem hidden in a maze of grey and shapeless masses that stretch toward the surrounding country in tentacular form. The very borders of the city are undefined, junk and refuse belts merging with the countryside. If on beholding this sight we pause to contemplate modern cities and consider what they could have been if planned, we must admit in the end that, in spite of their magnificent vitality, they represent one of man's greatest failures.

José Luis Sert

The unit of measurement for space in urban society is the individual. . . .

Arthur B. Gallion

The first step in adequate planning is to make a fresh canvass of human ideals and human purposes.

Lewis Mumford

From cradle to grave, this problem of running order through chaos, direction through space, discipline through freedom, unity through multiplicity, has always been, and must always be, the task of education, as it is the moral of religious philosophy, science, art, politics and economy.

Henry Adams

charm, their plazas, piazzas, courts, squares, and fountains and their distinctive, undefinable, uplifting spirit of *joie de vivre.* These cities were conceived as three-dimensional civic art and in terms of meaningful patterns of form and open spaces. Our cities, with few exceptions, are oriented to our traffic-glutted streets.

Whom are we to blame for this? Aristotle, in his *Rhetoric,* states that "truth and justice are by nature better than their opposites, and therefore if decisions are made wrongly, it must be the speakers who (through lack of effective powers of persuasion) are to blame for the defeat." For our purpose, this passage might well be paraphrased: "Facility, interest, and beauty are by nature better than chaos, the dull, and the ugly, and therefore if decisions are made wrongly, it must be we planners who, through lack of effective powers of persuasion (or more compelling concepts of urban living), are to blame. . . ."

In searching for a more enlightened approach to urban planning we must look back and reappraise the old values. While recognizing the fallacies of the "city beautiful" in its narrowest sense, we must rediscover the age-old art of building cities that inspire, satisfy, and work. And surely we will, for we are disturbed by the vapid nature of the cities we have planned or, worse, have allowed to grow unplanned in sporadic, senseless confusion.

We, in contemporary times, have lost the art and feeling of overall plan organization. Our cities lack coherent relationships and plan continuity. With our automobiles as the symbol and most demanding planning factor of our times, we have found the meandering streets, places, and plan forms of the ancient cities to be unsuitable. We have rejected (with good reason) the synthesizing device of the inexorable "grand plan" but have found, for the most part, few substitutes save the mechanical grid and other patterns of uninspired geometry. The transit, the protractor, and the compass have delineated for us a wholly artificial system of living areas and spaces. We must and will develop new types of plan organization better suited to our way of life. In future urban planning considerations the significant space is bound to return, and we will again have ways and places as important as the structures.

The desert character of our cities is concentrated in the downtown core. Here the average cityscape is a conglomeration of metal, glass, and masonry cubes set on a dreary base plane of oil-splattered concrete and asphalt. It is bleak, chill, and gusty in wintertime, and in summer it shimmers and weaves with its stored-up, radiating heat. Within view of its naked towers, the open countryside beyond is often many degrees warmer in winter and cooler in the summertime.

Such an oppressive and barren cityscape falls far short of the mark. Our cities must be opened up, refreshed, revitalized. Our straining traffic arteries must be realigned and bifurcated to bypass the city cores, to pass under or around the perimeter of great city parks or business squares in which the stores and restaurants and office buildings stand apart and breathe. In contrast with sharp building profiles and the hard surface and dull hues of pavement, the open park spaces must give the welcome relief of foliage, shade,

All good planning must begin with a survey of actual resources: the landscape, the people, the work-a-day activities in a community. Good planning does not begin with an abstract and arbitrary scheme that it seeks to impose on a community; it begins with a knowledge of existing conditions and opportunities. . . .

The final test of an economic system is not the tons of iron, the tanks of oil, or the miles of textiles it produces: The final test lies in its ultimate products—the sort of men and women it nurtures and the order and beauty and sanity of their communities.

Lewis Mumford

A city plan is the expression of the collective purpose of the people who live in it, or it is nothing.

Henry S. Churchill

It has become apparent that urban waterfronts, whether natural or artificial, are now prime pieces of real estate, essential ingredients in forming a community image, valuable stages for architectural display and great places for public recreation.

Grady Clay

Central Park in New York. Its effect on real estate values, its inestimable contribution to the city, its ineffable meaning to all who see and sense and use it—these lessons should never be forgotten by the urban planner. Yet how seldom, on even the smallest scale, do we find such urban parks envisioned.

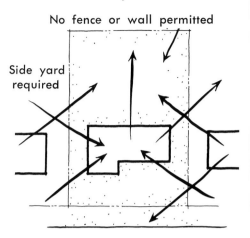
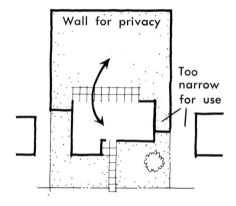
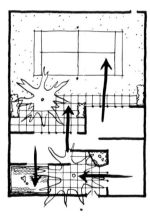
splashing water, flowers, and bright color. Like oases, such urban spaces will transform the city into a refreshing environment for vibrant urban life.

Problems

A common error in our city planning has been the assumption that the wider and straighter the street or avenue, the better. Thus was foreordained a city resembling a sieve, open and vacuous, where most outdoor activity is visible from the trafficways and where walled outdoor privacy within the residential area is often not even permitted. Most of the city's myriad side-yard or buffer spaces might better be consolidated for some significant uses. Air, sunlight, and open space are highly desirable features, but their distribution and treatment are as important as their extent.

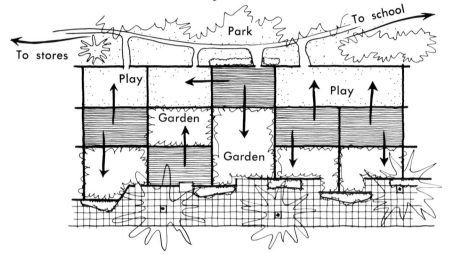

Minimum homes for maximum living.

People enjoy compression. Georgetown, in Washington, D.C., surely one of the most delightful residential areas of our country, has narrow brick homes set wall to wall along its narrow, shaded streets. Its brick walk pavements, often extending from curb to facade, are opened here around the smooth trunk of a sycamore or punched out there to receive a holly, a boxwood, a fig tree, or a bed of myrtle. In this compact community, where space is at such a premium, the open areas are artfully enclosed by fences, walls, or building wings to give privacy and to create a cool and pleasant well of garden space into which the whole house opens.

The great estates of Europe and the United States, with their vast expanses of turf and their sweeping vistas, are grand and impressive, but one soon becomes bored and finds in them little to make one wish to linger. They prove that spaciousness in itself is not always a desirable thing. The author in working with urban renewal and model cities programs has discovered that the openness of a new low-income-housing community was at first the thing with greatest appeal to families relocated from older neighborhoods or from cramped and aching slums. But the residents soon became dissatisfied with the severe buildings, the wide grass areas, and the play equipment set out on flat sheets of pavement. One would hear the officials ask, "What's wrong with these people? Why aren't they happy? What did they expect? What more do they want?"

What they wanted, what they missed, what they unconsciously longed for, were such congregating places as the carved and whittled storefront bench, the rear-porch stoops, the packed-clay, sun-drenched boccie courts, the crates and boxes set in the cool shade of a propped-up grape arbor or in the spattered shadow of a spreading ailanthus tree. They missed the meandering alleys, dim and pungent, the leaking hydrants, the hot, bright places against the moist, dark places, the cellar doors, the leaning board fences, the sagging gates, the maze of rickety outside stairs. They missed the torn circus posters, the rusting enameled tobacco signs, the blatant billboards, the splotchy patches of weathered paint. They missed the bakery smells of hot raisin bread and warm, sugared lunch rolls, the fish market smells, the clean, raw smell of gasoline, the smell of vulcanizing rubber. They missed the strident neighborhood sounds, the intermittent calls and chatter, the baby squalls, the supper shouts, the whistles, the "allee, allee oxen," the pound of the stone hammer, the ring of the tire iron, the rumbling delivery truck, the huckster's cart, the dripping, creaking ice wagon. They missed the shape, the pattern, the smells, the sounds, and the pulsing feel of life.

What they missed, what they *need*, is the compression, the interest, the variety, the surprises, and the casual, indefinable charm of the neighborhood that they left behind. This, in essence, is the appeal of the Left Bank of Paris, of San Francisco's Chinatown, of Beacon Hill in Boston. This same charm of both tight and expansive spaces, of delightful variety, of delicious contrast, of the happy accident, is an essential quality of planning that we must constantly strive for. And one of the chief ingredients of charm, when we find it, is a sense of the diminutive, a feeling of pleasant compression. Private or community living spaces become a reality only if they and the life within them are kept within the scale of pleasurable human experience.

A further error of our planning has stemmed from the lingering compulsion to force our cities into lots and blocks of uniform size and use. Such "ideal" cities of monotonous conformity are gray in tone. If we examine most recent city plans, we still find that one zone is designated for single-family homes, another zone for town-

The memorable cities of the world—London, Amsterdam, Paris, Copenhagen, Madrid, Athens, Rome, Montreal, New York, New Orleans, San Francisco—are those in which people live where they work. Civic and business centers are interspersed with townhouses, apartments, and cafés, with bakeries and boutiques, with wine, cheese, fruit, and florist shops, and with artists' studios.

The best way to promote security in a downtown area is to assure that the streets are alive with responsible urban residents who come out to enjoy the evening sights and activities. In such an atmosphere restaurants and theaters thrive, shops stay open, and people can linger or stroll about in relative safety.

Patterns of mix are important. The vibrant centers are those in which the old is intermixed with the new, the low with the high, the simple with the elaborate.

When rows of shops and homes are interrupted by blocks of stark office towers or by blank building walls, evening street life is diminished. To sustain street appeal and nighttime activity, office and apartment towers are best grouped around off-street plazas or courts. Business, residential, and commercial relationships are all thereby intensified.

The *layering* of shops, apartments, and offices is proving to be a successful means of keeping the evening streets alive, with people at hand to enjoy them.

Urban activity centers

New vitality in our cities

The best features of townhouse living are exemplified in this attractive residence.

houses, and another for high-rise apartments; an isolated district is set aside for commercial use; a green area will someday be a park. May we place in this residential area an artist's studio? It is not allowed! An office for an architect? A florist shop? A bookstall? A pastry shop? No! In a residential area such uses are usually not permitted, for that would be spot zoning, the sin of all planning

sins. These too often are the rules, and thus the rich complexities that are the very essence of the most pleasant urban areas of the world are even now still being regulated out of our gray cities. London, after the blitz, was replanned and rebuilt substantially according to this antiseptic planning order. The first new London areas were spacious, clean, and orderly, and all would have seemed to be ideal except for one salient feature: they were incredibly dull, and nobody liked them. Our zoning ordinances, which to a large degree control our city patterns, are still rather new to us. They have great promise as an effective tool and a key to achieving cities of vitality, efficiency, and charm when we have learned so to use our zoning powers as to ensure these qualities rather than preclude them.

Possibilities

The needs of the human beings who would work and live in our cities must come to have precedence over the insistent requirements of traffic, over the despoiling demands of industry, and over the callous public acceptance of rigid economy as the most consistent criterion for our street and utility layouts and for the development of our boulevards, plazas, parks, and other public works.

What are the human needs of which we speak? Some have been so long ignored or forgotten in terms of city planning and growth that they may now seem quaint or archaic. Yet they are *basic*. We human beings need and must have once again in our cities *a rich variety of spaces,* each planned with sensitivity to best express and accommodate its function, spaces through which we may move with safety and with pleasure and in which we may congregate. We must have *health, convenience,* and *mobility* on scales as yet undreamed of. We also must have *order*. Not an antiseptic, stilted, or grandiose order of contrived geometric dullness or sweeping emptiness but a functional order that will hold the city together

There are, certainly, ample reasons for redoing downtown—falling retail sales, tax bases in jeopardy, stagnant real-estate values, impossible traffic and parking conditions, failing mass transit, encirclement by slums. But with no intent to minimize these serious matters, it is more to the point to consider what makes a city center magnetic, what can inject gaiety, the wonder, the cheerful hurly-burly that make people want to come into the city and to linger there. For magnetism is the crux of the problem. All downtown's values are its by-products. To create in it an atmosphere of urbanity and exuberance is not a frivolous aim.

Jane Jacobs

The city in its complete sense, then, is a geographic plexus, an economic organization, an institutional process, a theatre of social action—and an esthetic symbol of collective unity. On the one hand it is a physical frame for the commonplace domestic and economic activities; on the other, it is a consciously dramatic setting for the more significant actions and the more sublimated urges of human culture.

Lewis Mumford

and make it work—an order as organic as that of the living cell, the leaf, and the tree. A sensed cohesive and satisfying order that permits of the happy accident, is flexible, and combines the best of the old with the best of the new. An order that is sympathetic to those structures, things, and activities that afford interest, variety, surprise, and contrast and that have the power to "charm the heart." We humans need in our cities *sources of inspiration, stimulation, refreshment, beauty, and delight.* We need and must have, in short, a *salubrious, pollution-free urban environment* conducive to the living of the whole, full life.

Such a city will not ignore nature. Rather, it will be integrated with nature. And it will invite nature back into its confines in the form of clean air, sunshine, water, foliage, breeze, wooded hills, rediscovered water edges, and interconnected garden parks.

The new urbanity

Gradually, but with quickening tempo, the face of urban America is taking on a new look. It is a look of wholesome cleanliness, of mopping up, renovation, or tearing down and rebuilding. There is a sense of urgency, directness, nonpretense, and informality. There is a new group spirit of concerted actions and of people enjoying the experience of making things happen, of coming and being together in pleasant city surroundings. There is a freshness, sparkle, and spontaneity as American as apple pie.

The movement was born partly of desperation—of the need by property owners to "save the city" and protect their threatened investments. It responds to the need for energy conservation and the contraction of overextended development patterns. It is a reaction also to revulsion at pollution, filth, decay, and delapidated structures. It is a strengthening compulsion to clean house, repair, and rebuild, mainly by private enterprise. There is a new vitality. There is a sense of competition, too, marked by inventiveness. Fresh winds are astir in our cities.

URBAN WAYS AND PLACES

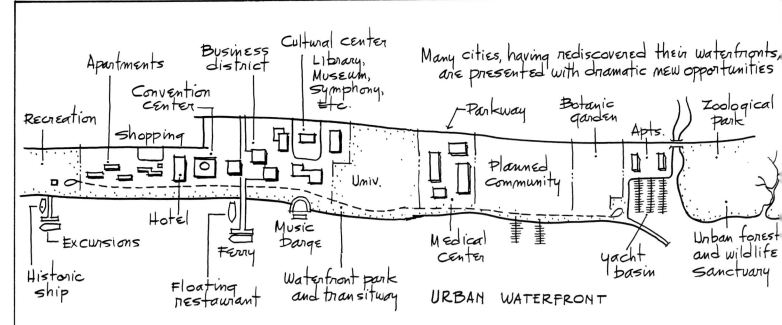

Recreation

Apartments

Convention center

Shopping

Business district

Cultural center
Library,
Museum,
Symphony,
etc.

Many cities, having rediscovered their waterfronts, are presented with dramatic new opportunities

Parkway

Botanic garden

Zoological Park

Apts.

Univ.

Planned Community

Hotel

Excursions

Ferry

Music barge

Medical Center

yacht basin

Urban forest and wildlife sanctuary

Historic ship

Floating restaurant

Waterfront park and transitway

URBAN WATERFRONT

The character and livability of a city are largely determined by the nature and arrangement of its open spaces.

<u>Possibilities:</u>

- <u>Waterfront</u>
  Beach, lake shore, or river edge

- <u>Blueways</u>
  Rivers, streams, and floodplains

- <u>Greenways</u>
  Freeways, parkways, transportation corridors, transmission easements, slopes, walkways, jogging paths, and bicycle trails.

- <u>Urban Parks and Recreation Areas</u>

- <u>Other Openspace Contributors</u>

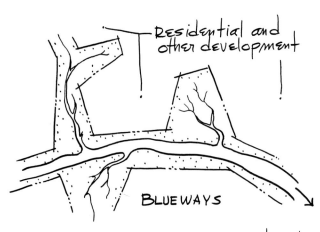

Residential and other development

BLUEWAYS

Streams and rivers form a network of interconnected drainageways. They provide the ideal opportunity for a cohesive open-space system — to accommodate parks, parkways, walks, trails, and nature preserves.

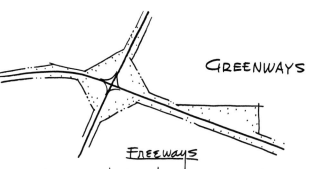

GREENWAYS

<u>Freeways</u>

With expanded interchange modes, widened rights-of-way, variable-width medians, and scenic easements, natural features and covers can be maintained to create lineal "motor parks" throughout the metropolitan region.

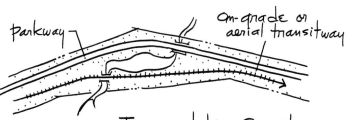

Parkway

On-grade or aerial transitway

<u>Transportation Corridors</u>

Transitways, often combined with arterial highways, provide welcome swaths of green and accommodate walks, trails, and bikeways.

<u>Utility Easements</u>

Transmission line easements and rights-of-way can contribute wide strips of open land for multiple public use.

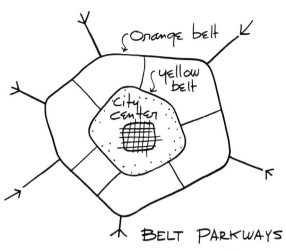

BELT PARKWAYS

Urban cores are best ringed with free-flowing parkways which intercept and distribute traffic.

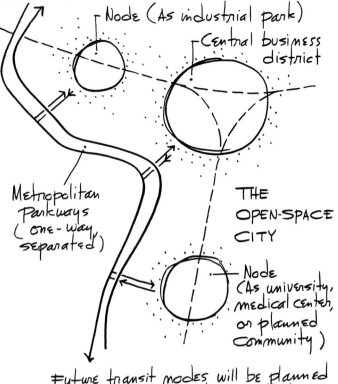

THE OPEN-SPACE CITY

Future transit modes will be planned as tiered activity centers - with towers and indoor-outdoor terraces. Each such concentrated urban core will be linked internally by rapid transit and externally by scenic parkways. It will turn inward to pedestrian courts, malls, and plazas and outward to forest, park, and recreation preserves. Within the broad openspace matrix low-intensity development of various categories will be clustered.

Each open area contributes refreshing breathing space and visual relief.

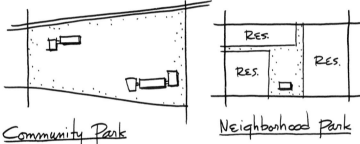

Community Park

As part of a Jr.-Sr. highschool campus it provides playfields and courts for the school athletic program.

Neighborhood Park

Often combined with an elementary school

Business Office/Industrial Parks

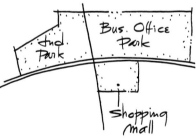

City Parks

The larger urban parks serve recreational needs beyond those provided for at neighborhood or community levels. These will include the full range of public congregating places and facilities - such as plazas, squares, pools, boating basin, zoological garden, historic landmarks, outdoor theaters, stadium, etc.

URBAN PARKS AND RECREATION

Institutional Campuses

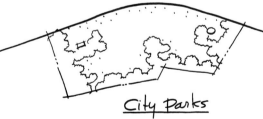

Churches
Hospitals   Universities
Libraries   Civic and
Museums   cultural centers

Each contributes openspace.

OTHER OPEN SPACE CONTRIBUTORS

· Urban forests
· Reservoirs
· Private golf, swim, and tennis clubs
· Roof tops
· Vacant lots
· Land-banked property
· Military installations
· Locks and dams
· In-city gardens and nurseries
· The unbuilt-upon space of all development sites

Ideally, the major openspace ways and places will be linked to create the blue-green frame within and around which the evolving city may take form.

14

Region

Rational land use planning can stop at no property line or jurisdictional boundary. For streams flow, trafficways must interconnect, and polluted air, for example, is wafted wherever the winds may blow it.

Every land or water holding abuts other properties and should respect the relationship. Every downstream use of property is influenced by all that transpires in the watershed above. Each habitation, community, and municipality affects and is affected by conditions within its surrounding social, economic, political, and physical region. Since these are not synonymous, what should the regional boundaries be? They will vary, depending upon the nature of the considerations or study. This principle of flexible and appropriate study boundaries is fundamental to all sound regional planning.

For too long the city has been considered a circumscribed entity. By tradition we have thought of the city *versus* the farmland, the city *versus* the suburbs, the city *versus* the townships or counties in which the city lies. Many serious and often needless frictions have resulted from a lack of coordinated planning. There have been costly duplications of administration and facilities. Animosities that will preclude for years intelligent cooperation on even the simplest of interarea issues have been generated. There is, however, a wise and growing tendency to plan for the development of the city and its contiguous matrix as a unified *region.*

Concurrent with the trend to broaden the scope of planning from an urban to a regional basis is the drive to structure or restructure residential districts into more self-sufficient neighborhoods. These, surrounded by greenbelts and connected by freeways to the manufacturing complexes, the urban cores, and the outlying region, give promise of a more humanized living environment.

If our lives and experiences are constantly being affected by sensed relationships, it would seem that these relationships could be given an expressive form order. They can be and are, whether we like it or not. Our homes, neighborhoods, and cities are telltale physical expressions of the way we think and live. Their plan layout and form are in a state of continuous evolution to reflect our changing ideas about living, as we constantly seek a better fit with our natural and built environment. With this in mind, it might be well to study the broad outlines of our present patterns of social and land use organization. Perhaps with better understanding we can improve the relationships and our way of life.

The family

In our democratic society, as in the highest cultures of the past, the family is the smallest and yet most significant social unit.

Family lifestyle patterns as we know them today are far different from those of the log cabin, the working farm, the row house, or the mansion. The free and rigorous life of the pioneer has given way to the more ordered routine of the farmers on their acreage or the conformity of the confined city dwellers. Parental attitudes have changed. The discipline of paternal- or maternal-dominated family living has become more relaxed and casual. Private fortunes

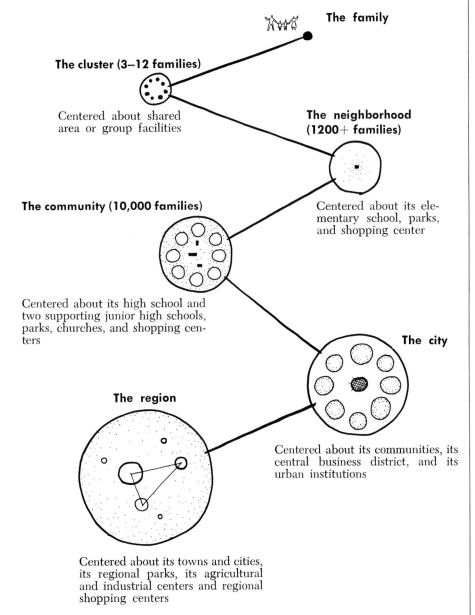

The family

The cluster (3–12 families)
Centered about shared area or group facilities

The neighborhood (1200+ families)
Centered about its elementary school, parks, and shopping center

The community (10,000 families)
Centered about its high school and two supporting junior high schools, parks, churches, and shopping centers

The city
Centered about its communities, its central business district, and its urban institutions

The region
Centered about its towns and cities, its regional parks, its agricultural and industrial centers and regional shopping centers

The problem of the landscape architect—even as of the architect, the town planner, the engineer, and indeed all men of good will—is now, and will be more acutely every day, the development of ways and means for bridging the gap between town and country, the antithesis between urban and rural life—more specifically between the masonry, the asphalt, and the dingbat construction of the town and the quiet greenery of meadow, forest, and shore. How to open up the town to the country, how to bring the town culturally to the country—that is our primary problem. . . .

Garrett Eckbo

To see the interdependence of city and country, . . . to appreciate that there is a just and a harmonious balance between the two—this capacity we have lacked. Before we can build well in any scale we shall, it seems to me, have to develop an art of regional planning, an art which will relate city and countryside. . . .

Lewis Mumford

As long as man's activities are in sympathy with nature, or are on so small a scale that they do not interfere with nature's self-renewing cycle, the landscape survives, either in a predominantly natural form or as a balanced product of human partnership with nature. But as soon as the growth of the population or its urban activities are sufficient to upset nature's balance, the landscape suffers, and the only remedy is for man to take a conscious part in the landscape's evolution.

Sylvia Crowe

have been for the most part taxed away. Salons, grand balls, and great dinners are almost a thing of the past, as are the chambermaid, the cook, and the well-trained staff of servants.

Life has become so automobile-oriented that many families have taken their cars into their homes or parked them at the front door. Homes and gardens are less pretentious, less ornate. They are mechanized, less cluttered, more open. Front and rear porches have disappeared along with the alley and the stable. The wide front lawn has been replaced by the walled garden courts of patio homes and townhouses. Exterior house walls have been opened up or "exploded" to let in more air and sunlight and to enframe the views of garden, sky, and landscape to provide more contact with nature and with the stone, water, and plants of the earth. As concepts of family living have changed, the forms of our dwellings have changed to reflect them.

Five cul-de-sac arrangements that provide a cluster of family dwellings.

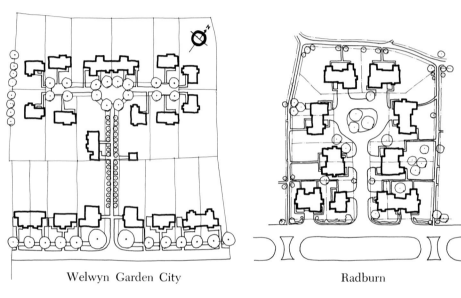

Welwyn Garden City

Radburn

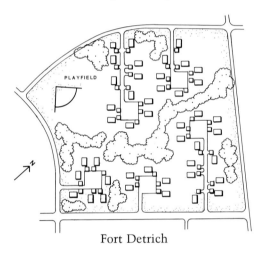

Fort Detrich

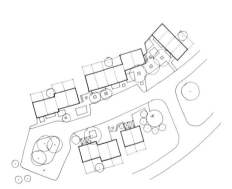

Valley Springs

East Hills

The cluster

It has been learned that from three to twelve families constitute the optimum interfamily social group. If their dwellings are clustered in a convenient plan arrangement, kaffeeklatsches, parties, children's play and games, and "get-togetherness" on a first-name basis are natural and spontaneous. Neighbors borrow cups of butter or sugar and exchange views and form friendships at the parking compound, while children share toys and "turf."

Ideally, the families in such a cluster would have the same general goals and standards but a diversity of individual status and interests.

As a group exceeds twelve to sixteen in number, it becomes unwieldy, tends to lose its cohesion, and automatically breaks up into smaller social alliances.

The most desirable plan arrangements for the cluster will afford an off-street parking compound, freedom from the noise and danger of passing traffic, pedestrian interaccess, and a focal place or feature such as a sitting area or a children's play court. The grouping will have harmonious site and architectural character and physical separation from adjacent clusters or structures. Compactness and the sharing of party walls are the mark of many successful clusters, where the normally unusable side-yard space is squeezed out and aggregated for group use and enjoyment.

The neighborhood

A neighborhood is at best a grouping of residential clusters around shared open space. It should be small enough to encourage participation of all families in group activities and large enough to contain a convenience-shopping center, playfields, and buffering. An enduring neighborhood plan and one that has accommodated changing concepts of social behavior and education is one formed around and providing safe walkway access to an elementary school. In size and population it is shaped to yield or contribute to the approximate number of students required for a balanced school facility. It is not

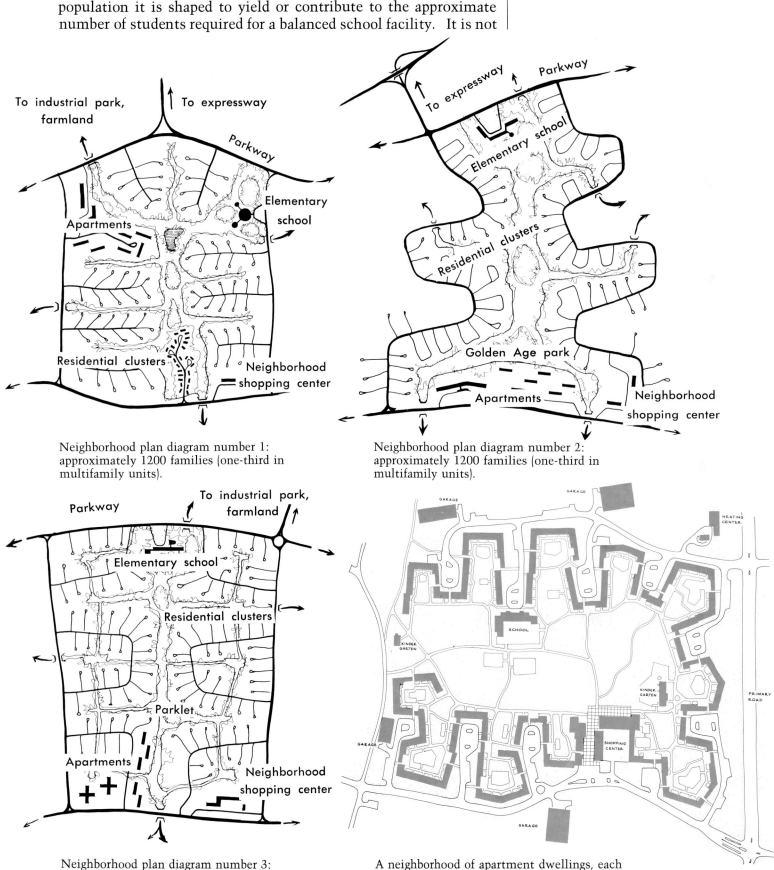

Neighborhood plan diagram number 1: approximately 1200 families (one-third in multifamily units).

Neighborhood plan diagram number 2: approximately 1200 families (one-third in multifamily units).

Neighborhood plan diagram number 3: approximately 1200 families (one-third in multifamily units).

A neighborhood of apartment dwellings, each related to an exterior approach and an interior social court and to a large central park area. The relatively high density of the apartment groups yields large open space where it counts.

Any architect worth his salt knows that a building is not designed by putting together a series of rooms. Any building that is good has an underlying design concept that binds all the parts together into a whole. Without this it is not architecture. Nor does a designed neighborhood consist of a series of "projects" that are strung together. There must be an underlying design plan that binds together the pieces and makes the neighborhood an entity.

Edmund N. Bacon

The physical plan can seldom if ever, create a "neighborhood" except in the most abstract use of the word. It can, however, very materially assist other forces in fostering a true neighborhood feeling.

Henry S. Churchill

essential, however, that either the school, shopping, or other shared amenities be centered within the single neighborhood confines. It is often more desirable that they be placed outside or between sub-neighborhood enclaves of varying character and size and be laced together with interconnecting greenways, walks, and bicycle trails.

In the well-conceived neighborhood peripheral roads will provide access and vehicular connection to free-flowing regional parkways. Through traffic will be precluded. Ideally, the neighborhood will be composed of planned tracts of from 3 to 30 acres, grouped around and between lobes of semiprivate park that open into the larger community park and school system. Each such tract, developed as an entity, would be freed of all individual lot restrictions. Its proposed layout would be subject to review by the planning agencies solely on the basis of livability. Land use patterns and densities, as approved, would then be fixed by covenants between the landowners and the municipality.

Reston, one of the better-planned American communities of the twentieth century.

The community

A *community*, as differentiated from the *neighborhood*, would at best comprise two or more neighborhoods separated by greenbelt spaces, interconnected with controlled-access parkways, and oriented to the more important communal features and nodes. It need not be contained within the limits of a city. Satellite communities or the larger new towns, spaced out in the open countryside and served by freeways and rapid transit, have many advantages.

Being more self-sufficient, they reduce the number of external vehicular trips required and thereby conserve fuel and energy. They are less disruptive of neighboring traffic networks, land uses, and established systems than if developed within or immediately contiguous to established residential areas. All planned communities, whether perforce impacted or formed more freely as satellites, have the great advantage of being brought on area by area and stage by stage in accordance with a balanced overall conceptual diagram. The ultimate capacities of roadways, schools, parks, and freshwater supply mains, for example, can be predetermined and facilities phased in without the need for costly periodic enlargement or reconstruction.

The land use patterns, traffic-flow diagrams, and population cap will be determined initially. There will be defined flexibility zones (the more extensive the better) within which the approved uses and number of dwellings may be freely arranged on the basis of subsequent and more detailed study and changing long-range needs. Environmental protection covenants, performance standards, and design guidelines are to be formulated and enforced from the start. Such planned communities, having clearly demonstrated their many benefits, are the promise of the future. There can be no better answer to regional growth and resource management.

Theoretically the ideal community will be composed of several to many interrelated neighborhoods of diverse social, architectural, and landscape character. Each neighborhood, while separate and unique, will share common pathways, amenities, and open space. When fully built out, in a process which may take several decades, a community will usually include and support a high school and two or more junior high schools, each within a school-park campus and community center, with game courts, sports fields, meeting rooms, auditorium, and library. There will be a community shopping and business office mall as well as the deployed neighborhood convenience centers. A transit station, airport and heliport, and light manufacturing or business campus are normally planned, and a wide range of cultural, recreational, and employment opportunities afforded.

Since physical forms and patterns can only express and help to provide a prescribed way of life, better communities will follow only as new and better concepts of community living, landownership, and land use are evolved. The superior community, as we envision it today, will be distinguished by the following features:

A natural periphery demarcated by highway, greenbelt, river, ridge, cliff, ravine, or other physical barrier

Community identity—orientation to a symbol, such as a high school, factory, church, shopping center, country club, or park—that gives it focus and meaning

Provision for outdoor communal activities in clean, sunlit, and shaded spaces uninterrupted by vehicular traffic flow

Minimum friction and danger in use of the automobile, coupled with maximum convenience and free-flowing trafficways with no on-grade crossings

Flexibility in forms and patterns to enable adjustment to new technological and socioeconomic development

Community open space zoned as farmland, forest, park, or preserve

Carl Koch has made this comment on the community: "There is a Chinese proverb that says, in effect, that by conforming to outward convention, we earn the right to be ourselves inwardly. The most beautiful places to live follow this principle—the old New England town or Louisburg Square in Boston are good examples. In

Every community needs a symbol of its existence. Much of modern community frustration has come into being because a symbol of the visual meaning for its life is missing. Because no symbol is found, there is no center on which to focus life.
Ralph Walker

In the creation of healthy environment nature's collaboration is not only important, but also indispensable.
Eliel Saarinen

Metropolitan diagram
(To be modified in response to topography)

A. Urba-center (central business district)
- Intensive governmental, business, and commercial uses with ancillary facilities
- Transit hub and interregional exchange
- Interconnected towers within a terraced pedestrian garden-park

B. Cultural
- Educational centers
- Museums
- Symphony hall
- Opera
- Theaters
- Religious institutions
- Civic auditorium
- Zoo, aviary, aquarium, planetarium
- Botanical garden
- Hospitals and health care
- Professional offices and studios
- Low- to high-rise apartments
- Restaurants, bars, and cafés
- Convenience and specialty shopping
- Other supporting uses

C. Residential communities
- Interrelated neighborhood clusters of varying size and character, grouped around shared spaces and amenities
- Full range of dwelling types, from detached single-family to patio homes, townhouses, and garden, low-rise, and mid-rise apartments
- A complete and diversified school-park and recreation system with blueway and greenway connectors

D. Open-space preserve
- Agricultural lands
- Forest
- Water management
- Parklands
- Game lands
- Wildlife sanctuary
- Conservation areas
- Planned satellite towns and cities
- Planned recreational, resort, and industrial nodes

(Other development precluded except by demonstration of need and compatibility)

E. Highway service centers
- Off-highway groupings with attractive approaches and environmental quality controls
- Rest stops, lodging, food services, convenience shopping, fuel, automotive sales and repair
- Transportation and storage terminals

contrast, a walk down the street of most of our subdivisions shows us that merely changing exterior details—the pitch of a roof, the color of the shingles, a porch here, an extra dormer there; all done to conceal a plan identical to the house next door—achieves only the monotony and standardized look that the designer has been at such pains to hide. Both Louisburg Square and the old New England village are in a sense made up of similar but homogeneous elements so assembled as to provide a unique and unified whole. In the proper context repetition of elements does not make for monotony. Nature isn't afraid of standardization. A flock of flying birds, each almost identical, is a thrilling sight. A tree covered with thousands of almost identical leaves is a thing of beauty.

"What makes the old New England town so attractive, and also satisfies us as we walk through Louisburg Square, is the outward conformity of the buildings to each other and the way they relate to each other to form the frame or walls of the total composition. The buildings, though well designed as units, are all part of a larger unified design. The community is the unit of design, not the individual house."

The city

A city is a large and densely populated center of economic, social, and political activity, having a relatively fixed geographic position and specific governmental powers granted to it in charter form by the state. It is the center of an urban culture.

Our cities can be only as good as enlightened public opinion permits or demands them to be. This education and persuasion toward civic action and progress is an often neglected phase in contemporary urban planning.

The form of a city will be, at best, the studied expression of its varied functions organized harmoniously in time, in nature, and in space. A good city plan must express our times, our technology, and our ideals. It must be an adaptable organic entity, with its roots in the past and its orientation to the future.

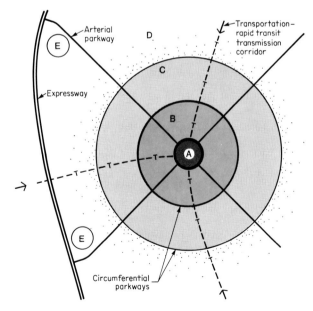

The urban nodes should be as compact as possible and should function as the nerve ganglia of the city and its region. Here are to be found the major governmental and business centers, offices, department stores, theaters, the opera, the symphony, the museums, and cathedrals. Many large areas of high population density cannot in the fullest sense be called cities because they lack many of the essential urban characteristics.

The city must be a growing, functioning organism, requiring and capable of providing light, air, water, food, circulation, elimination of waste, and regeneration, or else it will decay and die. It must have workable social, economic, and political structure, expressed in three-dimensional form. Desirable environmental features of the city include:

The most of those high qualities that civilization has attributed to urbanity; the least of those evils that the ages have condemned

Order, efficiency, beauty, and a milieu conducive to the development of full human powers

Significant art forms—architecture, bridges, sculpture, murals, and fountains

An expression of the city dweller's gregarious nature—congregating places where people can meet to exchange goods, services, and ideas and such communal spaces as the marketplace, the shopping mall, the park, the square, and the plaza

Separation, by alignment and level, of vehicular accessways and transportation routes

Traffic and parking accommodated but made incidental to the higher aspects of city life

Coordinated systems of traffic, transit, transportation, parks, and open space

An order of movement and nonmovement; planned sequences

Provision for pleasurable response to urban stimuli without undue friction or hazard

Clean and healthful surroundings

Opportunities for privacy

Individual freedom within cohesive social organization

Human scale, so that city dwellers, workers, and visitors feel themselves in agreeable proportion to what they see and hear and so that they share a sense of being pleasantly related to the city and thus to the ambient world

A highly developed and lucid rapport with the natural landscape forms and features

A cohesive and comprehensible metropolitan diagram

A free-flowing and easy transition between urban, suburban, and rural areas

The region

A region is a large and generally unified, but loosely defined, geographical area that provides the supporting base for one or more centers of population concentration. To simplify the complex problems of regional planning almost to the point of naiveté, it might be proposed that each region should be analyzed and planned for its highest and best use in relation to its projected population and inherent resources.

Regional planning Planning on a regional basis, whether in terms of geographic, political, social, or economic regions, provides a more

Will the city reassert itself as a good place to live? It will not, unless there is a decided shift in the thinking of those who would remake it. The popular image of the city as it is now is bad enough—a place of decay, crime, of fouled streets, and of people who are poor or foreign or odd. But what is the image of the city of the future? In the plans for the huge redevelopment projects to come, we are being shown a new image of the city—and it is sterile and lifeless. Gone are the dirt and noise—and the variety and the excitement and the spirit. That it is an ideal makes it all the worse; these bleak new Utopias are not bleak because they have to be; they are the concrete manifestation—and how literally—of a deep and at times arrogant, misunderstanding of the function of the city.
William H. Whyte, Jr.

The latent longing. . .for a life in mutual appreciation should be brought to blossom and fruit by education; but the external conditions needed for its fulfillment must also be created. The architects must be given the task to build for human contact, to build an environment which invites meetings and centers which give these meetings meaning and render them productive.
E. A. Gutkind

A regional plan that pieces together the disparate plans of the various member jurisdictions and blankets the whole with a layer of further restrictions does more harm than good.

Worthy regional planning starts with an understanding of human needs and the landscape.

The goal of regional planning is to develop through intergovernmental cooperation the best possible *diagrammatic framework* of land uses and trafficways, to provide the evolving *performance standards* required to ensure environmental integrity, and then to *encourage the free and creative expression of private enterprise.*

The comprehensive planning process is a systematic means of determining

where you are,

where you want to be,

and how best to get there.

Regional planning agencies can be effective only if

- The state officially prescribes the boundaries of each region.
- Regions are defined along county lines, since socioeconomic data are normally acquired on a countywide basis.
- County membership in, and support of, the regional agency is mandated by the state.

comprehensive and effective frame of reference than the consideration of any community, town, city, or county alone.

Regional planning agencies are at best nonpolitical and service-oriented. They provide planning coordination, regional information, and technical assistance to the member jurisdictions. Their primary functions are:

Data gathering, analysis, storage, and distribution

The preparation and updating of a comprehensive regional plan

The conduct of studies for various planning elements such as housing, transportation, and open space

The provision of liaison with state, federal, and local jurisdictions

The processing of state and federal grants-in-aid to local governments

The recording and coordination of all proposals relating to the protection, alteration, or development of salient land and water areas

Recommendations as to the significance of regional environmental impacts

Regional form   The land use and trafficway patterns of each region, if well considered, will respond to the "want to be" of the land. They will preserve the scenic superlatives, protect areas of ecological sensitivity, and ensure the integrity of the natural systems. They will recognize and adjust to the natural land and water forms. They will avoid the hazards, the obstacles, and the disruptive divisions and crossings. They will provide economies in travel time and distance and in construction, operation, and maintenance costs. They will provide a flexible matrix within which and around which development may take place freely and creatively as the direct expression of human needs and compatible uses.

Desirable environmental features of all regions will include:

Thriving neighborhoods, communities, and cities

Supporting lands reserved for food and goods production

Direct rapid transit interconnection of the regional hubs, with subsurface or overhead approaches to the station plazas

Separate and classified truck routes interconnecting the commercial, manufacturing, and agricultural districts, storage facilities, and distribution terminals

Linkage between all major activity centers by controlled-access freeways

Regional parkways, with scenic-historic byway loops traversing those areas of most significant natural and historical attributes

A complete park and recreation *system*

The location of all new activity centers in optimum relationships to land and water resources, energy generation facilities, transportation-transmission corridors, topographical features, and other planned uses

Wide, free, uninterrupted preserves zoned for forest, wildlife management, conservation, and recreation

Regional planning is the conscious direction and collective integration of all those activities which rest upon the use of earth as site, as resource, as structure. . . .

Lewis Mumford

The new regional pattern will be determined by the character of the landscape: its geographical and topographical features, its natural resources, by the use of land, the methods of agriculture and industry, their decentralization and integration; and by human activities, individual and social in all their diversity.

Ludwig K. Hilberseimer

It is foolish to permit satellite shopping malls to be built if they reduce the vitality of existing commercial centers.

New regional shopping nodes should be permitted only as their need can be demonstrated.

A complete regional recreation system provides insofar as feasible the whole range of opportunities, from the child's play lot within the residential cluster to the state or national park.

On the ascending order of social groupings—i.e., home, cluster, neighborhoods, community, etc.—each may be expected to provide for its own particular recreation needs. Beyond these, two or more groups or jurisdictions may jointly provide additional facilities such as public swimming pools, tennis centers, or golfing that perhaps neither could provide alone.

Larger installations such as zoos, botanic gardens, or major marinas require area-wide support, as do expansive regional parks and forest preserves.

On an even grander scale state and national parks provide for recreation within the context of scenic or historic superlatives.

The "land banking," in public or tax-adjusted private owner-ship, of all holdings not foreseeably needed or desirably suited for development

A long-range land and water management program based upon ongoing ecological studies and a regional resource inventory

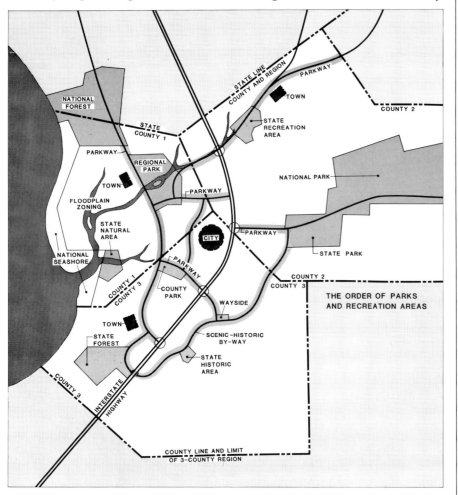

THE ORDER OF PARKS AND RECREATION AREAS

The Order of Parks and Recreation Areas
Within each region there will be a wide range of park and recreation areas in terms of both size and character. Each local government has the responsibility to provide the play lots, playfields, recreation centers, and local parks required to meet the particular needs of its people. Often, and ideally, two or more towns, cities, or counties may participate in a regional program to develop supplementary forest preserves, wildlife sanctuaries, campgrounds, and picnicking, hiking, fishing, swimming, and boating areas.

In addition to the local and regional facilities the state should provide an expanding system of state parks and recreation areas, natural areas, hunting lands, fishing lakes, parkways, scenic and recreation access roads, waysides, and historic landmarks.

The federal government is concerned with the preservation and development of natural and historic resources of national significance.

The essential requirement of a superior recreation system is that it be complete. It should be an interrelated complex of parks and open spaces of many diversified types, each contributing to the whole.

Regional open space The regional open-space framework will embrace and separate the various land uses and activity nodes. It will provide background, base, and breathing room, and when so arranged as to preserve the best of the landscape features, it will give each region its unique landscape character.

The essential spatial structure of a region comprises contribut-ing swaths, bits, and pieces fitted together. Aside from such major contributors as the water bodies, beaches, streams, wetlands, and floodplains, there are often military installations, highway and util-ity rights-of-way, conservation areas, campuses, school grounds, golf courses, and hiking, biking, and jogging trails. Lesser strips are added by vacated properties, extraction sites, and the un-built-upon portions of properties in use.

Perhaps the most important task of regional planning is to de-fine and help to bring into being a spacious, interconnecting, and permanent open-space preserve.

The essentials It is possible that the evaluation of sound regional development can be reduced to four simple tests:

1. **Is the proposed use suitable?** It must first be ascertained that the land or water area is to be devoted to its "highest and best use" consistent with federal, state, and regional land use plans (if these have been formulated) and with community goals.

2. **Can it be built without exceeding the carrying capacity of the land?** The use should not be permitted if it would impose

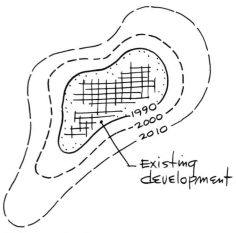

Urban service lines
As a device to ensure infill and protect open-space lands some municipalities are including as an element of their comprehensive plans a map of *urban service lines* showing by year the limit to which public services are to be extended. Within the period noted development will not be permitted beyond the designated line.

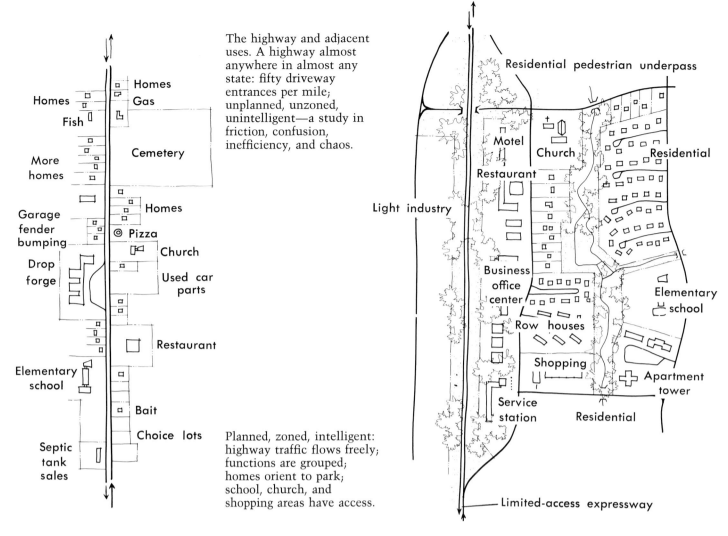

The highway and adjacent uses. A highway almost anywhere in almost any state: fifty driveway entrances per mile; unplanned, unzoned, unintelligent—a study in friction, confusion, inefficiency, and chaos.

Planned, zoned, intelligent: highway traffic flows freely; functions are grouped; homes orient to park; school, church, and shopping areas have access.

Zoning as commonly practiced is not workable.

Most municipalities and regions have zoned development land far in excess of foreseeable needs. Not only does this encourage scattered parcel-by-parcel construction, it results in tax assessments disproportionate to productivity and drives homeowners from their properties and farmers from their farms.

New construction would be better accommodated by the infill of existing centers until they were built out and unified. When additional land might then be needed for development, new cohesive communities could be defined through the process of comprehensive planning.

The open-space preserves of a region should be so designated and land-banked. Only those agricultural and recreational uses that would cause them no significant harm should be permitted, and land should be taxed accordingly.

When and only when adequate public services can be assured through the economic *extension* of existing trafficways or mains (or by a centralized installation, in the case of satellite communities) should "preserve" land be rezoned and development be allowed to proceed.

significant stress upon the natural systems. In case of question, the filing of a simplified environmental impact assessment could well be required. This would describe the nature of the project, its negative impacts (there are always some), and its benefits (which should outweigh the negative effects). The statement should address itself to at least the following checklist of environmental considerations:

a. Natural (eco) systems
b. Water supply and quality
c. Air quality
d. Noise pollution
e. Erosion
f. Flooding
g. Historic sites
h. Landscape features
i. Flora and fauna (rare or endangered species)
j. Open-space integrity

3. **Will it be a good neighbor?** Is the proposed use complementary and complimentary to the existing and proposed uses in the neighborhood? Or will it have harmful physical or visual effects? Will it reduce property values or force tax increases? Will it destroy or preserve cherished landmarks? A well-conceived, well-designed project—be it a bridge, service station, home, or play lot—should enhance, not harm its environs.

4. **Can adequate levels of public service be provided?** At all stages of its construction and use the proposed improvement should have available all public services required, without overloading of trafficways, power or water supply systems, storm sewers, waste treatment plants, fire and police facilities, and (in the case of residential development) schools and recreation areas. Not only should all such facilities be on-line when needed, but the local government should also be assured that the developers and users will bear their fair share of the cost.

If these four conditions can be satisfied, there should be no cause to oppose the project, for it should become a welcome regional asset.

15

Environment

To plan for the people of any culture or even to understand their simplest life patterns and art forms, it is necessary first to have some comprehension of their underlying beliefs.

This may be seen in the culture of the Athenians. Philosophically the Greeks understood and believed in the truth of utility and the beauty of function (which, from a close look at our cities, homes, automobiles, and other artifacts, most present-day Americans do not). And so, for their day-to-day living, they planned their streets, spaces, and structures in response to topography, for ease and directness of function, and for pleasurable convenience. Each form, each space, and each structure were designed to express and accommodate its use.

Philosophic orientation

Philosophically, the Greeks believed that the family lay at the inward center of their world; and so, with absolute logic, their homes were faced inward. From the outside, they were unostentatious. The entrance, often no more than a simple aperture in the wall that faced the winding street, opened into a private world of serenity and delight—into private spaces where living, conversing, and learning were cultivated as high arts.

Philosophically, the Greeks conceived of their civic buildings and temples in different terms. These were symbols of all that was high and noble and, as symbols, were set back or held up to be seen in the round. They were planned to embody and connote the ideal and the highest degree of order. They were consciously created focal points to which a whole city was tacitly oriented. To fully appreciate the ancient Greek cities, these things must be understood.

Philosophically, the Egyptians saw life as a march down a priestly and unswerving path, to come at last before the judges of the dead. The destiny idea controlled their thinking, their art, and even the plan layouts of their homes. Their whole existence was that of compulsive movement in a fixed line—the line of the processional, along which were spaced out vast masonry planes and columns and arches in rhythmic sequence and grandeur. The Egyptians' one aim was to extend themselves as far as possible in depth along this line. To understand the Egyptians and their cities, palaces, temples, and tombs, we must understand this central concept that runs through the whole form language of their culture. In contrasting the mode of the Egyptians with that of the Chinese, Oswald Spengler says in *Decline of the West:*

"But whereas the Egyptian treads to the end a way that is prescribed for him with an inexorable necessity, the Chinaman *wanders* through his world; consequently, he is conducted to his god or his ancestral tomb, not by ravines of stone, between faultless smooth walls, but by friendly Nature herself. Nowhere else has the *landscape* become so genuinely the material of the architecture."

To the Chinese, the temple is not a self-contained building but rather a temple-garden, in which ground forms, water, plants, and stones are as important as gates, walls, and structures. Gardening is intuitive. It is the architecture of the landscape that explains the building architecture.

To understand our American planning we must know that although the *way* was the prime symbol of the Egyptians, the *body* or *form* that of the classical age, and *people-nature* that of the orient, we inherit from northern Europe, as the prime symbol of our culture, the notion of *endless space.* Planned in this endless space, embracing it, and interrelated with it, we must contrive our own form world.

We must understand, too, that at the moment our society is hell-bent on an exuberant experimental binge. We are slightly tipsy with our heady new technology. We are reappraising and experimenting with all facets of our life. We are young and eager, and we are fired with the frontier spirit. If we seem to others (and sometimes even to ourselves) to have much energy but little direction, it is perhaps that as yet we have no cohesive directional philosophy of our own to serve us as a guide.

If society is paralyzed today it is not for lack of means, but for lack of purpose.
Lewis Mumford

The land that we love
Conservation at its best: Point Lobos State Park, California

In Florida at least 65 percent of all marine organisms including shrimp, lobsters, oysters, and commercial and game fish spend part of their life cycle in the brackish waters of tidal estuaries and coastal wetlands.

Within the past century over half of the state's wetlands have been dredged, filled, or drained.

The only way to protect fish and wildlife is to protect their habitat.

At the dawn of civilization, say 5,000 years ago, the population of the world cannot have numbered much more than 20 million. Today the yearly increase in world population is nearly twice this amount. Self-multiplying, like money at compound interest, world population reached the billion mark in the 1850's and the 2 billion mark in the 1920's. Even more disquieting the rate of increase has also been steadily increasing. At the present rate, today's population will double itself in less than 50 years.

Julian Huxley

A new planning order

Our country has passed, or perhaps is still passing, through a pioneering stage. Until very recently, one of our rugged freedoms has been our freedom to do with our land whatever we might wish. In the exercise of this dubious right we have voraciously exploited our natural wealth and ravished the land.

We have reduced millions upon millions of acres of forested watershed to eroded gullies and ruin. We have gouged enormous tracts of fertile land into barren wastes in our strip-mining operations. We have watched billions of cubic yards of rich topsoil wash out, irretrievably, to the sea. We have grossly polluted our streams and rivers with sewage and industrial waste. We have plundered our natural environment to a degree unprecedented in other civilizations. We have erred, and grievously. Now, late but at last, we have come to recognize the error of our ways.

In seeking to curb the waste and destruction, our present planning philosophy has been mainly one of restriction and prohibition. It has been, to a large degree, negative. No doubt such constraints have been helpful, but they are not enough. It is high time now that we reappraise our whole physical planning process, so that we may devise a *positive* approach more in keeping with our new understanding of land use.

Unless or *until* our exploding population growth is checked, more and ever more construction is inevitable. We can no longer, however, allow the uncontrolled development of our prime remaining natural or agricultural lands. We must first explore and maximize the possibilities of renewal and redevelopment. We must reclaim, redefine, reuse, and often reshape our obsolescent or depleted urban, suburban, and rural properties. We can and must create a whole new re-formed landscape within the grand topographical framework of protected mountain slopes, river basins, shores, desert, forest, and farmland.

In our *planning and replanning*, we must preserve intact such significant natural areas as are necessary to protect our watersheds and maintain our water table, to conserve our forests and mineral reserves, to check erosion, to stabilize and ameliorate our climate, to provide sufficient areas for recreation and for wildlife sanctuary, and to protect sites of notable scenic or ecological value. Such holdings might best be purchased and administered by the appropriate federal, state, or local agencies or conservancy groups.

We must ensure the logical *development* of the existing landscape. Such thinking points to a national resource planning authority. Such an authority would be empowered to explore and determine, on a broad scale, the best conceivable use of all major land and water areas and natural resources. It would recommend the purchase of those that should be so conserved. It would encourage, through zoning, enabling legislation, and federal aid, the best and proper development of these and all remaining areas for the long-range good of the nation. It would constantly reassess and keep flexible its program and master plans and engage for this work the best of the trained physical planners, geographers, geologists, biologists, sociologists, and experts in other related disciplines. Regional, state, and federal environmental advisory boards composed of distinguished scientists and thinkers might well be constituted, with participants nominated to this post of high honor by their respective professional groups.

Third, we must consciously and astutely *continue the evolution* toward a new system of physical order. This may be one of improved relationships, as of people to people, people to their communities, and all to the living landscape. Since we have now become in fact world citizens, the new order may stem from a philosophic orientation that borrows from and incorporates the most positive driving forces of the preceding cultures.

While the Athenians, as has been noted, faced their homes inward to family domains of *privacy*, while the Egyptians expressed a compulsion for *lineal progression*, while the Chinese designed their homes and streets and temples as *incidents in nature*, and while the western predilection was for a *continuum of flowing space*, perhaps the new universal philosophic guidelines may be a felicitous blending.

The value of the secure, private contemplative space may come to be generally recognized. The appreciation of lineal attainment may be translated into the design for pleasurable and rewarding movement along transitways, parkways, and paths. Whole cities and regions may be harmoniously integrated with the natural landscape, in which interconnecting open space may provide a salubrious setting for our new architectural and engineering structures.

For the first time in the long sweep of history, environmental protection is becoming at last a world concern. The wise management of our land and water resources and the earthscape is becoming a common cause. Fortunately, when the problems are nearing crisis proportions, the essential technology is at hand. Perhaps we

Any consideration of the future of open space, such as exists between our urban centers, requires a thoughtful appraisal of one of our most voracious consumers of land: housing. *Man's preference in housing, especially in urban fringe areas, results in the sprawl of single detached units in an awesome continuum across the countryside.*

What is the origin of the desire for this type of shelter expression—this compulsion to flee the city and to build cube on cube across the open land? Is it a desire for tax relief? Vested equity? Breathing space? Contact with the land? Or the poetics of "Home Sweet Home"? Regardless, is the solution largely that of better design within the acceptance of this preference? Or change from separated horizontal forms to unified collective density patterns? Perhaps as space between units decreases, space between our urban centers may be preserved, or may increase.

Walter D. Harris

The mistakes of planning are found in the overcautious concepts—not the bold.

Paul Schweikher

Make no little plans; they have no magic to stir men's blood, and probably themselves will not be realized; make big plans, aim high in hope and work, remembering that a noble logical diagram, once recorded, will never die, but long after we are gone will be a living thing, asserting itself with ever growing insistency.

Daniel Burnham

can pull it all together in time, and sooner than many might suppose, with enlightened, creative planning.

Significant environmental improvement does not necessarily require a monumental effort. It is sometimes achieved at a massive scale, as by effective and far-reaching flood control programs, clean air legislation, or the scientific management of regional farmlands, wetlands, or forest. For the most part, however, it is accomplished on a far lesser basis. It is the sum of an infinite number of smaller acts of landscape care and improvement. It is:

The advent of a well-designed park or parklet

The placing underground of power distribution and telephone cables in a new community

The cleanup and water-edge installation of paths and planting along a forgotten stream

Neighbors caring for their street

A linden tree installed beside the entrance of an urban shop

A vine planted on a factory wall

A scrap of blowing paper picked up by a child in the school yard

Each act generates others; together they make the difference.

A need for the visionary

The world is fast changing, and the tempo of change is accelerating. We struggle to keep abreast of the times. Experience has taught us that we can no longer base our long-range planning on simple projection. New concepts burst upon us, disrupting all established criteria. Ideas that seemed implausible yesterday are accepted and applied today and tomorrow will already be outmoded. As physical planners looking to and arranging the very framework for the future, we must be sensitive to the trends and alert to the signs that presage them. We must accept the fact that many revolutionary ideas, whether we now find them personally revolting or appealing, *may* become realities. Such ideas include:

Interplanetary travel

The colonization of outer space

Antigravitational devices

Man is a sun-roused dreamer, en route to tomorrow, a place he spins out of himself across the emptiness of time from gossamers of his imaginings.

John Lear

Designing is an intricate task. It is the integration of technological, social and economic requirements, biological necessities, and the psychophysical effects of materials, shape, color, volume, and space: thinking in relationships.

László Moholy-Nagy

We have begun to understand that designing our physical environment does not mean to apply a fixed set of esthetics, but embodies rather a continuous inner growth, a conviction which recreates truth continually in the service of mankind. . . .

Good planning I conceive to be both a science and an art. As a science, it analyzes human relationships; as an art, it coordinates human activities into a cultural synthesis.

Walter Gropius

To build intelligently today is to lay the foundations for a new civilization.

Lewis Mumford

Selective, instantaneous, and unlimited audiovisual communication

New sources and applications of vast power

The tapping of the energies of the tides, the sun, and the earth's molten core

Weather control

Hydroponic culture of food and raw materials

Large-scale mining and harvesting of the sea

Compulsory birth control

Euthanasia

Selective breeding of humans through artificial insemination

Planned ascendance of "advanced biologic types"

Hybridization of humans, as by nuclear radiation of chromosomes

Rapid and marked changes in the human mind and physique

Complete racial integration

The mastery of our technology

Low-cost, flexible shelters and vehicles, blown, woven, or fabricated of lightweight modular segments

New, intensified forms of domed urba-centers of commercial, civic, and cultural activity at the regional transit hubs

Clean and inspiring cities of pedestrian scale, on terraced decks above service levels, within a park and garden setting

Satellite towns and communities dispersed throughout the open countryside, well defined and interconnected with innovative systems of transportation and transmission

A reconsolidated American landscape in which pollution has been eliminated, depleted and eroded lands have been restored to productivity, and our natural superlatives have been protected for the use and enjoyment of all people of all generations to come

National resource planning

Leaseholding and controlled use of all property and resources

The first stage toward doing something is to know what is wrong.
Ian Nairn

Any plan is essentially the scheduling of specific means to definite ends. . . .
Any kind of planning implies conscious purpose. . . .
Catherine Bauer

To understand life, and to conceive form to express this life, is the great art. . . . And I have learned to know that in order to understand both art and life one must go down to the source of all things: to nature. . . .

Nature's laws—the laws of "beauty," if you will—are fundamental, and cannot be shaken by mere esthetic conceitedness. These laws might not be always consciously apprehended, but subconsciously one is always under their influence. . . .

The more we study nature's form-world, the more clearly it becomes evident how rich in inventiveness, nuances, and shiftings nature's form-language is. And the more deeply we learn to realize, in nature's realm, expressiveness is "basic."
Eliel Saarinen

World government, world law, world courts, and world enforcement and peacekeeping corps

New political, social, and economic structuring

Revolt against the increasing demands for conformity and a return to individualism

As an alternative, the complete subjugation of individuals to their society

Little time spent in the production of *goods;* much time spent in the production of *ideas*

Means of coordination and bringing to concerted focus on our planning problems the experience and accreting knowledge in all areas of inquiry

A highly developed science of environmental planning and protection

Greater insight into the forces that govern the cosmos and the development of a life attuned to these forces

Lifting our sights

It is time now that we advance to a higher concept of life and living within our circumambient universe.

Such a new concept will evince a greater respect for the human being and will seek a deeper insight into our true nature and requirements. It will seek, perhaps for the first time, to satisfy *all* our needs—of body, mind, and spirit.

Such a new concept will instill in us a better understanding of nature's compelling powers. It will not seek to conquer or imitate nature but will rather engender a sense of belonging.

It will encourage us to relearn the old truths and discover new truths of nature's law. We will, in time, regain the old instincts, experience again the glowing animal vitality and spiritual vibrancy that comes from a way of living attuned to the natural world. We will find our own *tao,* or way of life in harmony with nature.

Our new concepts of planning will look to the future to guide us into those areas of most promise and most meaning. Because we humans are the most highly developed organisms of which we so far know, the continuation of this development must surely be our purpose here. Our philosophers confirm this thinking when they tell us that to realize our full potential is our ultimate destiny.

Planning is that conceiving faculty which must recommend ways and means of transmuting the possibilities and impossibilities of today into the realities of tomorrow.

Eliel Saarinen

For planning of any sort our knowledge must go beyond the state of affairs that actually prevails. To plan we must know what has gone on in the past and what is coming in the future. This is not an invitation to prophecy but a demand for a universal outlook upon the world.

Siegfried Giedion

For to live, wholly to live, is the manifest consummation of existence.

Louis H. Sullivan

Epilogue

Looking back, I feel fortunate to have been in the Harvard Graduate School of Design during the period 1936–1939, in the tumultuous years of "the rebellion." At the time, I was somewhat puzzled and disappointed at first, for I had come to the school following the bright Beaux Arts star. Its particular brilliance in those times was perhaps like the last blazing of a meteor ending its orbit, for the Beaux Arts system[1] was soon to wane. But, blazing or waning, it was gone by the time I arrived there.

Dean Joseph Hudnut, one of the first of the architectural educators to read the signs, soon brought to the school three prophetic and vital spirits, Gropius and Breuer, late of Germany's Bauhaus, and Martin Wagner, a city planner from Berlin. They came as evangelists, preaching a strong new gospel. To the jaded Beaux Arts student architects, wearied of the hymns in praise of Vignola, beginning to question the very morality of the pilaster applied, and stuffed to their uppers with pagan acanthus leaves, the words of these new professors were both cathartic and tonic. Their vibrant message with its recurring and hypnotic text from Louis Sullivan, "Form must follow function," was strangely compelling. We began to see the glimmer of a beckoning light.

A fervor almost religious in quality seemed to sweep the school. As if cleansing the temple of idols, Dean Hudnut ordered the Hall of Casts cleared of every vestige of the once sacred columns and pediment. The egg-and-dart frieze was carted away. The holy Corinthian capital was relegated to the cobwebs and mold of the basement. We half expected some sign of God's wrath. But the wrath did not come, and the enlightenment continued.

---

[1]A system of architectural and design instruction that held almost complete sway over American schools from the beginning of the century to the early 1940s.

As the architects sought a new approach to the design of their structures, the landscape architects sought to escape the rigid plan form of the major and minor axis, which diagram, inherited from the Renaissance, had become the hallmark of all polite landscape planning. Inspired by the fervent efforts of our architectural colleagues, we assiduously sought a new and parallel approach in the field of landscape design.

Through the resources of Harvard's great library of planning we peered into history. We pored over ancient charts and maps and descriptions. We scanned the classic works of Europe and the orient for guidance. We searched for inspiration in the related fields of painting, sculpture, and even music.

Our motives were good; our direction, excellent. But, unknowingly, we had made a fatal error. In searching for a better design approach, we sought only to discover new *forms*. The immediate result was a weird new variety of plan geometry, a startling collection of novel clichés. We based plan diagrams on the sawtooth and the spiral, on stylized organisms such as the leafstalk, the wheat sheaf, and the overlapping scales of sturgeon. We sought geometric plan forms in quartz crystals. We adapted "free" plan forms from bacteria cultures magnified to the thousandth power. We sought to borrow and adapt the plan diagrams of ancient Persian courtyards and early Roman forts.

We soon came to realize that new forms in themselves weren't the answer. A form, we decided wisely, is not the essence of the plan; it is rather the shell or body that takes its shape and substance from the plan function. The nautilus shell, for instance, is, in the abstract, a form of great beauty, but its true intrinsic meaning can be comprehended only in terms of the living nautilus. To adapt the lyric lines of this chambered mollusk to a plan parti came to seem to us as false as the recently highly respectable and generally touted practice of adapting the plan diagram of, say, the Villa Medici of Florence to a Long Island country club.

We determined that it was not borrowed forms we must seek, but a creative planning philosophy. From such a philosophy, we reasoned, our plan forms would evolve spontaneously. The quest for a new philosophy is no mean quest. It proved as arduous as had been that for new and more meaningful forms. My particular path of endeavor led in a search through history for timeless planning principles. I would sift out the common denominators of all great landscape planning. At last, I felt sure, I was on the right track.

In retrospect, I believe this particular pilgrimage in search of the landscape architectural holy grail was not without its rewards, for along the way I met such stalwarts as Le Nôtre, Humphry Repton, Lao-tse, Kublai Khan, Pericles, and fiery Queen Hatshepsut. Many of their planning concepts so eagerly rediscovered (some to be set forth in this book) have served, if not in their whole as a planning philosophy, at least as a sound and useful guide.

Like good Christians who, in their day-by-day living, are confronted with a moral problem and wonder, "What would Christ do if he were here?" I often find myself wondering at some obscure crossroads of planning theory, "What would Repton say to that?" or "Kublai Khan, old master, what would you do with this one?"

But back to our landscape classes and our student revolution. Sure that we had found a better way, we broke with the axis. According to Japanese mythology, when the sacred golden phoenix dies, a young phoenix rises full-blown from its ashes. We had killed the golden phoenix, with some attending ceremony, and confidently expected its young to rise strong-winged from the carnage. We had never checked the mythological timing. But we found that, in our own instance, the happening was not immediate.

In lieu of the disavowed symmetry we turned to asymmetrical diagrams. Our landscape planning in those months became a series of graphic debates. Our professors moved among our drafting tables with wagging heads and stares of incredulity. We had scholarly reasons for each line and form. We battled theory to theory and principle to axiom. But, truth to tell, our projects lacked the sound ring of reality, and we found little satisfaction in the end result of our efforts.

Upon graduation, after 7 years' study in landscape architecture and a year of roaming abroad and with a hard-earned master's degree, I seemed to share the tacit feeling of my fellows that while we had learned the working techniques and terms of our trade, the indefinable essence had somehow escaped us. The scope of our profession seemed sometimes as infinite as the best relating of all mankind to nature, sometimes as finite as the shaping of a brass tube to achieve varying spouting effects of water. We still sought the poles to which our profession was oriented. For somehow it seemed basic that we could best do the specific job only if we understood its relationship to the total work we were attempting. We sought a revealing comprehension of our purpose. In short, what were we, as landscape architects, really trying to do?

Like the old lama of Kipling's *Kim*, I set out once again to wander in search of fundamentals, this time with a fellow student.[2] Our journey took us through Japan, Korea, China, Burma, Bali, and India and up into Tibet. From harbor to palace to pagoda we explored, always attempting to reduce to planning basics the marvelous things we saw.

In the contemplative attitude of Buddhist monks, we would sit for hours absorbed in the qualities of a simple courtyard space and its relationship to a structure. We studied an infinite variety of treatments of water, wood, metal, plant material, sunlight, shadow, and stone. We analyzed the function and plan of gardens, national forests, and parks. We observed people in their movement through spaces, singly, in small groups, and in crowds. We watched them linger, intermingle, scatter, and congregate. We noted and listed the factors that seemed to impel them to movement or affected the line of their course.

We talked with taper-fingered artists, with blunt-thumbed carpenters, with ring-bedecked princes, and with weathered gardeners whose callused hands bore the stains and wear of working in the soil. We noted with fascination the relationship of sensitive landscape planning to the arc of the sun, the direction and force of the wind, and topographical modeling. We observed the development of river systems and the relation of riverside planning to the river character, its currents, its forests and clearings, and the varying slopes of its banks. We sketched simple village squares and attempted to reduce to diagram the plan of vast and magnificent cities. We tested each city, street, temple group, and marketplace with a series of searching questions. Why is it good? Where does it fail? What was the planner attempting? Did he achieve it? By what means? What can we learn here? Discovering some masterpiece of planning, we sought the root of its greatness. Discovering its overall order, we sought the basis of order. Noting unity in order, we sought the true meaning of unity.

This consuming search for the central theme of all great planning was like that of the old lama in his search for truth. Always we felt its presence to some degree, but it was never clearly revealed. What were these planners really seeking to accomplish?

---

[2]Lester A. Collins, later chairman of Harvard's department of landscape architecture.

How did they define their task? How did they go about it? Finally, wiser, humbled, but still unsatisfied, we returned to America to establish our small offices and be about our work.

Years later, one warm and bright October afternoon I was leaning comfortably in the smooth crotch of a fallen tree, hunting gray and fox squirrels, the timeless sport of the dreamer. My outpost commanded a lazy sunlit hollow of white oak and hemlock trees. The motionless air was soft and lightly fragrant with hay fern. Close by, beyond a clump of dogwood still purple with foliage and laced with scarlet seed pips, I could hear the squirrels searching for acorns in the dry, fallen leaves. An old familiar tingling went through me, a sense of supreme well-being and an indefinable something more.

I half recalled that the same sensation had swept through me years ago, when I first looked across the city of Peking, one dusky evening, from the Drum Tower at the North Gate. In Japan it had come again in the gardens of the Katsura Detached Palace, overlooking the quiet water of its pine-clouded pond. And again I recalled this same sensation when I had moved along the wooden-slatted promenade above the courtyard garden of Ryōanji, with its beautifully spaced stone composition in a panel of raked gravel simulating the sea.

Now what could it be, I wondered, that was common to these far-off places and the woodlot where I sat? And all at once it came to me!

The soul-stirring secret of Ryōanji lay not in its plan composition but in what one *experienced* there. The idyllic charm of the Silver Pavilion was sensed without consciousness of contrived plan

Katsura.

forms or shapes. The pleasurable impact of the place lay solely in the responses it evoked. The most exhilarating impacts of magnificent Peking came often in those places where no plan layout was evident.

What must count then is not primarily the designed shapes, spaces, and forms. What counts is the *experience!*

The fact of this discovery was for me, in a flash, the key to understanding Le Corbusier's power as a planning theorist. For his ideas, often expressed in a few scrawled lines, dealt not so much with masses or form as with experience creation. Such planning is not *adapted* from the crystal. It is crystalline. It is not *adapted* from the organism. It is truly organic. To me, this simple revelation was like staring up a shaft of sunlight into the blinding incandescence of pure truth.

With time, this lesson of insight (perception and deduction) becomes increasingly clear. One plans not places, or spaces, or things; *one plans experiences*—first, the defined use or experience, then the empathetic design of those forms and qualities conceived to achieve the desired results. The places, spaces, or objects are shaped with the utmost directness to best serve and express the function, to best yield the experience planned.

By this criterion, a highway is not best designed as a strip of pavement of given section, alignment, and grade. A highway is properly conceived as an experience of movement. The successful highway is planned, in this light, to provide for the user a pleasant and convenient passage from point to point through well-modulated spaces with a maximum of satisfaction and a minimum of friction.

One plans not places, or spaces, or things . . . one plans experiences: Mellon Square, Pittsburgh.

Many of the serious failures of American roadways stem from the astounding fact that, in their planning, the actual experience of their use was never even considered.

The best community, by this test, is that which provides for its habitants the best experience of living.

A garden, by this standard, is not designed as an exercise in geometry; it is not a self-conscious construction of globes, cubes, prisms, and planes within which are contained the garden elements. In such a geometric framework the essential qualities of stone, water, and plant materials are usually lost. Their primary relationship is not to the observer but to the geometry of the plan. Final plan forms may be, in some rare cases, severely geometric, but to have validity a form must be derived from a planned experience rather than the experience from the preconceived form.

A garden, perhaps the highest, most difficult art form, is best conceived as a series of planned relationships of human to human, human to structure, and human to some facet or facets of nature, such as the lichen-encrusted tree bole of an ancient ginkgo tree, a sprightly sun-flecked magnolia clump, a trickle of water, a foaming cascade, a pool, a collection of rare tree peonies, or a New Hampshire upland meadow view.

A *city*, also, is best conceived as an environment in which human life patterns may be ideally related to natural or constructed elements. The most pleasurable aspects of cities throughout history have not derived from their plan geometry. Rather, they have resulted from the essential fact that, in their planning and growth, the life functions and aspirations of the citizens were considered, accommodated, and expressed.

To the Athenian, Athens was infinitely more than a pattern of streets and structures. To the Athenian, Athens was first of all a glorious way of life. What was true of Athens should be no less true of our "enlightened" urban planning of today.

The design approach then is not essentially a search for form, not primarily an application of principles. The true design approach stems from the realization that a plan has meaning only to people for whom it is planned, and only to the degree to which it brings facility, accommodation, and delight to their senses. It is a creation of optimum relationships resulting in a total experience.

We make much of this matter of relationships. What then is an optimum relationship between a person and a given thing? It is one that reveals the highest inherent qualities of that which is perceived.

In the final analysis, in even the most highly developed areas or details one can never plan or control the transient nuances, the happy accidents, the minute variables of anything experienced; for most things sensed are unpredictable and often hold their very interest and value in this quality of unpredictability. In watching, for instance, an open fire, one senses the licking flame, the glowing coal, the evanescent ash, the spewing gas, the writhing smoke, the soft splutterings, the sharp crackle, and the dancing lights and shadows. One cannot control these innumerable perceptions that, in their composite, produce the total experience. One can only, for a given circumstance or for a given function, plan a pattern of harmonious relationships, the optimum framework, the maximum opportunity.

The perception of relationships produces an experience. If the relationships are unpleasant, the experience is unpleasant. If the relationships sensed are those of fitness, convenience, and order, the experience is one of pleasure, and the degree of pleasure is dependent on the degree of fitness, convenience, and order.

Fitness implies the use of the right material, the right shape, the right size, and the right volumetric enframement. *Convenience* implies facility of movement, lack of friction, comfort, safety, and reward. *Order* implies a logical sequence and a rational arrangement of the parts.

The perception of harmonious relationships, we learn, produces an experience of pleasure. It also produces an experience of *beauty*. What is this elusive and magical quality called beauty? By reasoning, it becomes evident that beauty is not in itself a thing primarily planned for. Beauty is a result. It is a phenomenon that occurs at a given moment or place when, and only when, all relationships are perceived to be harmonious. If this is so, then beauty as well as usefulness should be the end result of design.

All planning of and within the landscape should seek the optimum relationship between people and their living environment and thus, per se, the creation of a paradise on earth. Doubtless this will never be fully accomplished. Humans are, sadly, too human. Moreover, because the very nature of nature is change, such planning would be continuing, without possible completion, without end. And so it must be. But we may learn from history that the completion is not the ultimate goal. The goal for all physical planners is an enlightened planning *approach.* Again, for instruction on this point, we may turn to the wisdom of the orient. Because of the dynamic nature of their philosophies, the Zen and Taoist conceptions of perfection lay more stress upon the process through which perfection is sought than upon perfection itself. The Zen and Taoist art of life lies in a constant and studied readjustment to nature and one's surroundings, the art of self-realization, the art of "being in the world."

In every area of human endeavor, the most successful projects are those best planned and designed.

Plan not in terms of meaningless pattern or cold form. Plan, rather, a human experience. The living, pulsing, vital experience, if conceived as a diagram of harmonious relationships, will develop its own expressive forms. And the forms evolved will be as organic as the shell of the nautilus; and perhaps, if the plan is successful, it may be as beautiful.

Nautilus.

Bibliography

1. History and theory

The references listed provide an insight into landscape-planning history and thought. They give no more than a glimpse of the broad range and wealth of material available.

Bring, Mitchell, and Josse Wayembergh: *Japanese Gardens*, McGraw-Hill Book Company, New York, 1981.

Bronowski, Jacob: *The Ascent of Man*, Little, Brown and Company, Boston, 1973.

Brubaker, Sterling: *To Live on Earth*, published for Resources for the Future, Inc., Johns Hopkins University Press, Baltimore, 1972.

Ching, Francis D. K.: *Architecture: Form Space & Order*, Van Nostrand Reinhold Company, New York, 1979.

Clark, Kenneth: *Civilisation*, Harper & Row, Publishers, Incorporated, New York, 1969.

Clifford, Derek: *A History of Garden Design*, Frederick A. Praeger, Inc., New York, 1963.

Downing, Andrew Jackson: *The Theory and Practice of Landscape Gardening*, facsimile of the 1859 edition, Funk & Wagnalls, New York, 1967.

Eaton, Leonard K.: *Landscape Architect in America: The Life and Work of Jens Jensen*, The University of Chicago Press, Chicago, 1964.

Eckbo, Garrett: *Landscape for Living*, McGraw-Hill Information Systems Company, McGraw-Hill, Inc., New York, 1950.

Fein, Albert: *Frederick Law Olmsted and the American Environmental Tradition*, George Braziller, Inc., New York, 1972.

Gothein, Marie Luise: *A History of Garden Art*, 2 vols., E. P. Dutton & Co., Inc., New York, 1928.

Hubbard, Henry Vincent, and Theodora Kimball: *An Introduction to the Study of Landscape Design*, rev. ed., Hubbard Educational Trust, Boston, 1959.

Hyams, Edward: *Capability Brown and Humphry Repton*, Charles Scribner's Sons, New York, 1971.

Jackson, J. B.: *Landscapes: Selected Writings*, ed. by Ervin H. Zube, University of Massachusetts Press, Amherst, 1970.

Jellicoe, Geoffrey, and Susan Jellicoe: *The Landscape of Man: Shaping the Environment from Prehistory to the Present Day*, The Viking Press, Inc., New York, 1975.

Le Corbusier, *Oeuvre complète*, 8 vols., Les Éditions d'Architecture, Zurich, 1964–70.

Marsh, George Perkins: *Man and Nature*, Harvard University Press, Cambridge, Mass., 1965 (originally published in 1864).

Mumford, Lewis: *The City in History: Its Origins, Its Transformations, and Its Prospects*, Harcourt, Brace & World, Inc., New York, 1961.

Newton, Norman T.: *Design on the Land*, The Belknap Press, Harvard University Press, Cambridge, Mass., 1971.

Oldham, John, and Ray Oldham: *Gardens in Time*, Lansdowne Press, Sydney, Australia, and New York, 1980.

Rasmussen, Steen Eiler: *Towns and Buildings*, Harvard University Press, Cambridge, Mass., 1952.

Reps, John W.: *The Making of Urban America: A History of City Planning in the United States*, Princeton University Press, Princeton, N.J., 1965.

Tobey, George B.: *A History of Landscape Architecture: The Relationship of People to Environment*, Elsevier Publishing Company, New York, 1972.

White, Stanley: *A Primer of Landscape Architecture*, University of Illinois, Urbana, 1956.

2. Environment

The field of environmental protection and planning has recently assumed increased significance as world conditions become ever more critical. The following publications are believed to be among those most pertinent.

Braun, Ernest, and David E. Cavagnaro: *Living Water*, The American West Publishing Company, Inc., Palo Alto, Calif., 1971.

Brower, David (ed.): *Wildlands in Our Civilization*, Sierra Club, San Francisco, 1964.

Burchell, Robert W., and David Listokin: *Environmental Impact Handbook*, published by the Center for Urban Policy Research, Rutgers University, New Brunswick, N.J., 1975.

Carson, Rachel: *The Sea around Us*, Oxford University Press, New York, 1951.

———: *Silent Spring*, Houghton Mifflin Company, Boston, 1962.

Clark, John: *Coastal Ecosystems; Ecological Considerations for Management of the Coastal Zone*, The Conservation Foundation, Washington, 1975.

Clawson, Marion: *Forests for Whom and for What?* Johns Hopkins University Press, Baltimore, 1975.

Commoner, Barry: *Science and Survival*, The Viking Press, Inc., New York, 1966.

Curry-Lindahl, Kai: *Conservation for Survival: An Ecological Strategy*, William Morrow & Company, Inc., New York, 1972.

Dubos, René: *So Human an Animal: How We Are Shaped by Surroundings and Events*, Charles Scribner's Sons, New York, 1969.

Fairbrother, Nan: *New Lives, New Landscapes*, Alfred A. Knopf, Inc., New York, 1970.

Kepes, Gyorgy (ed.): *Arts of the Environment*, George Braziller, Inc., New York, 1972.

Leopold, Aldo: *A Sand County Almanac*, Oxford University Press, Fair Lawn, N.J., 1969.

Little, Charles E.: *Challenge of the Land: Open Space Preservation at the Local Level*, Pergamon Press, New York, 1969.

McHarg, Ian L.: *Design with Nature*, The Natural History Press, Garden City, N.Y., 1969.

Mann, Roy: *Shoreline Appearance and Design*, planning handbook prepared for the National Park Service and the New England River Basins Commission by Roy Mann Associates, Inc., New England River Basins Commission, Boston, 1975.

Odum, Eugene P.: *Fundamentals of Ecology*, W. B. Saunders Company, Philadelphia, 1971.

Olgyay, Victor, and Aladar Olgyay: *Design with Climate*, Princeton University Press, Princeton, N.J., 1963.

Pilkey, Orrin H., Jr., Orrin H. Pilkey, Sr., et al.: *How to Live with an Island*, handbook to Bogue Banks, North Carolina, North Carolina Department of Natural and Economic Resources, Raleigh, N.C., 1976.

Porter, Eliot: *In Wilderness Is the Preservation of the World*, Sierra Club, San Francisco, 1962.

Reid, Keith, et al.: *Man, Nature and Ecology*, Doubleday & Company, Inc., Garden City, N.Y., 1974.

Robinette, Gary O.: *Plants, People and Environmental Quality*, published by the U.S. Department of the Interior and the National Park Service in collaboration with the American Society of Landscape Architects Foundation, Government Printing Office, Washington, 1972.

Simonds, John Ormsbee: *Earthscape: A Manual of Environmental Planning*, McGraw-Hill Book Company, New York, 1978.

Teal, John, and Mildred Teal: *Life and Death of the Salt Marsh*, Little, Brown and Company, Boston, 1969.

Udall, Stewart L.: *The Quiet Crisis*, Holt, Rinehart and Winston, Inc., New York, 1963.

Veri, Albert R., William W. Jenna, Jr., and Dorothy Eden Bergamaschi: *Environmental Quality by Design: South Florida*, in cooperation with the Center for Urban and Regional Studies, University of Miami, University of Miami Press, Coral Gables, Fla., 1975.

White House Conference on Natural Beauty, *Beauty for America*, Government Printing Office, Washington, 1965.

3. Community

The arrangement and design of more agreeable homesites, neighborhoods, and communities are treated in the following publications.

Aronovici, Carol: *Community Building: Science, Technique, Art*, Doubleday & Company, Inc., Garden City, N.Y., 1956.

Bailey, James (ed.): *New Towns in America: The Design and Development Process*, John Wiley & Sons, Inc., New York, 1973.

Burby, Raymond J., III, et al.: *New Communities U.S.A.*, Lexington Books, Lexington, Mass., 1976.

Chermayeff, Serge I., and Alexander Tzonis: *Shape of Community: Realization of Human Potential*, Penguin Books, Inc., Baltimore, 1971.

Dowden, C. James: *Community Associations: A Guide for Public Officials*, published jointly by the Urban Land Institute and the Community Associations Institute, Washington, 1980.

Engstrom, Robert, and Marc Putman: *Planning and Design of Townhouses and Condominiums*, The Urban Land Institute, Washington, 1979.

Fagin, Henry, and Robert Weinberg (eds.): *Planning and Community Appearance*, Regional Plan Association, New York, 1958.

Freedman, Jonathan: *Crowding and Behavior: The Psychology of High Density Living*, The Viking Press, Inc., New York, 1975.

Harman, O'Donnell, and Henninger Associates: *New Approaches to Residential Land Development: A Study of Concepts and Innovations*, The Urban Land Institute, Washington, 1961.

Howard, Ebenezer: *Garden Cities of Tomorrow*, The M.I.T. Press, Cambridge, Mass., 1965 (first published in 1946 by Faber & Faber, Ltd., London).

Huntoon, Maxwell C., Jr.: *PUD: A Better Way for the Suburbs*, The Urban Land Institute, Washington, 1971.

McKeever, J. Ross, Nathaniel M. Griffin, et al.: *Shopping Center Development Handbook*, The Urban Land Institute, Washington, 1977.

Macsai, John, et al.: *Housing*, John Wiley & Sons, Inc., New York, 1976.

Miller, Brown, et al.: *Innovation in New Communities*, The M.I.T. Press, Cambridge, Mass., 1972.

National Association of Home Builders: *Cost Effective Site Planning: Single Family Development*, National Association of Home Builders, Washington, 1976.

O'Mara, W. Paul: *Residential Development Handbook*, The Urban Land Institute, Washington, 1978.

Smart, Eric, et al.: *Recreation Development Handbook*, The Urban Land Institute, Washington, 1981.

Untermann, Richard, and Robert Small: *Site Planning for Cluster Housing*, Van Nostrand Reinhold Company, New York, 1977.

Whyte, William H.: *Cluster Development*, American Conservation Association, New York, 1964.

4. Urban and regional patterns and form

Urban and regional patterns and form receive attention in these references on land use, transportation, recreation, and resource planning.

Abrams, Charles: *The Language of Cities,* The Viking Press, Inc., New York, 1971.

Bacon, Edmund N.: *Design of Cities,* rev. ed., The Viking Press, Inc., New York, 1974.

Basile, Ralph, et al.: *Downtown Development Handbook,* The Urban Land Institute, Washington, 1980.

Bell, Gwen, and Jacqueline Tyrwhitt: *Human Identity in the Urban Environment,* Penguin Books, Inc., Baltimore, 1972.

Blunden, John, et al. (eds.): *Regional Analysis and Development,* Harper & Row, Publishers, Incorporated, New York, 1973.

Bosselman, Fred, and David Callies: *The Quiet Revolution in Land Use Control,* Government Printing Office, Washington, 1972.

Brahtz, J. F. Peel (ed.): *Coastal Zone Management: Multiple Use with Conservation,* John Wiley & Sons, Inc., New York, 1972.

Bush-Brown, Louise: *Garden Blocks for Urban America,* Charles Scribner's Sons, New York, 1969.

Chapin, F. Stuart, Jr.: *Human Activity Patterns in the City: Things People Do in Time and in Space,* John Wiley & Sons, Inc., New York, 1974.

Clawson, Marion: *America's Land and Its Uses,* Johns Hopkins University Press, Baltimore, 1972.

Clay, Grady: *Close-Up: How to Read the American City,* Frederick A. Praeger, Inc., New York, 1973.

Crowe, Sylvia: *The Landscape of Roads,* The Architectural Press, Ltd., London, 1960.

Gruen, Victor, and Larry Smith: *Centers for the Urban Environment: Survival of the Cities,* Van Nostrand Reinhold Company, New York, 1973.

Halpern, Kenneth: *Downtown U.S.A.,* Whitney Library of Design, New York, 1978.

Harr, Charles M.: *Land-Use Planning: A Casebook on the Use, Misuse, and Re-Use of Urban Land,* 3d ed., Little, Brown and Company, Boston, 1976.

Jacobs, Jane: *The Death and Life of Great American Cities,* Random House, Inc., New York, 1961.

Laurie, Ian C.: *Nature in Cities,* John Wiley & Sons, Inc., New York, 1979.

Lochmoeller, Donald C., et al.: *Industrial Development Handbook,* The Urban Land Institute, Washington, 1975.

Lynch, Kevin: *The Image of the City,* The Technology Press of the Massachusetts Institute of Technology and Harvard University Press, Cambridge, Mass., 1960.

Mackaye, Benton: *The New Exploration: A Philosophy of Regional Planning,* University of Illinois Press, Urbana, 1962.

Mann, Roy: *Rivers in the City,* Frederick A. Praeger, Inc., New York, 1973.

Meier, Richard L.: *Planning for an Urban World: The Design of Resource Conserving Cities,* The M.I.T. Press, Cambridge, Mass., 1974.

Okamoto, Rai Y., and Frank E. Williams: *Urban Design Manhattan,* The Viking Press, Inc., New York, 1969.

Owen, Wilfred: *The Accessible City,* The Brookings Institution, Washington, 1972.

President's Council on Recreation and Natural Beauty: *A Proposed Program for Scenic Roads and Parkways,* U.S. Department of Commerce, Government Printing Office Washington, 1966.

Rapuano, Michael, P. P. Pirone, and Brooks E. Wigginton: *Open Space in Urban Design,* report prepared for the Cleveland Development Foundation and sponsored by the Junior League of Cleveland, Inc., The Spiral Press, New York, 1964.

Robinson, John: *Highways and Our Environment,* McGraw-Hill Book Company, New York, 1971.

Safdie, Moshe: *For Everyone a Garden,* The M.I.T. Press, Cambridge, Mass., 1974.

Shomon, Joseph James: *Open Land for Urban America: Acquisition, Safe-Keeping and Use,* Johns Hopkins University Press, Baltimore, 1971.

Simonds, John Ormsbee (ed.): *The Freeway in the City: Principles of Planning and Design,* Government Printing Office, Washington, 1968.

Spreiregen, Paul D.: *Urban Design: The Architecture of Towns and Cities,* for the American Institute of Architects, McGraw-Hill Book Company, New York, 1965.

Stein, Clarence S.: *Toward New Towns for America,* The M.I.T. Press, Cambridge, Mass., 1971.

Strong, Ann Louise: *Open Space for Urban America,* Government Printing Office, Washington, 1965.

Tunnard, Christopher, and Boris Pushkarev: *Man-Made America: Chaos or Control?* Yale University Press, New Haven, Conn., 1963.

U.S. Conference of Mayors Special Committee on Historic Preservation, *With Heritage So Rich,* Random House, New York, 1966.

Urban Land Institute, *Air Rights and Highways,* The Urban Land Institute, Washington, 1969.

Von Eckhardt, Wolf: *The Challenge of Megalopolis,* based on the original study by Jean Gottman, The Macmillan Company, New York, 1964.

Whittick, Arnold (editor in chief): *Encyclopedia of Urban Planning,* McGraw-Hill Book Company, New York, 1974.

Whyte, William H.: *The Last Landscape,* Doubleday & Company, Inc., Garden City, N.Y., 1968.

————: *The Social Life of Small Urban Spaces,* The Conservation Foundation, Washington, 1980.

Wolf, Peter: *The Future of the City: New Directions in Urban Planning,* Whitney Library of Design, Watson-Guptill Publications, Inc., New York, 1974.

5. Applied site planning

Among the many excellent source books on site and landscape planning and design the following have been selected as a checklist.

Allen, Marjorie: *Planning for Play,* The M.I.T. Press, Cambridge, Mass., 1968.

American Society of Landscape Architects: *Landscape Architect's Handbook of Professional Practice,* American Society of Landscape Architects, McLean, Va., 1972.

Appleyard, Donald, et al.: *The View from the Road,* Joint Center for Urban Studies, The M.I.T. Press, Cambridge, Mass., 1964.

Baerwald, John E. (ed.): *Transportation and Traffic Engineering Handbook,* Prentice-Hall, Inc., Englewood Cliffs, N.J., 1976.

Bardi, P. M.: *The Tropical Gardens of Burle Marx,* Reinhold Publishing Corporation, New York, 1964.

Brambilla, Roberto, and Gianni Longo: *For Pedestrians Only: Planning, Design and Management of Traffic-Free Zones,* Whitney Library of Design, New York, 1977.

Bush-Brown, James, and Louise Bush-Brown: *America's Garden Book,* rev. by New York Botanical Garden, Charles Scribner's Sons, New York, 1980.

Callender, John Hancock: *Time-Saver Standards for Architectural Design Data,* 5th ed., McGraw-Hill Book Company, New York, 1974.

Carpenter, Jot (ed.): *Handbook of Landscape Architectural Construction,* Landscape Architecture Foundation, McLean, Va., 1973.

Center for Design Research, *Streetscape Equipment Sourcebook 2,* The Urban Land Institute, Washington, 1979.

Church, Thomas D.: *Gardens Are for People,* Reinhold Publishing Corporation, New York, 1955.

Clay, Grady (ed.): *Water and the Landscape,* a *Landscape Architecture* book, McGraw-Hill Book Company, New York, 1979.

Clouston, Brian: *Landscape Design with Plants,* Van Nostrand Reinhold Company, New York, 1981.

De Chiara, Joseph: *Site Planning Standards,* McGraw-Hill Book Company, New York, 1978.

————and Lee Koppelman: *Urban Planning and Design Criteria,* Van Nostrand Reinhold Company, New York, 1975.

Dirr, Michael A.: *Manual of Woody Landscape Plants: Their Identification, Ornamental Characteristics, Culture, Propagation and Uses,* Stipes Publishing Company, Champaign, Ill., 1977.

————: *Photographic Manual of Woody Landscape Plants: Form and Function in the Landscape,* Stipes Publishing Company, Champaign, Ill., 1978.

Eckbo, Garrett: *Home Landscape,* rev. ed., McGraw-Hill Book Company, New York, 1978.

Everett, Thomas H.: *The New York Botanical Garden Illustrated Encyclopedia of Horticulture,* 10 vols., Garland Publishing, Inc., New York, 1981.

Gold, Seymour M.: *Recreation Planning and Design,* McGraw-Hill Book Company, New York, 1980.

Hackett, Brian: *Planting Design,* McGraw-Hill Book Company, New York, 1979.

Hay, Roy, and Patrick M. Synge: *The Color Dictionary of Flowers and Plants for Home and Garden,* Crown Publishers, Inc., New York, 1969.

Jorgenson, Jay: *Landscape Design for the Disabled,* U.S. Department of Housing and Urban Development, Washington, 1975.

Landphair, Harlow, and F. Klatt, Jr.: *Landscape Architecture Construction,* Elsevier Publishing Company, New York, 1979.

Lovejoy, Derek (ed.): *Land Use and Landscape Planning Techniques,* Barnes & Noble, Inc., New York, 1973.

Munson, Albe: *Construction Design for Landscape Architects,* McGraw-Hill Book Company, New York, 1974.

Parker, Harry, and John MacGuire: *Simplified Site Engineering,* 4th ed., John Wiley & Sons, Inc., New York, 1967.

Ramsey, Charles G., and Harold R. Sleeper: *Architectural Graphic Standards,* 7th ed., John Wiley & Sons, Inc., New York, 1981.

Robinette, Gary O.: *Off the Board/Into the Ground: Techniques of Planting Design Implementation,* William C. Brown Company, Dubuque, Iowa, 1968.

Rutledge, Albert J., and Donald J. Molnar: *Anatomy of a Park,* McGraw-Hill Book Company, New York, 1971.

Schmertz, Mildred F.: *Campus Planning and Design,* McGraw-Hill Book Company, New York, 1972.

Seely, Elwyne E.: *Design: Data Book for Civil Engineers,* John Wiley & Sons, Inc., New York, 1968.

Sunset Magazine: *Sunset Gardening and Outdoor Books,* an enduring series of paperback publications on such subjects as *Annuals, Basic Gardening Illustrated, Fences and Gates, Garden Pools, Fountains and Waterfalls, Patio Book,* etc., Lane Publishing Company, Menlo Park, Calif.

Tourbier, Joachim, and Westmacott, Richard: *Lakes and Ponds,* The Urban Land Institute, Washington, 1976.

U.S. Department of Agriculture, Forest Service: *National Forest Landscape Management,* vol. 1, Government Printing Office, Washington, 1973.

————: *National Forest Landscape Management,* vol. 2, chap. 1, "The Visual Management System," Government Printing Office, Washington, 1974.

————: *National Forest Landscape Management,* vol. 2, chap. 2, "Utilities," Government Printing Office, Washington, 1974.

U.S. Department of the Army, Headquarters: *Planning and Designing of Outdoor Recreation Facilities* (The Environmental Planning and Design Partnership, consultants), Government Printing Office, Washington, 1975.

U.S. Federal Highway Administration: *A Manual for Planning Pedestrian Facilities,* Government Printing Office, Washington, 1974.

U.S. Outdoor Recreation Resources Review Commission: *Outdoor Recreation for America,* study report in 27 vols. on specific topics, Government Printing Office, Washington, 1962.

Ward, Colin (ed.): *Vandalism,* Van Nostrand Reinhold Company, New York, 1973.

Wyman, Donald: *Shrubs and Vines for American Gardens* The Macmillan Company, New York, 1969.

————: *Trees for American Gardens,* The Macmillan Company, New York, 1959.

————: *Wyman's Gardening Encyclopedia,* The Macmillan Company, New York, 1971.

Zion, Robert L.: *Trees for Architecture and the Landscape,* Reinhold Book Corporation, New York, 1968.

Quotation sources (page)

Adams, Henry: *The Education of Henry Adams*, Houghton Mifflin Company, Boston, 1928 (279)

Ardrey, Robert: *African Genesis*, Dell Publishing Co., Inc., New York, 1961 (7)

Aristotle: *Rhetoric* (279, 285)

Bacon, Edmund N.: *Planning*, The American Society of Planning Officials, Chicago, 1958 (293)

Beck, Walter: *Painting with Starch*, D. Van Nostrand Company, Inc., Princeton, N.J., 1956 (240)

Bel Geddes, Norman: *Magic Motorways*, Random House, Inc., New York, 1940 (213, 215)

Benét, Stephen Vincent: *Western Star*, Farrar & Rinehart, Inc., New York, 1943 (6)

Borissavliévitch, Miloutine: *The Golden Number*, Alec Tiranti, Ltd., London, 1958 (242)

Bowie, Henry P.: *On the Laws of Japanese Painting*, Dover Publications, Inc., New York, 1952 (republication of 1911 edition) (110)

Braun, Ernest, and David E. Cavagnaro, *Living Water*, The American West Publishing Company, Inc., Palo Alto, Calif., 1971 (11)

Breuer, Marcel: In conversation (111)

——: *Sun and Shadow*, Dodd, Mead & Company, Inc., New York, 1955 (165)

Bronowski, Jacob: *Arts and Architecture*, February and December 1957 (3, 110, 192)

Carson, Rachel: *The Sea around Us*, Oxford University Press, New York, 1951 (24)

Carver, Norman F., Jr.: *Form and Space of Japanese Architecture*, Charles E. Tuttle Co., Inc., Rutland, Vt., 1956 (207)

Church, Thomas D.: *Gardens Are for People*, Reinhold Publishing Corporation, New York, 1955 (219, 257)

——: Quoted in article by Dr. Joseph E. Howland in *Southern Florist and Nurseryman*, Jan. 30, 1981 (259)

Churchill, Henry S.: *The City Is the People*, Harcourt, Brace and Company, Inc., New York, 1945 (280, 293)

Clawson, Marion: *Man and Land in the United States*, University of Nebraska Press, Lincoln, 1964 (36, 37, 38)

Clay, Grady: *Water and the Landscape*, McGraw-Hill Book Company, New York, 1979 (24, 280)

Crowe, Sylvia: *Tomorrow's Landscape*, Architectural Press, Ltd., London, 1956 (290)

Cullen, Gordon: *Townscape*, Reinhold Publishing Corporation, New York, 1961 (155)

Danby, Hope: *The Garden of Perfect Brightness*, Henry Regnery Company, Chicago, 1950 (194)

Eckbo, Garrett: *Landscape for Living*, McGraw-Hill Information Systems Company, McGraw-Hill, Inc., New York, 1950 (105, 136, 290)

Eiseley, Loren: *The Immense Journey*, Random House, Inc., New York, 1957 (48)

Gallion, Arthur B.: *The Urban Pattern*, D. Van Nostrand Company, Inc., New York, 1949 (279)

Gardner, James, and Caroline Heller: *Exhibition and Display*, McGraw-Hill Information Systems Company, McGraw-Hill, Inc., New York, 1960 (198)

Giedion, Siegfried: *Space, Time and Architecture*, Harvard University Press, Cambridge, Mass., 1941 (19, 306)

Goshorn, Warner S.: In correspondence with Harold S. Wagner (37)

Granger, Frank Stephen (translator): *Vitruvius on Architecture*, G. P. Putnam's Sons, New York 1931 (246)

Gropius, Walter: "The Curse of Conformity," *The Saturday Evening Post*, Sept. 6, 1958 (305)

——: *Scope of Total Architecture*, Harper & Brothers, New York, 1955 (281)

Gutkind, E. A.: *Community and Environment*, C. A. Watts & Co., Ltd., London, 1953 (10, 296)

Hayakawa, S. I.: *Language in Thought and Action*, Harcourt, Brace and Co., Inc., New York, 1939 (3, 198)

Hilberseimer, Ludwig K.: *The New Regional Pattern*, Paul Theobald and Company, Chicago, 1949 (213, 297)

Hubbard, Henry V., and T. Kimball: *An Introduction to the Study of Landscape Design*, The Macmillan Company, New York, 1917 (187, 191)

Huxley, Julian: "Are There Too Many of Us?" *Horizon*, September 1958 (303)

Kennedy, John F.: Quoted in *Hydroscope*, publication of the Southwest Florida Water Management District, December 1979 (49)

Kepes, Gyorgy: *Language of Vision*, Paul Theobald and Company, Chicago, 1944 (190, 198)

Lawrence, D. H.: *Etruscan Places*, Martin Secker, Ltd., London, 1932 (5)

Le Corbusier: *The Radiant City*, republication, The Orion Press, Inc., New York, 1964 (20, 111)

Leopold, Aldo: *A Sand County Almanac*, reprint, Oxford University Press, Fair Lawn, N.J., 1969 (40, 217)

Li, H. H.: Translation of Chinese manuscript (7)

McHarg, Ian L.: *Landscape Architecture* (quarterly magazine of the American Society of Landscape Architects), January 1958 (295)

McPhee, John: *Coming into the Country*, Bantam Books, Inc., New York, 1979 (37)

Mendelsohn, Eric: *Perspecta* (the Yale architectural journal), 1957 (192)

Michener, James: *Return to Paradise*, Random House, Inc., New York, 1951 (5)

Moholy-Nagy, László: *The New Vision*, Wittenborn, Schultz, Inc., New York, 1928 (141, 192, 305)

Mumford, Lewis: *The Culture of Cities*, Harcourt, Brace and Company, Inc., New York, 1938 (9, 279, 284, 290, 297, 305)

——: *Faith for Living*, Harcourt, Brace and Company, Inc., New York, 1940 (280, 302)

Nairn, Ian: *Outrage*, The Architectural Press, Ltd., London, 1956 (306)

Neutra, Richard J.: *Survival through Design*, Oxford University Press, New York, 1954 (9, 144)

Newton, Norman T.: *An Approach to Design*, Addison-Wesley Press, Inc., Cambridge, Mass., 1941 (8, 192)

Niemeyer, Oscar: *Modulo* (241)

Ognibene, Peter J.: "Vanishing Farmlands," *Saturday Review*, May 1980 (37)

Okakura, Kakuzo: *The Book of Tea*, Charles E. Tuttle Co., Inc., Rutland, Vt., 1958 (125)

Pope, Alexander: *Of the Use of Riches* (7)

Rasmussen, Steen Eiler: *Towns and Buildings*, Harvard University Press, Cambridge, Mass., 1951 (277)

Read, Sir Herbert: *Arts and Architecture*, May 1954 (160)

Reed, Henry H., Jr.: *Perspecta* (the Yale architectural journal), 1952 (183)

Russell, Bertrand: "The Expanding Mental Universe," *The Saturday Evening Post*, July 18, 1959 (13)

Saarinen, Eliel: *Search for Form*, Reinhold Publishing Corporation, New York, 1948 (189, 193, 238, 294, 306, 307)

Santayana, George: *The Sense of Beauty*, Dover Publications, Inc., New York, 1955 (188, 191)

Sert, José Luis, and C.I.A.M.: *Can Our Cities Survive?* Harvard University Press, Cambridge, Mass., 1942 (238, 279)

Severud, Fred M.: "Turtles and Walnuts, Morning Glories and Grass," *Architectural Forum*, September 1945 (9)

Shigemori, Kanto: In conversation (256)

Simonds, John Todd: In conversation (3)

Sitte, Camillo: *The Art of Building Cities*, Reinhold Publishing Corporation, New York, 1945 (193, 238, 242, 285)

Spengler, Oswald: *Decline of the West*, Alfred A. Knopf, Inc., New York, 1939 (146, 302)

Sullivan, Louis H.: *Kindergarten Chats*, Wittenborn, Schultz, Inc., New York, 1947 (192, 306)

Sze, Mai-mai: *The Tao of Painting*, The Bollingen Foundation, Inc., New York, 1956 (24)

Taut, Bruno: *Fundamentals of Japanese Architecture*, Kokusai Bunka Shinkōkai, Tokyo, 1936 (146)

Tunnard, Christopher: *Gardens in the Modern Landscape*, Charles Scribner's Sons, New York, 1948 (9, 19)

Van Loon, Hendrik: *The Story of Mankind*, Boni and Liveright, New York, 1921 (8)

Veri, Albert R., et al.: *Environmental Quality by Design: South Florida*, University of Miami Press, Coral Gables, Fla., 1975 (12, 54)

White, Stanley: *A Primer of Landscape Architecture*, University of Illinois, Urbana, 1956 (8, 10, 31)

Whyte, Lancelot Law: "Some Thoughts on the Design of Nature and Their Implications for Education," *Arts and Architecture*, January 1956 (4)

Whyte, William H., Jr.: *The Exploding Metropolis*, Doubleday & Company, Inc., New York, 1958 (295)

Wittkower, Rudolph: *Architectural Principles in the Age of Humanism*, University of London, Warburg Institute, 1949 (246)

The World's Great Religions, Time Inc., New York, 1957 (9)

Zevi, Bruno: *Architecture as Space*, Horizon Press, New York, 1957 (143)

Illustration credits

All drawings and photographs not otherwise credited are the work of the author. Position on page is indicated as follows: T = top; B = bottom; M = middle; L = left; R = right.

Page and position	
2	Grant Heilman
4B	Arthur Rothstein
5L	Grant Heilman
5R	Underwood and Underwood
6	Grant Heilman
8T	Underwood and Underwood
8B	Ansel Adams
9TL, TR	Harry Callahan
9B	Carl Struwe
10TL	Grant Heilman
10TR, ML, MR	Carl Struwe
10BL, BM, BR	Hermann Eisenbeiss; courtesy LIVING LEICA
11	Hermann Eisenbeiss; courtesy LIVING LEICA
13L	Aero Service Corporation
13R	Siegfried Hartig; courtesy LIVING LEICA
14	Grant Heilman
15TL	Grant Heilman (Alan Pitcairn)
15TR, M, B	Grant Heilman
17T	Courtesy Miller, Wihry, Lee, Inc., Landscape Architects, Engineers and Planners
17BM	Lawrence Halprin and Associates
18T	Norman F. Carver, Jr.
18BM	Jack R. Scholl
19T	Sasaki Associates, Inc., Watertown, Massachusetts; Washington, D.C.; and Coral Gables, Florida
20T	Courtesy Arvida Corporation
21T	Courtesy Dr. Siegfried Giedion and the Swiss National Tourist Office, New York City
21M	Allen Freeman
22T	Courtesy Mount Wilson and Palomar Observatories
22BM	Royston, Hanamoto, Beck and Abey
22BR	Philip D. Simonds
23T	U.S. Atomic Energy Commission
25T	Underwood and Underwood
25B	Courtesy Italian State Tourist Office, New York City
26B	Underwood and Underwood
27	Courtesy Burnham Hoyt, Architect
28TL	Underwood and Underwood
28TR	Rollie McKenna
29	Michio Fujioka
32, 33	Grant Heilman
34	Grant Heilman
35	Grant Heilman
36	Grant Heilman
38BL	Grant Heilman
39R	Grant Heilman
46, 47	Grant Heilman
48M	Grant Heilman
48B	Photographs courtesy of Kim Lighting
49	Photographs courtesy of Kim Lighting
50	Photographs courtesy of Kim Lighting
51	Photographs courtesy of Kim Lighting
52T	Grant Heilman
52B	Photographs courtesy of Kim Lighting
53M	McFadden Air Photos, courtesy Sengra Development Corporation
53B	Photographs courtesy of Kim Lighting
55T	Courtesy The Springs, Longwood, Florida
57R	Commercial Place, Norfolk, Virginia. Courtesy Sasaki Associates, Inc.
62, 63	Grant Heilman
65	Grant Heilman
66, 67	Photographs and design by Theodore Osmundson & Associates, Landscape Architects
76, 77	Grant Heilman

Page and position	
79T	Courtesy Northstar-at-Tahoe
79B	Courtesy Sasaki Associates, Inc.
80	Grant Heilman
82	Grant Heilman
84T	Photograph and design by Theodore Osmundson & Associates, Landscape Architects
84BL	Philip D. Simonds
85BM	Geoffrey L. Rausch
87L, R	Geoffrey L. Rausch
94	Morley Baer
100	Courtesy Northstar-at-Tahoe
110	Courtesy Sasaki Associates, Inc.
111	© Walt Disney Productions
117	Hedrich-Blessing
118	Photos: John E. Hoffman
119	Photo: C. Richard Hays
122T	Courtesy Sasaki Associates, Inc.
123	Pedro E. Guerrero
124T	G. E. Kidder Smith
125	Rollie McKenna
136L	Julius Shulman
137T	Courtesy Rockefeller Center, Inc.
137M	Courtesy Sasaki Associates, Inc.
138L	Courtesy Museum of Modern Art, New York City
139B	Julius Shulman
140T	© Courtesy Spacenet by Gametime, Inc., Fort Payne, Alabama
140B	Julius Shulman
141	Courtesy Museum of Modern Art, New York City
142R	Leonard Schugar
143L	Julius Shulman
143R	© Walt Disney Productions
144T	Gateway Film Productions, Ltd.
145ML	Ezra Stoller, © ESTO
147T	G. E. Kidder Smith
149T	Courtesy Sasaki Associates, Inc.
149M	Rondal Partridge
151TR	Charles J. Ott, courtesy National Park Service
151MR	G. E. Kidder Smith
152	Ezra Stoller
153TL	Courtesy General Motors Technical Center, Detroit
153TR	David Gates, Landscape Architect
153BL, BR	Grant Heilman
154T	Underwood and Underwood
154B	Ernest Braun
155	Yoshinobu Yoshinaga
157T	Phil Palmer, courtesy California Redwood Association
157BL	Jeffrey Lindsay, designer
157BR	Douglas M. Simmonds
158	Photo: Norman F. Carver, Jr.
159LB	David Gates, Landscape Architect
159R	A. B. Hosmer
160BL	Geoffrey L. Rausch
160BR	Courtesy Reinhold Publishing Corporation
161T	Courtesy Museum of Modern Art, New York City
162T	Julius Shulman
163T	William A. Graham, courtesy Reston, Virginia
165	Courtesy Sasaki Associates, Inc.
172, 173	Julius Shulman
174T	Julius Shulman
182	Courtesy French Embassy and Information Division, New York City
184T	Fairchild National, Inc.
186L	Underwood and Underwood
188T	Y. Yamakawa
188B	Underwood and Underwood

Page and position	
196, 197	Original design for Three Rivers Stadium, Pittsburgh. Courtesy Deeter, Ritchey, Sippel Associates, Architects
206B	Norman F. Carver, Jr.
213B	Courtesy Clarke + Rapuano Inc., New York City
215M, B	Courtesy Clarke + Rapuano Inc., New York City
228	© Walt Disney Productions
231T	Newman-Schmidt Studios, Inc.
231B	Michael Wolgensinger
234	Photograph and design by Theodore Osmundson & Associates, Landscape Architects
235	Manhattanville study, sponsored by Columbia University. Courtesy Clarke + Rapuano Inc., New York City
236, 237	Ezra Stoller, © ESTO
239L	E. Funk, courtesy LIVING LEICA
244T	Ezra Stoller
244B	Norman F. Carver, Jr.
250L	Courtesy Burt, Hill, Kosar and Rittelman Associates, Architects
251T	Falcón & Bueno, Landscape Architect, Architect, Engineer
251MR, BR	Courtland P. Paul, Peridian Group
253T	David E. Scherman, courtesy Museum of Modern Art, New York City
253B	Soichi Sunami, courtesy Museum of Modern Art, New York City
254, 255	Courtesy California Redwood Association
256L	Robert L. Shaheen
256R	Falcón & Bueno, Landscape Architect, Architect, Engineer
257L, MT, R	Douglas and Maggie Baylis
257MB	Falcón & Bueno, Landscape Architect, Architect, Engineer
258L	A. E. Bye and Associates
258R	H. Russell Hanna, Jr.
259LT, RB	Courtland P. Paul, Peridian Group
259LB, M	Douglas and Maggie Baylis
259RT	James L. Loper
260L	Douglas and Maggie Baylis
260R	Falcón & Bueno, Landscape Architect, Architect, Engineer
261L, MT, R	Douglas and Maggie Baylis
264, 265	Village of Cedarwood, Boca West, Florida. Courtesy Arvida Corporation
269T	Julius Shulman
270	Julius Shulman
273T	Courtesy Pelican Bay, Coral Ridge–Collier Properties, Inc.
273BL, BM, BR	Ed Chappell, Courtesy Pelican Bay, Coral Ridge–Collier Properties, Inc.
276, 277	© Steve Rosenthal. Benjamin Thompson & Associates, Architects for the Pavillion
278	Fairchild National, Inc.
279	Map of Rome by Nolli, 1784; from *Towns and Buildings* by Steen E. Rasmussen
280	Fairchild Aerial Surveys, Inc.
282L	Stewart Simonds
283TL, TR	Marvin Rand
283BL	Dennis A. Poluha
283BMT	Leslie Barr
284L	Richard O. Hagan
284MT	Newburyport Downtown. Courtesy Sasaki Associates, Inc.
284MB	Dennis A. Poluha
284R	Geoffrey L. Rausch
285L	Geoffrey L. Rausch
288, 289	Grant Heilman (William Felger)
293	Lois M. Weissflog, courtesy Reston Gulf Oil Corporation
300, 301	© The Bettman Archives, New York City
308, 309	© The Bettman Archives, New York City
313	Geoffrey L. Rausch
315	Photograph by H. Landshoff from THE SHELL by Hugh and Margaret Stix, published by Harry N. Abrams, Inc. All rights reserved.

Index

Abstract line expression, variations in, *illus.*, 149–150
Abstract spatial expression, 146–148
Abstract variables in line of approach, *illus.*, 199
Accentuating elements, addition of, 17, 232
Activity, induced, 138–140
Activity areas (nodes), 297
 illus., 282–285
 (*See also* Use areas)
Adams, Henry, quoted, 279
Adaptation of project to site, 25, 91–100, 105, 108–109, 111, 120, 122
 by introduction of compatible land uses, 6, 16, 19, 34
 by site analysis, 25, 39–40, 94–96, 100–105
 site-structure diagram, *illus.*, 108
 site-structure integration, 7, 109, 111, 120, 121–126
 illus., 108
 (*See also* Site; Site planning and design; *entries beginning with the term:* Site-structure)
Advanced planning of borrow pits and extraction sites, 53, 54
Afforestation and reforestation, 54, 66, 67, 73
Agriculture, start of, 63
Air:
 as the earth's atmosphere, 12, 84
 as a trafficway, 232–233
Air currents (wind and breeze), 77–83, 85–88
 (*See also* Breeze; Climate; Wind)
Air pollution, 40, 66, 285, 306
 (*See also* Environment; Visible landscape)
Airport planning, 232
Alaska, 37, 38
Alberti, Leon Battista, quoted, 144
Alignment of paths and trafficways (*see* Circulation; Visible landscape)
Amenity in home and garden design, 259–260
Amusement park, design of, 146–147
Analogy of state as a developing farmstead, 39
Analysis, site (*see* Site analysis)
Animal:
 as creature of nature, 3, 65
 the human, 3–9, 315
Anthropomorphic module, 245
 illus., 246
Approach court, 120
Approach drive, planning of, 218–220
 (*See also* Circulation; Trafficways)
Aquifer, 48, 152
 illus., 50
Arbor, 158
Architects, 142, 241, 245, 246, 293, 296, 309, 310
 Japanese, planning approach of, 97, 99
Architectural composition, plan arrangement for, 111, 114, 122, 198, 241, 243, 247, 302
 (*See also* Composition of structures)
Architecture:
 buildings and structures (*See* Climate; Spaces; Structures)
 climatic factors in planning and design, 77–89
 as planning and design discipline, 8, 9, 11, 97, 106–107, 192
 (*See also* Landscape architecture as planning and design discipline)
 as space definer, 165
Ardrey, Robert, quoted, 7
Aristotle, quoted, 7, 279, 285
Art, 68, 78, 296, 301
Asymmetry, 191–192, 311
 (*See also* Symmetry and symmetrical plan arrangement)
Athens, Greece, *illus.*, 300–301
Atmosphere, 12, 78, 84
 (*See also* Air; Climate)
Atomic devices, nuclear power, 23

Attiret, Jean-Denis, quoted, 194–195
Automobile:
 as a planning factor, 83, 213, 291
 as a safety hazard, 30, 213, 294
 (*See also* Circulation; Parking; Trafficways)
Automobile traffic, 213–227
 (*See also* Circulation)
Axis as linear plan element, 148, 180–187, 192, 310

Bacon, Edmund N., quoted, 293
Base map, 100
Base plane, 117, 142, 152–155, 166–169, 212
 in relation to traffic, 212–213
 of site volumes or spaces, 135, 152–155, 212
 illus., 166–167
Bauer, Catherine, quoted, 306
Beauty:
 examples of, 13, 110, 145, 176, 189, 248, 259, 279
 in nature, 13, 14, 17
 sensed, 16, 19, 99, 139, 245, 314, 315
 of symmetry, 186–187, 189
Beaux Arts as system of architectural instruction, 309
Beck, Walter, quoted, 240
Behavior of humans (*See* Human, behavior of)
Bel Geddes, Norman, quoted, 213, 215
Belluschi, Pietro, quoted, 183
Benét, Stephen Vincent, quoted, 6
Bicycle paths and trails, 71, 74, 130, 234, 293
 (*See also* Circulation; Trafficways)
Bigger, Frederick, quoted, 221
Bilateral symmetry, 187, 188, 192
 illus., 191
Biological factors in planning and design, 65
 (*See also* Ecology)
Biomass of earth, 36
Biosphere of earth, 11, 64
Birds, 47, 57, 65
 (*See also* Conservation; Wildlife)
Blight: urban, 266, 267
 (*See also* City; Environment; Pollution; Visible landscape)
Blueway (*See* Water, blueway)
Borissaviévitch, Miloutine, quoted, 242, 245
Borrowed space and borrowed scenery, 259, 260
Botanic garden, 63
Botany, brief history of, 63
Boulevard (*see* Circulation; Streets; Trafficways)
Bowie, Henry P., quoted, 110
Braun, Ernest, quoted, 11
Breeze, 78, 87
 utilization of, 83–85, 87, 164
 illus., 86, 89, 99
Breuer, Marcel, quoted, 111, 165
Bridges, 43, 262
Bronowski, Jacob, quoted, 3, 110, 192
Building identification (*see* Signs)
Building orientation (*see* Climate; Structures)
Buildings (*see* Climate; Spaces; Structures)
Built environment (*see* Environment, built, constructed, or planned; Landscape)
Burbank, Luther, 63
Burchard, John Ely, quoted, 182
Burnham, Daniel, quoted, 304

Camps and campsites, 50, 52
Carrying capacity of land, water, and natural systems, 40, 52, 298
Carson, Rachel, quoted, 24
Carver, Norman F., Jr., quoted, 207
Cavagnaro, David, quoted, 11
Cemetery, design of, 147–148
Central business district (center city, urba-center), 287, 295, 306
 (*See also* City; Region; Urba-centers)
Central Park, New York City, *illus.*, 280

Champs Élysées, Paris, 181–183
Changing landscape, 31
Child's play lot, design of, 135, 139
China:
 landscape planning in, 17, 25, 184–185, 194–195, 302
 (*See also* Oriental planning and design; Peking, China)
Church, Thomas D., quoted, 219, 257, 259
Churchill, Henry, quoted, 280, 283
Circulation, 117, 125, 127, 197–235
City, 277–287, 295–296
 blight and deterioration of, 266, 267
 as environment for living, 5, 112–113, 277, 279–285, 296, 314
 function of, 295–296
 historical evolution of, 278
 lot or site in, characteristics of, 112–113
 metropolitan diagram, *illus.*, 295
 the new urbanity, 285
 planning of, 7, 8, 24, 136, 277–287, 295–296
 (*See also* Community; Environment; Regional planning; Site; Visible landscape)
 possibilities in, 284–285
 problems of, 281–282
 in the region, 289, 295–296
 renewal and redevelopment of, 281, 285
 urban ways and places, *illus.*, 286–287
 (*See also* Landscape; Open space; Parks and recreation; Region; Urban areas)
Cityscape, 136, 277–281
Civilization, planning and, 7, 63, 303
Clawson, Marion, quoted, 36, 37, 38
Clay, Grady, quoted, 24, 280
Clients, reporting to, 93
Climate, 77–78
 amelioration, modification, and control of, 68, 71, 84–87
 illus., 84–87
 plants in, 64, 73, 74
 atmosphere, 12, 78, 84
 breeze (*see* Breeze)
 climatic regions, 78
 cold, 78, 80, 81
 cool-temperate, 78, 80, 81
 hot-dry, 78, 82, 83
 warm-humid, 78, 82, 83
 as factor in planning and design, 77–89, 220, 256, 257
 humidity, 87
 microclimate, 50, 57, 71, 112–113, 256
 microclimatology, 84–89
 planetary framework, 77
 precipitation (dew, rainfall, frost, or snow), 78, 80–83, 85, 89
 response to, 78–83
 storms, 78, 80–83, 85, 87
 sun and sunlight (*see* Sun)
 temperature, 79–83, 86–89
 wind (*see* Wind)
Cluster, plan arrangement, 81, 83, 238–241, 270, 291, 292, 295
 (*See also* Community; Habitations; *entries beginning with the term:* Site-structure)
Coastal wetlands, estuaries, and dunes, 47, 50–52, 65, 67, 303
Cold climatic region, 78, 80, 81
Collaboration in landscape planning and design, 105
Collins, Lester A., quoted, 165
Color, design application of, 79, 81, 83, 84, 87, 117, 125, 135–139
 Chinese theory, 146
 spatial, 146, 157
 Spengler's theory, 146
Community, 113, 265–275, 293, 295
 checklist of desirable community features, 93, 267, 273
 climatic factors in planning and design of, 80–83

Community (*Cont.*):
  development guidelines, 272, 294
  planned, 7, 66, 67, 70, 79, 295, 314
  planning of: form order in, 267, 290
    new directions in, 267, 273
  satellite, 293, 294, 299, 306
Community symbol, need of, 294
Comparative analysis of site development
    plans, 109
Composition of structures, 237–249
  (*See also* Architectural composition, plan
    arrangement for; *entries beginning
    with the term:* Site-structure; Site vol-
    umes)
Comprehensive land planning, 296–299
Compression in planning, 41, 138, 141, 281,
    282
Computer technology in planning and design,
    39
Concealment and revealment, 176–177
Conceptual plan, 105, 109, 120
Condemnation of land (*see* Eminent domain)
Conditioned perception, 205
  (*See also* Planned experiences)
Conservation, 295, 298, 303
  of energy, 87, 229, 285, 293
  of forests, 65, 81
  of land, 12, 34, 38, 39, 49, 66
  of nature, 271
  as strategy for resource management, 297
  (*See also* Environment; Region)
Construction (*see* Materials, of construction)
Contemplation as conditioned response, 138
Contour plowing, 153
Contours (*see* Topography)
Contrast in landscape planning, 20–21, 138,
    139
Convenience as factor in planning and de-
    sign, 314, 315
Cool-temperate climatic region, 78, 80, 81
Court of the Concubine, Peking, China,
    203–204
Court of the Lions, Granada, Spain, *illus.*,
    186
Creative aspect of planning, 109–110, 315
Cribbing, 44
Crowe, Sylvia, quoted, 290
Cullen, Gordon, quoted, 155
Culs-de-sac, 291
  (*See also* Trafficways)
Cultural values (*see* Social activity)
Cycles of nature, 23, 77, 78, 126, 290

Dams (*see* Water, impoundments; Water-
    related construction)
Danby, Hope, quoted, 194
Datum in topographic survey, 95
da Vinci, Leonardo, quoted, 246
Decks, docks, platforms, and overlooks, 43,
    55, 56, 116
  illus., 262
  (*See also* Terraces)
Defined open space, 205–253
Definition of site volumes (*see* Site volumes,
    definition of)
Design, 111, 212, 303
  abstract qualities in, 137–139
  approach to, 97, 314
  community (*See* Community)
  fitness as quality in (*see* Fitness as design
    quality)
  home and garden (*see* Climate; Habita-
    tions; Planning; Plants; Site)
  light as factor in, 137–139
  modular, 246, 247, 263
  process, methods, and procedures of, 97,
    110, 135
  regional (*see* Region)
  site (*see* Climate; Site)
  urban (*see* City)
  (*See also* Architecture; Planning).
Design review board, 272

Development of land, 12, 38, 39, 49, 52
  planned, 303, 304
  unplanned or uncontrolled, 303
Development rights, transfer of, 267, 268
Dispersion of plan elements, 83, 124, 125
Displeasure as a conditioned response, 139
Distance:
  as a negative factor, 202–203
  positive qualities of, 203
Drainage of land, 40, 49, 51, 54, 65, 81, 83,
    116, 127, 131, 167
Drawings, technical (*see* Architecture; Plan,
    schematic; Planning)
Drive, approach, planning of, 218–220
  (*See also* Circulation; Trafficways)
Dubos, René, quoted, 7
Dudok, Willem, quoted, 141
Dunes, 52, 67
Dwelling (*see* Habitations)
Dwelling-nature relationships, 255–258
Dynamic tension, 240

Earth, the:
  atmosphere of, 12, 84
  as human habitat, 6, 22, 37, 255, 259
  as planet, 78
Earth forms (shaping, mounding, and sculp-
    ture), 42, 43, 74, 114, 118
  illus., 42–43
Earthscape, 22–24, 36, 66, 304
Earthwork, 40, 41
  (*See also* Excavation, filling and grading;
    Land)
Eckbo, Garrett, quoted, 136, 290
Eco-environs plan set, 97
Ecology:
  ecological analysis, 104
  ecological base or framework, 5, 7, 11, 12,
    65, 66, 78, 81
  ecological communities, 40
    (*See also* Natural systems)
  ecological determinants as plan set, 97,
    101, 104, 105
  ecological imperative, 36
  ecological stress, 68
  ecological survey for regional planning, 93
  life-support systems, 12, 52
Economic factors in planning and design, 78,
    266–267, 280, 284, 289, 295, 298, 303
Egyptian plan forms, 302, 304
Eiseley, Loren, quoted, 48
Elements of volumetric containment,
    148–149, 151, 161
Eminent domain, 37, 267
Emotional response, predetermined (*see*
    Planned experiences)
Empathy for project, necessity of, 111
Enclosure:
  axiom for, 165
  degrees of, *illus.*, 136
  functions of, 162–165
  for privacy, 158–159
    (*See also* Privacy)
  qualities of, 159
    (*See also* Site volumes; Spaces)
Energy:
  conservation of, as function of planning
    and design, 87, 229, 285, 293
  solar, 12, 22, 36, 77, 78, 306
  wind as source of, 85
Engineer, 9, 11, 106–107
Entrance court, 219–220
Environment, 301–307
  abuse of, 4–5, 7–8
  artificial, 6
  built, constructed, or planned, 6, 7, 29–31,
    66, 94, 289, 290
  extensional, 12, 19
    (*See also* Landscape, extensional)
  and health, 78
  as human habitat, 6, 23, 64, 67, 77, 84, 296
  human interaction with, 3, 10, 315

Environment (*Cont.*):
  landscape as living, 6, 12, 16–19
    illus., 290
  as natural habitat, 5
  optimum, 141
  (*See also* Natural environment)
Environmental control officer, 272
Environmental impact assessment, 96–105,
    297, 299
  checklist, *illus.*, 98
  statement on, 48–49
Environmental planning:
  goals and objectives of, 7, 136
  guidelines for, 296–298
  lifting our sights, 307
  a need for the visionary in, 305–307
  a new planning order for, 303–305
Environmental protection, 294, 304
Environs, site, 95, 120
Erosion, control of, 39, 40, 44, 45, 48, 49, 51,
    54, 64–66, 72, 81–83, 127, 303
Estuaries and estuarine systems, 47, 65, 303
  (*See also* Water, wetlands)
Ethic, land (*see* Land)
Evapotranspiration and evaporation, 12, 50,
    64, 71, 83, 85, 87
Excavation, filling, and grading, 40, 43, 51,
    53–54, 81, 130
  (*See also* Earth forms; Earthwork)
Exotic plants, 70
Expansion-contraction of conceptual plan,
    120
Experience and perception, 110, 136, 312, 313
Experiences, planned (*see* Planned experi-
    ences)
Exploded plan arrangement, 124, 291
Exposure to view, breeze, wind, or storm, 89,
    115, 116
Extensional landscape, 95, 238, 239
Exterior spaces or volumes (*see* Spaces; Site
    volumes)
Extraction sites, preplanning of, 53–54

Fairchild, David, 63
Falling Water, Bear Run, Pa., *illus.*, 21
Family as social unit, 290–291
Farms, farming, and farmland, 34, 35, 39
  (*See also* Agriculture)
Fences, 159
  illus., 170
  (*See also* Screens; Site volumes)
Fibonacci, Leonardo, 245
Fills and embankments as engineered struc-
    tures, 45
  (*See also* Earthwork; Land)
Fish, 65
Fitch, James, quoted, 146
Fitness:
  as a design quality, 100, 137, 162, 255, 314,
    315
  law of, 248
Flags and banners, 139
Fleeting landscape as seen from vehicles, 230
  (*See also* Circulation)
Flexibility zoning, 267, 268, 294
Flight, airplane, 232–233
Flooding, flood prevention and control of (*see*
    Water, floods and flooding)
Floodplain, 52, 81, 83
Flow diagram, *illus.*, 108
Focal points, 139, 291, 301
Food, plants as, 36, 63–66
Food chain, 36, 64, 65
Footpaths (*see* Paths, trails, and walkways)
Forces, natural (*see* Nature, forms, forces, and
    features of)
Forests:
  afforestation and reforestation, 54, 66, 67,
    73
  conservation of, 65, 81
  destruction of, 65
  as human habitat, 6, 23

Form:
  in nature (see Nature, forms, forces, and
    features of)
  plan, two-dimensional, 135
  spatial, three-dimensional volumetric,
    144–145, 156, 252
  (See also Spaces)
Form creation, principles of, 6, 10, 11, 110,
    125, 310, 315
Form order in community planning, 267, 290
France, Raoul, quoted, 10
Franklin, Benjamin, 24
Fright as an induced response, 138
Function:
  as factor in planning and design, 6, 17, 19,
    71, 94, 121, 125, 126, 129, 135, 139,
    141, 142, 144–146, 152, 158, 162, 239,
    252, 309
  unsuitable land uses, 19, 94

Gabions, 44, 49, 56
Gaiety as a conditioned response, 138
Gallion, Arthur B., quoted, 279
Garden:
  botanic, 63
  design of, 60, 314
  as extension of habitation, 12
  rooftop, illus., 66, 67
  of Ryōanji, Kyoto, Japan, 312
    illus., 251
  (See also Habitations; Plants)
Gardening, 67
Gardner, James, quoted, 198
Geology, 39, 78, 256
Geomancy, 11
Geometry in landscape design, 73, 116, 123,
    190, 195, 241–243, 247, 248, 280, 284,
    310, 314
Giedion, Siegfried, quoted, 19, 307
Glare, 74, 82, 83
Goals and objectives of planning and design,
    7, 77, 106, 296
Goethe, Johann Wolfgang von, quoted, 191
Golden rectangle, 242, 243
Goshorn, Warner S., quoted, 37
Grade and gradient (see Slopes)
Gravity, 24, 116
Greek cities and culture, 300–302, 304, 314
  illus., 90–91, 210–211, 300–301
Greenough, Horatio, quoted, 9
Greenway, 286, 293
  (See also Blueway; Open space; Parks;
    Parkways)
Grid pattern of trafficways (see Circulation)
Gropius, Walter, quoted, 281, 305
Ground covers and mulches, 69, 72, 167
Ground plane (see Circulation; Land; Site;
    Spaces)
Ground-surface treatment:
  drainage (see Drainage of land)
  grading (see Earthwork; Excavation, filling,
    and grading; Site)
  ground cover planting, 69, 72, 167
    (See also Plants)
  mulches, 167
  paving 166
    illus., 263
    (See also Circulation; Climate; Habita-
      tions; Trafficways; Site)
Group imperative, 265–267
Gulf Stream, 24
Gutkind, E. A., quoted, 10, 296

Habitat, 36–37, 50, 64
  as amenity, 259–260
  as protection, 258
  as shelter, 258
  as utility, 258–259
  (See also Environment; Human, needs and
    habitat of)
Habitations, 12, 83, 255–263, 270

Handicapped, the, design for, 130, 203, 221
Harbor analogy, illus., 218
Harmony in architectural and landscape plan-
    ning, 20, 21, 114, 120, 139, 148, 203,
    243, 244, 315
Harris, Walter D., quoted, 304
Harvard Graduate School of Design, 309
Hayakawa, S. I., quoted, 3, 198
Hazard, 6, 112, 127, 138
  automobile as, 30, 213, 294
  traffic as, 213, 266
  trafficways as, 29, 30, 213
  (See also Safety)
Health, environment and, 78
Height and depth, connotation of, illus., 201
Heller, Caroline, quoted, 198
Heredity as planning factor, 7
Highway service center, 295
Highways, 6, 7, 313, 314
  (See also Circulation; City; Community;
    Region; Trafficways)
Hilberseimer, Ludwig K., quoted, 213, 297
Hill, landscape development of, 26–28
  illus., 26
Historic features and landmarks, 271, 297,
    298
Homeowners' association, 272–273
Horizon, design expression and, 118
Horticulture, 64
Hot-dry climatic region, 78, 82, 83
Howard, Ebenezer, quoted, 285
Hubbard, Henry V., quoted, 187, 191
Hudnut, Joseph, 309
Human(s):
  as animal, 3–9, 315
  behavior of, 3, 78, 79, 113, 142, 144, 156,
    163, 174, 265, 301, 311, 315
  as earth dweller, 136
  history, development, and migrations of,
    23, 63, 65, 78, 301–302
  interaction with environment, 3, 10, 315
  needs and habitat of, 7, 113, 258–261, 284,
    285, 297, 304, 307
  survival of, 35
Human body as module in planning and de-
    sign, 92
Human eye and vision, 190–191
Human-nature relationship, 6, 7, 22, 24, 33,
    47, 92, 125, 261, 302, 315
Human scale, 41, 72, 82, 119, 143, 163, 282,
    296
Hunter, the, and the philosopher, 1
Huxley, Julian, quoted, 303
Hydrologic cycle, 12

Idealism, expression of, 148
Impact assessment (see Environmental impact
    assessment)
Incongruous elements, elimination of, 16–17
Indians (American), 36, 37, 79
Indoor-outdoor living, illus., 256–261, 281
Insects, 65, 82, 83
Integral planning, 120–121
  (See also Site-structure plan development)
Integrated systems of circulation, 235
  trafficways as, 215, 269, 289, 296
Integration of structures and site, 123, 126
Intelligence, defined, 3
Introduced plantations, 65–66, 68
Inward plan progression, 120
Ios, Greece, illus., 210–211
Islands, closeness to nature on, 24

Jacobs, Jane, quoted, 284
Japan:
  landscape planning in, 97, 99, 143, 155,
    176–177, 247, 251, 312
  (See also Kyoto, Japan; Oriental planning
    and design)
Japanese home, 18, 125
Japanese painting, principles of, 110, 247
Johnstone, B. Kenneth, quoted, 109

Katsura Palace, Kyoto, Japan, 239, 312
Keats, John, quoted, 145
Kennedy, John F., quoted, 49
Kepes, Gyorgy, quoted, 190, 198
Kinematics of motion, 147, 198, 200
Kipling, Rudyard, quoted, 6
Koch, Carl, quoted, 294
Kublai Khan, 184–185, 310
Kump, Ernest J., quoted, 165
Kyoto, Japan, 11
  garden of Ryōanji, 312
    illus., 251
  Katsura Palace, 239, 312
  Silver Pavilion, illus., 155

Lakes (see Water, lakes)
Land, 33–45
  abuse of, 40
  acquisition of, for public use (see Eminent
    domain)
  carrying capacity of, 40, 52, 298
  clearing of, 65
  conservation of, 12, 34, 38, 39, 49, 66
  development (see Development of land)
  drainage of (see Drainage of land)
  excavation and grading of (see Excavation,
    filling, and grading)
  as food source, 36
  form (see Earth forms; Topography)
  as habitat, 36–37
  as heritage, 33–35
  management of, and water, 39, 49, 51, 52
  overstressed, 34
  ownership of, 36, 38, 40
  planning of, 12, 28, 36, 68, 135
    (See also Landscape architecture as plan-
      ning and design discipline; Landscape
      planning and design; Planning)
  preservation of, 12, 39
  profile of, illus., 42–43
  reclamation of, 37, 66
  regulation of, 38, 40
  as resource, 35–38
  simpatico feeling for, 97–99, 122
  as soil bank, 35–36
  stewardship and husbandry of, 11, 35, 36, 65
  subdivision of, 37
  surveying (see Survey)
  use of, 17, 34, 39–41, 289, 294, 304
  unsuitable, 19, 94
  (See also City; Community; Habitations;
    Landscape planning and design, fun-
    damentals of; Region; Site planning
    and design)
"Land banking," 298, 299
Land grants, 37–38
Land reform, 38
Land rights, 37, 38, 40
Landscape(s), 66, 68, 105
  accentuation of natural form of, 17, 26, 27,
    41–43, 124
  alteration of natural form of, 26, 34
  beauty of, 13, 14, 17
  built or constructed, 66, 94, 290
  character of, 13–21, 99, 114, 120, 257, 298
  conservation of, 49
  continuity in, 68
    (See also unity and order in, below)
  cultivated, 12
  curve in earth shaping, illus., 42–43
  development of, 49
  ecological factors and (see Ecology)
  elements of: major, 24–26
    minor, 26–29
  exemplary outdoor places and space, illus.,
    16–23
  extensional, 95, 238, 239
  features of, 24, 26, 94, 102–104, 114
  fleeting, 230
    (See also Circulation)
  harmony in, 13
  humanized, 11, 20

Landscape(s) (*Cont.*):
  for living, *illus.*, 16–23
  as living environment, 6, 12, 16–19
    illus., 290
  natural, 17, 47, 94, 113
  organization in, 19–20
  planned, 20, 68–75
  preservation of, 49
  preservation of natural forms, 26, 114
  protection of, 12
  quality of, 16
  renewal and redevelopment of, 37, 52–53
  in repose of equilibrium, 19, 20
  restoration of, 49
  rural, 66
  structures in, 247–250
  trees in, 69, 72–75
  type of, 16, 146
  unity and order in, 13, 31, 105, 142, 203,
    311
  urban, 66
  visible, 173–195
  water and (*see* Water, as landscape feature)
  (*See also* Land)
Landscape architecture as planning and design
    discipline, 8, 31, 106–107, 310, 311
Landscape character, 13, 16, 20, 249
  accentuated, 17, 232
  and contrasting elements, 20–21, 138, 139
Landscape planning and design, 28, 66, 71,
    105, 256, 294, 310, 311
  climatic factors in, 77–78
  contrast in, 20–21, 138, 139
  fundamentals of, 3–31
  geometry in (*see* Geometry in landscape
    design)
  harmony in (*see* Harmony in architectural
    and landscape planning)
  sound in, 61, 137–139, 147
  symmetry in, 189–190, 311
  taxes and, 298, 299
  utilities in, 81, 305
  water in, 48–49, 54–61, 127
  wind in (*see* Wind, as factor in landscape
    planning and design)
  (*See also* Oriental planning and design; Site
    planning and design)
Lao-tse, quoted, 141
Law of fitness, 248
Law of the same, 243–245
Law of the similar, 243–245
Lawn and seeded areas, 130
Lawrence, D. H., quoted, 5
Leakey, L. S. B., quoted, 7
Lear, John, quoted, 305
Le Corbusier, 313
  quoted, 20, 111
Léger, Fernand, quoted, 192
Leopold, Aldo, quoted, 40, 217
Level site, characteristics of, 116–119
Life-support systems, 12, 52
  (*See also* Natural systems)
Lifting our sights, 307
Light:
  as design factor, 137–139
  qualities of, 69, 137–139, 157
Lighting:
  site, 127, 128
  of street, *illus.*, 274–275
Line expression, abstract, *illus.*, 149–150
Line of approach, abstract variables in, *illus.*,
    199
Line of sight (sight line), 179, 180, 217
Linnaeus, Carolus, 63
Load-bearing capacity, 153
Location appraisal checklist, *illus.*, 93

Maillart, Robert, 20, 21
Maintenance needs, 129, 271
Malls and plazas, 57, 60, 271
Maps, 92–93, 100
  (*See also* Plan, schematic; Planning; Survey)

Marinas (*see under* Water)
Marshes and bogs, 48, 54, 65, 67
  (*See also* Water, wetlands)
Materials:
  of construction, 57, 81, 83, 87, 113, 115,
    117, 125, 126, 129, 135, 138, 139,
    148, 151–153, 166, 170, 171, 255, 311
  indigenous, 129
Mathematics as basis of order, 190, 242, 243,
    247
  (*See also* Geometry in landscape design)
Meadow, 57
Mendelsohn, Eric, quoted, 192
Metropolis (*see* City; Region)
Metropolitan diagram, *illus.*, 295
Michener, James, quoted, 5
Microclimate, 50, 57, 71, 112–113, 256
  (*See also* Climate)
Microclimatology, 84–89
Mies van der Rohe, Ludwig, quoted, 141
Military crest, 116
Modular design, 246, 247, 263
Module, anthropomorphic, in planning and
    design, 245
  illus., 246
Moholy-Nagy, László, quoted, 141, 192, 305
Monumentality, civic, 183, 184
Motion, 197–208
  downward, 200
  horizontal, 200
  impelled by form and concept, 198,
    200–202, 311
  as induced response, 138–139, 201, 250
  kinematics of, 147, 198, 200
  upward, 200
Mountains, 22, 33, 51
Movement, paths of, 127
  (*See also* Circulation; Traffic, flow and
    movement of)
Mumford, Lewis, quoted, 9, 279, 280, 284,
    290, 297, 302, 305
Museum of Modern Art, New York City, 137,
    253

Nairn, Ian, quoted, 306
National parks, 38, 124
National resource planning, 304, 306
Natural areas, preserved and protected, 54, 66
Natural environment, 289, 303
  (*See also* Climate; Land; Landscape planning
    and design, fundamentals of; Plants;
    Water)
Natural forces, forms, and features (*see* Nature,
    forms, forces, and features of)
Natural systems, 12, 36, 37, 48, 66, 126–127,
    216, 256, 297
  carrying capacity of, 40, 52, 298
Nature, 9–11, 315
  appreciation of, 114, 125, 181, 260–261
  as base for all planning, 11
  beauty in, 13, 14, 17
  conservation of, 271
  cycles of, 23, 77, 78, 126, 290
  dwelling-nature relationships, 255–258
  forms, forces, and features of, 2, 6, 10,
    22–29, 35, 64, 86, 114, 120, 261, 296,
    306
  human-nature relationship (*see* Human-
    nature relationship)
  immutable way of, 23
  laws of, 307
  not to be conquered, 22, 23, 307
  plant and animal communities in, 36
    (*See also* Animal; Plants)
  rediscovered, 9
  as revealed to the physical planner, 11
  subjugated, 6
  symmetry in, 186, 187
  violated, 4
  (*See also* Climate; Land; Landscape planning
    and design, fundamentals of; Plants;
    Water)

Nature preserves, 52, 271
Need for the visionary in planning, 305
Neighborhood appraisal checklist, *illus.*, 93
Neighborhood planning, 292–293
  illus., 292
Neutra, Richard J., quoted, 6, 144
New directions in community planning,
    267–273
New planning order, 303–305, 307
New towns, 267
New urbanity, 285
New York City, streets in, *illus.*, 278
Newton, Norman T., quoted, 8, 192
Niemeyer, Oscar, quoted, 241
Noise, abatement and control of, 69, 71, 74
Nuclear power, devices of, 23

Occidental (western) planning, and design,
    241, 247
Occult balance (*see* Visual balance)
Oceans, ocean basins, and seas, 22, 23, 47,
    50, 64, 77
  thermal currents of, 77, 78
  (*See also* Water)
Ognibene, Peter J., quoted, 37
Okakura, Kakuzo, quoted, 125, 176
Open space (open-space systems), 50, 67, 71,
    87, 136, 269, 286, 294, 295, 297, 298,
    304
  defined, 250–253
  for parks and recreation, 66, 81, 83
Open-space planning and design, 67, 71, 267,
    269
Order:
  mathematics as basis of, 190, 242, 243, 247
    (*See also* Geometry in landscape design)
  of parks and recreation areas, *illus.*, 298
  in planning and design, 147, 148, 243, 284,
    285, 311, 314, 315
    (*See also* Landscape, unity and order in)
Ordered approach, 207–208
Organic growth, 192, 245, 295, 296, 315
Organic order, 165, 245, 285, 313, 315
Organic planning and design, 192
  (*See also* Planning)
Organisms, interrelationship of, 11
Orient, influence on contemporary planning,
    9, 10
Oriental planning and design, 29, 158, 165,
    184, 207, 240, 255, 260
  (*See also* China; Japan)
Orientation:
  of buildings, site-use areas, and trafficways,
    81, 83, 84, 86–88, 113, 114, 116, 118,
    139, 141, 293, 301
  to view or vista, 116, 125
Ornamentation, plants as, 67
Outdoor living spaces, *illus.*, 262–263
Outdoor recreation (*see* Parks and recreation)
Outdoor spaces (volumes) (*see* Spaces; Site
    volumes)
Outward plan progression, 120
Overhead plane, 84, 156–158
  illus., 156, 158
  (*See also* Sky as overhead plane)
Overlays, plan, 101–105

Parking:
  areas and compounds, 71, 131, 220–221,
    224–227, 291
  layout and design for, *illus.*, 224–227
Parks and recreation:
  amusement, design of, 146–147
  areas, *illus.*, 287
  a balanced system of, 297, 298
    illus., 298
  camps and campsites, 50, 52
  Central Park, New York City, *illus.*, 280
  community, 271
  national, 38, 124
  open space for, 66, 81, 83

Parks and recreation (*Cont.*):
  order of, *illus.*, 298
  playgrounds, 135, 139
  regional system, 297
  urban, 67
  water-based, 50, 51, 54, 55, 57, 231
  (*See also* City; Community; Region)
Parkways, 7, 51, 293, 295, 297, 298
  (*See also* Circulation)
Paths, trails, and walkways, 55, 58, 74
  (*See also* Bicycle paths and trails; Circulation; Trafficways)
Paths of movement (*see* Circulation)
Patio, 262
Pedestrian movement, things seen, 212
Pedestrian traffic, 208–213
  (*See also* Circulation; Site; Visible landscape)
Pedestrian ways and places, *illus.*, 210, 211
  (*See also* Circulation)
Pedregal, Mexico, *illus.*, 144–149
Peking, China, 184–185, 312
  Court of the Concubine, 203–204
  Sea Palace Gardens, 241
  Temple of Heaven, 185
People (*see* Human)
People movers, 233–235
Perception, 197, 314, 315
  conditioned, 205
    (*See also* Planned experiences)
  and deduction, 4, 6
Philosophic orientation in environmental
  planning, 301–302, 310
  Chinese, 302, 304
  Egyptian, 302, 304
  Greek, 301–302, 304
  western, 302, 304
Photogrammetry, 39
Photosynthesis, 12, 36, 64
Physical planning (*see* Planners; Planning)
Piazza San Marco, Venice, 308
Piling, 44, 56, 59
Pix, vertical in relation to, 163–164
Plan:
  continuity of, 280
  elements of: dispersion of, 83, 124, 126
    relationship of, 141, 314, 315
  organization of, 280
  progression of, sequential, 205–207
    (*See also* Sequence)
  proving the, 121
  reinforcement of, 69
Plan, schematic, 92–93, 100–105, 108–109,
  120–121, 126
  illus., 108, 120
Planetary framework, 77
Planned communities (*see* Community,
  planned)
Planned community development (PCD), 268
Planned experiences, 110, 136–141, 148, 151,
  163, 190, 198, 207, 208, 287, 312–315
Planned landscape, 20
  and planted landscape, 68–75
Planned unit development (PUD), 268
Planners, 11
Planning:
  airport, 232
  approach to, 258, 279, 303, 310, 315
  biological factors in, 65
    (*See also* Ecology)
  city (*see* City, planning of)
  climate as factor in, 77–89, 220, 256, 257
  community (*see* Community)
  comprehensive, 296–299
  compression in, 41, 138, 141, 281, 282
  computer technology in, 39
  concept of, 95, 105
  conservation of energy and, 87, 229, 285,
    293
  creative aspect of, 109–110, 315
  economic considerations in (*see* Economic
    factors in planning and design)
  environmental (*see* Environmental planning)

Planning (*Cont.*):
  errors of, 281, 282
  function in (*see* Function, as factor in planning and design)
  goals and objectives of, 7, 77, 106, 296
  in harmony with nature, 6
  integral, 120–121
    (*See also* Site-structure plan development)
  landscape (*see* Landscape planning and design)
  to meet human needs, 7
  national resource, 304, 306
  nature as base for all, 11
  new order of, 303–305, 307
  occidental, 241, 247
  open-space, 67, 71, 267, 269
  order in (*see* Order, in planning and design)
  organic, 192
  philosophic orientation in, 301–302, 304,
    310
  political factors in, 78, 289, 295
  principles of, 35
  regional (*see* Regional planning)
  sequence in (*see* Sequence, in planning and
    design)
  site (*see* Site planning and design)
  social considerations in (*see* Social activity)
  suburban, 7, 41
  sun as planning and design factor (*see* Sun)
  trafficway (*see* Trafficway planning)
  urban (*see* City, planning of)
  waterscape, 53–54
  (*See also* Plan; Planners)
Planning attitude, 110–111
Planning process, systematic approach to, 4, 7,
  30, 99, 101, 105, 109, 111, 135, 280,
  296, 305
  illus., 106–107
Plant materials, 165, 217
Planting:
  design and, 68–70, 72–75, 128–129, 131,
    227
  diagram of, 69
  introduced plantations, 65–66, 68
  theme species, examples by region, *illus.*, 70
  (*See also* Plants; Vegetation)
Plants, 63–75
  in climate control, 64, 73, 74
  cultivation and propagation of, 65
  as detritus, 65
  exotic species of, 70
  as food, 36, 63–66
  in food chain, 36, 64, 65
  in gardening, 67
  as ground covers, 69, 72, 167
  identification of, 66–67
  indigenous (native), 64, 69, 70, 73, 217
  naturalized, 70
  in nature, 64–65
  in the planned and planted landscape, 68–75
  in reforestation and afforestation, 66
  as screens and windbreaks, 71, 72, 74
    (*See also* Erosion, control of; Views and
    viewing)
  soil building by, 65
  transpiration by, 64
  water retention by, 64
  (*See also* Garden; Vegetation)
Platform construction (decks, docks, and
  raised walkways), 55, 56, 58, 81, 83
Plato, quoted, 144
Playgrounds, 135, 139
  (*See also* Parks and recreation)
Pleasure as a conditioned response, 139
Point Lobos, California, *illus.*, 302–307
Political factors in planning and design, 78,
  289, 295
Pollution:
  air, 40, 66, 285, 306
  water (*see* Water, pollution and contamination of)
  (*See also* Environment; Visible landscape)
Ponds, 48, 51–54, 59

Pope, Alexander, quoted, 7
Possibilities of the city, 284–285
Power of suggestion, 176
Prairie, 1, 51
Precipitation, 78, 80–83, 85, 89
Preplanning of excavation sites, 53–54
Principles of planning, 35
Privacy:
  through enclosure and orientation, 118, 139,
    158–159, 281, 296
  need for, 113, 260, 304
Problems of the city, 281–282
Professional service agreement, 106–107
Profile of the land, *illus.*, 42–43
Program, design and preparation of, 92, 94, 95,
  126
Progressive realization of vista, 179–180, 197
Property appraisal checklist, *illus.*, 93
Property lines and coordinates, 101
Proportion and scale, 125, 138, 139, 142, 306
Psychological attributes of exterior spaces, 142
Psychological response, predetermined (*see*
  Planned experiences)
Public domain, 37, 267
Public services, 299
Public squares, courts, plazas, and spaces, 162,
  163

Qualities:
  of enclosure, 159
  of light, 69, 137–139, 157
  spatial, 141–143
  of water, 50, 57, 60
Quality:
  of landscape, 16
  of life and environment, 322
  of water, 12, 49, 51

Radburn, New Jersey, *illus.*, 266
Rai, Sanyō, quoted, 11
Rail, water, and air traffic, 228–233
Rainfall (*see* Precipitation)
Ramps, 115, 168, 203
Random path layout, *illus.*, 212
Rapid transit (*see* Transit, rapid)
Rasmussen, Steen, quoted, 240–241, 277
Read, Sir Herbert, quoted, 160
Recharge swales, ponds, and basins (*see under*
  Water)
Reclamation of land, 37, 66
Reconnaissance of site, 40, 92, 93
Recreation (*see* Parks and recreation; Region)
Redevelopment (*see* Renewal and redevelopment)
Reed, Henry H., Jr., quoted, 183
Reefs and sandbars, 52
Reforestation and afforestation, 54, 66, 67, 73
Region, 95, 100, 289–299
  activity centers in, 295
  communities within, 293–295
  comprehensive plan for, 296–299
  family in the, 290–291
  metropolitan districts in, 289, 295–296
  neighborhoods within, 292
  open space in, 298
  parks and recreation in, 297
    illus., 298
  residential clusters in, 291–292
  residential uses in, 93
  towns and cities in, 289–290, 295–296
  transportation in, 289, 293–297
Regional development, criteria and tests for,
  298–299
Regional form, 297–298
Regional open space, 295, 298–299
Regional planning, 296–299
  authorities, commissions, and departments
    of, 297
  data gathering and recording for, 93, 297
  defined, 297
  ecological survey for, 93

Regional planning (*Cont.*):
goals of, 296
life-style objectives in, 290, 298–299
test of development suitability, 298–299
Relationship:
optimum, 314
of plan elements, 141, 314, 315
site-structure (*see* Site-structure relationship)
Relaxation as a conditioned response, 137–138
Renaissance, the, 8, 121, 122, 188, 194, 241, 247, 260
Renewal and redevelopment:
landscape, 37, 52–53
urban, 267, 281, 285, 303
Repose through equilibrium, 240
Reservoirs, dams, and impoundments (*see under* Water)
Residential location appraisal checklist, *illus.*, 93
Residential site planning and design, 255–263, 267, 269, 270, 272
Resort communities, 52
Resource management, 37, 195, 294, 297
Resource planning, national, 304, 306
Response, predetermined (*see* Planned experiences)
Reston, Virginia, *illus.*, 293
Riprap, stone, 56
Rivers (*see* Water, rivers and river basins)
Roads (*see* Circulation; Streets; Trafficways)
Roadway and street sections, *illus.*, 216, 222–223
Rockefeller Center, New York City, 136, 137
Rome, Italy, 277
map of, by G. B. Nolli, *illus.*, 279
Rooftop gardens, *illus.*, 66, 67
Rubble in slope retention, 44
Rudolph, Paul, quoted, 238
Rules of composition, 241–247
Rural site, 114–115
Russell, Bertrand, quoted, 8
Ryōanji, garden of Kyoto, Japan, 312
illus., 251

Saarinen, Eliel, quoted, 189, 193, 238, 294, 306, 307
Safety:
as site-planning criterion, 54, 57, 258, 282
in trafficway planning and design, 70, 75, 127, 294
(*See also* Hazard)
Santayana, George, quoted, 94, 188, 191
Sasaki, Hideo, quoted, 126
Satellite community, 293, 294, 299, 306
Satellite plan form, 120, 124
Scale:
induction of, 69, 112, 119, 139
proportion and, 125, 138, 139, 142, 306
Scenic features, resources, and values (*see* Views and viewing; Visible landscape)
Schematic site plan (*see* Plan, schematic)
School-park combination, 270, 294
School as planning factor, 292
Schweikher, Paul, quoted, 304
Science and physical world, 12, 22, 38, 63, 64, 68, 84, 246, 272, 304, 307
Screens:
visual, 69, 71, 72, 74, 83, 118
illus., 171
wind (shelterbelts), 43, 66, 68, 69, 81, 85, 87, 153, 164
illus., 89
Sculpture and sculptural quality, 160, 161, 192, 253
Seas (*see* Oceans, ocean basins, and seas)
Seasons in climatic regions, 80, 81
Sedimentation and siltation, 48, 55, 64
(*See also* Erosion, control of)
Sei do, 110
Seneca, quoted, 5

Sequence:
in planning and design, 71, 139, 148, 203, 205–207, 296
of visual unfolding, 162, 205–207, 208, 219
(*See also* Space; Visible landscape)
Sequential progression and transition, 113, 126, 148, 162, 204–208
Sert, José Luis, quoted, 238, 279
Severud, Fred M., quoted, 9
Sewers (*see* Drainage of land)
Shade, 69, 74, 83, 86, 158
(*See also* Climate)
Shadows, patterns of, 83–86, 117, 125, 158, 165
Shelter, habitat as, 258
Shigemori, Kanto, quoted, 256
Shopping centers and malls, 270, 271
(*See also* City; Community; Region)
Shrubs, 69, 72, 74
(*See also* Plants)
Sidewalks (*see* Circulation)
Sight line in trafficway design, 179, 180, 217
Signs:
as information system, 127
illus., 128, 132–133
as landscape component, 127
illus., 132–133
for trafficways, 217
Siltation and sedimentation, 48, 55, 64
(*See also* Erosion, control of)
Silver Pavilion, Kyoto, Japan, *illus.*, 155
Simonds, John Todd, quoted, 3
Simonds, Philip Douglas, quoted, 213
Simpatico feeling for land, 97–99, 122
Site(s), 91–133
adaptation of project to (*see* Adaptation of project to site)
alternative, 92–94
appraisal checklist for, 93
building, 81, 83
character of, 16, 20, 68, 97, 99, 117
compatible uses of, 91, 99
constraints and limitations of, 99, 103
construction of, 55, 56, 58, 59, 71, 74, 107
development alternatives for, 26
development guidelines checklist, *illus.*, 130–131
drainage of, 116, 167
ecological considerations (*see* Ecology)
environs, 95, 120
extensional aspects of, 95, 97
features of, 102, 114
(*See also* Landscape, features of)
furnishings for, 131
hazards at, 112, 127
(*See also* Safety)
highest and best use of, 91, 99
the ideal, 94
level, 116–119
lighting and illumination, 127, 128
illus., 274–275
location appraisal checklist, *illus.*, 93
negative aspects eliminated, 28
optimum, 92
plan and planning of (*see* Site planning and design)
reconnaissance of, 40, 92, 93
rural, 114
selection of, 85, 91–94
steeply sloping, 115–116
total, 95
unsuitable uses of, 92
urban, 112–113
Site analysis, 25, 28, 29, 93–105, 109, 255, 256
process of, 100–105
Site analysis map, 102–104
illus., 103, 108
Site plan (conceptual), *illus.*, 109
Site planning and design:
comparative analysis of plan alternatives, 109
data gathering for, 95, 97, 100

Site planning and design (*Cont.*):
development guidelines, *illus.*, 130–131
as an orderly process, 106–107
program development in, 94–95
residential (*see* Habitations; Residential site planning and design)
safety as criterion in, 54, 57, 258, 282
survey requirements in, 95–96
visual aspects of (*see* Visible landscape)
water-related, 54–61, 81, 83, 231
(*See also* Architecture; Landscape Architecture; Planning; Site)
Site potential, 126
Site spaces (*see* Site volumes)
Site-structure diagram, 108–109, 115, 238, 241
Site-structure expression, 111–119
Site-structure plan:
development of, 114, 120–121, 124, 135, 250
illus., 108
Site-structure relationship, 41–115, 121, 237–253
Site-structure unity, 105, 122–127, 250, 255–257, 261
Site systems, 126–129, 235, 273, 275, 296
illus., 132–133
Site use areas (*see* Function; Use areas)
Site volumes, 135–171
abstract spatial expression of, 146–148
base plane of, 135, 152–155, 212
illus., 166–167
definition of, 135, 136, 151–152, 156, 157, 164, 170, 171, 250–252
illus., 144–149
(*See also* Space, definition and enclosure of)
design qualities of, 137–139, 147, 148
elements of containment, 148–149, 151, 161
overhead plane, 156–158
as space, 84, 145
spatial color of, 146, 157
(*See also* Color)
spatial form of, 144–145, 156, 252
spatial impact of, 136–141, 146, 147
spatial qualities of, 141–143
spatial size of, 142–144, 259
suited to function, 136, 160, 252
verticals as component of, 158–165
(*See also* Site; Spaces)
Sitte, Camillo, quoted, 193, 238, 241, 242, 385
Sky as overhead plane, 115, 117, 122, 144, 156, 161, 260
Slopes:
design treatment of, 115–116, 130
illus., 55
dynamics of, *illus.*, 44–45
in nature, 86
retention of, 55, 56, 68
illus., 44–45
steeply sloping site, 115–116
(*See also* Earthwork; Land; Site; Water)
Social activity (behavior), 291, 292, 295, 296
characteristics of, 78, 289, 290
(*See also* Human, behavior of)
Soil, 35–36, 47, 49, 54, 64, 67, 68, 78, 81, 153, 301
(*See also* Erosion, control of; Land; Topsoil; Water)
Sound in landscape planning and design, 61, 137–139, 147
Space:
"borrowed," 259, 260
between buildings, 238–340
cadence and, 207
character of, 238, 302
definition and enclosure of, 68, 69, 71, 74, 112, 160, 161, 170, 171, 237–242, 250
(*See also* Site volumes, definition of)
dimensions of, 143, 259
modulation of, 74, 203–205, 313
site volumes as, 84, 145
in urban areas, 277–281
Spaces, 135–171

Spaces (*Cont.*):
   organization of, 79, 135, 136, 165, 237
   (*See also* Site volumes)
Spaciousness, sense of, 260
Spatial character, 137–142
Spatial color, 146, 157
   (*See also* Color, design application of)
Spatial expression, abstract, 146–148
Spatial form, 144–145, 156, 252
   (*See also* Spaces)
Spatial impact, 136–141, 147
Spatial penetration of structure, 238
Spatial qualities, 141–143
Spatial size, 142–144, 259
Spatial variety, *illus.,* 164
Spengler, Oswald, quoted, 146, 302
Stairs, exterior (*see* Steps)
Standardization, 295
   (*See also* Site systems)
Steps:
   in combination with ramp (perrons), *illus.,*
      169
   design criteria for, 130, 168–169
      (*See also* Trafficways, pedestrian)
   in Greek village of Ios, *illus.,* 210–211
   as site design feature, 210, 213
      illus., 168–169
Stewardship and husbandry of natural land-
   scape, 11, 35, 36, 65
Stonehenge, England, *illus.,* 144
Storm-water drainage (*see* Drainage of land;
   Erosion, control of; Land; Water)
Streams and waterways (*see* Water, streams
   and brooks)
Streets:
   lighting of, *illus.,* 274–275
   in New York City, *illus.,* 278
   planning and design of, 269
   as residential frontage, 269
      (*See also* Community)
   typical sections of, *illus.,* 222–223
      (*See also* Circulation; City; Community;
      Trafficways)
Strip development of highways, *illus.,* 6
   (*See also* Trafficways; Visible landscape)
Strip mining, 53–54
   (*See also* Earthwork; Land)
Structures, 237–253
   clustering of, 238–241
   composition of, 237–249
   as exterior space definers, 161, 237–238
   in the landscape, 247–250
   as vertical elements, 161–162
      (*See also* Climate; *entries beginning with
      the term:* Site-structure; Spaces)
Subdivision planning and design (*see* Com-
   munity)
Suburbs (suburbia), 7, 41, 66, 266
Sullivan, Louis H., quoted, 192, 307, 309
Sun:
   angle of incidence, 78
   as planning and design factor, 79, 81–83, 85,
      86, 89, 99, 117, 125, 158, 211
      illus., 86, 88, 89
   as source of energy (*see* Energy, solar)
Superblock street layout (*see* Circulation;
   City; Community)
Survey, 38–39
   site reconnaissance by field inspection (*see*
      Site analysis)
   topographic, 95–96, 100, 108
   U.S. Geological, 92
Swale, 71
Symbiotic balance (symbiosis), 66
Symbols, symbolism, and association, 57, 71,
   127, 138, 139, 148, 162, 207, 294, 301,
   302
Symmetry and symmetrical plan arrangement,
   139, 181, 186–190, 192, 194
   beauty of, 186–187, 189
   bilateral, 187, 188, 192
      illus., 191
   despotism of, 187–189

Symmetry and symmetrical plan
      arrangement (*Cont.*):
   dynamic, 187
   in landscape planning and design, 189–190,
      311
   in nature, 186, 187
   nature of, 189–190
Systems (*see* Site systems)
Sze, Mai-mai, quoted, 24

Taliesin West, 123
Tao as the governing force of the universe, 9,
   24, 307, 315
Taut, Bruno, quoted, 146
Taxes as related to landscape planning, 298,
   299
Technology, 302, 304
   (*See also* Science and physical world)
Temperature, 79–83, 86–89
   and comfort, 88
   modified by design, 88, 89
      (*See also* Microclimatology)
   ranges of, 86, 88
      (*See also* Climate)
Tension:
   as conditioned response, 137
   and repose, 240
Terminus of vista, 178
Terraces, 55, 116, 263
Texture in design, 135, 137–139
Thermodynamics, 24, 87
   illus., 88–89
Tidal estuaries and marshes (*see* Water, estuary; Water, marshes)
Topographic survey, 95–96, 100, 108
   specification for, 95–96
Topography, 7, 40, 52, 65, 71, 81, 88, 101, 311
   analysis of, 88–89
   effect on wind, 43, 83, 86
   response to, 52, 65, 71, 81
   revisions to, 40
Topsoil, 35, 40, 65, 153, 303
   (*See also* Earth, the; Environment; Erosion,
      control of; Land)
Traffic:
   flow and movement of, 208, 209, 212, 213,
      218
   grade separation of, 213–215, 296
   as hazard to safety, 213, 266
   patterns of, and land use areas, 103, 127, 294
   pedestrian, 208–213
      (*See also* Circulation; Site; Visible land-
         scape)
   rail, water, and air, 228–233
   vehicular, 103, 104
      (*See also* Circulation; Trafficways; Transit,
         rapid)
   (*See also* Circulation; Trafficways)
Trafficway(s):
   air as, 232–233
   approach drive and entrance court, 218–220
   capacity of, 216
   classified, 268, 269
   as hazard, 29, 30, 213
   as integrated system, 215, 269, 289, 296
   parking bays and compounds, 71, 131,
      220–221, 224–227, 291
   pedestrian, 208–213
   planning of (*see* Trafficway planning)
   sight line in design of, 179, 180, 217
   signage for, 217
   streets, residential, *illus.,* 222–223
   urban, 112, 215, 277, 280
      illus., 278, 286–287, 295
   vehicular, 213–230
      (*See also* Circulation; Parkways; Streets;
         Transit, rapid)·
Trafficway planning:
   arterial parkways in, 295
   circumferential beltways in, 295
   classified truckways and freightways in,
      203, 297

Trafficway planning (*Cont.*):
   in communities, 266
   grade separation of crossings, 296
   highways in, 6, 7, 313, 314
   interchanges in, 295
   location and design in, 12, 130–131
   safety in, 70, 75, 127, 294
Transit, rapid, 269, 293, 295, 297
   advanced modes of, 228
   direct interconnection of urban and regional
      centers by, 229
   integration with other trafficway types, 230
   nodes and terminals, 229
   reasons for lagging acceptance of, 228–229
   as urban and regional form giver, 228, 230,
      235
Transition:
   designed, 232, 296
   modulated, 126
   sequential (*see* Sequential progression and
      transition)
Transportation, 66
   classified truck routes and freightways, 203,
      268–269, 297
   improved modes and concepts of, 228, 266
   planning for, 266
      (*See also* Trafficway planning)
   separation of pedestrians and vehicles,
      213–215, 222
   and traffic-free communities, 266, 268–269
      illus., 291–292
   urban trafficway patterns, 280
      illus., 278, 286–287, 295
      (*See also* Circulation; Region; Trafficways;
         Transit, rapid)
Transportation corridors, 286, 295
Transportation routes, 79
Travel:
   by air, 232–233
   by automobile, 213–227
   by bicycle, 234
   by pedestrians, 208–213
   by people movers, 233–235
   by rail, 228–230
   by water, 50, 230–232
      (*See also* Circulation)
Trees:
   canopy, 69, 72
   in landscape design, 69, 72–75
   theme, 69
      (*See also* Planting; Plants)
Tunnard, Christopher, quoted, 9, 19

Ugliness, 6, 19, 20, 139, 145
   defined, 16
U.S. Forest Service, 195
U.S. Geological Survey maps, 92
Unity:
   with diversity, 128
   landscape, 13, 31, 105, 142, 203, 311
   of site and structure (*see* Site-structure
      unity)
Universe, vitality of, 5
Urba-centers, *illus.,* 229, 235, 295, 306
Urban areas, 66, 67
   activity centers, *illus.,* 282–285
   possibilities in, 284–285
   redevelopment and renewal of, 267, 281,
      285, 303
   service lines in, *illus.,* 298
   space in, 277–281
   spaces in, 279
      as corridors, 277
   sprawl of, 277, 304
   trafficways in (*see* Trafficways, urban)
   waterfront, 286
      (*See also* Water)
   (*See also* City; Region; Transit, rapid)
Urban courts, malls, and plazas, 57, 60
   (*See also* City, planning of)
Urban planning (*see* City, planning of)
Use areas, 108, 114, 126, 135, 145

Use as a landscape planning determinant, 17–19
  (See also Function)
Use volumes, 135, 145
  (See also Site volumes; Spaces)
Utilities in landscape planning and design, 81, 305

Van Loon, Hendrik, quoted, 8
Vegetation, 51, 78, 80–83, 85, 86
  water-related, 52, 59, 60, 71, 232
  (See also Plants)
Vehicular trafficways, 213–230
  (See also Circulation)
Veri, Albert R., et al., quoted, 12, 54
Versailles, garden and Palace of, France, 180–181,
  illus., 241
Verticals, 136, 158–165
  as point of reference, 162–163
  in visual screening, enframement, and control, 118
  in volumetric definition, 136, 164
Vetter, Hans, quoted, 8
Vicinity, site, 95, 100
Views and viewing, 6, 43, 51, 52, 55, 68, 71, 72, 80, 81, 83, 104, 129, 137, 230
  design treatment of, 117, 120, 125, 173–177, 190, 252, 260
  sequential aspects of, 117, 173
  from a sloping site, 116
  (See also Circulation; Visible landscape; Water, scenic value of)
Villa d'Este, Tivoli, Italy, 124
Villa Gamberaia, Italy, 30–31
Vines, 69–72
Visible landscape, 173–195
Vista, 177–180
  enframement of, 178–179
  progressive realization of, 179–180, 197
  terminus of, 178
  (See also Axis as linear plan element; Views and viewing)
Visual (occult) balance, 148, 189, 190–191
  illus., 191, 240
Visual control, 138, 159–160
  (See also Spaces; Visible landscape)
Visual resource management, 195
Visual screens (see Screens, visual)
Vitruvius, Marcus, quoted, 245–246
Volumes (see Site volumes)

Walk intersections, reinforcement of, illus., 212
Walker, Ralph, quoted, 294
Walks, walkways, and trails (see Paths, trails, and walkways)
Walls, 43, 55, 56, 158, 164
  illus., 44, 170
Warm-humid climatic region, 78, 82, 83

Water, 47–61
  access to, 52, 55, 56, 58
  aquifer, groundwater, and water table, 48, 50, 152
  beaches, shores, and water edges, 54–56, 58
    illus., 55, 56, 58
  blueway, 53, 286
    (See also rivers and river basins, streams and brooks, waterways and water bodies, below)
  in constructed pools, fountains, and cascades, 57, 116, 179
    (See also fountains, below)
  detention, percolation, and recharge of, 50, 57
  dredge and fill, 52, 53
  drought, 48, 80
  erosion by (see Erosion, control of; siltation and sedimentation, below)
  estuary, 47, 65, 303
    (See also wetlands, below)
  falls and cascades, 47, 48, 51, 57, 59–61
  floodplain, 52, 81, 83
  floods and flooding, 47, 48, 55, 56, 58, 81, 83, 87
  flow of, 47, 56–61
  fountains, 48–53, 57, 60, 61, 84
  frontage along, 51–52
  as habitat, 50
  impoundments, 52, 54–55, 57
  irrigation, 47, 49, 79, 82–85
  lakes, 47, 48, 50, 53, 54, 66, 80
  as landscape feature, 51–54, 57–59, 124,127
    illus., 60–61
  in landscape planning and design, 48–49, 54–61, 127
  management of, 48–52, 268
  marshes, 48, 54, 65, 67
    (See also wetlands, below)
  in microclimate moderation, 50, 57
    (See also Microclimate)
  oceans, ocean basins, and seas, 22, 23, 47, 50, 64, 77, 78
  pollution and contamination of, 48, 49, 53, 57, 303
    illus., 48
  ponds, 48, 51–54, 59
  pools, 47, 57, 59, 60, 84
  qualities of, 50, 57, 60
  quality of, 12, 49, 51
  rapids, 47, 59
  recreational use of, 50, 51, 54, 55, 57, 231
  rivers and river basins, 47, 49, 58, 231, 232, 311
    river basin studies, 48
    (See also blueway, above; streams and brooks, below)
  scenic value of, 47, 48, 50, 51, 55, 57–60
  seas (see oceans, ocean basins, and seas, above)
  siltation and sedimentation, 48, 55, 64
  springs, 47, 48, 52, 54, 57
  streams and brooks, 47, 48, 50–52, 54, 56–59, 65, 80

Water (Cont.):
    (See also blueway, rivers and river basins, above)
  supply of, 49–51, 80, 82, 83
  surface runoff, 49, 50
  travel by, 50, 230–232
  waterfalls (see falls and cascades, above)
  waterscape, 47, 53–54, 57
  watershed, 57, 66–68
  waterways and water bodies, 49–51, 54–59, 66, 71, 81, 85, 231–232
  wetlands, 50–52, 65, 303
Water features:
  altered and improved, 54–56, 58, 59
  developed, 52, 55–60
  protected, 52, 54, 56
  rediscovered, 52
  restored or reclaimed, 52, 53
Water-related construction, 55–59
Water-related site design, 54–61, 81, 83, 231
Water-related vegetation, 52, 59, 60, 71, 232
Weather (see Climate)
Wells and well fields (see under Water)
White, Stanley, quoted, 8, 10, 31
Whyte, Lancelot Law, quoted, 4
Whyte, William H., Jr., quoted, 296
Wild rivers, 49
  (See also Water, rivers)
Wilderness, 49, 66, 67
  (See also Environment; Land; Region)
Wildlife, 47, 65, 66, 78, 303
Wildlife preserve or sanctuary, 52, 127, 297
Wilson, E. H., 63
Wind, 78, 89, 115, 116
  effect of topography and structures on, 43, 83, 86
  erosion by, 66
  as factor in landscape planning and design, 43, 66, 68, 69, 80, 81, 82, 83, 86, 87, 164, 311
  as source of energy, 85
  windscreens (shelterbelts) (see Screens, wind)
  (See also Climate)
Wittkower, Rudolph, quoted, 246
Wright, Frank Lloyd, 21

Yin and yang, 126
Yoshida, Hiroshi, quoted, 247
Yuan Ming Yuan, China, 194–195

Zen Buddhism, 176, 207, 315
Zevi, Bruno, quoted, 143
Zoning, 37, 283, 284, 297, 299, 304
  flexibility, 267, 268, 294

About the author

John Ormsbee Simonds has distinguished himself in all three areas of his professional life, as teacher, author, and landscape architect. His degrees from Michigan State University and the Harvard Graduate School of Design were followed by years of travel, research, and observation which provided him with a firsthand knowledge of worldwide landscape development and a thorough understanding of the most advanced land-planning approaches and technology. He served for many years on the architectural faculty of Carnegie Mellon University, is a fellow of the Royal Academy of Design, Great Britain, was a member of the President's Task Force on the Environment, and has been president of the American Society of Landscape Architects, which awarded him its highest honor, the ASLA medal. The Chicago Botanic Garden and the new Pelican Bay community in Florida are among his firm's many award-winning projects.

John Simonds's articles have appeared in the *AIA Journal, Architectural Record, Parks and Recreation, Perspecta, Modulus, Landscape Architecture* magazine, *Consulting Engineer,* and other leading planning and design publications. He is the editor of *Freeway in the City* and the author of *Earthscape,* a best-selling book on environmental planning.